全球开发性金融发展报告（2015）

中国开发性金融促进会（CAPDF）
北京大学国家发展研究院（NSD）联合编写组　编著

GLOBAL
DEVELOPMENT FINANCING
REPORT
(2015)

中信出版集团·CHINACITICPRESS·北京

图书在版编目（CIP）数据

全球开发性金融发展报告. 2015／中国开发性金融促进会，北京大学国家发展研究院联合编写组编著. —
北京：中信出版社，2016.1
ISBN 978 – 7 – 5086 – 5675 – 5

Ⅰ.①全… Ⅱ.①中… ②北… Ⅲ.①金融业 – 经济发展 – 研究报告 – 中国 – 2015　Ⅳ.①F832

中国版本图书馆CIP数据核字（2015）第272033号

全球开发性金融发展报告（2015）

编　　著：中国开发性金融促进会、北京大学国家发展研究院联合编写组
策划推广：中信出版社（China CITIC Press）
出版发行：中信出版集团股份有限公司
　　　　　（北京市朝阳区惠新东街甲4号富盛大厦2座　邮编　100029）
　　　　　（CITIC Publishing Group）
承　印　者：北京画中画印刷有限公司

开　　本：787mm×1092mm　1/16　　印　张：31.25　　字　数：720千字
版　　次：2016年1月第1版　　　　　印　次：2016年1月第1次印刷
书　　号：ISBN 978 – 7 – 5086 – 5675 – 5/F·3535　广告经营许可证：京朝工商广字第8087号
定　　价：76.00元

版权所有·侵权必究
凡购本社图书，如有缺页、倒页、脱页，由发行公司负责退换
服务热线：010 – 84849555　　服务传真：010 – 84849000
投稿邮箱：author@citicpub.com

编委会

主　任：陈　元
副主任：胡怀邦　郑之杰　李吉平
　　　　　袁　力　林毅夫
主　编：邢　军　姚　洋
编　委：张　帆　徐佳君　王　茜
　　　　　靳宝华　王春来

序

在亚信非政府论坛首次年会的"开发性金融与亚洲发展"圆桌会议召开之际，我谨对《全球开发性金融发展报告（2015）》的正式发布表示祝贺。

这是一份具有开创性和前瞻性的报告，对增进各界了解开发性金融的现状以及发展趋势有重要意义。开发性金融历史悠久，发源于两百年前的欧洲，并在第二次世界大战后蓬勃发展，为推动各国经济增长、可持续发展、维护经济金融安全做出了卓越贡献。据粗略统计，世界开发性金融机构联盟、各区域开发银行协会的成员累计达328家，是国际金融体系举足轻重的力量。当前，全球发展对开发性金融提出了新的要求，但是人们对开发性金融的认识还不全面，对开发性金融运作原理和主要功能的理解还有待深入，这份报告及时地呈现了开发性金融机构的总体面貌和发展趋势，是开发性金融领域的一项重要报告。

同时，该报告也为开发性金融机构之间相互交流与学习提供了契机。开发性金融的主要特征是服务政府发展目标，以中长期投融资为手段，依托政府信用支持，通过市场化运作缓解经济社会发展的瓶颈制约，维护经济金融稳定。由于各国的政治制度、法律体系、经济政策和优先发展任务等不同，因此各开发性金融机构结合本地实际，形成了各自的运作模式、实践经验和专业优势。开发性金融发展的差异化和多样化是国际开发性金融创新发展的源泉，各开发性金融机构只有相互借鉴、取长补短，才能共同促进全球开发性金融的健康发展，该报告对全球主要开发性金融机构的持续关注恰恰体现了互鉴互学的精神。

随着各国相互联系日益紧密、相互依存日益加深，区域和跨区域合作蓬勃兴起，互联互通建设加速推进，加强开发性金融机构的互信与合作变得越来越重要，这既是维护地区金融稳定和金融安全的重要保障，也是增强经济中长期发展动力的重要支撑，更是亚洲各经济体良性互动、协调发展，共建亚洲命运共同体的重要推动力。过去20年，以国家开发银行为代表的中国开发性金融把国际经验与中国国情和发展的阶段性特征相结合，为国际金融的创新发展贡献了中国经验和中国智慧；展望未来，随着政府对开发性金融的重视以及市场对开发性金融的需求，开发性金融将有更大的发展空间。同时，由于各国市场规则不统一，市场体系不完善，因此需要各国开发性金融机构加强合作，共同建设市场，共同应对风险与挑战，携手开创未来，这正是本报告所追求的目标，也是本报告将持续开展下去的根本动力。

衷心希望各开发性金融机构为推动全球可持续发展、增进人类福祉做出新的贡献。

第十二届全国政协副主席
中国开发性金融促进会会长

目 录
CONTENTS

序 / V

第一篇　开发性金融综述

第一章　绪论 / 3

第二章　多边开发性金融机构 / 17

第三章　高收入国家的开发性金融机构 / 50

第四章　中低收入国家的开发性金融机构 / 76

第五章　与中国相关的开发性金融机构 / 130

第六章　开发性金融机构协会 / 149

第二篇　开发性金融机构的分析与展望

第七章　全球开发性金融机构的结构与发展趋势 / 163

第八章　转型进程中开发性金融机构的作用 / 180

第九章　结论 / 204

机构名称简写 / 207

致　谢 / 210

Preface / 213

Part One　Overview of Development Financing

Chapter 1　Introduction / 219
Chapter 2　Multilateral DFIs / 236
Chapter 3　National DFIs in High Income Countries / 279
Chapter 4　National DFIs in Medium-/Low-Income Countries / 311
Chapter 5　China-Related DFIs / 380
Chapter 6　Associations of DFIs / 406

Part Two　Analysis and Outlook of Development Financing Institutions

Chapter 7　Structure and Trends of Global Development Financial Institutions / 421
Chapter 8　The Role of DFIs in a Transformation Agenda / 440
Chapter 9　Conclusion / 469

Acronyms and Abbreviations / 472
Acknowledgements / 482
References / 484

第一篇　开发性金融综述

在新一轮绿色增长、工业化和城市化浪潮的刺激下，为了支持可持续发展目标的新方略，世界各国对大规模、长时间、可持续的开发性金融提出了更高的要求。第一章绪论对开发性金融的需求与供给以及开发性金融机构的战略角色进行了介绍。根据规模、目的、功能以及商业模式的不同，世界各地的开发性金融机构采用了多样化的形式。从第二章到第五章，我们将介绍世界上主要的开发性金融机构，并按照功能和地理位置将它们分成4类：多边开发性金融机构、高收入国家的开发性金融机构、中低收入国家的开发性金融机构，以及与中国相关的开发性金融机构。第六章进一步介绍了3家开发性金融机构协会。我们从机构官方网站、年报及新闻报道等多种渠道，收集了这些开发性金融机构的最新数据。

报告一共选取了30家开发性金融机构，并简要介绍了每一家的创立、使命、股权和资金、商业模式和金融产品。我们尝试选取了尽可能具有代表性的样本，但我们并不试图囊括所有的开发性金融机构。为了平衡报告的广度和深度，我们选取在规模、影响力和运营模式的创新方面都较为突出的开发性金融机构。另外，由于本报告的定位是亚洲相互协作与信任措施会议（亚信论坛）第五届峰会圆桌讨论的背景文件，因此相比其他地区，我们更多选取了位于亚洲的开发性金融机构。简而言之，报告本身对于任何类型的开发性金融机构持中立的态度。

第一章　绪论[*]

新一轮绿色增长、工业化和城市化浪潮正以前所未有的规模和速度席卷全球，世界各国正迎来历史性的转型机遇。时代变革的强音对大规模、长时期、可持续的开发性金融提出了更高的要求。

开发性金融涵盖了广泛的金融工具。其中，既有公共资金，也有社会资本；既涉及国内资源，又包含国际融资。一个较为普遍的共识是，开发性金融的发展方向，是善用政府支持的"杠杆"和"催化剂"作用，使融集到的大额资金发挥最大功效，以满足可持续发展目标（SDGs）的要求。可持续发展目标是继千年发展目标后全球发展的新方略，包括经济发展、社会进步和环境保护三大支柱，并且已经于2015年9月在联合国各成员国间签署。

本报告旨在对开发性金融机构的战略角色做宏观描述。为转型发展进程提供融资支持是我们必须面对的挑战，开发性金融机构将为此做出贡献。

开发性金融需求的前瞻性分析

未来全球发展的三大趋势决定了世界各国对长期转型性投资有较大需求。首先，地区发展加速融合需要开发性的引导资金，以启动项目并促进变革进程的实现；其次，加速推进的工业化和城市化需要大量的长期融资；最后，大规模的可持续发展需要积极培育市场、建设市场以实现融资。

---

[*] 本报告执笔人为张帆、徐佳君、王春来。

地区发展加速融合需要开发性引导资金

进入21世纪,世界多极化、经济全球化、文化多元化和加速信息化成为时代的主题,与之相应的区域一体化也不断加深。在后经济危机时代,开放性区域合作对维护全球自由贸易体系、建立开放型世界经济至关重要。从经济的角度看,区域一体化旨在推动经济要素的自由有序流动,各种资源的合理高效配置,以及各国各地区市场的深度融合。

为传承和弘扬"和平合作、开放包容、互学互鉴、互利共赢"的"丝绸之路精神",中国政府于2015年3月制定并发布了《推动共建丝绸之路经济带和21世纪海上丝绸之路的愿景与行动》。丝绸之路经济带和21世纪海上丝绸之路(简称"一带一路")建设是一项系统工程,致力于"亚欧非大陆及附近海洋的互联互通,建立和加强沿线各国互联互通伙伴关系,构建全方位、多层次、复合型的互联互通网络,实现沿线各国多元、自主、平衡、可持续的发展"。

秉承同样的精神,亚太经济合作组织(APEC)各经济体领导人于2014年11月共同发布了题为"北京纲领:构建融合、创新、互联的亚太"的领导人宣言。这一纲领旨在"推动区域经济一体化,促进经济创新发展、改革与增长,加强全方位基础设施与互联互通建设,共商拓展和深化亚太区域经济合作之大计,实现亚太和平、稳定、发展和共同繁荣"。

作为加强区域一体化的重要一步,博鳌亚洲论坛2015年年会宣布启动"中国东盟海洋合作年",旨在在中国和东南亚各国间深化互信、加强对接,共建21世纪海上丝绸之路。中国已与印度尼西亚(简称"印尼")、泰国、马来西亚、印度、斯里兰卡等国家开展了形式多样的海洋合作,中国—东盟海上合作基金和中国—印尼海上合作基金支持的项目稳步推进。

2015年5月8日,中国与俄罗斯发表了《关于丝绸之路经济带建设和欧亚经济联盟建设对接合作的联合声明》。双方一致同意扩大贸易合作,促进双向投资便利化,在物流、基础设施、区域生产网络等领域加强互联互通,共同打造产业园区和跨境经济合作区。

除了亚洲和欧洲外，非洲也在加快区域一体化进程。非洲开发银行制定了《区域一体化战略书》（*Regional Integration Strategy Paper*），跨境基础设施已在建设之中。近期，非洲联盟宣布，计划于2017年建成大陆自由贸易区（Continental Free Trade Area，CFTA），为非洲建立统一市场，使非洲10亿人员、物资、服务和技术得以自由流动，为贸易和投资创造更大、更具活力的经济空间。

所有这些推进区域一体化的努力共同开辟了合作的新领域——基础设施互联互通、产业投资、资源开发、经贸合作以及金融合作。首先，跨境基础设施建设需要长期、大规模的融资。其次，建设工业园区和跨境经济合作区能有效推进区域和跨区域产业集群的开发。最后，金融合作是实施区域一体化战略的重要基础。其中非常关键的一点是要建立国际信用体系，这样才能改进风险响应和危机管理体系，建立区域金融风险预警机制，为跨境风险危机管理建立交流合作机制。

一般而言，新合作领域的开拓是商业资本力所不能及的。私人投资者的经营决策往往取决于短期风险回报率，因而商业资本在复杂的大规模跨境项目上往往迟疑不前。

因此，加快区域一体化进程，需要长期、大规模的投资来启动关键性的战略项目。成功的实例可以彰显变革型投资的价值，从而吸引和激励更多的商业资本参与其中。

加速推进的工业化和城市化进程需要长期投资

随着工业化和城市化进程在全球范围内加速推进，各国正面临着对长期投资的极大需求。工业化进程的加速意味着必须增加长期投资，以提高劳动生产率，升级产业结构，实现向全球价值链上游的攀升。与此同时，新型城市化浪潮对可持续的、耐风险考验的城市基础设施和社会服务的需求也日益高涨。预计到2030年，各新兴经济体的城市人口数量将比2000年翻一番，新增20亿。大量人口向城市迁徙，意味着对水、能源、交通等城市基本服务的需求也相应增长。长期投资存在着巨大的供给缺口，这成为推动转型的主要阻碍因素。世界银行的研究显示，每增加10%的基础设施投入，GDP将增长1%。因此，如何弥补长期融资缺口，就成为实现经济增长、就业增加、产业升级和经济转型的关键。

比如，在基础设施建设领域，其投资缺口就十分惊人。经济合作与发展组织（简称"经合组织"，OECD）在《关于全球基础设施建设的发展报告及未来预测（至2030年）》中估计，到2030年，全球范围内陆路交通、电信、电力、供水和公共卫生等部门所需的基础设施投入将高达53万亿美元。每年所需投资几乎相当于全球GDP的2.5%。据世界经济论坛发布的《基础设施投资政策蓝图》（the Infrastructure Investment Policy Blueprint）预计，全球基础设施领域的债权和股权投资存在每年近1万亿美元的缺口。亚洲开发银行做出的估算则是，2010~2020年，亚洲国家整体基础设施，如能源、交通、电信、供水和公共卫生，共需投入约8万亿美元。

筹集和维持长期投资，需要应对一些挑战。首先，较长的投资期需要应对周期性金融危机的冲击。在全球金融陷入困顿低迷的情况下，国际长期信贷流动性收紧，此时的资金供给者能起到"减震器"的作用，有助于维护金融稳定。比如，世界银行的研究显示，开发性金融机构（DFIs）能起到"反周期"的作用，因为在商业银行遭遇暂时性困难、私营部门融资受限时，这一类机构通常会加大贷款力度。其次，由于银行可担保、融资的项目严重短缺，制约了这些国家获得长期融资的规模。因此，提升项目规划和落地执行能力非常关键。最后，一个国家的中长期发展动力十分有利于保持对长期投资的吸引力。长期投融资常常与实体经济发展密切相关。因此，发现经济增长点并实施促进战略，对推动产业升级和结构调整至关重要，这有助于在长期投资和可持续增长之间实现积极的双向互动。

长期投融资短缺的症结不在于资本总额不足，而在于缺乏有效的融资中介，融资中介能够引导资本投向复杂、期限长、风险更高的项目。世界银行的研究显示，长期投融资渠道的开发很不充分，现有的金融工具、金融机构和金融政策必须经历改革，才能适应长期投融资的需求规模，满足经济增长的需要。因此，在全球储蓄和长期投资间建立更加紧密的关联尤为重要。

规模化的可持续发展需要培育市场以实现融资

可持续发展目标是全球发展方略，包括经济发展、社会进步和环境保护3个维度，并且已经于2015年9月在联合国各成员国间签署。一个较为广泛的共识是，开发性金融的可持续发展方向是依托政府支持，融集大额资金，推进转型进程。这需要国家在培育前沿市场方面主动作为、发挥积极作用。

第一，可持续经济增长需要持续的技术革新和产业升级，从而不断为中长期经济发展注入新的动力。在新的全球价值链的宏观图景下，经济转型期的产业政策不能被保护"幼稚产业"那些固有观念所局限，而应综合考虑技术、金融、基础设施和政治经济学等各方面因素。新型的产业政策要求我们主动建立技术习得的流程，这是攀登增长阶梯的核心驱动力。事实上，今天许多变革性技术都源于公共资金资助的研究活动。简而言之，经济转型需要具备企业家精神的国家（entrepreneurial state）。

国家要具备开拓性的企业家精神，这一观念对正在经历转型的低收入国家实现经济起飞尤为重要。经过10年的经济稳步增长，低收入国家数量大大减少，已从2000年的63个减至今天的34个，而这一进程在可预见的未来仍将持续。然而，低收入国家在经济逐步发展、摆脱贫困地位的过程中，有可能陷入两端落空的困境：既得不到官方发展援助，又无法从市场上获得融资。一方面，这些国家不再满足从多边援助机构获得软贷款和资金补贴的限定条件；另一方面，它们尚不具备通过全球资本市场建立可靠融资渠道的能力。可以预见的是，伴随着工业化和城市化进程的深化，转型中的低收入国家将形成巨大的投资需求，这更加凸显了融资缺口之大。因此，我们面临的迫在眉睫的挑战，是如何帮助转型中的低收入国家完成市场培育，逐步过渡到可以主要依靠市场机制来获得可靠的融资，从而实现跨越式的经济转型。

第二，社会发展对公共品供给提出的需求，仅靠私营部门是无法满足的。公共品的正外部性意味着收益不由提供者独享，因而逐利的私营企业可能动力不足，不愿提供诸如教育、卫生、减贫、保障性住房等公共服务。换言之，公共品市场往往发育不成熟。

公共服务供给不足可能会带来严重后果。社会不公会导致社会动荡乃至冲突，教育和卫生品质低下可能会阻碍人力资本的积累，破坏机会均等，威胁人们追求幸福生活的权利。今天，城市化的新浪潮席卷全球，人们对公共服务的需求比以往任何时候都大得多，因而这些问题也更为严峻。

因此，激励开发性金融为公共品供给提供融资，对维护社会稳定、提供高品质社会福利和保持长期经济增长都有重大意义。

第三，绿色增长至关重要，因为不可持续的生产将威胁公众健康，触发一连串灾难性的环境恶化后果，最终危及经济的长期增长和社会福利的改善。在高级别国际论坛和国家发展战略中，绿色增长都占据显著位置。经合组织举办了"绿色成长与可持续发展论坛"（the Green Growth and Sustainable Development Forum），以期在经合组织成员国和非成员合作伙伴中推进绿色增长。在中国，正如国家"十二五"发展规划（2011—2015）显示，快速发展的工业化、日益增强的农业生产和城市化都使其越来越重视绿色经济的发展。实现绿色增长需要在各个领域做出努力，包括农业可持续增长、产业升级、可再生能源创新以及可持续性基础设施建设。

推动向绿色增长模式转变，绿色投资应当具备可扩展性，但在转型的最初阶段，私人资本往往无法满足这一要求。比如，据国际能源机构（IEA）估算，2011~2050年，全球仅能源一个领域就需追加年均低碳投资1.1万亿美元。新型可再生能源的开发在早期往往需要承担巨大的风险，这意味着短期内很难收回成本并赢利。私人机构追求的是投资回报，其决策在很大程度上受利润最大化和风险最小化原则的支配，而且仅当技术突破使成本显著降低、大规模生产成为可能时，风险收益比才会越过拐点，从而大规模地吸引私人投资。

简而言之，加大对可持续发展的融资支持，国家应当主动作为，培育前沿市场。由于私营部门具有投资期短和风险规避的特性，因而公共部门的参与必不可少。它可以通过培育前沿市场，降低投资风险，增强投资者信心，从而为经济发展释放商机。

总之，在未来的转型进程中，为了更好地发挥三大发展趋势的积极作用，大规模的长期转型性融资必不可少。对开发性金融需求的前瞻性分析，使我们清晰地看到其中孕育的崭新机遇和潜伏的未知挑战：（1）地区发展加速融合需要开发性引导资金；（2）加速推进的工业化和城市化进程需要长期投资；（3）规模化的可持续发展需要培育市场以实现融资。

大规模、长时期的开发性金融供给存在短缺

从上面的分析可以看到，世界对长期转型性投资的需求巨大，然而从供给的角度看却存在短缺。为什么官方发展援助和私人资本无法给经济提供充足的长期发展融资？下文将做简要阐释。

官方发展援助总量少且规模小

开发性金融往往与官方发展援助相联系，这一援助方式其实是由较富裕国家的纳税人提供资金，再转移支付给贫穷国家。各主要援助国的援助政策由经合组织的发展援助委员会（DAC）统一协调。

官方发展援助的规模很小，依靠其自身远不能满足受援国对资金的需求。2013年，官方发展援助的总支付额约为1 500亿美元。但是，即便各援助国都能信守承诺，将国民总收入（GNI）的0.7%用作官方发展援助，其支付总额大概也仅在4 000亿美元左右。0.7%是国际援助承诺的参考值，由大多数发达国家（美国除外）于1970年在联合国一致同意通过，并在其后的最高级别国际援助和发展会议上多次重新签署。由此可见，官方发展援助远远无法提供足够的外部资金，用以支持基础设施建设，满足城市化和绿色增长进程

的需要，而这对转型增长来说极为关键。

进一步说，由于自身存在一系列问题，现有的国际援助体系尚不能适应实现大规模、长时期转型性投资的需要。首先，援助机构有达成短期业绩目标的压力。其次，援助机构本身的激励机制存在问题，导致它们不愿意投入精力来帮助受援国实现项目的规模化经营，并由此构建受援国的系统能力。最后，最根本的问题在于，过去30年间最受欢迎的发展模型对政府的作用重视不足。作为一国宏观经济蓝图的缔造者，以及对相互关联投资的统筹协调者，政府的作用不应被忽视。

简而言之，官方发展援助远远不敷所需：数额上太小，不足以应对大规模开发性融资需要；结构上太零散，不足以承载转型所需的长远愿景。

私人资本市场受短视主义困扰

各资本市场短视主义的盛行，使得中长期投资的市场供给低于需求。近年来的记录显示，私人资本不会自动流入发展中国家，支援基础设施建设。20世纪90年代，对私人资本市场的迷信使人们相信，在基础设施投资领域，私人投资者会扮演引领者、开拓者的角色。然而这一期待落空了：随着政府支持的逐步退出，私人资本并未像人们预计的那样涌入发展中国家。在实际投资过程中，私人投资者往往高估了现实中的风险，从而导致人人持观望的态度，没有人愿意成为第一个投资者。

针对私人资本市场固有的短期行为盛行的问题，现行的解决方案是着力释放机构投资者的潜力，鼓励它们开展长期投资。机构投资者包括养老基金、保险商以及主权财富基金等，通常，它们持有的是长期债务，因而投资眼光也相对长远些。比如，经合组织于2012年2月启动一项计划，试图为机构投资者和长期投资项目建立联系。2013年9月，在二十国集团圣彼得堡峰会上，各成员国元首共同宣布支持经合组织起草的《二十国集团/经合组织关于机构投资者长期投融资的高级原则》（*High-Level Principles of Long-Term Investment Financing by Institutional Investors*），随后还研究制定了落实这些高级原则的方法。尽管机构投资者们拥有巨大的潜力，但要想有效地发挥政策杠杆的作用，降低投资风险，进而清除投资障碍，受援国政府的干预仍被认为是不可或缺的因素。

总之，私人资本市场短期行为的盛行阻碍了长期融资的顺利进行。

开发性金融机构的战略角色

开发性金融机构的战略定位是弥补长期转型性投资的巨大缺口。下面我们将首先就开发性金融机构给出一个一般性定义，随后对其在促进长期转型性投资方面承担的三大战略角色做详细阐释。

开发性金融机构的定义

开发性金融机构是指以主权信用为依托，利用市场机制开展活动，以实现某国、某地区或某几个国家的公共政策或战略性目标为宗旨的金融机构。开发性金融机构可以是单一国别的，也可以是区域性或全球性的，这主要取决于所涉及国家的数量和地理分布。

与传统的政策性银行相比，开发性金融机构有以下特点：

第一，传统政策性银行以政府转移支付或补贴作为最主要的资金来源，很少关注自身业绩表现。相比之下，开发性金融机构更强调资产质量、风险管理和财务可持续性，强调融资渠道的多样性，其资金来源包括资本市场上发行的债券、公众存款、实收资本以及政府出资，还可以向其他金融机构借款或合作融资。

第二，传统政策性银行依据行政命令进行资源配置，运作资金依赖政府补贴。与之相反，开发性金融机构在实际业务中拥有更大的自主权，它们更主动地利用市场机制实现公共政策（或国际发展）的既定目标。

第三，与传统政策性银行相比，开发性金融机构的经营更有效率，其经营产出更具规模、更具有可持续性、影响力更大。因此，开发性金融机构在推动公共使命和战略目标实现方面更为积极主动。

事实上，尽管这两类机构都是为了实现公共使命而设立，但是在风险管理、财务可持续性以及推动可扩展、有影响力的发展成果等方面，开发性金融机构的表现都优于传统政策性银行。

与商业银行相比，开发性金融机构有以下几个特点：

首先，在企业目标方面，商业银行是为了使利润和股东权益最大化而设，而开发性金融机构则主要是为了实现政府所确定的公共政策和战略性目标。因此，商业银行的运作遵循安全性、流动性、收益性原则，而开发性金融机构在努力实现公共目标的同时仅追求收支平衡或略有盈余，以实现可持续经营。

其次，在金融工具方面，商业银行受期限错配的制约，主要开展短期零售融资业务，但开发性金融机构可以依托主权信用在资本市场上发行债券，因而可以为基础设施建设、核心产业部门、公共项目以及国际开发合作提供长期、大额的融资支持。

最后，在市场角色定位方面，商业银行专注于在成熟的市场环境中扩大市场份额；但在那些很难在较短时间内取得投资回报的领域，比如贫民区改造等项目，它们就不情愿或没有能力补上融资缺口。相反，开发性金融机构正是在市场失灵的地方发挥作用，从而建立市场信用体系和制度，为私营部门的参与奠定基础。

开发性金融机构的三大战略角色

开发性金融机构的首要责任是汇聚中长期投资，谋求经济社会的可持续发展。在资本市场短视主义盛行的当下，这一责任尤为重大。本节将从汇集中长期投资这一基本任务出发，探讨开发性金融机构在推进转型进程中的三大战略角色。

从传统观点来看，开发性金融机构的角色仅限于补救市场失灵。在那些利润太过微薄、不足以吸引私人资本进入的领域，开发性金融机构可以提供融资服务。比如，增加医疗和教育领域的投入，从而提升社会福利。

但这一看法忽略了开发性金融机构在转型发展过程中承担的三大战略角色，即长期规划、市场培育以及聚合各方力量，促成政府与社会资本的合作。

长期规划

长期综合性规划对一个国家或一个地区实现跨越式发展来说至关重要。首先，要以战略视角来制定长期的战略发展目标。这一点对发展中国家来说尤为重要，因为唯有如此，这些国家才能释放巨大潜能，发挥后发优势，追赶发达经济体。目标明确的规划能帮助人们发现并解决资源、技术和制度领域的瓶颈。突破这些瓶颈对实现规模化经营、产业和技术升级以及跨越式发展至关重要。其次，制度化的规划工作有助于减少政治权力的滥用，确保长期综合性发展规划能严格落实。最后，良好的规划应当与时俱进，及时迎接新挑战，根据实际情况修正已有的战略和路径。

开发性金融机构可以成为这方面的融智银行，因为它们具备制定长期综合性规划的专长。开发性金融机构可以与不同层级的政府开展合作，帮助它们设立长期发展目标、发现关键的瓶颈问题、制定各种创新性战略、实施发展规划。从这个意义上说，开发性金融机构不仅为发展提供融资服务，也提供高度专业化的知识。

随着越来越多的国家从低收入步入中低收入行列，长期规划的重要性日益凸显。大量国家从劳动生产率较低的传统经济体转向劳动生产率较高的大型现代经济体。今天，这一转型的速度之快前所未见，只需要一代人的时间就能完成。对赶超经济体而言，要发挥后发优势，公共部门必须以前瞻性的眼光主动作为，打造经济起飞必需的基础设施"软件"和"硬件"。所谓的亚洲经济奇迹就是一个范例：20世纪70年代起，亚洲"四小龙"（韩国、中国台湾、中国香港、新加坡）的腾飞，以及近几年中国的快速发展都是明证。在拥有全球超过3/4低收入国家的非洲，各国已将经济转型列入首要日程。《非洲联盟转型规划》将2063年定为目标年，到那时整个非洲大陆应达到中等收入水平。只有以宏大愿景和战略远见制定发展规划,才能合理调度公共资源、协调社会资本,共同实现长远目标。

但请注意,国家能力对能否制定高效的长期规划有很大影响。宏大的愿景固然能使一国发挥后发优势,释放巨大潜力,赶超发达经济体,但这样的共同愿景能否获得国家支持,则取决于该国的国家能力。事实上,脆弱国家(fragile states)"履行基本治理职能的能力都很成问题",更缺乏"与社会建立建设性互动关系的能力"。在国家局势不稳定的情况下,政府连自身的合法性都受到质疑,就更不必奢谈建立共同愿景,制定和实现长期规划了。

总之,开发性金融机构可以成为专业化知识的提供者,协助各国政府,尤其是赶超型发展中国家的政府制定长期综合性规划,实现跨越式发展。

市场培育

发展中国家的一个紧约束是市场机制不成熟、不健全,甚至根本不存在,这将严重阻碍转型进程。大规模转型投资涉及的问题往往空前复杂、空前庞大,需要长远眼光。转型投资往往在技术或结构上被认为存在风险,因此,一般来说,受中短期业绩表现制约的私人机构往往无法参与。这一问题对那些市场仍处于萌芽乃至休眠状态的发展中国家而言尤为严重。因此,发展中国家应当主动加强市场建设,为转型投资铺平道路。

市场培育的核心是良好信用的培育。由于缺少可靠的历史记录,投资发展中国家的风险往往被过分高估。错误的高估风险会导致无人愿意冒险成为第一个投资者——他们都不愿或不能承担实验失败的风险和损失。这样一来,为经济腾飞和价值的规模增长创造条件就尤为关键了,唯有如此才能解决"无信心"和"不作为"的问题。

对发展中国家而言,主权信用是非常有价值的信用资本。凭借主权信用,它们可以主动建立市场、培育社会信用。开发性金融机构以主权信用为依托、利用市场机制开展活动,以启动和扩张投资。开发性金融机构可以担当市场先行者的角色,它们可以承担风险、厘清误解,乃至克服低迷状态,为投资者建立信心,以较小规模的投资吸引更大规模的私人投资。这些先行先试的努力可以改善借款方的信用状况和项目公司的治理结构，还可以为市场参与设计各种模型，从而超越商业银行的局限，实现市场培育。

总之，开发性金融机构能够推动绿色投资，增强投资者信心，从而培育市场，为大规模、可持续投资创造条件。

聚合各方力量，促成政府与社会资本的合作

开发性金融机构是公共和私营部门之间的桥梁。这类机构是准公共部门，以实现公共使命和战略目标为宗旨，通常依托主权信用在资本市场上以较低的价格融得资金。而且，它们还基本遵循风险管理、项目管理和财务表现等市场化原则。这种双重角色使开发性金融机构获得公共和私营部门的双重信任，能够与双方都建立起富有成效的合作关系。因此我们可以说，要使政府和社会部门实现协同增效，开发性金融机构是最佳媒介。

实现政府与市场、公共部门与私营部门间的协同增效，是吸引长期融资必不可少的环节。以基础设施建设投资为例：由于在投资的不同阶段存在各种各样的风险，因此没有哪家机构能独力承担全部投资。这时，开发性金融机构就为政府、多边开发银行、私人投资者和融资人提供了合作的平台。这样的合作不仅能调动许多金融工具，包括（但不限于）补贴、贷款、股权、担保以及保险，而且还能构建知识共享平台，将各领域专家的意见汇集起来。

总之，作为公共和私营部门合作互动的桥梁，开发性金融机构可以在各个资金供应方之间建立合作伙伴关系，解决复杂的长期投资问题。

报告结构概览

本报告将遵循以下思路展开：第二章到第五章选取了部分多边、国别和与中国相关的开发性金融机构，回溯它们各自的历史，展示其基本经营信息，特别突出介绍了它们最新的关键性和创新项目。第六章对国际开发性金融机构协会进行了介绍，这些组织的设立是为了促进各开发性金融机构的相互学习与合作。第七章就所选各开发性金融机构的模式进行数据分析，内容包括所有制、规模、资金来源、资产质量及其他指标。第八章为案例分析,这一部分案例的选取和分析重点包括:开发性金融机构如何通过参与跨越式发展的长期规划,解决重大发展问题;如何充分利用主权信用培育市场;以及如何聚合各方力量,促成政府与社会部门的合作。第九章展望了开发性金融的良好前景,呼吁各方妥善运用开发性金融机构日益增强的资金实力,在各开发性金融机构间增加互信、加强合作。

第二章 多边开发性金融机构

多边开发性金融机构由多个国家建立，受国际法约束，其所有者或股东一般为国家政府，偶尔也由其他国际机构和组织担任。多边开发性金融机构的主要使命是降低世界或某一广大区域的贫困程度。这些机构通过提供低息贷款来支持一系列广泛的投资，其中大多是长期投资。目前，最著名的多边开发银行是世界银行和各大洲的区域性多边开发银行，其中大多数是在"二战"后成立的，旨在帮助世界经济的重建以及为长期国际合作的发展提供机制。

世界银行集团

基本信息

世界银行（简称"世行"）是为发展中国家资本项目提供贷款的联合国国际金融机构。世行是世行集团（World Bank Group，WBG）的组成部分、联合国发展集团的成员之一。世行集团由国际复兴开发银行（the International Bank for Reconstruction and Development，IBRD）、国际开发协会（the International Development Association，IDA）、国际金融公司（the International Finance Corporation，IFC）、多边投资担保机构（the Multilateral Investment Guarantee Agency，MIGA）以及国际投资争端解决中心（the International Centre for Settlement of Investment Disputes，ICSID）5个成员机构组成。现任世行行长为金

埔。世行成立于1944年的布雷顿森林会议，总部设在美国华盛顿特区，截至2014年年底，共有131家代表分支机构与17 139位员工。2010年，根据各成员国的贡献，世行调整其成员的表决权以增加发展中国家的话语权。目前，表决权最高的世行成员为：美国（15.85%）、日本（6.84%）、中国（4.42%）、德国（4.00%）、英国（3.75%）、法国（3.75%）、印度（2.91%）、俄罗斯（2.77%）、沙特阿拉伯（2.77%）和意大利（2.64%）。

使命与战略

世行的官方目标是消除贫困，它为全世界设定了到2030年要实现的两大目标：第一，终结极度贫困，将日均生活费低于1.25美元的人口比例降低到不超过3%，中期目标是到2020年将极度贫困人口比例降低到9%以下；第二，促进共享性繁荣，推动各国底层40%人口的收入增长。为了实现这些目标，世行进行了大范围的机构再调整，以强化国际复兴开发银行、国际开发协会、国际金融公司、多边投资担保机构以及国际投资争端解决中心之间的合作。

股权结构与治理

世行由其成员国及地区所有。IBRD和IDA分别拥有188个成员国和172个成员国。这些成员国由世行的最终决策者——理事会代表。理事一般由成员国及地区的财政部长或发展部长担任。他们于每年的世行和国际货币基金组织的理事会年会期间会面。理事们授权给25位在世行工作的执行理事。世行的董事会由世行行长及25位执行理事组成。前五大股东（美国、日本、中国、德国、英国）各自任命一位执行理事，而其他成员国及地区则由选举产生的执行理事作为代表。董事会每两年进行一次行长选举，选举产生的世行行长同时也是整个世行集团行长。行长负责主持董事会会议和银行的全面管理，董事会负责银行的日常运营和决策。

资金来源

世行资金有 4 个主要来源：各成员国缴纳的股本、国际金融市场借款、成员国的拨款以及商业收入。IBRD 在国际资本市场发行债券，为中等收入国家和资信可靠的低收入国家的经济改革项目提供贷款、担保、其他风险管理产品及技术援助。2014 财年，IBRD 发行了 22 种货币债券，共筹集相当于 510 亿美元的资金。尽管市场存在波动，但是世行凭借其在资本市场的地位与资金实力，仍能以非常优惠的条件筹集到大量资金。IBRD 筹集资金的能力来源于它稳健的资本状况、股东的支持，以及审慎的财务政策与行动。正因如此，世行保持着 3A 信用等级。IBRD 的股本主要包括实收资本与储备金。根据 2011 年 3 月 16 日世行理事会通过的《一般和选择性增资决议》（General and Selective Capital Increase Resolutions），增资总额达到 870 亿美元，其中实收资本将在 5 年内增加 51 亿美元。2014 财年，IBRD 的认缴资本已达到 2.32 亿美元，可用的实缴资本达到 1 400 万美元，股本占贷款的比例为 25.7%。截至 2014 年 6 月 30 日，总认购资本达 426 亿美元，相应实收资本达 25 亿美元。IDA 的资金主要来自合作伙伴政府的捐款，其他资金来源包括 IBRD 净收入转移、IFC 赠款和借款国所偿还的 IDA 信贷回流资金。IDA 第 16 期的增资时间跨度为 2012～2014 年，增资规模（根据增资讨论最新情况更新）为 338 亿特别提款权（相当于 508 亿美元）。

经营数据

2014 财年，世行的总资产达到 3 588.83 亿美元，总股本达 404.67 亿美元。IBRD 的年收入来自股权收益及低利润率的贷款。这些收入用于支付运营费用和 IDA 对最贫困国家的转移支付。IBRD 在 2014 财年的净亏损为 9.78 亿美元。世行集团向其成员国和私人部门共承诺 656 亿元的贷款、拨款、股权投资和担保。IBRD 承诺资金总额为 186 亿美元，而专门为最贫困国家提供资金的 IDA 所承诺的资金总额为 222.4 亿美元。IFC 为私人部门发展提供了 220

亿美元的资金,其中 50 亿美元是从投资合作伙伴中募集的。MIGA 提供了 32 亿美元的政治风险和增信投资担保,包括对一些转型项目的投资担保。世行的标普评级为 AAA,穆迪评级为 AAA。

商业模式与产品

世行贷款分为批发贷款和零售贷款。中国大城市拥堵和碳减排项目就是世行批发贷款项目的一个例子,其目的在于通过发展公共交通和管理交通需求,帮助建立政策框架,减少中国大城市的交通拥堵和温室气体排放。世行资金使用分为两种模式:发放贷款和提供拨款。世行集团通过向发展中国家提供零利率或低利率信贷以及拨款,支持了众多领域的投资,包括教育、健康、公共管理、基础建设、金融和私人部门发展、农业以及环境与自然资源管理。其中,公共管理和司法领域得到了 22% 的 IBRD 和 IDA 贷款投资,交通占比为 17%,能源和矿产占比为 16%。有些项目是由世行与政府、其他多边机构、商业银行、出口信贷机构以及私人部门投资者共同出资。

IBRD 主要的目标投资区域是欧洲、中东、拉美、东亚以及亚太地区,而 IDA 主要覆盖非洲、南亚、亚太地区。世行也可通过与双边和多边捐助机构合作建立的信托基金提供或调动资金。很多合作伙伴要求世行帮助管理一些旨在解决跨行业、跨地区需求的计划和项目。IDA 提供的资助拨款是世行集团的另一项重要工作。IBRD 也向客户提供金融衍生品。另外,世行集团还通过政策咨询、研究分析和技术援助支持发展中国家。

专栏 2-1　发挥世行集团在承担变革项目中的协同作用

为了增加用于支持发展中国家的资金储备和类型,特别是支持转型项目,世行采取了新的措施。这些措施旨在充分利用整个世行集团的金融资源和工具，发挥国际复兴开发银行、国际开发协会、国际金融公司和多边投资担保机构之间的协同作用。

提供政治风险担保的世行分支机构——MIGA 正和 IBRD 达成一项创新性的敞口互换协议。该协议将增加双方的资产组合的多样性，从而为开展额外业务创造条件。早期的一个合作案例是 IBRD 和 MIGA 达成的一项总值 1 亿美元、具有创新性的敞口掉期交易，互换确保双方在巴西和巴拿马开展额外业务。MIGA 的职责是降低直接投资发展中国家的政治风险，提供指导和咨询，在线交流投资信息，并妥善解决投资者与政府的争端。MIGA 通过排除跨国投资的潜在政治风险，确保 IBRD 和其他世行集团成员贷款的有效性。2014 年，MIGA 计划在未来 4 年内增加约 50% 的担保。

IBRD、IDA、IFC 和 MIGA 正在探讨共同制定并实施高影响力的变革项目。"一个真正成功的合作伙伴关系需要合作各方诚实、坦率和真诚，建立和发挥各自的优势将是关键。"

亚洲开发银行

基本信息

根据亚洲开发银行（the Asian Development Bank，AsDB，简称"亚行"）的成立协议，亚行于 1966 年成立，目前拥有 67 个成员国，其中 48 个来自亚太地区。前五大股东分别为日本（15.7%）、美国（15.6%）、中国（6.5%）、印度（6.4%）和澳大利亚（5.8%）。亚行总部设在菲律宾首都马尼拉，并在全世界设有办事处，代表机构包括北美（华盛顿特区）、欧洲（法兰克福）和日本（东京）。截至 2014 年 12 月 31 日，亚行共有员工 3 051 人，他们分别来自其 67 个成员国的 61 个国家。

亚行的最高决策机构为理事会，由每个成员国的一位代表组成。相应的，理事会从中选举产生由12位成员组成的董事会及代理人，其中8位来自亚太地区的成员国，其余来自亚太地区以外的成员国。理事会选举产生亚行行长，由其担任董事会主席并负责管理亚行。行长任期为5年，任期届满后可继续参选。由于日本是最大股东之一，传统上行长一直由日本人担任。现任行长为中尾武彦（Takehiko Nakao），他于2013年接替黑田东彦（Haruhiko Kuroda）。亚行在亚洲设有11处常驻代表办事处，在东京、华盛顿、法兰克福均设有代表办事处。

使命与战略

亚行的愿景是使"亚太地区脱离贫困"，使命是帮助发展中成员国减少贫困，提高人民生活水平。为实现这一愿景，亚行致力于三大战略发展议程：包容性经济增长、环境可持续发展和区域一体化。

2008年，亚行在长期战略框架下明确了其角色与战略方向，指导直到2020年的业务，并提高对发展中成员国援助的作用与效率。亚行通过广泛的活动和倡议以促进发展中成员国的经济增长和社会发展。在亚行"2020战略"中，亚行聚焦以下5个关键领域：发展私营部门，鼓励改善治理，支持性别平等，帮助发展中国家获取知识，加强与其他开发机构、私营部门以及社区组织的合作伙伴关系。这些领域与亚行的三大战略发展议程（包容性经济增长、环境可持续发展和区域一体化）密切相关。

股权结构与治理

亚行股东由来自48个亚太地区和19个非亚太地区的发展中国家和发达国家组成。每个股东国都在亚行的最高权力机构——理事会设有代表。

资金来源

亚行的资金来源分为普通资金（Ordinary Capital Resources，OCR）和特

别资金（Special Funds Resources，SFR）。普通资金包括实收资本、营业余额和债券发行收益。亚行在国际和国内资本市场发行债券以募集资金，亚行债券获得国际主要评级机构的最高评级。特别资金来自亚行的专项基金，比如亚洲发展基金、亚行研究所以及日本特别基金。2014 年，亚行共募集 119.75 亿美元的中长期资金和 25.18 亿美元的短期资金。据估计，亚行今后 3 年的年借款需求将达到 130 亿～150 亿美元。

经营数据

截至 2014 年年底，亚行总资产达到 1 540.92 亿美元，所有者权益总计为 169.38 亿美元。2014 年，亚行投资的项目总额达 229.3 亿美元，其中 136.9 亿由亚行自行承担，92.4 亿由共同出资伙伴承担。主权投资项目为 159.9 亿美元，非主权投资项目为 69.4 亿美元。核定股本、认购股本分别为 1 540.9 亿美元和 1 530.6 亿美元。2014 年，亚行贷款额共计 73.68 亿美元（其中主权贷款 62.8 亿美元，非主权贷款 10.88 亿美元），与 2013 年 59.85 亿美元的贷款额（其中主权贷款 51.78 亿美元，非主权贷款 8.07 亿美元）相比，增幅为 23.1%。

从成立到 2013 年 12 月 31 日，亚行在 OCR 上批准贷款总额为 1 554.91 亿美元（已终止的项目除外），其中 92.7% 为主权贷款，即发放给公共部门（成员国、由相关成员国担保的机构、政府机构和其他公共机构）的贷款。近 7.3% 为非主权贷款，即发放给私人企业、金融机构和选定的非主权公营单位的贷款。

商业模式与产品

亚行的商业模式包括贷款、股权投资、技术支持以及与其他机构联合融资。亚行根据普通资金的商业条款提供"硬"贷款，而隶属于亚行的亚洲开发基金（Asian Development Fund，ADF）则从专项资金中提供附带优惠条件的"软"贷款。亚行贷款分为批发贷款和零售贷款。包括联合融资在内的前五位受助对象分别是印度（26.6亿美元）、巴基斯坦（25.8亿美元）、中国（23.6亿美元）、越南（20.6亿美元）和印度尼西亚（20.5亿美元）。不计联合融资，前五位受助对象依次为：印度（24.5亿美元）、中国（20.5亿美元）、巴基斯坦（15.4亿美元）、印度尼西亚（10.2亿美元）和菲律宾（8.8亿美元）。亚行将更有选择性地继续致力于卫生、农业、灾难和紧急援助发展。亚行还将促进政策对话，提供咨询服务，并通过共同出资的方式利用官方、商业以及出口信贷资源来调动资金，这些活动将最大化其援助开发的影响。运营资金由普通资金和特别资金共同提供。亚行规定，普通资金和特别资金需分开设立及使用。

专栏2-2　2014格鲁吉亚—土耳其跨边境水电项目

亚行与世行集团成员之一国际金融公司以及欧洲复兴开发银行（EBRD）合作，于2014年9月投资舒阿海维（Shuakhevi）水电站的建设和运营，帮助格鲁吉亚开发本国水电潜力，实现能源自给。

国际金融公司提供的2.5亿美元债务融资是格鲁吉亚历史上规模最大的民营水电投资，包括亚行和欧洲复兴开发银行的两笔9 000万美元长期优先贷款，以及国际金融公司的7 000万美元长期优先贷款。国际金融公司的项目投资总额为1.04亿美元，其中包括对佐治亚（Adjaristsqali Georgia）企业的3 400万美元股权投资。该企业为合资企业，印度的塔塔电力（Tata Power）和挪威的清洁能源投资（Clean Energy Invest）各占40%，国际金融公司占20%。

舒阿海维水电站将满足格鲁吉亚的冬季电力需求，减少对进口燃料的依赖，增加可再生能源的产量。在其他季节，水电厂将通过欧洲复兴开发银行资助的传输线向土耳其出口电力，促进电力跨境交易。该项目通过创造就业机会，提高市政收入和升级地区道路，使当地社区受益。该项目表明，以无追索权的跨境融资模式在格鲁吉亚开展绿色领域的水电项目是可行的，并且对该领域乃至格鲁吉亚的发展都具有重要意义。同时，该项目也促进了区域合作，提升了格鲁吉亚的能源贸易收入。这一突破性的可再生能源投资体现了亚行在支持能源安全和环境可持续发展方面的重要作用。

亚行对亚洲私营部门的9 000万美元融资中有1 500万由加拿大气候基金（the Canadian Climate Fund）提供，该基金由加拿大政府资助，亚行负责管理，用于私营部门。有EBRD参与投资的格鲁吉亚至土耳其跨境输电线路项目展现了银行是如何通过促进私人领域投资来帮助国家转型成为开放经济体的，这将刺激能源发电领域的私人投资。舒阿海维项目预计将提振投资者对格鲁吉亚的信心，并刺激该领域更多的私人投资。

该项目是格鲁吉亚第一个通过联合国气候变化框架公约碳减排认证的水电项目。预计年发电量为4 500亿瓦特时，年温室气体减排量为20万吨以上。该项目总装机容量为187兆瓦，包括位于格鲁吉亚西南部的阿扎尔（Adjara）地区的舒阿海维和斯科哈塔（Skhalta）水电厂。水电厂于2013年9月开工，计划于2016年投入使用。

美洲开发银行

基本信息

美洲开发银行（Inter-American Development Bank，IADB，简称"美开行"）是拉丁美洲和加勒比地区重要的开发性资金来源。根据1959年签署的《美洲开发银行成立协议》，美开行通过向政府和政府机构（包括国有企业）提供贷款，支持拉丁美洲和加勒比地区的经济发展、社会发展和区域一体化。美开行的总部位于华盛顿特区，在其 26 个债务国设有分支机构，共有员工 2 000 人。该行董事会包括 14 位执行董事，以及对应的 14 位候补执行董事。现任行长为路易斯·阿尔韦托·莫雷诺（Luis Alberto Moreno），负责主持董事会。

使命与战略

美开行有五大目标：减少贫困和社会不平等、解决小国弱国的需求、通过私人部门促进发展、应对气候变化、促进可再生能源和环境可持续发展、推动区域合作和一体化。自 2012 年以来，根据美洲开发银行第九次增资（the Ninth General Increase in the Resources of the Inter-American Development Bank，IADB-9），美开行一直致力于战略和部门规范性文件的修订。同年，IADB 制定了部门框架文件，为每个部门提供：（1）一个灵活的框架，可以应对广泛的挑战和面向 26 个成员国借款的制度环境；（2）对项目团队有意义的战略性指导，明确银行每个部门的目标。

财权结构与治理

美开行由其成员国所有，包括 26 个借款成员国和 22 个非借款成员国。其前五大股东依次为：美国（29.34%）、阿根廷（10.77%）、巴西（10.77%）、墨西哥（6.92%）和加拿大（6.29%），而投票权份额位居前五的成员国依次为：美国（30.0%）、阿根廷（11.0%）、巴西（11.0%）、墨西哥（7.1%）和日本（5.0%）。

资金来源

美开行通过从其 48 个成员国、金融市场和管理的信托基金借款以及共同融资获得资金。美开行的债务评级为最高的 3A 级。IADB 的通知即缴资本由 22 个非借款成员国担保，包括世界上最富有的发达国家，这是美开行发行债券的保证。这种安排确保了美开行债券的 3A 信用评级，并且使借款成员国的借款利率接近商业银行对其最大借款企业利率。此外，22个非借款成员国只提供担保，不实际出资，因此它们用于支持美开行的贷款业务对本国预算的影响很小。美开行以标准商业利率向机构投资者发行债券以募集贷款资金。债券由该行的48个成员国实缴资本和22个非借款成员国担保的通知即缴认购资本构成。上述这些资本一起构成了美开行的普通资本1 010亿美元。其中，已缴部分为4.3%，剩余的95.7%为通知即缴。除了向成员国提供贷款，美开行还积极开展对私营企业的贷款业务，以促进拉丁美洲和加勒比地区的中小企业发展。具体实施方式既可通过IADB的结构化企业融资部门，或IADB的"多数人机会"这一倡议活动进行，也可以经由IADB成员国成立的、旨在帮助拉美及加勒比地区中小企业融资的多边贷款机构——美洲投资公司进行。

经营数据

截至2014年年底，美开行的总资产为1 062.99亿美元，而在2013年年底这一数字为970.1亿美元；所有者权益为236.97亿美元，而在2013年年底为235.5亿美元。该机构资产收益率在2014年和2013年分别为0.52%和1.36%。IADB充足资本政策巩固了理事会所确立的目标——维护3A信用评级。根据贷款违约时间长度，美开行对由主权担保的不良贷款有不同处理。

商业模式与产品

IADB采取零售贷款模式。此外，它通过在拉美和加勒比地区的26个借款成员国的经济发展项目，每年在成员国中为商业机构和咨询机构创造了2万~3万个合同机会。IADB集团通过私人部门促进拉美和加勒比地区的发展。通过向那些对社会和经济发展有积极影响的企业项目提供资金和技术援助，美开行对微型企业、大型公司和金融机构、各类市场参与者均提供广泛支持。

2014年美开行审批的贷款集中在IADB-9下的5个优先领域，并有助于实现框架内设立的目标。就行业而言，42%的贷款用于发展制度支持，38%用于基础设施和环境领域,16%用于社会部门项目,5%用于一体化和贸易计划。此外,新批准的业务中,35%用于发展的配套制度支持方面,34%用于基础设施和环境部门,17%用于一体化和贸易,14%用于社会领域。

治理与监管

IADB监督每一笔贷款资金的使用情况。银行工作人员通过美开行在26个借款成员国的办事处监控每一项业务的进展。执行董事会有权对流动性政策做出修改,并通过提高政策上限、增加资金灵活度,加强流动性。政策允许银行管理层基于未来现金流的需求预期,对流动性资产进行动态管理。

专栏2-3 扩大对厄瓜多尔女企业家的金融服务

融资困难已成为阻碍厄瓜多尔地区企业发展的最大问题,小型企业受限于融资难以充分发挥潜力。此外,世行的数据显示,在厄瓜多尔,仅有28.5%的小企业由女性所有,15%的贷款被授予由女性领导的企业。企业家的性别所导致的贷款额度差距可以通过提供专业化的理财产品来缩小。"扩大对厄瓜多尔女企业家的金融服务"项目于2013年获得批准,并于2014年签署。作为向拉美和加勒比地区的民营企业提供技术援助的牵头者,美开行集团的多边投资基金(MIF)通过提供无偿技术合作资金,加强厄瓜多尔皮钦查银行(Banco Pichincha)对由女性领导的中小企业融资的支持。这将促进皮钦查银行改进风险分析工具,开发针对女性的专业化产品及服务,以提升细分市场的服务能力。此外,皮钦查银行还将加入女性全球银行业联盟(GBA)——一个为女性企业家提供融资的经验交流和实践的全球平台。"扩大对厄瓜多尔女企业家的金融服务"项目的可持续性是基于由女性领导的中小企业所面临的融资不平等。考虑到与由男性领导的企业之间巨大的融资差距，尚未得到融资服务的潜在客户对皮钦查银行而言是发展的机遇。

该项目是多边投资基金与皮钦查银行在2008年建立的合作伙伴关系的延续。在第一阶段，MIF通过提供无偿技术合作资金来支持皮钦查银行扩展面向小企业的融资服务，成功帮助皮钦查银行进行规模缩减。银行将小额信贷的对象扩展到了32 465家中小企业，远超项目的原定目标。此外，由女性领导的中小企业获得的贷款远少于男性，这种不平等正是"扩大对厄瓜多尔女企业家的金融服务"项目所希望改善的。

该项目还将和MIF的另一个项目"应用心理测量工具扩大小企业融资"（Rolling Out a Psychometric Tool for Expanding Small Business Finance）开展合作，在风险分析模型中引入创业金融实验室开发的心理参数。该模型将作为风险分析方法的补充，使银行能够帮助目前不符合借款条件的企业。

欧亚开发银行

基本信息

根据俄罗斯和哈萨克斯坦签署的《欧亚开发银行成立协议》，欧亚开发银行（Eurasian Development Bank，EDB）成立于2006年，总部设在哈萨克斯坦的阿拉木图，目前拥有6个成员国：俄罗斯（2006年）、哈萨克斯坦（2006年）、塔吉克斯坦（2006年）、亚美尼亚（2009年）、白俄罗斯（2010年）和吉尔吉斯斯坦（2011年）（括号内年份是各成员国加入欧亚开发银行的时间）。EDB的现任主席是德米特里·潘金（Dmitry Pankin）。

欧亚开发银行是欧亚共同体反危机基金（EAF或ACF）的管理者，该基金于2009年由亚美尼亚、白俄罗斯、哈萨克斯坦、吉尔吉斯共和国、俄罗斯和塔吉克斯坦共同创立。EAF的主要目标是帮助成员国克服全球金融危机的影响，以确保长期经济稳定和促进经济一体化。EAF通过贷款支持预算、收支和本国货币平衡，并提供投资信贷为国际项目融资。

2014年年底，欧亚开发银行的股权占比分别为：俄罗斯（65.97%）、哈萨克斯坦（32.99%）、亚美尼亚（0.01%）、塔吉克斯坦（0.03%）、白俄罗斯（0.99%）、吉尔吉斯共和国（0.01%）。此股权结构表明，EDB主要由俄罗斯和哈萨克斯坦控制，服务独联体区域的经济发展。EDB在圣彼得堡设有分支机构，在其成员国的首都设有6个代表办事处。截至2014年年底，EDB共有员工294名。

使命与战略

《欧亚开发银行成立协议》的第一章确立了该银行的使命：促进成员国市场经济的发展，通过投资加强贸易和经济一体化。通过参与其他国际金融及银行业机构、工会的活动，EDB力图积极促进国际金融和经济合作。EDB的任务是通过投资活动促进市场经济发展、拉动经济增长、扩大贸易以及加强成员国的经济联系。EDB投资活动的目标包括：促进国家间关系，为欧亚区域一体化提供技术援助，为推动区域一体化进程和发展金融市场的金融和投资提供机制支持；提高环境管理，保护和改善环境状况。根据该行委员会于2014年7月批准的2013—2017战略，EDB将致力于以下几个方面：成员国的发电项目、运输以及市政基础设施建设的融资；通过资助降低企业能源消耗、提高资源节约的项目以提升能源利用效率；对有利于贸易和经济联系的项目追加融资；提升经贸关系和相互投资的吸引力，以增强成员国之间的经济一体化。除此之外，EDB不资助诸如学校和医院建设等社会项目。

所有权

根据协议，欧亚开发银行在其任何一个成员国享有法律豁免权。同样，在最终判决前，该银行的财产和资产也免于搜查、征收、逮捕、没收、征用或任何其他形式的撤回和转让。该银行在成员国的领土内享受税收豁免（特定类型服务的应交税款除外）。

根据协议第九条，欧亚开发银行应当使用自有或借入的资金维持运营。但是如有需要，该银行可以接受其成员国政府的直接支持。EDB 在国内发行地方债券，亦根据欧元中期票据计划在国内外市场发行欧洲债券，并通过欧元商业票据项目筹集资金，从其他金融机构通过双边银行借款募集资金。成员国政府为欧亚开发银行的债务提供担保。其信用评级独立于成员国。例如，目前，穆迪对欧亚开发银行的评级为 Baa1/（P）Baa1，而对俄罗斯的评级为 Ba1。

资金来源

欧亚开发银行的注册资本总额为 70 亿美元，其中包括已缴资本 15 亿美元和通知即缴资本 55 亿美元。

经营数据

截至 2014 年年底，欧亚开发银行的总资产为 39.155 0 亿美元，2013 年年底为 45.936 6 亿美元。2014 年年底，欧亚开发银行的所有者权益为 16.382 7 亿美元，2013 年年底为 16.321 6 亿美元。2014 年年底，总负债为 22.772 亿美元，2013 年年底为 29.615 亿美元。2014 年，实现净利润 1 778 万美元，2013 年则亏损 7 251 万美元。2014 年，银行客户的平均贷款利率是 8.58%。2013 年年底，欧亚开发银行的资产收益率（ROA）为 -1.8%，净资产收益率（ROE）为 -4.3%。另据穆迪估算，2014 年年底，该行的不良贷款率为 4.5%。

商业模式与产品

欧亚开发银行发放的贷款分为批发贷款和零售贷款。银行贷款可采取的形式有：一次性贷款（one-off loan）、循环信用证（revolving credit）和非循环信用证（non-revolving credit）以及银团贷款等。贷款最长期限为15年。实体经济可以获得3 000万~1亿美元的信贷。欧亚开发银行在项目上的平均投资额约为5 000万美元。该银行提供咨询、技术援助、研究分析工作以及国际合作。

欧亚开发银行建立了以下项目融资流程：项目初步评估；融资决议；资金支持准备；开展项目融资；项目监控、落实和偿付。同时，对涉及投资者选择（竞争性招标，涉及公私合作的项目）和组织银团融资的项目还建立了特殊流程。欧亚开发银行的所有融资项目几乎都位于成员国领土内。当前投资组合的国家分布情况分别是：俄罗斯（45.18%），哈萨克斯坦（36.76%），白俄罗斯（12.58%），亚美尼亚（1.57%），塔吉克斯坦（0.38%），吉尔吉斯斯坦（0.9%），其他欧亚经济共同体国家占2.63%。

组织与管理

根据《成立协议》第二条，欧亚开发银行受以下章程的约束：国际法的通用原则和标准、可适用的国际条约、《欧亚开发银行成立协议》以及银行纲领。《成立协议》以及成员国之间缔结的其他协议相较各成员国法律优先适用。根据《成立协议》第五条，成员国的投票权由各自持股比例决定。EDB的法定资本为150万股，每股1 000美元。每一股代表一票投票权。EDB的管理委员会由9人组成，主席为德米特里·潘金。EDB委员会成员由各成员国财政部或相应部门的部长和副部长担任，并负责任命管理委员会及管委会主席。根据公司治理规定第7.3条，EDB每年需要进行外部审计。根据公司治理规定第4.5条，EDB有两个对委员会负责的监管机构：修订委员会——委员会的监督机构，负责监督银行的财务和经营；内部审计服务部——银行的独立部门，通过系统性和一致的措施，协助理事会和执行机构进行风险评估，提高风险管理、内部控制和公司治理的效率，以实现银行的战略目标。

专栏2-4　哈萨克斯坦的铁路行业融资项目

哈萨克斯坦是一个正在蓬勃发展的出口导向型内陆国。石油和石油产品、金属、众多其他原料以及半制成品、谷物是其最重要的出口产品。然而，哈萨克斯坦距离海洋和许多目标市场有数千公里之远。

2013年4月，欧亚开发银行和Trans-telecom JSC（哈萨克斯坦国家铁路公司的子公司）签署了一项协议。根据该协议，欧亚开发银行将投资开发自动牵引供电调度控制系统。因此，欧亚开发银行向Trans-telecom JSC提供175亿哈萨克坚戈（1.13亿美元）的贷款，为期7.5年。项目成本总计255亿坚戈（1.65亿美元），包括发展哈萨克斯坦自动化轨道交通控制系统。哈萨克斯坦国家铁路公司正在安装精密设备，分别用于测量火车的柴油和电力消耗，收集、分析实时数据。分析人士预测，使用自动化控制系统将减少最多13%的柴油消费量和7%的用电量。

项目预计将对该国经济的可持续发展产生积极影响。据欧亚开发银行的分析人士预测，该项目将为哈萨克斯坦带来每年超过4 000万美元的经济增长。然而，由于铁路建设是长期投资，现在判断项目成效为时尚早。

2014年10月，欧亚开发银行增加了项目融资份额，在2013年的175亿坚戈（1.02亿美元）的基础上向Trans-telecom JSC追加贷款75亿坚戈（4 400万美元）。

本案例展示了开发性金融机构是如何通过基础设施投资帮助发展中国家突破发展瓶颈的。

非洲开发银行

基本信息

1963年7月,非洲高级官员及专家会议和非洲国家部长级会议在苏丹首都喀土穆召开,会议通过并签署了建立非洲开发银行的协议。1966年7月1日,非洲开发银行(the African Development Bank,AfDB)开始正式运营。AfDB旨在促进成员国的经济发展和社会进步,其法定资本由79个成员国认缴,其中包括53个独立的非洲国家和26个非洲以外的国家。

AfDB的董事会包括20名执行董事和代理执行董事,现任行长为唐纳德·卡贝鲁卡(Donald Kaberuka),同时也是董事会主席。截至2014年年底,银行前五大股东依次为:尼日利亚(9.3%)、美国(6.6%)、日本(5.5%)、埃及(5.4%)、南非(4.8%)。执行董事会负责日常决策,包括贷款和资金捐助的批准以及指导工作决策。每个成员国均在董事会设有代表,但他们的投票权和影响取决于其所在国家向AfDB投入的资金。非洲开发银行的总部位于科特迪瓦首都阿比让,并设有13个分支机构。

根据AfDB成立协议的第8条,AfDB还被授权建立或委托管理与其目的、功能一致的专项基金。按照这一规定,1972年非非洲国家(non-African states)成立了非洲发展基金(African Development Fund,ADF),1976年尼日利亚成立了尼日利亚信托基金(Nigeria Trust Fund,NTF)。

使命与战略

非洲开发银行的使命是促进非洲的经济可持续增长和减少贫困。该银行的十年战略(2013—2022)强调了全球价值链在连接非洲与世界经济中的重要性。同时,该银行在私人部门、区域一体化、农业和人类发展方面的政策和战略也与上述目标一致。

股权结构与治理

非洲开发银行的法定资本由 79 个成员国认缴，包括 53 个非洲国家和 26 个非洲以外的国家。非洲以外的国家占总股权的 40%，而非洲国家占 60%。

资金来源

非洲开发银行董事会批准的年度贷款计划旨在提高资源的成本效益，进而为集团客户融资以及满足流动性需求。这是因为不同于有中央银行作为最后贷款人的商业银行，非洲开发银行完全依赖自身流动性履行债务。该银行通过绑定全球大型基准债券与满足特定需求业务的方式发行中长期债券。标准普尔将该银行全球债务发行机构下的所有优先级债券评为 AAA 级。该银行的充足股本由其通知即缴资本支持，尽管非洲开发银行从未发出缴纳通知。非洲开发银行并不吸收存款或政府转移支付，它和多边合伙人、双边机构、政府和当地企业开展联合融资业务。

经营数据

2014 年年底和 2013 年年底，非洲开发银行的总资产分别为 332.52 亿美元和 323.35 亿美元，所有者权益分别为 88.09 亿美元和 89.8 亿美元，总资产收益率分别为 0.14% 和 0.35%，净资产收益率分别为 0.52% 和 1.25%。银行 2% 的非主权贷款和证券组合具有很高的风险，每个项目都有特定的贷款利差，最长贷款期限为 50 年。

商业模式与产品

非洲开发银行的贷款模式为零售贷款。其部门级业务表明，该银行有选择地开展业务，并注重结果。基础设施建设在非洲开发银行批准项目中所占比例最大，其中最主要子类为交通设施，其次是能源、用水及卫生设施。非洲开发银行提供大量的融资业务，包括信贷、贸易融资及对中小企业的支持

（非洲发展基金则不主要承担此类业务）。非洲开发银行提供如下产品：为主权担保借款人提供的增强型可变利差贷款（Enhanced Variable Spread Loan）产品、单一货币贷款、担保和一系列风险管理产品（包括利率和货币掉期交易、利率上限协议、利率上下限协议、大宗商品对冲和指数化贷款）。非洲开发银行通过定制债务偿还方式为借款人提供便利，包括年金、递增或递减的分期偿还或者期终一次偿还。

治理与监管

非洲开发银行风险管理的政策和程序随着市场、信用、产品和其他发展而持续改进。非洲开发银行管理风险的指导原则由银行的充足资本政策、银行金融产品和服务的一般授权以及银行信用风险管理的指导方针来确定。

欧洲复兴开发银行

基本信息

欧洲复兴开发银行（European Bank for Reconstruction and Development，EBRD）成立于冷战结束后的1990年，是一个多边开发性金融机构，总部设在伦敦。该银行领导层由5个部分组成：总裁、董事会、理事会、执行委员会和高级领导小组。截至2014年年底，欧洲复兴开发银行的成员已经扩展到中亚和地中海南部及东部的国家。迄今为止，共有64个国家和地区以及欧盟、欧洲投资银行加入了欧洲复兴开发银行。

使命与战略

欧洲复兴开发银行的使命是："不同于一般的开发银行，欧洲复兴开发银行负有政治使命，即仅援助那些承诺和奉行多党民主和多元化原则的国家。此外，EBRD同样致力于保护环境和可持续能源发展工作。"

股权结构与治理

EBRD 的所有权归属于全体成员国和成员机构,前五大股东分别是:美国(10.1%)、法国(8.6%)、德国(8.6%)、意大利(8.6%)、日本(8.6%)和英国(8.6%)。

资金来源

EBRD 的资金来自政府、国际机构(双边援助)和各种基金组织(多边基金)。主要捐赠者和基金包括主权国家、国际金融机构、欧盟、EBRD 股东特别基金(shareholder special fund,SSF)和融资优惠(气候变化)。

在过去的 5 年中,EBRD 经营稳健。自 2011 年以来,标准普尔、穆迪和惠誉三大国际评级机构始终对 EBRD 的债务给予 3A 的信用评级。因此可以认为,在过去的 5 年中,EBRD 从未发生过贷款减值或逾期的状况,也未曾让成员国政府协助解决这类问题。由于 EBRD 是由各成员国政府出资成立的机构,因而其债务是以成员国的主权信用为担保的。除政府以外,EBRD 也通过其全球中期票据项目和基于成员国主权信用的商业票据从资本市场募集资金。

经营数据

2014 年年底,EBRD 的总资产为 635.63 亿美元,较 2013 年同期的 674.45 亿美元下降了 5.76%。2014 年年底,EBRD 的所有者权益由 2013 年的 204.93 亿美元减少到 171.35 亿美元,同比下降 16.4%。2014 年年底,EBRD 的贷款组合余额为 250.63 亿美元,与 2013 年年底的 271.13 亿美元相比下降了 7.56%。2014 年 EBRD 的资产收益率为 -0.9%,而 2013 年这一指标为 1.8%。相比 2013 年 7.2% 的净资产收益率(基于净利润计算得到),2014 年 EBRD 的净资产收益率仅为 -3.8%,同年不良贷款率为 5.6%,较 2013 年的 3.3% 有大幅上涨。EBRD 的贷款利率是基于当前市场利率水平制定的,包括固定利率和浮动利率两种。其贷款的最长期限可达 15 年。

商业模式与产品

EBRD 不是零售银行，不提供存款、储蓄账户或抵押贷款等商业性服务和产品。EBRD 资助的领域包括农业、金融机构、信息和通信技术行业、制造业、服务业、市政基础设施、自然资源、核安全、房地产、旅游业、可持续资源、气候变化和运输业。EBRD 项目的主要目标是促进成员国的经济发展。同时，EBRD 也向大型私人企业提供金融支持，比如 2013 年分别对土耳其的两家互联网和电话公司 Evim.net 与 TurkNet 提供资金支持。EBRD 注重以下业务领域的决策：资助早期转型国家和新加入成员国，如地中海南部和东部地区国家；促进环境和社会可持续发展；消除被投资国的性别差异，倡导男女平等；促进本币贷款和资本市场的发展。

专栏 2-5 中西亚的可持续资源和能源项目

环境保护和能源可持续发展被欧洲复兴开发银行视为核心问题。经济的快速增长提高了各国对能源和资源的需求，也增加了人们对环境的可持续发展和气候变化的关注。因此，欧洲复兴开发银行的各成员国的当务之急是制定和落实解决资源问题的政策。

欧洲复兴开发银行致力于提高成员国的资源效率优先意识。继 2006 年发起可持续能源倡议（SEI）后，欧洲复兴开发银行于 2013 年发起了可持续资源倡议，作为 SEI 的拓展。2014 年，一系列可持续资源和能源项目在中亚和西亚投入运营。该区域有大量的基础设施融资需求，而可持续发展的概念尚未得到应有的关注。

以下是 2014 年欧洲复兴开发银行启动的 5 个关键项目：

1. 吉尔吉斯斯坦能源效率项目

作为吉尔吉斯斯坦的主要银行之一，吉尔吉斯斯坦投资和信贷银行（KICB）自 2001 年以来一直与欧洲复兴开发银行开展合作，并于 2014 年 7 月获得了欧洲复兴开发银行通过当地银行提供的 500 万美元贷款。这笔贷款将被用于改进和升级企业和家庭的节能设备。

该项目旨在提高能源效率，提升能源安全意识，降低能源消耗。未来计划包括促进私人部门的能源结构转型和提升能源使用效率。据报道，KICB 将获得欧洲复兴开发银行提供的 200 万美元贷款，用于购买和安装家庭和民营企业的节能设备。

2. 格鲁吉亚水电发展

2014 年 11 月，格鲁吉亚东北部的 Dariali 峡谷正在建设一个新的水电站（HPP）。这是欧洲复兴开发银行帮助格鲁吉亚发展可再生能源的一个主要环节。而格鲁吉亚有望成为世界上水力资源最丰富的国家之一。

Dariali 能源公司是格鲁吉亚的一家民营水电站，已经获得了欧洲复兴开发银行提供的 8 000 万美元银团贷款。项目完成后，该水电站预计在利用水力潜力和碳减排方面起到至关重要的作用。

3. 约旦太阳能发电厂

2014 年 11 月，欧洲复兴开发银行与法国开发性金融机构法国经合投资公司（PROPARCO）合作，向约旦提供 1 亿美元贷款（各出资 5 000 万美元），用于兴建位于约旦南部的 3 个太阳能光伏发电厂。

这项计划旨在提升约旦的可再生能源发电量。在约旦，像太阳能这样的可持续能源还没有得到充分开发。这些发电厂预计发电容量约为 40 兆瓦，从而减少约旦对能源进口的依赖。

4. 哈萨克斯坦的风力发电厂

哈萨克斯坦可再生能源领域实施的一个重大项目是它受 EBRD 资助的

第一个大型风力发电厂。2014年11月，欧洲复兴开发银行和清洁技术基金（CTF）向Wind Power Yereymentau（哈萨克斯坦的一个特殊目的机构）提供了140亿坚戈（7 170万美元）的贷款。这笔贷款由哈萨克斯坦的国有能源企业JSC Samruk-ENERGO担保。

通过实施该项目，哈萨克斯坦的风力发电量预计将从45兆瓦增至95兆瓦。目前，哈萨克斯坦正处于能源转型期，煤炭提供了70%以上的发电量。风力发电厂的使用预计每年将减少12万吨二氧化碳的排放。

5. 波黑（BiH）生物质锅炉厂

2014年12月，欧洲复兴开发银行向波黑提供了一笔700万欧元（850万美元）的主权贷款，用于建设普里耶多尔（Prijedor）的生物质锅炉厂。该项目还得到了瑞典国际发展合作署（SIDA）200万欧元（240万美元）的资金支持。

该项目最先在波黑市政当局投入运营，旨在通过安装单独的热变电站增加供暖服务。预计将有超过13 000人从中获益。

为表彰其对可持续资源和能源的贡献，欧洲复兴开发银行于2014年被授予美国财政部颁发的发展成果奖。欧洲复兴开发银行的可持续资源和能源项目促进了中亚和西亚地区经济的强劲与可持续发展。

加勒比开发银行

基本信息

加勒比开发银行（Caribbean Development Bank，Caribbean DB）成立于1969年，是一家区域性金融机构，总部设在巴巴多斯。加勒比开发银行的领导层由行长、董事会和理事会组成。截至 2014 年年底，加勒比开发银行共有 19 个本地区借款成员国，3 个本地区非借款成员国和 5 个非本地区非借款成员国。

使命与战略

加勒比开发银行的使命是："旨在成为提供区域发展资金的主要媒介，以高效、负责、合作的方式与借款成员国和其他发展伙伴协作，通过经济与社会发展系统地消除这些国家的贫困。"

股权结构

加勒比开发银行的所有权归属于全体成员国。前六大股东分别是：牙买加（18.62%）、特立尼达和多巴哥（18.62%）、加拿大（10.02%）、英国（10.02%）、德国（6.00%）、中国（6.00%）。

资金来源

作为一个开发性金融机构，加勒比开发银行不经营商业银行的存款业务。加勒比开发银行在国际资本市场发行债券，也从多边机构获得信贷。其主要资金来源包括普通资金（ordinary capital resources，OCR）和特别资金（Special Funds Resources，SFR）。其中，OCR 包括从欧洲投资银行、美洲开发银行、世界银行以及国际资本市场认购的资本和债务。SFR 又可分为两类：特别开发基金（Special Development Fund，SDF）和其他专项基金（Other Special Funds）。用于 SFR 的资金由成员国每 4 年补充一次。为 SFR 出资的成员国会就下一个 4 年中将要开发的优先领域与加勒比开发银行展开磋商。在过去的 5 年中，加勒比开发银行在不良贷款管理方面表现稳定。2009～2013 年，不良贷款率最高为 2012 年的 4.0%，最低为 2013 年的 0.1%。2013 年，加勒比开发银行的长期债券被穆迪评为 Aa1 级。因此，加勒比开发银行不需要成员国政府帮助解决不良贷款的问题。由于加勒比开发银行是一个由成员国政府出资成立的机构，因此其债务由成员国政府的主权信用担保。除了政府方面，加勒比开发银行也会凭借成员国的主权信用等级在国际资本市场募集资金。

经营数据

2013年年底，加勒比开发银行的总资产为14.52亿美元，较2012年年底的16.41亿美元下降了11.5%。总所有者权益为7.436亿美元，较2012年年底的7.07亿美元增长了5.2%。贷款组合余额为9.727亿美元，较2012年年底的9.799亿美元下降了0.73%。2013年，加勒比开发银行的资产收益率为1.17%，而在2012年，这一指标是1.52%。相比2012年2.17%的净资产收益率，2013年的净资产收益率仅为0.39%。不良贷款率在2013年是0.1%，而2012年这一指标为4.0%。其贷款利率视不同基金而定。在2013年，特别开发基金的平均贷款利率为2.44%，而其他专项基金为2.23%。加勒比开发银行发放的贷款最长期限是22年。

商业模式与产品

加勒比开发银行为非零售银行，不开展存款储蓄等商业银行业务。加勒比开发银行投资的领域包括农业和农村发展、制造业和工业、交通和通信、电力、能源、水利、环境卫生、社会基础设施和服务、环境可持续性和灾害风险降低、金融以及商业。加勒比开发银行的区域发展援助分为若干层次。加勒比开发银行的借款成员国拥有直接借用财政资源的权利。加勒比开发银行重视以下业务领域：促进农业生产和贸易、促进私人和公共投资以及创业和发展、提供技术援助、支持区域和本地金融市场与资本市场的发展；支持教育、培训和人力资源事业的发展。

专栏2-6 作为筹集外部资金桥梁的加勒比开发银行

加勒比地区包含二十多个国家和政治实体。大多数国家经济规模较小且不稳定。一些国家，如海地，仍然面临生活必需品短缺的问题。大多数国家的金融活动规模相对较小，资金短缺成为普遍现象。

意识到单纯依靠内部成员的局限性，加勒比开发银行在过去几年致力于通过与多边国际机构和世界其他地区的合作建立一个强大的融资支持体系。其大量项目是与加勒比地区以外的实体签订，并且获得外部资金支持的。

以下是2014年加勒比开发银行实施的几个重大项目：

- 2014年1月，加勒比开发银行与国际金融公司（世行集团成员）签署了一份谅解备忘录，以支持"对加勒比地区建设更好的基础设施至关重要的公私合作伙伴关系"。该备忘录将鼓励私人部门更广泛地参与基础设施建设。

- 2014年4月，加勒比开发银行和加勒比灾害应急管理机构得到了2 000万欧元（2 420万美元）的灾害管理拨款。该补助资金预计将加强加勒比地区抵御自然灾害、提升灾害风险管理水平的能力。

- 2014年7月，加勒比开发银行、美洲开发银行和日本国际协力机构签署合作备忘录，以促进东加勒比地区可再生能源和能源使用效率的发展。该方案旨在解决高能耗问题，减少对传统燃料的依赖。

- 2014年9月，欧盟、西班牙和美洲开发银行承诺帮助加勒比开发银行发展可再生能源，以加速经济发展，缓和气候变化的影响，确保能源安全。

- 2014年10月，加勒比开发银行和加拿大就区域发展问题展开讨论。讨论主要围绕如何提升加勒比开发银行的影响和能力，从而为借款成员国面临的挑战提供解决方案。

在所有的合作项目中，能源和资源领域的项目表现最为突出。跟随倡导可持续能源的趋势和考虑到加勒比地区能源利用的现状，加勒比开发银行高度重视"可持续能源倡议"（Sustainable Energy Initiatives），并于2014年8月制定了发展蓝图：加勒比开发银行将作为可持续能源和资源项目的执行机构，而美洲开发银行、日本国际协力机构和欧盟将负责提供资金支持。

区域合作不仅带来了稳固的金融资源，还带来了先进的管理方法和理念，提高了加勒比开发银行的运营效率。开发性金融机构应该顺应和利用金融全球化的发展潮流和机会。借助外部资金和管理手段对小型多边开发性金融机构而言尤为重要。未来，加勒比地区将加强与其他地区的合作，并在区域和全球事务中提升参与度和话语权。

伊斯兰开发银行

基本信息

伊斯兰开发银行（Islamic Development Bank，IsDB）是一家国际金融机构，于1973年12月在沙特阿拉伯王国吉达举行的伊斯兰国家财长会议上成立。1975年10月20日，IsDB正式运营，总部设在吉达。伊斯兰开发银行先后在摩洛哥的拉巴特、马来西亚的吉隆坡、哈萨克斯坦的阿拉木图和塞内加尔的达喀尔设立了4个区域办事处，在安卡拉（土耳其）和雅加达（印度尼西亚）设有两个国家关口局（gateway office），在14个成员国设有代表机构。IsDB的前五大股东分别是沙特阿拉伯（23.52%）、利比亚（9.43%）、伊朗（8.25%）、尼日利亚（7.66%）和阿拉伯联合酋长国（7.51%）。现任行长是艾哈迈德·穆罕默德·阿里（Ahmad Mohamed Ali），他自 1975 年便担任此职务。当前，IsDB 的执行董事会由 18 位成员组成：9 位由主要股东国家任命，而另外 9 位由其余国家选举产生。根据 IsDB 纲领，银行将按照伊斯兰教法的原则来促进其成员国和非成员国穆斯林社群的经济社会发展。

专栏 2-7　伊斯兰金融的本质

伊斯兰金融从属于伊斯兰教法。伊斯兰教法是一个泛用术语，尽管学者们同意其中的主要原则，但伊斯兰教的各个流派以及不同辖区之间的理解仍不尽相同。在许多国家，服从伊斯兰教规定的机构和传统主流金融机构并行。就其核心而言，伊斯兰金融是一个金融的道德体系。

- 伊斯兰金融是一个金融领域的道德体系。
- 天课是强制性的慈善，必须每年支付一次。在其他方面，每年对闲置资金收取 2.5% 的费用，捐赠给穷人和有需要的人。
- 贷款或高利贷的利息受到各种形式的规制。所有天赐的宗教（指伊斯兰教）严禁收取贷款利息。
- 双方必须共担商业交易的风险，共享商业交易的回报。
- 交易应当有真实的经济目的，而非不适当的投机，并且不能包含对任何一方的剥削或者任何有罪的活动。
- 伊斯兰交易往往基于资产，虽然标的资产并不一定构成抵押品。

使命与战略

伊斯兰开发银行的使命是促进人类全面发展，重点领域是减轻贫困、改善治理和提高人民福祉。IsDB 的"愿景之旅"（Vision Journey）计划分为两个阶段：中期战略1.0版（2009~2012年）或基础阶段，以及中期战略2.0版（2013~2015年）。中期战略2.0版于2012年批准通过。2013年，IsDB还制定了详细的十年战略框架。十年战略框架包含3个战略目标、五大战略支柱或优先领域，以及一个贯穿始终的主题。3个战略目标为：广泛团结、增长连通、促进伊斯兰金融业的发展。五大战略支柱为：经济和社会基础设施、私人部门增长、包容的社会发展、伊斯兰金融业发展、伊斯兰国家和非伊斯兰国家中穆斯林群体的合作。

股权结构与治理

伊斯兰开发银行由其成员国所有，目前由56个成员国组成。成为成员国的基本条件是该国家是伊斯兰合作组织（OIC）的成员。

与其他多边开发银行一样，伊斯兰开发银行只受国际法约束，而不受任何特定主权管辖。伊斯兰开发银行的大多数经营性资产与其他多边开发银行相同，得益于主权担保和国有事业单位或者高评级的银行及商业的担保。此外，作为一个超主权国家机构，伊斯兰开发银行享有税收豁免优惠政策。

资金来源

伊斯兰开发银行的资本来自成员国缴纳的资金。沙特阿拉伯认缴的资本最多，占全部通知即缴股本的23.9%。截至2013年年底，认购资本达180亿第纳尔（275.6亿美元），其中已缴纳部分为178亿第纳尔（272.6亿美元）。最初，伊斯兰开发银行的运营资金主要来自其股东权益。IsDB 46.3%的认购股本由Aaa、Aa和A级的国家持有，这一比例低于大多数Aaa级多边开发银行。其成员国通过定期注入新资本以表明对银行的持续支持。然而，随着成员国项目对资金需求的增长，伊斯兰开发银行开始通过发行伊斯兰债券来募集资金。运营资金的另一个来源是与合作伙伴共同出资，如阿布扎比发展基金、科威特基金、沙特发展基金等。

专栏2-8 伊斯兰债券（Sukuk）

最初，伊斯兰开发银行的运营资金主要来自股东权益。然而，随着其成员国融资需求的增加，伊斯兰开发银行决定从资本市场筹集资金。2003年8月，伊斯兰开发银行发行了价值4亿美元的信托证券，该证券于2008年到期。伊斯兰债券的出现丰富了伊斯兰开发银行调动资金的手段。除了补充内部资源，发行伊斯兰债券也旨在促进伊斯兰债券业在全球资本市场的发展。

伊斯兰债券有类似于传统债券的特征，根据伊斯兰教法设计，该类债券将出售给那些限于伊斯兰教法而无法投资传统债券的投资者。伊斯兰债券和传统债券之间的主要区别如下：

- 伊斯兰债券表明资产所有权；传统债券表明债务。
- 伊斯兰债券的担保资产符合伊斯兰教法；传统债券的担保资产可能会包括违背伊斯兰教法的产品或服务。
- 伊斯兰债券根据担保资产价值定价；传统债券根据信用评级定价。
- 当资产价值增加时，伊斯兰债券的价值也会增加；传统债券对应固定收益。
- 当卖出伊斯兰债券时，卖出的是担保资产所有权；当卖出传统债券时，卖出的是债务。
- 由于伊斯兰教法禁止收取利息费用，因此伊斯兰债券投资者只收取债券投资资产所产生的利润份额。

尽管伊斯兰债券的发行规模与传统债券相比仍然偏小，但伊斯兰债券正在经历快速增长（见图2.1）。迄今为止，这些债券主要由主权国家（特别是巴林、马来西亚、卡塔尔和巴基斯坦）、企业、超主权国家组织发行，少量由伊斯兰银行发行。

单位：百万美元

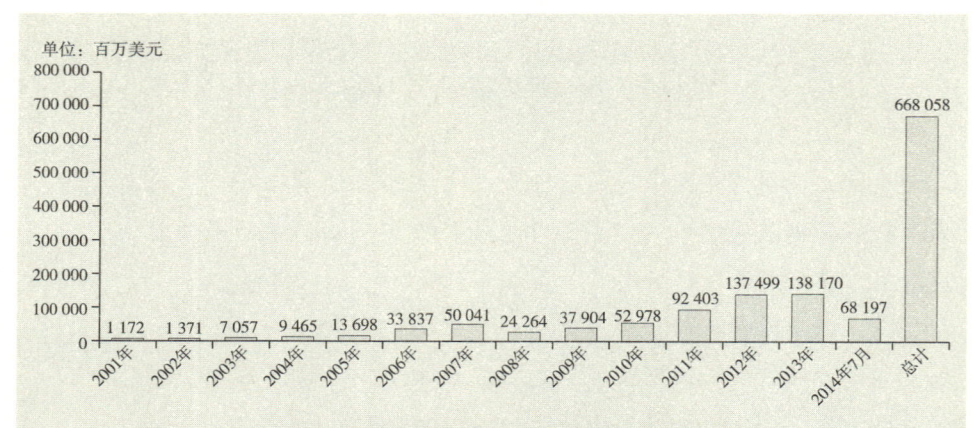

图 2.1 全球伊斯兰债券总额（2001 年 1 月～2014 年 7 月）

数据：2001年 1 172；2002年 1 371；2003年 7 057；2004年 9 465；2005年 13 698；2006年 33 837；2007年 50 041；2008年 24 264；2009年 37 904；2010年 52 978；2011年 92 403；2012年 137 499；2013年 138 170；2014年7月 68 197；总计 668 058。

2005 年，伊斯兰开发银行设立了 10 亿美元中期票据（MTN）项目，以便更频繁和有组织地利用全球资本市场资源。该项目允许伊斯兰开发银行发行不同面额的伊斯兰债券。2010 年 9 月，伊斯兰债券项目从 10 亿美元增至 35 亿美元，并于 2013 年 11 月进一步扩大至 100 亿美元。该项目通过满足伊斯兰开发银行的资金需求来支持其业务增长。根据中期票据计划，到 2012 年 11 月，伊斯兰开发银行发行了 13 个系列的伊斯兰债券，其中 5 个系列分别通过 4 家私募基金和 1 家公募基金于 2012 年发行。

2014 年，伊斯兰开发银行发行了两只价值各为 15 亿美元的伊斯兰债券，发行期为 5 年，利息为 1.8%。2014 年发行的两只伊斯兰债券是历史上超主权国家机构规模最大的私募业务。过去 10 年，伊斯兰开发银行致力于发展伊斯兰债券市场，频繁进入公共市场。截至 2014 年 6 月，伊斯兰开发银行已发行约 70 亿美元的伊斯兰债券。

伊斯兰开发银行可以通过伊斯兰债券募集运营资金，减少对股权筹资的依赖。如今，该银行具有更加成熟的为其成员国和非成员国的穆斯林群体的开发性项目融资的能力。此外，发行伊斯兰债券符合伊斯兰教法，这有助于促进伊斯兰金融在全球资本市场的发展。

经营数据

尽管受全球经济危机和一些成员国政治不确定的持续影响，伊斯兰开发银行的财务表现依然稳定。然而，如同大多数多边开发银行，IsDB 不以利润为导向，也不实行分红。相比商业银行，其利润表现较为平淡，但相比同类银行，其表现较为稳定。IsDB 的资产收益率在 2012 年和 2013 年分别为 1.19% 和 1.44%，而同期净资产收益率分别是 1.91% 和 2.51%。尽管如此，在过去 5 年中，伊斯兰开发银行的净利润为平均每年 1.43 亿第纳尔（占盈利资产的 1.7%）。IsDB 属于资本状况最好、杠杆率最小的多边开发银行之一，其权益资产比为 54%，债务股本比为 79.5%。IsDB 的资本充足率是 43.3%，最低要求为 35%。尽管处于高风险的运营环境，IsDB 的经营性资产持续表现良好，减值水平相当低。不良贷款率也维持在非常低的水平，在 2013 年约为 1%。IsDB 对高收入、中等收入和低收入国家的贷款期限不尽相同。最长贷款期限为 30 年，包括对最贫困国家的 10 年宽限期。

商业模式与产品

伊斯兰开发银行根据伊斯兰教法运营，因此不接受存款，只靠股本、留存收益以及通过对外交易和项目融资业务自创的资金维持运营。IsDB 通过提供符合伊斯兰教法的金融产品来支持成员国的发展。通过这些金融产品，IsDB 向农业、工业、农业产业和基础设施以及其他各领域项目提供资金。其银行贷款不收取利息，仅通过每年收取 0.75%～2.0% 的服务费来支付管理成本。IsDB 向亚洲、非洲以及中东的成员国和非成员国中的穆斯林群体提供贷款审批和财务协助，主要集中于能源、交通和其他基础设施领域。

治理与监管

伊斯兰开发银行的治理包括理事会和执行董事会的活动，以及旨在提升制度效率和发展效益的银行集团评估、风险管理、内部审计以及整合。

第三章 高收入国家的开发性金融机构

除了多边的开发银行外，开发性金融机构还包括国别开发银行。国别开发银行通常是由国家建立的金融机构，其创立的目的是为经济、社会和环境的发展而融资。国别开发银行在各国国内的长期经济发展中扮演了重要角色，对世界经济也产生了积极的影响。目前，世界各国均建立了各自的国别开发银行，这些国别开发银行的组织结构、资金来源、商业模式各不相同。本书选取了亚、非、欧、拉美的18家重点开发银行，并按世行定义的高、中、低收入国家进行分类。本章将对高收入国家的开发性金融机构进行探讨。

德国复兴信贷银行

基本信息

德国复兴信贷银行（Kreditanstalt für Wiederaufbau，KfW）是"二战"后德国在马歇尔计划下于1948年组建的政府所有的开发银行。KfW的总部位于德国法兰克福，分布在全球的办事处超过80个。德意志联邦共和国以30亿欧元（36.3亿美元）的名义资本，占KfW 80%的股份，而联邦各州以7.5亿欧元（9.1亿美元）入资，占股20%。KfW的股东中没有个人或私人机构。

KfW集团包括KfW和5个子公司：（1）国际项目融资和出口信贷银行（IPEX-Bank），提供项目和公司理财服务，负责德国境内和境外贸易以及出口金融服务。自2004年1月1日起，IPEX-Bank作为法律上依存KfW集团的内部机构运作。自2008年1月1日起，作为法律上独立的子公司运作。(2) 德国投资发展公司（DEG），推动发展中国家和转型国家的私营经济发展。(3) 技术参与公司（Tbg），专门解决历史遗留的银行合约问题。(4) 融资和咨询公司（FuB），处理和德国东部货币兑换相关的业务以及前德意志国家保险清算银行的代理业务。(5) 德国能源局有限公司（Dena），推广环保型产品，推动资源节约及可再生能源的发展。

使命与战略

作为一家"公共法律机构"，KfW的主要任务有4个：(1) 拉动内需，促进个人和中小企业投资，推动市政设施建设；(2) 出口和项目融资，支持德国和欧洲企业在全球市场的发展；(3) 开发性金融，支持发展中国家和转型国家的经济和社会进步；(4) 代表德国联邦政府执行特定任务。

KfW致力于支持经济、生态和社会的可持续发展。其工作重点包括：(1) 推动中小企业（SMEs）和新兴企业的发展；(2) 提供股权资本；(3) 为住宅安置节能设施；(4) 支持环保举措；(5) 为零售客户提供教育资金；(6) 支持市政公债和地区性发展银行；(7) 出口和项目融资，推动发展中国家和新兴经济体的发展。

KfW的具体任务根据时间所需不断调整。"二战"后，KfW受马歇尔计划支持，推动灾后重建，为德意志联邦共和国的建设做出了巨大贡献。自20世纪70年代以来，德意志联邦共和国进入稳定发展时期，KfW开始支持中小企业，尤其在高新技术和环保领域，为中小企业提供条件优惠的长期贷款，也因此为德国2/3的人口创造了就业机会。东西德合并后，KfW在部分德国公司私有化过程中也扮演了重要角色，包括汉莎航空、德国电信等。2000年以后，以原KfW为基础形成了KfW集团。如今，KfW的业务领域不断扩大：不仅关注教育和中小企业，还关注气候和环保（见表3-1）。2014年，KfW提供了741亿欧元（897.4亿美元）的发展资金，其中36%用于应对气候变化和环境保护。

表 3.1　2012～2013 年 KfW 的资金投向

	2014 年		2013 年	
	金额（百万欧元）	占比（%）	金额（百万欧元）	占比（%）
社会基础设施和服务	1 609	31	1 955	40
教育	257	5	329	7
健康	297	6	212	4
人口政策和计划以及生育健康	110	2	66	1
水供应与卫生废物/水处理	726	14	1 145	23
市民社会	176	3	198	4
其他社会基础设施和服务	43	1	5	0
经济基础设施和服务	2 906	55	2 251	46
交通和仓储	202	4	60	1
能源生产与分配	1 461	28	1 025	21
金融	1 243	24	1 159	24
商业与其他服务	0	0	7	0
生产部门	161	3	208	4
农业、林业、水产	160	3	122	2
工业、建设、采矿	1	0	86	2
其他	592	11	503	10
总计	5 268	100	4 917	100

政府支持

KfW 的原始资金来自联邦共和国和联邦政府的财政预算。KfW 代表联邦共和国推动发展，尤其在环境保护和发展中国家等问题上发挥重要作用。

再融资方面，资本市场是 KfW 最重要的资金来源，占其全部资金的 90%。作为一家国有机构，KfW 拥有政府担保，因此在资本市场信用良好。

KfW 也接受来自联邦政府的预算转移。预算转移通常发放到经济地位较为重要的地区，或者以非偿还性补助的形式发放。

联邦共和国为 KfW 的所有债务提供担保，包括 KfW 发放的贷款、债务证券、固定远期交易、KfW 参与的期权，以及其他涉及 KfW 的信用和涉及第三方由 KfW 担保的信用。

KfW 免交所得税。在房屋建设、居住和租用方式上，KfW 和德国中央银行（德意志银行）享有同等权利。

资金来源

KfW 的再融资是在国际资本市场上完成的。KfW 是世界上最大、最活跃的债券发行人之一，基本上只通过国际货币和资本市场为商业活动提供资金。通过其第一等级的信用评级，KfW 能够获得低息借款，并维持融资的可持续性。

KfW 集团在国际资本市场的融资策略依靠三大支柱：欧元和美元的基准债券、基准之外的公开募集债券和私募债券。2014 年，用债务进行的融资依旧占据着举足轻重的地位，占总资产的 83%，与前一年相比没有太大变化。由于利率一直维持在较低水平，因此 KfW 希望在总融资额中提高外国货币的比例，并计划在 2015 年扩大绿色债券发行量。

2014 年，KfW 在长期资金中为国际资本市场的相关行业募集了 574 亿欧元（695 亿美元）（2013 年为 654 亿欧元，即 901 亿美元），在 13 个国家发行了 250 种债券，并从大量的投资者流动性债券（基准债券）中获利。这些债券约占三大支柱的 57%，是融资十分重要的一部分。2014 年，KfW 的资本市场活动受到了两大产品的影响——在法兰克福发行的 KfW 首只人民币债券以及用美元、欧元发行的首只绿色债券。KfW 也因此设立了市场标准，为新的市场领域奠定了基础。

经营数据

截至 2014 年年底，KfW 的总资产达到 4 891 亿欧元（5 923 亿美元），股权合计 216 亿欧元（262 亿美元）。2014 年的资产收益率和净资产收益率分别为 0.31% 和 7.01%。作为风险报告的一部分，其信用程度分为 4 个方面：投资等级、非投资等级、监视清单和违约。2014 年年底，后两项占总信用的 7%（见图 3.1）。KfW 持有 14.1% 的一级资本。来自惠誉、穆迪、标准普尔的长期信用评级均达到最高级。

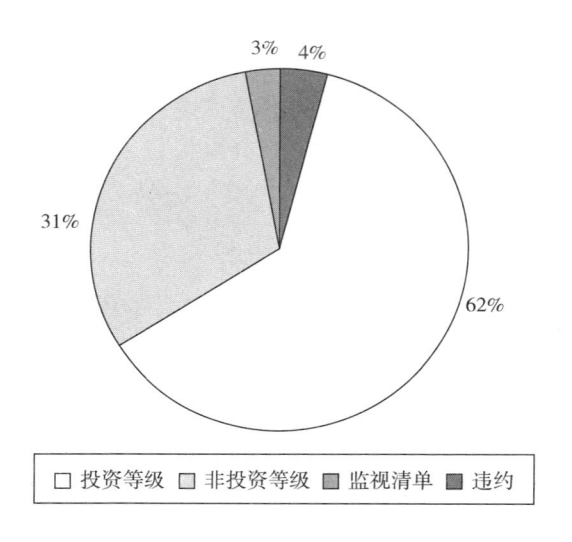

图 3.1 以净风险敞口衡量的 KfW 信用程度（2014 年 12 月 31 日）

商业模式与产品

KfW 的业务涵盖国内和国际两部分。国内业务包括：（1）KfW 中小企业银行，为中小型企业提供贷款；（2）KfW 市政和私人银行/信贷机构，为个人客户提供房产、环境、教育方面的服务，同时为政府服务；（3）政府特殊项目和大公司的战略性股票持有。国际业务包括：

（1）KfW开发银行的国际投资；（2）KfW国际项目融资和出口信贷银行的国际贸易。

作为开发银行，KfW用于促进发展的资金在2014年上升至741亿欧元（897亿美元），其中476亿欧元（576亿美元）用于推动商业发展，255亿欧元（321亿美元）用于国际金融。中小企业约占国内发展业务的44%。个人客户、公司、公共组织以及国际客户都是KfW的目标市场。

KfW为个人购买、建造住房以及创立企业提供贷款。KfW提倡能源有效利用，其融资可以帮助企业创立、巩固发展、扩张业务，范围涵盖了公司发展的全过程。KfW尤其鼓励节约能源、环境保护、可再生能源的发展（见专栏3-1）。比如，KfW的环境保护专项组为环保项目提供长达3年的免还款期，并为小企业实行较低的利率。其他对中小企业优惠的政策还包括提供顾问服务。

KfW提供的贷款通常通过其他普通银行转贷款。储蓄银行、合作银行和商业银行是KfW的主要合作伙伴。目前，KfW对国内能源节约方面的项目投资直接发放给用款方。通常，KfW直接为公共借款人提供贷款，比如城市和市政府。

公司治理

作为一家国有的、长期性金融机构，KfW的监管模式与普通商业银行有所不同。KfW的主管部门由董事会和监管委员会组成。董事会负责KfW的业务，根据KfW的公司章程管理资产，及时履行义务，执行监管委员会的决议。监管委员会和委员负责审查公司运营和资产，主要任务包括任命和解雇董事会成员、审议通过财务报表以及为高层监察部门选拔审计人员。

专栏 3-1　KfW 对位于摩洛哥的世界最大太阳能电厂的融资

摩洛哥是北非最大的能源进口国，一直致力于减少对进口化石能源的依赖。2013 年，摩洛哥经济增长超过 4%，国家经济逐渐起步。受基础设施投资和工业企业发展的推动，摩洛哥对能源的需求不断增加。目前，该国发展高度依赖高价的进口化石能源。

摩洛哥政府一直推行积极的能源策略。其目标是到 2020 年，太阳能、风力和水力发电单项年发电量达到 2 000 兆瓦。除此之外，摩洛哥也是可再生能源方面的领导者，逐步向可再生能源过渡，既有利于解决全球气候变化问题，也能保证摩洛哥的能源安全。

作为摩洛哥金融合作的伙伴之一，KfW 一直代表联邦经济合作发展部（BMZ）及联邦环境自然保护和核安全部（BMUB）与摩洛哥进行合作，并与其他国际资助方一道，资助瓦尔扎扎特（Ouarzazate）的发电厂。

瓦尔扎扎特位于撒哈拉边缘，阳光强度可达每年每平方米 2 500 千瓦时，是建立太阳能发电厂的理想位置。瓦尔扎扎特将建成世界上最大发电厂之一，年发电量达到 560 兆瓦，通过 4 个独立发电站发电，占地 3 000 公顷。

第一发电站"努尔 1 号"（Noor I）（阿拉伯语中，Noor 是"光"的意思）于 2013 年 6 月开工。该系统的亮点是熔盐能源储存设备，该设备能够有效存储热量达 3 小时，只要有阳光就能发电。如果项目按照计划进行，努尔 1 号将于 2015 年 10 月开始发电（见图 3.2）。

努尔 1 号的总投资额约 6.33 亿欧元（7.67 亿美元）。摩洛哥无法单独完成这样庞大的项目。在多家金融机构中，德国提供了 1.15 亿欧元（1.39

图 3.2　努尔 1 号所在地——抛物面反射镜
图片来源：KfW／叶苏斯·瓦奎斯·塞拉诺，埃尔斯·英吉尼拉，S.A.

亿美元)。预计努尔 2 号和努尔 3 号发电站的总投资额约 18 亿欧元 (21.8 亿美元)，其中 KfW 将提供 6.54 亿欧元 (7.92 亿美元)。

"瓦尔扎扎特的工程是一个参考方案，目标是低碳环保技术的革新，不仅对摩洛哥，对其他北非国家也意义重大。尽管目前发电厂主要为摩洛哥服务，但是将来有望将太阳能输送到欧洲，这个想法还停留在设想阶段，摩洛哥希望能够推动这个想法的实现，为摩洛哥的发展提供巨大机遇。"

北莱茵威斯特法伦州银行

基本信息

北莱茵威斯特法伦州银行（NRW. BANK）成立于2002年8月1日，在杜塞尔多夫和明斯特都设立了总部。该银行没有在德意志联邦共和国之外的国家或地区设立分部，截至2014年年底在德国境内共有30家分支机构，1 283名员工。克劳斯·纽豪斯自2014年5月1日起担任执行委员会主席。

北莱茵威斯特法伦州银行承担的是德意志联邦共和国地方银行的任务，该行始建于19世纪中期，2002年，德意志联邦共和国地方银行分为West LB股份公司（一家私有银行）和北莱茵威斯特法伦州地方银行（一家公有银行）。北莱茵威斯特法伦州地方银行成立于2002年8月1日，成立的基础是《关于北莱茵威斯特法伦州公有银行重组法律关系的法案》，2004年5月31日，《关于将北莱茵威斯特法伦州地方银行重组为北莱茵威斯特法伦州发展银行法案及其他修订案》生效后，北莱茵威斯特法伦州地方银行变为北莱茵威斯特法伦州银行，是北莱茵威斯特法伦州的开发银行。

北莱茵威斯特法伦州银行的管理层包括执行委员会、监管委员会和担保人。银行的执行和监管层从住房推广委员会和北莱茵威斯特法伦州顾问委员会获得具体建议。2011年，莱茵州和威州—利珀县联合作为银行担保人，北莱茵威斯特法伦州成为北莱茵威斯特法伦州银行的唯一担保人。

使命与战略

北莱茵威斯特法伦州银行的公共任务是"支持唯一担保人——北莱茵威斯特法伦州的市政建设，以满足公共需要，尤其在经济发展、结构调整、社会民生、住房政策等方面，实施并监管欧盟的发展政策"。根据可持续发展政策，北莱茵威斯特法伦州银行加大对居住条件、社会发展、气候变化、环境保护等项目的支持。

资金来源和政府支持

北莱茵威斯特法伦州银行与国内投资者的资金交易主要包括：不记名债券、记名债券以及期票。该行也利用融资项目在国际上筹集资金。该行构成投资的股票大多为北莱茵威斯特法伦州联邦持有，并于银行成立之日转移至银行。此外，在 2010 年，北莱茵威斯特法伦州批准了一项 24.14 亿欧元（31.62 亿美元）的免息后偿贷款，偿还期至 2044 年。北莱茵威斯特法伦州须对州承担的贷款、银行发行的债券、期货、期权、发放给北莱茵威斯特法伦州银行的贷款以及其担保的贷款直接负责。包括 8 项促进发展的融资在内，2014 年该行的总风险敞口约 1.39 亿欧元（1.68 亿美元），2013 年为 1.21 亿欧元（1.66 亿美元），来自北莱茵威斯特法伦州联邦的担保降低了其信用风险，涵盖了相应融资总额的 49%。良好的信用、专业的投资者服务，加上利息较低，北莱茵威斯特法伦州银行发行的债券十分具有吸引力，为未来长期融资打下了良好的基础。2014 年，惠誉对北莱茵威斯特法伦州银行的评级为 AAA。

经营数据

2013 年，北莱茵威斯特法伦州银行的总资产为 1 438 亿欧元（1 742 亿美元），不良贷款率约为 0.5%，最长贷款期限为 30 年，是德国第二大开发银行。2014 年，该行总权益为 179 亿欧元（217 亿美元），资产收益率和净资产收益率分别为 0.01% 和 0.09%。

商业模式与产品

北莱茵威斯特法伦州银行既提供零售银行业务，也提供批发银行业务，是一家很大程度上预算独立的开发银行，其经营政策是在整体上促进和支持发展。该银行利用预期获利在国际资本市场融资。北莱茵威斯特法伦州银行采取稳健的投资策略，利润用来支持银行的发展及推广活动，保证银行的长期发展，包括免息贷款和储备金及银行的运作。为了完成公共任务，银行主要批准贷款、承保担保，并进行股权投资。利用自身资源（比如，对推动发展的贷款降低利息）是银行商业模式的关键一环。

北莱茵威斯特法伦州银行提供优惠政策的领域有3个：新兴企业、发展与保护政策、住房与民生，3个领域下总共有9个促进发展项目，体现了银行的工作重点（见图3.3）。2014年，北莱茵威斯特法伦州银行提供了89亿欧元（108亿美元）的资金推动商业发展，相比2013年（92亿欧元，合127亿美元）下降了3.7%。北莱茵威斯特法伦州银行希望投入更多资金进行高额、长期的贷款（比如，支持具备规模的中小企业和北莱茵威斯特法伦州的基础设施建设）。同时，该银行也致力于促进向绿色能源的转型。

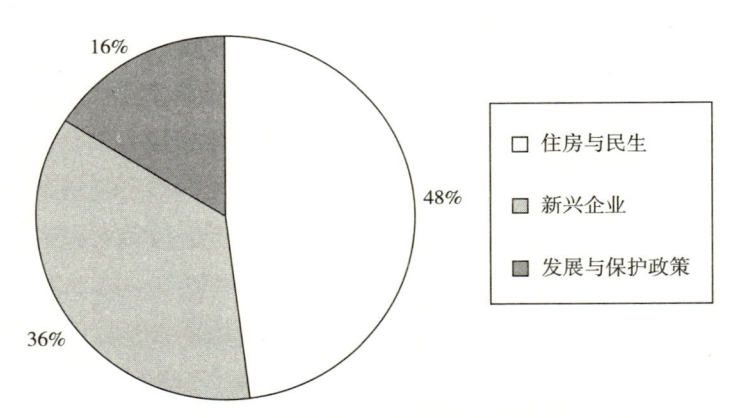

图 3.3　北莱茵威斯特法伦州银行提供优惠政策的领域

治理与监管

根据法律，北莱茵威斯特法伦州银行具有法定身份，是一家公法认定的信贷机构。该银行需要遵循商业银行的审慎原则（比如，资本充足率、贷款等级划分、贷款拨备），其设立的基础是《关于北莱茵威斯特法伦州公有银行重组法律关系的法案》。由州内政部施行政府对该银行的监管，政府对社会住房推广的监管,经与住房管理相关部门协议完成。

法国储蓄托管机构

基本信息

法国储蓄托管机构(Caisses des Dépôts et Consignations,CDC)创立于 1816 年路易十八时期,当时颁布了法国历史上第一部金融法,希望重振法国人民对国家信用的信心。根据法律,CDC 是"维护国家利益、促进公司发展的长期投资人和资助方"。作为国家的一部分,CDC 完全国有化,在法国议会监督委员会的监管和担保下,集中存款投资支持项目发展。CDC 在国家战略、公共利益及支持创新、促进可持续发展等方面发挥了重要作用。CDC 的总部位于法国巴黎里尔街 56 号,有 10 家分支机构和 10 家下属机构,包括 Bpifrance 集团、CNP 保险、威立雅运输和法国邮政,在保险、银行、地产、运输和休闲等不同竞争性行业运营。CDC 通过地区机构和法国当地政府协调,开展集团的管理和金融业务。CDC 同样将存款投入到长期"公共项目(包括补贴住房)及当地政府成立的促进城镇发展的半公共企业"。

自 1816 年成立后,CDC 于 1822 年发放了第一笔地方开发性贷款。1868 年,CDC 筹集了第一家寿险基金。1890 年,CDC 启动了律师存款管理项目。1910 年,CDC 开始推行第一个义务退休金计划。1945 年,CDC 开始为战后重建筹集资金。1950~1980 年,CDC 支持了法国"光荣三十年"计划。2007 年,CDC 发布了"ELAN 2020 战略计划",关注领域从基础设施建设扩大到支持中小企业发展、社会住房、教育、可持续发展以及其他关系到民生、具有战略意义的领域。

使命与战略

依照机构成立时的定义,CDC 是"法国国家利益和经济发展的长期投资者"。CDC集团"通过特定机构管理政府委托资金以及集团资金"。CDC的活动领域包括：保护公民储蓄、提供可靠的银行服务、管理退休金计划、为个人提供保险、支持当地政府、发展房地产、为企业融资、进行长期投资以及应对气候变化。

政府支持

CDC处在"法国议会的监管和担保之下"。由于其特殊的法律地位，CDC受到了法国公共部门的高度保护，享受法国政府的支持。法律保障让CDC避免了流动性和破产的风险，保护了偿付能力。评级机构认为，CDC作为一家与政府相关的金融机构，受益于法国的信用评级。惠誉指出："考虑到法国政府对CDC提供支持，并依据法律条文80-539，CDC可依靠当地法律和金融支持及时履行债务服务的义务，因此该银行的违约评级和法国主权信用紧密相关。"

资金来源

"CDC主要从存款和储备金中获得长期投资的资金，但也会进入有期债项市场，使债务形式多元化。"截至2013财年年底，CDC的客户存款金额占总负债的44%，银行同业拆借占18.2%，债务证券占24.7%。"CDC维持着185亿欧元（255亿美元）的欧洲中期债券项目，每年发行30亿~40亿欧元（42亿~57亿美元），期限为2~30年。"

资助模式方面，由于CDC得到了政府支持，因此主要将法定准备金、对冲工具和养老金等作为资金来源。CDC综合业务和信托业务的资金来自不同的法定资本。

CDC的总体业务资金包括：（1）法定准备金和公共部门存款——CDC由法国立法部门指定，为法国社会资金管理部门、非政府组织、社会住房建设机构、捐赠基金和其他公共部门管理资金等提供银行服务，CDC的主要资金来源是储备金和其他存款；（2）发行债券——作为一家长期投资机构，CDC

通过发行债券改善资产负债结构，并接受稳定的储蓄存款。

对应于总体业务的资金，CDC 总债务由多个部分组成：法定准备金和其他公共部门存款（37.5%）、累计未分配利润（22.5%）、法定存款中得到的债务证券（40%）。对于债务证券，其中长期发行债务占 7.5%，短期债务占 22.5%，回购资金占 10%（见表 3.2）。

表 3.2　CDC 集团（经合并的）资产负债表

资产		负债及所有者权益	
子公司和战略股权	20.0%	累计留存收益	22.5%
地方发展性项目	2.5%	法定存款准备金	37.5%
股权投资	12.5%	长期融资	7.5%
投资性资产	5.0%	回购	10.0%
证券投资组合	60.0%	短期融资	22.5%

除上述业务外，CDC 还涉及信托业务，比如政府监管的储蓄账户和养老金业务。

经营数据

CDC 从事批发借款。2014 年年底，其净收益为 17.93 亿欧元（21.71 亿美元），2013 年应占利润为 21.37 亿欧元（29.44 亿美元）。2013 年总资产为 1 430.9 亿欧元（1 971.2 亿美元），2012 年总资产为 2 866.5 亿欧元（3 779.4 亿美元）。2013 年年底，总权益为 310.9 亿欧元（428.4 亿美元），资产收益率和净资产收益率分别为 1.49% 和 6.87%。根据 2015 年 1 月出版的《惠誉对 CDC 的完整评级报告》，CDC 的减值贷款占总贷款的比例在 2013 年和 2014 年分别为 9.13% 和 6.84%。2013 年平均利率为 2.18/%。2014 年，惠誉、穆迪和标准普尔对 CDC 的信用评级分别为 AA/F1+、Aa1/P1+、AA/A1+。

商业模式与产品

CDC 的运营领域主要包括：公民储蓄保护、提供可靠的银行服务、管理退休金计划、为个人提供保险、支持地方政府、房地产开发、企业融资、进行长期投资以及应对气候变化。

（1）公民储蓄保护。CDC 集中并管理大部分法国公民的储蓄，成为其"储蓄基金"。利用这一资金，CDC 向对国计民生重要的部门发放贷款，比如居民住房、城镇建设。一部分资金用来支持国家整体发展作为回报。CDC 的主要任务是保证大量储蓄的安全性和流动性。CDC 实现了管理储蓄基金和为公共项目融资的双重作用。

（2）促进长期投资。每年 CDC 将利润的 1/3 投入到公共服务项目，通过股权投资，支持地方政府和公共部门的发展政策。与其他投资者不同，CDC 利用金融手段进行公共服务投资。CDC 是金融市场上最大的长期投资者之一。管理证券投资组合的主要目标就是持续发放收益，促进金融稳定，支持公共事业投资。

（3）融资业务。通过股权资本投入，CDC 帮助建立了法国的新公共投资银行——Bpifrance，以促进经济和地区发展。CDC 为中小企业提供投资、整合股权资本，促进创新，支持投资市场，通过 OSEO（法国创新署）为中小企业发放贷款。CDC 支持了新兴企业的发展，推动了社会经济的进步。

（4）支持地方政府。在住房、交通、工程、可再生能源和电子技术方面，CDC 支持地方政府和跨地区机构发展。

（5）管理养老金计划。作为广受推崇的资金管理者，CDC 管理着法国 47% 的养老金和社会福利基金。这些基金涵盖了 730 万就业人口和 350 万老龄人口，在法国，每五个人中就有一个人的养老金由 CDC 管理。CDC 能够提供高附加值的服务，是中央政府、地区政府和医疗服务部门 75 000 名公共服务人员的首选。

（6）为个人承保。CNP 保险是 CDC 的子公司，在为个人提供保险业务方面已有 150 年历史，是法国保险市场的领头羊。为帮助客户应对风险，CNP 保险提供了一系列保险产品：人寿储蓄保险、退休保险、应急基金和贷款付偿。如今，共 2 300 万人参加了储蓄和应急基金的保险，1 700 万人参加了贷款付偿。

（7）支持房地产开发。CDC 和当地政府合作，促进房地产建设，保障人民的居住权利，促进可持续发展。

（8）提供银行服务。自成立以来，CDC 同时是受法律保护的私募基金管理机构。今天，CDC 不仅提供法律方面的服务，同时帮助实现社会保障、维护公共利益。CDC 针对客户需求提供个性化服务，保障服务的安全性和高质量。

公司治理

法国储蓄托管机构由首席执行官皮埃尔－勒内·勒马（Pierre-René LE-MAS，2014 年 5 月 21 日上任）负责。首席执行官任期 5 年，由法国总统经内阁会议任命。CDC 管理委员会还包括其他 14 名成员。

监管委员会负责监督 CDC 管理层，为主席和首席执行官提供建议、辅助管理，但主席并不一定要采纳这些建议。董事会主席每年向议会递交报告，经议员审批。"监管委员会的职责是审查 CDC 的重大决策、战略方向、股权计划、储蓄基金管理和审计账目。"

CDC 监管委员会包括主席亨利·伊玛纽力（Henri Emmanuelli）和其他 12 名成员，其中 3 名不属于政府机构。监管委员会 13 名成员中，包括 3 名议员和 3 名专业人员，这些人员中 2 名由下议院主席提名，1 名由上议员主席提名。

法国议会通过监管委员会监督 CDC。"法国银行监管组织——法国金融审慎监管局（ACPR）认为，尽管 CDC 不是一家银行，但就银行监管方面而言，CDC 在资本充足率、内部偿债比方面都表现良好。"

日本政策投资银行

基本信息

日本政策投资银行（Development Bank of Japan，DBJ）的前身是成立于1951年的日本开发银行（Japan Development Bank，JDB）。20世纪50年代，JDB的主要作用是为钢铁、煤炭等重要工业的合理化改革、现代化和培育提供贷款。历经几次改革，1999年6月，《日本政策投资银行法》颁布。北海道东北发展金融公共公司是一家为地区发展项目提供资金的机构，同年10月，它与JDB一并转入DBJ。之后，根据《日本政策投资银行公司法案》（2007年，第85号法案；《新政策投资银行法案》），日本政策投资银行于2008年10月1日正式成立。

根据《新政策投资银行法案》，DBJ有望在成立5～7年内实现完全私有化。而法案修订之后，实现私有化的目标被延迟。由于2007～2008年金融危机的爆发，DBJ认为有必要将资金从政府转入民间，以重振日本经济。近期，DBJ决定自2015年4月1日起，在5～7年内实现完全私有化，但由于某些特定原因，日本财政部目前仍对DBJ享有完全控制权。

DBJ拥有10家分行，在日本境内有8家办事处，在纽约有1家海外办事处，以及3家分别位于新加坡、伦敦和北京的附属机构。

使命与战略

基于"运用金融手段开创未来之路"的公司理念，DBJ的新使命是"通过创新的金融业务解决问题、建立客户信任、实现社会富裕"。根据《新政策投资银行法案》，银行将提供组合投资和贷款服务。

政府支持

DBJ 目前属于日本国有，并完全处于日本财政部的控制之下。

资金来源

无论政府是否提供担保，DBJ 都可以直接向政府和借款人（如地区性银行）发行国内和国际债券。2014 年，日本政府为 DBJ 的境外债券提供了预算为 1 500 亿日元（14.56 亿美元）的担保。该债券 70% 发行于国内资本市场，30% 发行于国际资本市场。大多数债券以日元标价，但是 DBJ 希望增加美元债券发行量，同时增加美元资产。

DBJ 的信用评级分别是 A1 级（穆迪投资服务公司）、A+级（标准普尔公司）、AA 级（日本评级和投资信息公司）和 AAA 级（日本信用评级机构）。DBJ 减值贷款一直维持在较低水平，其贷款投资组合多为借贷给日本基础设施行业的私人企业。

经营数据

截至 2014 年 3 月 31 日和 2014 年 9 月 30 日，DBJ 整合后总资产分别为 163 107 亿日元（1 584.79 亿美元）和 162 109 亿日元（1 477.94 亿美元）。2014 年，DBJ 的净资产收益率和资产收益率分别为 0.33% 和 2.02%，不良资产率为 0.93%。信托基金和股票基金分别为 1 342 150 亿日元（13 027.29 亿美元）和 16 400 亿日元（159.18 亿美元）。总负债为 136 800 亿日元（1 327.82 亿美元）。借贷和债券分别为 91 800 亿日元（891.04 亿美元）和 42 400 亿日元（411.55 亿美元）。净利润为 1 243 亿日元（12.06 亿美元），资产充足率为 15.23%（《巴塞尔协议Ⅲ》，国际清算银行的指导方针）（截至 2014 年 3 月）。

商业模式与产品

DBJ 希望作为高度专业化的金融机构运作,提供组合投资和贷款服务。

DBJ 的主要资金来源是政府资金支持和债券发行。在金融危机和 2011 年日本地震之后,DBJ 建成了危机应对网络。根据《日本公共金融公司法案》,特定金融机构的成立意义是为了在自然灾害及其他重大危机之后提供信贷,DBJ 就是其中之一。此类金融机构从日本公共金融公司获得信贷后发放贷款。作为具有特殊使命的金融机构,DBJ 计划继续利用自身在灾后重建方面的专业能力提供贷款(见专栏 3-2)。

DBJ 最近开始在金融模式方面进行转变,试图降低对政府资金的依赖,但目前其主要资金来源仍为政府支持。此外,DBJ 还大力推进资金来源的多元化,增加私人机构资金的比重。

专栏 3-2 DBJ 在日本灾后管理中的作用

由于日本是灾害多发地,因此灾后重建和管理一直具有重要意义。尤其在 2008 年金融危机和 2011 年日本大地震之后,灾后管理的地位更加显著。

DBJ 帮助企业建立灾后应对措施以抵御灾难风险,并提供应急资金,从业务持续性计划、抗震设施建设到 IT 备份系统等多方面入手应对灾难。此外,DBJ 还提供新金融手段帮助受灾重创企业恢复经营。

2006 年,DBJ 启动财务管理系统,全面评估灾难重建工作的准备情况。该系统包括灾难评估体系和财务计划,用户可以在系统中自估企业法人的灾后重建管理计划,并基于评级结果分配融资优惠利率。除文档材料外,DBJ 在与客户讨论灾后重建工作的过程中也会决定评级的分配。通过客观的第三方评估，了解企业的灾后重建准备。这个系统主要用于减少灾后重建工作的内部阻碍。企业也可以在公司的宣传中使用评估结果，例如在网站上发布信息，总结自己在防灾准备方面所做的工作。

自2011年起，DBJ开始利用金融手段帮助日本从大地震的影响中恢复。

2014年4月，DBJ和岩手银行共同向日本东部两家企业提供贷款以帮助它们走出震后危机。2011年，DBJ和岩手银行合作成立东日本基金，为受到大地震影响的企业提供资金支持。

上述事实无疑证明了政策性银行能够给予的特殊支持。当下，金融危机和自然灾害频发，因此保证对危机的快速反应和及时处理能力至关重要。作为政府的一部分，政策性银行有责任提供应对危机管理的服务，建立直接、有效的应急系统，以帮助受影响企业渡过危机。

治理与监管

根据日本国会于2007年6月6日通过的《新日本政策投资银行法案》的相关条款，作为《关于推动管理改革实现精简高效政府的法案》（2006年，第47号法案，行政改革推进法案）和以政策性金融为基准的改革的一部分，DBJ在其成立之初接管了JBD所有资产，但不包含根据《新日本政策投资银行法案》附录第15条第2款规定的转移到政府的财产。同样，DBJ接受源于JBD的所有权利和义务，除前述法案附录第15条第2款规定的转移到政府的财产。

对于DBJ关键事务，财政部长具有监管权，例如年度业务计划、针对债券发行和借贷的基本政策，以及DBJ公司章程的修改。

韩国产业银行

基本信息

根据《韩国产业银行法》，韩国产业银行（Korea Development Bank，KDB）成立于1954年4月1日，其目标是为主要工业项目提供融资和管理，以促进国家工业化进程，推动经济发展。根据国家政策，KDB通过向问题企业提供重组和咨询服务，为战略性地区发展项目提供资金，辅助企业的管理正常化。KDB拥有82家国内分行、8家海外分行（东京、北京、上海、广州、沈阳、新加坡、伦敦和纽约）、5家海外附属机构（KDB亚洲有限公司、KDB爱尔兰有限公司、KDB欧洲银行有限公司、KDB巴西银行和KDB乌兹别克斯坦银行）和6家全球代表处，共有3 398名员工。KDB的总部设在韩国首尔，其董事会成员共11名，董事会主席为洪起泽。

KDB早期主要是为基础设施建设提供政策性资金支持，包括电力、煤炭及港口建设，也为国内企业提供银团贷款。1955年，KDB首次发行了工业金融债券。20世纪六七十年代，KDB重点扶持重化工业，以促进国家工业结构调整，增加法定资本，并成为韩国首家发行外币债券的金融机构。20世纪八九十年代，KDB开始大力向国际资本市场和投资银行领域扩张，建立基金会，通过向高新技术行业提供资助，成为一家具有全球竞争力的投资银行。90年代末的亚洲金融危机到2008年，KDB采取了一系列措施以稳定国内金融市场，消除市场焦虑，促进工业增长（见专栏3-3）。

2007年，韩国政府决定对KDB进行改革，将KDB分为韩国金融公司（KoFC）和KDB金融集团（KDBFG）。KoFC负责政策性业务，而KDBFG负责商业银行业务。2013年，新一届政府决定停止KDB的商业化运营，重新确立其为完全国有化的政策性银行，KDB所有权属于韩国政府，其监管部门系韩国企划财政部。KDB将通过快速、有效的增长来提升利润率和资产质量，从而进一步加强金融稳定性。2014 年 5 月《韩国产业银行法》修订后，"KDB 于 2014 年 12 月 31 日将 KDBFG 与 KoFC 进行合并，以增强银行竞争力，促进自身可持续发展。"

> **专栏 3-3　KDB 在金融危机中为经济复苏采取的预先性措施**
>
> 在应对 2008 年金融危机时，韩国实施了一定的政策性措施以帮助韩国金融和房地产行业抵御危机的直接影响。这些措施包括：运用政策和金融手段稳定货币、证券、债券市场，为企业和金融实体提供融资服务，以及扶持中小型企业和小微金融部门。
>
> 在上述政策性措施中，KDB 扮演了重要角色。"1998 年亚洲金融危机时 KDB 在稳定金融市场方面的丰富经验在 2008 年国际金融危机中显示出其重要性。在金融危机席卷全球导致公司拖欠贷款激增的情况下，KDB 通过提前公布违约贷款、及时处理拖欠贷款等措施，在公司重建方面提供了支持。自 2008 年金融危机以来，KDB 实行了一系列预先性重组措施，开启快速通道项目为中小型企业提供流动性资产，同时 KDB 还是"债权银行集体协议"的签署方，以防止国内建筑工业无力偿还债务或破产。此外，KDB 还主动为缺乏流动性的中小型造船企业提供援助；KDB 通过贷款修改和企业重整，帮助公司正常化经营，或为破产企业处理不良信用清偿、资产支持证券的发行、并购重组和拍卖等问题制定项目计划。

使命与战略

KDB 的主要任务是"自主运营，通过推行先进政策促进韩国金融业和经济的发展"。2013 年 8 月，KDB 开始建立"韩国发展的金融引擎，全球 KDB"

的新愿景。为了实现这一目标，KDB确定了五大核心价值观：信任、热情、合作、客户导向和市场领导（见专栏3-4）。

该银行还根据市场状况、政策金融需求、私人金融状况等确立了五大中期和长期商业策略：（1）促进创新型经济发展，具体包括支持创新型高风险行业，例如风险企业和新兴企业；（2）成为金融服务的领导者，作为饱和金融市场的突破口；（3）在金融危机中强调其市场安全网的角色，以更好地应对未来的金融风险；（4）通过提高盈利以强化可持续政策金融的基础；（5）为朝韩半岛统一做准备，并以此为跳板寻求更好的经济发展机遇。

专栏3-4　KDB为促进创新经济的新使命

2013年重组后，KDB的新使命是推动经济创新，尤其要为风险相对较高的行业提供融资，以及通过创新金融产品，加强与具有发展前景且具备先进科技的中小企业合作。

为了让2015年成为促进创新经济的开局之年，KDB将为新增长引擎业务及新兴企业提供180万亿韩元（1 648.3亿美元）的资金支持。

在政府的政策支持下，KDB的大部分资金将于2015年上半年在17个城市建立创新经济中心，这些中心对新兴企业实行友好政策，创业者可以享受一站式服务，方便新兴企业的运作。

KDB还将为韩国科技部推出的"制造业创新计划3.0"提供金融支持。该计划旨在将IT技术与制造过程结合，目标是鼓励10 000家制造企业设立"智能"工厂，将信息通信技术（Information Communication Technology，ICT）融入设计、生产、配送过程，降低成本。

政府支持

自 1954 年成立以来，KDB 在政府的支持下一直表现出色，并制定了支持韩国经济发展的政策，成为韩国首屈一指的政策性银行。KDB 的预算和运营计划必须经政府批准，政府信用为 KDB 债券提供保障，并为 KDB 提供损失赔偿和信用支持，例如，政府为产业金融债券和外币债券提供担保。如果 KDB 年度储备金无法弥补财政赤字（尽管过去 5 年从未出现），韩国政府将为其提供资金。

资金来源

KDB 通过以下途径获得必要资金：（1）储蓄存款和零存整取存款；（2）发行产业金融债券、其他证券和债务金融工具；（3）如果 KDB 对政府的债务从属于 KDB 运营造成的其他债务，则 KDB 接收来自政府、韩国银行和其他金融机构的借款；（4）外国资本。KDB 最重要的资金来源是发行产业金融债券。回归政策性银行之后，KDB 减少了银行零售业务。

经营数据

截至 2013 年年底，KDB 的总资产为 2 588 020 亿韩元（2 451.25 亿美元），2014 年 6 月，KDB 的总资产为 2 772 780 亿韩元（2 539.12 亿美元）。截至 2013 年年底，KDB 的总股本为 288 120 亿韩元（272.89 亿美元），2014 年 6 月，KDB 的总股本为 302 040 亿韩元（1 276.59 亿美元）。截至 2013 年年底，KDB 的资产收益率为 -1%，2012 年年底，其净资产收益率为 5.4%，2014 年年底，不良贷款率为 2.5%。KDB 的最长贷款期限为 10 年。

商业模式与产品

KDB 的主要业务是政策金融：强化创新经济发展；满足风险企业融资需求；提高银行科技的竞争力；对公业务及重组，包括提供贷款和投资担保，同时作为市场安全网，提供企业债券的重新募集资金；投资银行，提供的服务包括重组并购、风险资本、证券包销、项目金融；国际银行业务，包括企业联合、结构化金融、贸易金融和其他金融服务；养老金和信托，退休金津贴和信托业务；以及小额银行业务、研究和咨询业务。

近年来，KDB 一直支持中小企业、新兴企业和基础设施的建设。过去4年，KDB 超过一半的信用资金投入到中小企业和新兴企业中。为金融服务、造船业、交通运输、钢铁、批发零售业提供的贷款占总贷款金额的比例分别为 26.5%、6.9%、5.1%、5.0%、和 4.8%（见表3.3）。

表3.3　KDB 贷款的行业分布（最主要的5个行业）

行业	金融服务	造船业	交通	钢铁	批发和零售	总比值
占比	26.5%	6.9%	5.1%	5.0%	4.8%	48.3%

公司治理

2009年10月，KDB 被拆分为韩国金融公司（KoFC）和 KDB 金融集团（KDBFG），KDBFG 重点做商业性业务。朴槿惠2013年2月就任总统后，果断终止 KDB 商业化改革进程，将 KDB、KDBFG、KoFC 合并，退回到改革前的状态。2014年5月，韩国国会通过了最新修订的《KDB 法》，KDB 于2015年1月1日按新的法案运行，其子公司包括：KDB 资产管理、KDB 投资公司、大宇证券、KIAMCO（KDB 基础设施）、KDB 人寿保险。具体结构如图3.4所示。

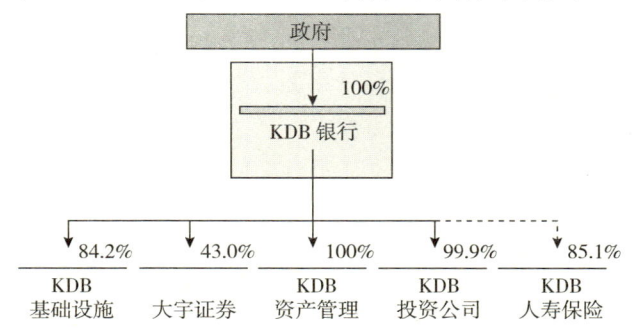

图3.4　KDB 组织结构（2014年12月31日之后）

KDB下属机构介绍如下：

（1）大宇证券。大宇证券中间人业务的市场占有率居第一位，其收入来自高附加值的交易，如IPO、新股增发等，成为表现良好的投资银行，增强了韩国市场在债券和衍生品市场的影响力。

（2）KDB投资公司。KDB投资公司通过国内风险企业寻求风险资本家和战略合作伙伴。其下属机构已经在绿色和新增长领域开发了强大的业务能力，扩大了风险投资交易网。

（3）KDB资产管理。自1996年以来，KDB资产管理就以联合投资管理、投资顾问和全权委托投资服务等形式提供优质服务。其下设机构扩大营销渠道，吸引养老基金和大企业的资金，开发稳定的资产管理规模，以及有效的销售能力。

（4）KIAMCO（KDB基础设施）。KIAMCO是韩国最大的专业管理基础设施建设基金的机构。该公司已经积累了丰富的管理经验，也和道路、铁路、港口建设及其他基础设施工程的投资方建立了长期稳定的合作关系。

（5）KDB人寿保险。KDB人寿保险的保险产品包括人身保险、死亡保险、集体保险等。2010年6月，KDB银行接管锦湖人寿保险之后，公司从"锦湖人寿保险有限公司"更名为"KDB人寿保险有限公司"。

第四章　中低收入国家的开发性金融机构

不同的发展阶段对开发性金融机构的组织架构、战略定位和商业模式的影响会很大。开发性金融机构在发展中国家扮演着重要角色。发展中国家的金融市场亟须发展，对金融产品服务的需求也很旺盛。本章将聚焦于中低收入国家的开发性金融机构。

俄罗斯发展与对外经济事务银行

基本信息

作为国有企业，俄罗斯发展与对外经济事务银行（Vnesheconombank，VEB，又称"俄罗斯外经银行"）的宗旨是增强并推动俄罗斯经济竞争力的多样化，刺激投资活动。VEB 是一家国有专业银行，依据 2007 年 6 月 4 日生效的俄罗斯联邦法律《发展与对外经济事务银行法》（简称《外经银行法》）开展经营活动。现任监事会主席是德米特里·梅德韦杰夫（Dmitry Medvedev，俄罗斯联邦政府总理），董事会主席是弗拉基米尔·德米特夫（Vladimir Dmitriev）。

VEB 的主要业务领域是商业银行无法承担的资本密集的长期项目融资。VEB 不与商业金融机构竞争，只参与那些无法从私人投资者获得融资的项目。根据金融政策备忘录，VEB 在 5 年回报期的项目上开展了总值超过 20 亿卢布（6 000 万美元）的信贷、抵押和担保业务。

目前，VEB 集团已经成立，囊括了 VEB 旗下旨在贯彻落实《外经银行法》各项条款的各附属机构。

VEB 通过持续经营发挥了俄罗斯联邦政府代理人的功能；管理并偿还俄罗斯主权外债，以及对外国借款人的国家债务；确保俄联邦的各法律实体、地方实体和自治州市等偿还对俄联邦所负的债务；VEB 还通过持续分析记录政府所提供的担保，承担着提供和执行俄联邦政府担保的功能。

使命与战略

VEB 是国家级开发银行，通过增强国民经济竞争力、以创新方式实现现代化来贯彻政府的社会经济政策。它的使命是通过资助具有国家意义的投资项目，推动俄罗斯经济多样化并提升其效率，是俄罗斯发展的重要推动力。按照《外经银行法》条款 3.1 的规定，VEB 应该采取行动以促进俄联邦经济竞争力的多样性，鼓励通过投资、保险、咨询和其他投资性活动来实施俄联邦国内外的项目，其中包括涉及外资、基础设施、创新、经济特区、环保、支持俄罗斯产品、工程和服务出口以及支持中小企业等项目。

当前，VEB 贷款投向的结构为：工业领域占 49.2%，基础设施领域占 41.5%，农工综合体占 9.3%。

作为一家开发性金融机构，VEB 需要在封闭的外国资本市场、加速的俄罗斯资本外流和银行业减缓的流动性水平的条件下，满足实体经济对长期融资的需求。它的活动具有明显的反周期效果。作为实现现代化背景下的产物，VEB 旨在充分增加大规模投资项目，以及创新、进口替代、基础设施发展等项目。

VEB 计划，到 2020 年，支持国民经济的融资总额占俄罗斯 GDP 的 4.5%，其中包括次级贷款、租赁业务以及附属银行信贷。除此之外，VEB 在总固定资本投资量中的贡献将达到 2.3%。VEB 占银行贷款总量的比例将达到 6%，并且在银行长期贷款总量中占比 14%。VEB 贷款余额将达到 3 万亿卢布（900 亿美元），通过中小银行（VEB 的附属银行）对中小企业提供金融支持的金额将达到 7 500 亿卢布（225 亿美元）。

政府支持

根据《外经银行法》第 4 章规定,"VEB 的法律地位受到该法、其他俄联邦法和监管法的制约,并在此基础上采取行动。其他银行及银行业务法仅当其不与本法冲突时对 VEB 适用,并且要充分考虑在这一领域立法的特殊性。关于银行及银行业务立法程序的条款,涉及以下流程的不适用于 VEB:(1) 国家信贷机构登记和这类机构的银行许可证发行;(2) 信贷机构清算或重组;(3) 信贷机构活动信息的提供;(4) 与《外经银行法》或银行及银行业务法相冲突的银行业务操作和交易规则;(5) 信用机构稳定性和财务稳健性标准的应用,以及其他强制性要求和规定。"

资金来源

VEB 的资金来源包括:联邦预算、中央银行和国家财富基金。这些国家机关与 VEB 共同持有储蓄,并且该银行是俄罗斯唯一有资格获得此类资金的机构。

根据《外经银行法》第 5 章规定,VEB 不对俄联邦债务负责,俄联邦也不对 VEB 债务负责。VEB 应当利用其特性独立实现自身设立的目标。

2013 年年底,VEB 从资本市场募集的资金总额为 8 134 亿卢布(244 亿美元),其中全年从银行获得的信贷资金为 3 427 亿卢布(103 亿美元),通过发行债券获得的资金为 4 707 亿(141 亿美元),包括 3 118 亿卢布(94 亿美元)的欧债、以卢布为标的的 1 425 亿卢布(43 亿美元)国内债券和以外汇为标的的 164 亿卢布(5 亿美元)国内债券。

经营数据

2013 年年底,VEB 的总资产为 33 139.58 亿卢布(1 007.44 亿美元),总股本为 5 768.59 亿卢布(175.37 亿美元),注册资本为 3 880.69 亿卢布(117.97 亿美元)。

2013 年年底，VEB 的贷款余额为 3 291.77 亿卢布（100.73 亿美元）。2015 年 2 月 24 日，穆迪下调了俄罗斯七大金融机构的评级，使 VEB 的长期本币（LC）和外币（FC）发行人评级从 Baa3 降到 Ba1，前景在修正后变得消极，短期 LC 和 FC 发行人评级从 p-3 降低到 NP。2015 年 2 月 20 日，穆迪将俄罗斯政府债务评级从 Baa3 下调到 Ba1，反映了俄罗斯逐步降低的信用形象。作为与政府相关的机构，VEB 的债务评级也被降级。

商业模式与产品

根据《外经银行法》3.3 条规定，VEB 承担以下基本功能：（1）为旨在完善基础设施和实现创新的投资项目融资，包括贷款的形式，或者对商业组织资本给予利率支持；（2）根据俄联邦法律发行债券或其他类型证券；（3）安排贷款及引导借贷资金，包括那些金融市场中的借贷资金；（4）购买商业实体、投资基金以及相互投资基金的股权；（5）行使货币控制代理方的权利和义务，并为其他授权银行做出示范；（6）为第三方法人实体提供担保；（7）从第三方购买应偿金融债务的权益，以及发行该权益支持的债券；（8）提供出口信贷支持，为有商业风险或政治风险的项目提供投资保险；（9）综合考虑受商品和证券价格、汇率、利率及通货膨胀率水平影响的收益率，以最小化经营风险为目标，谨慎参与交易；（10）参与支持俄联邦的目标项目和政府投资项目；（11）参与具有国家意义的公私合营投资项目，以及旨在完善基础设施和其他保障经济特区运行设施的项目；（12）租赁业务；（13）为支持俄罗斯工业产品出口提供预算贷款服务，包括国外设施的建设和全套安装设备的供给，为俄罗斯公司参与国际招标提供银行担保和保险服务，支持履行已签署的出口合同；（14）组织、实施对投资项目的专家检查，协助俄罗斯出口商起草合同；（15）通过为信用组织和支持中小企业的合法实体融资的方式，参与中小企业信贷融资支持计划；（16）监控各法律实体履行与 VEB 达成的相关项目的实施程度；（17）与国际开发组织、外国企业和发展机构合作，参与国际发展协会在俄联邦项目的实施；（18）参与俄联邦内外的协会、工会,以及其他正在建立或已经建立的旨在促进经济发展与投资的非盈利组织;(19)在俄联邦内外建立分支机构,开设代表处与法律实体登记处;(20)对俄国制造的产品出口提供金融和担保支持;(21)参与登记、使用、服务并偿还俄罗斯联邦对外国的政府性债务等操作。

根据《外经银行法》第 4 章规定,VEB 可以开展下列银行业务:(1)以存款形式吸引参与 VEB 项目实施的各法律实体的货币基金;(2)开立并维护参与 VEB 项目实施的各法律实体的银行账户,以及俄联邦中央银行、俄联邦信贷机构、外国银行及国际结算中心的代理账户;(3)投资有吸引力的基金;(4)清算法人支付订单;(5)购买、出售现金和非现金形式的外币;(6)归集参与 VEB 项目实施的各法律实体的现金、账单、付款单据等;(7)为参与 VEB 项目实施的各法律实体提供银行担保。

VEB 的优先投资领域有:飞机结构、航天工业、造船业、电力、原子工业、国防、涉农产业、计算机技术、通信系统和医学。

VEB 在俄罗斯经济发展中发挥了重要作用,参与投资项目和支持工业出口的形式包括:信贷、抵押和担保、授权资本、租赁交易、出口信贷保险、支持出口的融资和担保等。

VEB 也参与创新活动。如今,VEB 正在参与实施 66 个旨在开发创新的项目,这些项目分布于如下工业领域:国防工业园区、飞机结构、医疗设备和制药学、火箭和航天工业、电子工业和引擎建设。目前,创新项目占银行贷款余额的 34.5%。2014 年 7 月,VEB 决定为 26 个创新项目提供总额大约为 1 990 亿卢布(57.31 亿美元)的资金支持,其中 VEB 参与的份额超过 1 699 亿卢布(48.93 亿美元)。

VEB 多元化的投资还包括运输(例如,布伦瑞克铁路)、电力(例如,OGK-5 和 GSR 能源)和电信(例如,俄罗斯塔)等。

自 2007 年以来,VEB 附属的中小企业银行(SME 银行,2011 年前为俄罗斯开发银行)一直在实施中小企业项目中扮演代理角色。通过区域伙伴银行网络和基层组织(租赁、保理公司、小额信贷机构和其他机构),把对中小企业的贷款和其他形式的金融支持推广到俄罗斯各个地区。同时，VEB 的信贷期限被延长至 7 年，数额高达 1.5 亿卢布（450 万美元）。SME 银行旗下由伙伴银行发放的贷款加权平均贷款余额占比为 12.6%。

治理与监管

根据《外经银行法》第 13 章规定，VEB 管理委员会是一个学院式的执行机构，由一位主席和其他 8 位成员组成。主席直接领导管理委员会的工作，其成员由主席推荐，由 VEB 监事会任命或除名。管理委员会成员应为 VEB 正式员工，即每个委员会成员都是业务主管人员。

VEB 管理委员会行使以下权利：（1）向 VEB 监事会准备并呈送有关 VEB 活动主要方向和投融资业务影响因素的提案，以待批准；（2）批准 VEB 管理部门提供的额度内投资项目的决定；（3）起草并向 VEB 监事会呈送金融收入与支出计划（预算），以待批准；（4）审查年度报告并提交监事会，以待批准；（5）向监事会提交利润分配的提案；（6）批准员工名单，根据俄联邦法律制定员工雇用、解雇条例和条件、社会保障、权利义务、纪律处分体系、工薪形式及规模；（7）批准 VEB 的组织结构；（8）行使不在 VEB 其他管理机构能力范围内、需谨慎考虑由委员会行使的权利。

根据《外经银行法》第 15 章规定，管理委员会主席是 VEB 的唯一执行负责人并管理其日常运营。主席应由俄罗斯总统任命或解除，且主席任期不应超过俄罗斯政府推荐的 5 年。新任主席候选人名单应在现任主席期满前一个月呈递总统。如果总统驳回该候选人，VEB 监事会主席应该在 15 天内向总统呈递另一位候选人。

根据《外经银行法》第 16 章规定，管理委员会主席具有以下权利：（1）无须授权即代表 VEB 及其利益与政府机关、地方当局、国外和国际组织及其他组织开展工作；（2）领导并贯彻实施委员会决议；（3）发布 VEB 范围内的命令和指令；（4）在其副手之间分配职权；（5）向 VEB 监事会提交管理委员会成员的任命或解任提案；（6）雇用或解雇 VEB 员工；（7）在 VEB 范围内的其他决策，不包括 VEB 监事会和管理委员会管辖内的议题。

根据《外经银行法》第 10 章规定，VEB 监事会是其最高管理机构，由主席和其他 8 位成员组成。VEB 监事会主席应由俄罗斯政府总理担任。VEB 监事会成员任期 5 年并应由俄罗斯政府任命。除监事会主席外，其他监事会成员不应是 VEB 正式员工。俄罗斯政府有权在任期终止前解除 VEB 监事会的成员任命，且若该情况发生，政府应在两个月内任命新成员。

根据《外经银行法》第 11 章规定，VEB 监事会应由监事会主席或其他得到主席授权的成员召开，至少每季度一次。超过一半的成员出席方可通过监事会决议。决议的通过采取出席者中的多数投票原则。若投票平局，取监事会会议主持者意见。监事会会议应由 VEB 监事会主席主持，如果主席缺席，由得到授权的监事会成员主持。

根据《外经银行法》第 12 章规定，VEB 监事会具有以下权利：（1）基于俄联邦政府通过的备忘录确认 VEB 活动的原则性方向；（2）批准有关 VEB 管理部门的条款；（3）批准有关 VEB 分支和代理机构的条款；（4）批准 VEB 年度报告；（5）批准 VEB 的金融收入和支出计划（预算）、储备金和基金的构成，以及收入、储备金、基金的配置程序；（6）决定分支机构的建立、代表处的开设和法律实体的注册；（7）选定对 VEB 年度财务报表进行审计的公司；（8）听取 VEB 管理委员会主席关于 VEB 活动的报告；（9）决定 VEB 内控负责人的任命及其权力的提前终止；（10）决定 VEB 发行债券，并依据俄联邦法律制定债券发行流程；（11）在备忘录赋予的授权范围内明确 VEB 开展投融资活动的限制因素；（12）当 VEB 的财产购买、转让或可能转让涉及账面价值超过 VEB 股票（资产）10% 及以上时，批准相关交易，账面价值应截至该交易被批准前的最新报告；（13）其他考虑在此行使的权利。

哈萨克斯坦开发银行

基本信息

2001 年 5 月 18 日颁发的哈萨克斯坦共和国政府法令第 659 条，"关于整合哈萨克斯坦开发银行（Development Bank of Kazakhstan，DBK）封闭股份公司"，规定了 DBK 的独家法律地位。作为哈萨克斯坦共和国政府为非基础部门提供资金的投资机构，DBK 有着特殊的法律地位，并具有以下优势：（1）在特定问题上不受国家监管机构对银行的规定；（2）可以使用开发银行授权的资本放贷。

DBK 的总部位于哈萨克斯坦阿斯塔纳。DBK 由国家全资持有，这确保了国家的有力支持。有了 Baiterek 国家管理控股股份公司（Baiterek National Management Holding JSC）作为新股东，DBK 致力于改善资产管理效率和优化信贷程序。2005 年，DBK 全资参与的附属租赁公司——DBK 租赁股份公司（DBK Leasing JSC）成立，旨在为在建的工业、生产和基础运输设施项目提供租赁融资。DBK 的立法基于《哈萨克斯坦共和国宪法》、《哈萨克斯坦开发银行法》和其他监管法文件。

使命与战略

DBK 的使命是"通过投资国家非能源部门，促进国民经济可持续发展"。DBK 定义的目标是改善和提高公共投资活动的效率、发展工业基础设施和加工行业、通过提高内部和外部投资来促进国家经济发展。DBK 的长期发展战略在 2014 年 7 月 14 日的银行董事会上决议通过（第 156 条记录），并制定了到 2023 年的战略目标和主要趋势。DBK 的战略目标是向现代、独立的国家开发企业转型，作为财务稳定、具有活力的银行，在提高国家经济的非能源领域竞争力方面扮演重要角色。DBK 的战略方向是贷款、金融资源管理和企业管理，主要为3个重点支持领域提供金融援助：企业直接融资，通过基础设施投资促进地区/集群的发展，以及通过银行间贷款为优先分支机构提供融资渠道。

根据DBK到2020年的长期发展战略，第一阶段的首要任务是为国家重点项目下的战略投资项目和贸易融资提供贷款；第二阶段，DBK将着重在非项目领域吸引社会资本，组织融资交易，以及建议客户进入资本市场、作为财政代理为政府和商业银行的工业项目吸引"廉价"贷款。

政府支持

若DBK遇到财务困难，哈萨克斯坦政府将提供及时、特殊的支持。DBK与政府和银行的整体联系使得它可以接收政府直接的预算转移支付。DBK在2014年10月收到500亿坚戈（2.76亿美元）的政府预算贷款，并期望在2014年年底之前获得额外的500亿坚戈（2.76亿美元）贷款和250亿坚戈（1.38亿美元）欧元注资。DBK的公共政策角色越来越集中在为政府的产业化项目融资。

作为国家计划FIID（Forced Industrial-Innovative Development，强制工业创新开发）的关键运营商，DBK贷款组合中的80%涵盖了这些工业项目和创新开发。DBK约60%的贷款用于石油加工和冶金领域。2013年，DBK的股权从哈萨克斯坦主权财富基金Samruk-Kazyna（萨姆鲁克—卡泽纳）转移到Baiterek，保持了政府对银行的间接所有权以改善治理。

Baiterek是政府在2013年成立的股份制公司，为非商品部门提供金融和投资支持，并管理着10家开发性机构。DBK是这10家机构中最大的一家，占控股总资产的58%。成立Baiterek旨在使政府能够更加关注开发性机构，并帮助政府提高这些机构的效率和公司治理。

DBK的独立信用反映了其作为国家开发性金融机构的公共政策角色，它受到单独的法律、对其有利的资金到期日、充足的流动性缓冲和可接受的资本充足率的规范。DBK与政府的密切联系为该银行提供了定期获取资本和流动性资源的渠道。该银行免于哈萨克斯坦国家银行（NBK）的监管。目前，支持该银行所需的成本相对于国有财政资源来说并不大。

资金来源

基于现有立法对哈萨克斯坦开发银行活动的细则和限制，哈萨克斯坦开发银行信贷投资项目的唯一融资来源是借入资金。银行信贷业务的资金基础决定了信贷投资项目的基本条件和出口业务。为了确保必要的基础资金，DBK 在国内和国际资本市场上使用不同的借贷工具——发行和增发债券、吸引银行间拆借和公共预算额度、银团贷款、信贷额度利用及其他工具。根据 2013 年的统计结果，该银行对债权人的债务是 57 亿美元。

除此之外，在面临"昂贵"来源资金的情况下（早些时候在比较不利的市场条件下获得的资金），DBK 与现有的债权人就提前还款或互换达成协议以降低融资成本。例如，2013 年上半年，DBK 的负债管理交易总量超过 7.7 亿美元，这使得 DBK 融资的平均成本显著降低。

2013 年，从金融工具角度看，DBK 的债务结构包括欧元债券（34%）、银行间贷款（43%）、初级债券（13%）、贷款和 FSA 基金（9%）以及伊斯兰债券（1%）。

经营数据

截至 2014 年年底，DBK 的总资产为 1.31 万亿坚戈（71.6 亿美元），总股本为 3 129.68 亿坚戈（17.15 亿美元），总贷款余额为 8 151.87 亿坚戈（44.67 亿美元），净利润是 112.62 亿坚戈（6 200 万美元），资产收益率是 0.86%，净资产收益率是 3.60%。银行的投资项目在 2013 年年底的加权平均利率为 6.6%。截至 2013 年年底，从 DBK 转移到哈萨克斯坦投资基金股份公司的有问题的项目占银行贷款组合的 12.5%，2012 年同期是 41.9%。2014 年年中，DBK 不良贷款率下降到 7.8%。经过 13 年的业务开展，DBK 通过投资，引导了 86 亿美元支持国家经济发展，建立了 75 个在实施项目，创造了 1.89 万个永久性就业岗位。

DBK 的管理机构包括：（1）最高权威——唯一股东；（2）管理机构——董事会；（3）执行机构——管理委员会；（4）监督机构——内部审计服务。董事会由 6 名成员组成，其中包括 3 名独立董事。阿谢特·伊谢克舍夫（Asset Is-sekeshev）从 2009 年 5 月起任 DBK 董事会主席。

该银行同时设有风险管理委员会，并在银行战略决策中发挥重要作用。设立风险管理委员会的主要目的是协助董事会履行以下职责：确保银行的风险管理发挥应有的可用性和功能，以及完善和加强风险管理系统。

商业模式与产品

DBK 为零起点项目融资——包括在基础设施和加工行业新启动和未开发项目。该银行也为现代化和重建工业设施进行融资。作为国家基础设施和非能源领域发展的金融机构，该银行为诸如农业、建筑、工业、基础设施等行业提供贷款。

DBK 的服务包括：（1）为中期（5 年和更长时间）和长期（10～20 年）大型项目（不少于 3 000 万美元）提供融资，也包括为投资项目的实施提供临时融资；（2）出口（出口前操作）融资；（3）夹层融资、项目融资、项目实施下借款人融资；（4）发行担保贷款，由其他贷款机构提供以及联合融资提供的服务，其他金融组织发行的贷款；（5）银行间贷款。DBK 通过其他金融机构直接向终端客户发放贷款。

2013 年，该银行服务项目的领域结构是：金融活动（22%）、能源（40%）、太空部门（12%）、运输和通信（26%）。从区域结构来看，有相当一部分由区域间项目（56%）和阿拉木图城及阿拉木图地区（21%）的项目组成。

专栏 4-1　DBK 与中国之间的合作

随着两国之间商业和战略合作的加深，哈萨克斯坦共和国和中华人民共和国之间的双边关系已成为重要的战略议题。中华人民共和国主席习近平在 2013 年的讲话中提出，中国将与中亚国家建立一个"丝绸之路经济带"。"一带一路"的倡议关系着 65 个国家、44 亿人。哈萨克斯坦计划在中亚发挥中国产品通往欧洲路径的关键中转国作用。实际上，2014 年，从中国通过哈萨克斯坦到欧盟的集装箱运输体积比 2012 年增长了 4.5 倍。中国政府也致力于建设和管理第二和第三阶段的中哈项目物流。

哈萨克斯坦开发银行加强了与中国的银行之间的合作。

根据 DBK 新闻报道，哈萨克斯坦开发银行董事会主席 B·扎米舍夫（Bolat Zhamishev）和中国国家开发银行（CDB）主席郑之杰在阿斯塔纳会谈期间就两个金融机构最具前景的合作领域展开了讨论。目前，两家开发银行已经确定进一步合作的领域。DBK 负责人向中国同行分享了在哈萨克斯坦非资源经济和基础设施的资助项目机会。目前，DBK 潜在项目的投资组合（渠道）已超过 1 万亿坚戈。DBK 之前曾与 CDB 签署（2008 年和 2009 年）总额为 3 亿美元的 3 个贷款合同。所有公布的贷款设施都已完全兑现，特别是在电力、冶金、交通、纺织领域的项目。此外，2014 年 5 月，DBK 和 CDB 签署了信用额度总计 5 亿美元的总体协议。B·扎米舍夫和郑之杰对这个协议的实施表达了共同的兴趣和期望。2014 年 5 月 19 日至 21 日，中国进出口银行向 DBK 提供了价值 10 亿美元的贷款，用于奇姆肯特（Shymkent）炼油厂的现代化和重建。在纳扎尔巴耶夫（Nursultan Nazarbayev）总统国事访问中国期间，双方在中哈两国元首的共同见证下签署了一份贷款协议。贷款将依照优惠条款分配给上海合作组织成员国。

乌兹别克斯坦共和国国家对外经济活动银行

基本信息

1991年9月7日,乌兹别克斯坦共和国国家对外经济活动银行(National Bank for Foreign Economic Activity of the Republic of Uzbekistan,NBU)依据乌兹别克斯坦共和国总统法令成立。1991年10月25日,NBU依据乌兹别克斯坦共和国法律注册成为封闭式股份有限责任公司。NBU的总部位于塔什干阿米尔特莫街101号(101,Amir Temur Street.Tashkent)。银行的理事会由政府代表担任,负责批准和修改章程及其他重要决策。银行委员会主席由内阁任命。董事会是执行代理,成员包括:董事会主席——拉希莫夫·波列维奇(Rakhimov Saidakhmat Borievich),董事会第一副主席——阿齐姆·阿克迈德哈齐(Azim Akhmedkhadjaev),董事会副主席——阿利舍·米斯托夫(Alisher Mirsoatov)和其他部门人员。

使命与战略

NBU的主要任务是"服务外贸业务、增加国家出口潜力和吸引外国投资"。主要目标包括吸引外部融资,支持国家导向型经济的发展和改革。近期,NBU最重要的发展战略是49%的股份私有化,这是该国政府改革国有银行业计划的一部分。这一举措将使NBU获得更大的透明度,鼓励现代技术和管理技术的使用,并有助于NBU利用国际资本市场,提高服务质量,实现更大的独立性,以及在业绩方面更加向股东负责。

股权结构

1993年3月,NBU注册成为由乌兹别克斯坦共和国政府全资控股的金融机构。

资金来源

NBU 的资金来源主要包括：法定资本金，资源基金和其他基金，客户的账户资金，银行间信贷，别国的公司、企业和银行的资金，债券和证券的利润，以及居民储蓄。同时，政府也向 NBU 提供贷款并为贷款提供担保。然而，依据法律，政府不需要承担银行的债务，除非这些债务连带政府责任。

经营数据

截至 2013 年年底，NBU 的总资产达 11.23 万亿苏姆（50.98 亿美元），其中盈利资产占总资产的 83%。信贷业务占资产结构的权重很大——信贷业务占银行总净资产的 59.5%。截至 2014 年年底，NBU 的资产总额达 12.83 万亿苏姆（51.32 亿美元），负债 11.73 万亿苏姆（46.9 亿美元），股东权益 1.10 万亿苏姆（4.42 亿美元）。2013 年，NBU 的净利润为 1 021.81 亿苏姆（0.51 亿美元）。截至 2013 年年底，NBU 的资产收益率为 0.9%，净资产收益率为 10.1%，总股本为 1.01 万亿苏姆（5.02 亿美元）。截至 2013 年年底，NBU 的贷款投资组合总值为 68.22 万亿苏姆（36.5 亿美元），相比 2012 年各个时期增加了 30%。NBU 的最长贷款期限为 15 年。

2013 年 5 月 3 日，NBU 被穆迪投资服务公司评级为 B1/B2/E +/NP。2013 年 11 月 26 日，被标准普尔评级为 B +/B。所有评级机构对该行的相关评级都很稳定。截至 2015 年 4 月，穆迪、标准普尔和惠誉尚未发布新的乌兹别克斯坦主权信用评级。

商业模式与产品

NBU 提供批发银行和零售银行业务。它为乌兹别克斯坦的外贸、担保提供、福费廷、保理业务和国内出口商直接贷款等领域提供了 70% 以上的服务。通过运用欧洲复兴开发银行、亚洲开发银行和国际金融公司提供的信贷额度，NBU 在建筑、产业现代化和技术升级以及原材料购买等领域开展项目投资。

同时，NBU 也是乌兹别克斯坦最大的投资银行，其投资组合包括飞机制造商股权、纺织和食品工业、农业、交通和旅游业以及金融行业。特别要提出的是，NBU 在支持中小企业上尤为努力。此外，NBU 提供传统的零售服务，是现有私人存款领域的领先者，依靠创新的产品和在国家银行体系中高水平的公众信任，NBU 的私人存款额度仍在不断提升。

NBU 的产品可分为 3 类：个人产品、小型及私人企业产品，以及企业客户产品（包括汇款、小额贷款、项目融资等）。

治理与监管

NBU 由政府直接监管，理事会成员包括乌兹别克斯坦财政部长、对外经济关系部长等，负责人是董事会主席与董事会副主席。

专栏 4-2　NBU 获得"可持续项目融资"国际奖项

2014 年，经过与几十个国家的 200 多个银行和金融机构的角逐，NBU 获得"可持续项目融资"国际奖项，证书授予了正在建设的"Angren-Pap"电气化铁路项目。

为了在可持续发展中发挥作用，NBU 专注于基础设施建设项目。为长为 124 公里的"Angren-Pap"电气化铁路提供建设融资是 NBU 里程碑式的一步。经过精心挑选，该项目选择在没有稀有本土植物和动物且不适宜农业的土地上开展，以确保在施工期间不会对环境造成无法弥补的破坏，同时确保周边地区不受影响。

"Angren-Pap"项目的主要环境效益是通过对货运的再分配减少了超过一半的二氧化碳排放量。该项目为超过 900 个家庭提供了就业，并为费尔干纳山谷（Fergana Valley）的居民创造了更多的创收机会。该项目还连接了当地居民与其他社区，并提供了通向外界的更便捷的途径，减少了当地人口的出行时间，增强了社会凝聚力。"Angren-Pap"项目给乌兹别克斯坦带来了众多经济效益，除了创造就业机会外，还减少了货物的运输成本，进而降低了产品的成本，提高了乌兹别克斯坦的经济竞争力。

蒙古开发银行

基本信息

蒙古开发银行（Development Bank of Mongolia，DBM）成立于2011年5月12日，总部位于蒙古首都乌兰巴托。它的成立基于两个重要文件，一个是蒙古政府于2010年7月20日发布的第195号决议，另一个是2011年2月10日通过的《蒙古开发银行法》，该法案旨在正式建立、管控和监督DBM。作为一家完全国有的金融机构，DBM是一家在工业及基础设施发展项目上落实国家政策的重要银行。其目标是促进区域发展，减少城乡差距，促进国内外投资者的合资项目。

DBM有70多位员工，以及一个由9人组成的董事会，董事会成员由政府任命，任期3年。DBM直属蒙古最高行政机关——内阁领导，也接受蒙古经济发展部（the Ministry of Economic Development）以及财政部（the Ministry of Finance）的监管。

使命与战略

DBM的使命：一是促进蒙古的经济发展和基础设施建设，为符合政府宏观发展战略的政府鼓励项目提供长期融资；二是鼓励经济可持续发展；三是支持高附加值产业；四是传播现代财务解决方案及理念。

根据《蒙古开发银行法》，DBM 有责任为重大项目融资。蒙古议会每年都会批准一批重大项目，依据《蒙古开发银行法》，这些项目都能从 DBM 得到贷款，而其他没有政府保证的项目必须通过 DBM 董事会的调查。

DBM 遵循以下战略：（1）为最重要的产业部门提供中长期贷款以及其他财务解决方案，这些产业部门包括能源、电网、加工业以及基础设施；（2）引进内外部投资，促进外资投资；（3）鼓励有助于优化经济结构的投资，比如增强出口产业和新的出口企业竞争力的投资；（4）通过减少城乡差距、增加就业机会以及引进有效的管理方法，支持社会可持续发展；（5）与金融行业声誉较好的机构以及其他组织合作共赢。

股权结构

作为一家完全国有化的银行，DBM 通过以下 3 种方式得到政府支持：首先，DBM 是基于《蒙古开发银行法》而组建的，在 DBM 为议会批准的项目提供资金的过程中，蒙古政府和议会依法支持、领导和监督 DBM。其次，DBM 以低于市场利率的价格（4.79%）从政府手中直接获得资金，因此，DBM 有能力以更低的利率和更长的还款期限提供贷款。最后，蒙古政府以国家身份保障贷款，"政府保证所有贷款都会由国家预算偿还，从而所有贷款的信誉评级与蒙古政府一致"，因此，贷款无违约风险。

资金来源

DBM 的筹资渠道包括 DBM 发行的中期票据以及蒙古政府的借款。DBM 已签署欧洲中期票据项目（Euro Medium-Term Note program），并且在 2012 年 3 月以 5.75% 的票息发行五年期政府担保票据，成功融资 5.8 亿美元。

2012 年，蒙古政府发行了"成吉思汗债券"（"Chinggis Bond"），以相对低的票息（5.25%）发行十年期债券（五年期债券票息为 4.25%），获得 15 亿美元融资。该债券旨在为重大项目融资，推进蒙古产业发展及基础设施建设。

另外，2013年，DBM发行了以日元计价的十年期武士债券（Samurai bond），成功从日本资本市场上获得融资。这是蒙古金融机构首次发行的武士债券，同时DBM也是发行武士债券的首家B级评级金融机构。此外，DBM与外国金融机构签署了众多谅解备忘录，包括中国的国家开发银行以及科威特阿拉伯经济发展基金（Kuwait Fund for Arab Economic Development）。

DBM贷款投向的行业主要包括采矿业、公路、建筑材料、能源、铁路、航空运输以及公共事业工程。由"成吉思汗债券"筹措的资金大部分用于公路建设，而DBM的最大投资项目用于支持额尔登塔班陶勒盖公司（ETT），该公司是一家专门从事采矿业的国有公司——额尔登蒙古矿业公司（Erdenes MGL）的子公司。

在2014年年末，DBM拥有价值2 465.36亿图格里克（MNT）（约13.06亿美元）的股本。

专栏4-3　成吉思汗债券：转型投资与债务可持续性

与中国及许多发展中经济体相似，蒙古经历了GDP的持续高速增长，并且在2011年达到17.3%。然而，在2012年这一情况发生了变化。议会通过法律限制主要经济领域中外资的投资，确保所有企业中蒙古所有者的股权至少为50%。该法案严重打击了外国投资者的积极性。而且，蒙古最大的目标市场——中国逐渐减少煤炭进口，导致蒙古经济增长减速。此外，蒙古落后的国内基础设施进一步妨碍了经济增长，影响了投资的引进，缺少资金又恶化了投资环境。蒙古政府急需解决上述恶性循环。

为解决困境，蒙古政府认为有必要从资本市场上引入资金。在2012年年末，蒙古政府通过DBM在国际市场上发行了"成吉思汗债券"。"成吉思汗债券"是蒙古政府在国际市场上发行的第一只国债,它为蒙古政府筹措了15亿美元的资金。该债券旨在为重大项目融资,促进蒙古产业发展和基础设施建设。

"成吉思汗债券"成功发行后:首先,已经支持了数个大型基础设施建设项目。"新铁路"(The New Railroad)项目获得了4亿美元的贷款,该项目将通过建立1 800公里铁路来增加采矿业产品的出口。其次,增加了蒙古外汇储备,并且增强了投资者对蒙古经济发展的信心。最后,提高了蒙古人民的生活水平。例如,"Buyant Ukhaan-1"区在融资后能够以相对较低的价格(128万MNT/m^2)为年轻家庭、老人和公务员提供1 764所公寓。

但是,世界银行和国际货币基金组织近期警告蒙古政府,扩张性的财政政策和货币政策会威胁经济的稳定。2014年7月17日,穆迪将蒙古外币政府债务的评级从B1下调至B2,评级展望至今仍然保持负面。在相关评级中,穆迪将DBM的高级无担保评级从B1下调至B2,并且展望依然保持负面。由于DBM的债务拥有蒙古政府的信用保证,因此它的债务评级与蒙古政府的评级保持一致。

经营数据

截至2014年年底,蒙古开发银行的总股本为2 465.36亿蒙古图格里克(1.31亿美元),相较于2013年的1 438.79亿蒙古图格里克(0.88亿美元)增长20%。2013年和2014年,其总资产分别为3.23万亿蒙古图格里克(19.68亿美元)和5.51万亿蒙古图格里克(29.17亿美元)。2014年年底,DBM的总负债为5.259 497万亿蒙古图格里克(27.86亿美元),而在2013年为3.09万亿蒙古图格里克(18.8亿美元)。

2014年,蒙古开发银行的综合收益为1 026.57亿蒙古图格里克(5 400

万美元），相较于 2013 年的 268.88 亿蒙古图格里克（1 600 万美元）增长明显。

蒙古开发银行的资产收益率在 2012 年年底为 -0.6%，而在 2013 年年底为 0.8%，在 2014 年第一季度为 0.5%。银行的净资产收益率在 2012 年年底为 -8.5%，在 2013 年年底为 18.7%。2013 年年底的资本充足率（CAR）为 12.8%。

商业模式与产品

蒙古开发银行主要以 3 种方式参与开发性金融项目：第一，债务融资。在法律允许的范围内，中小型项目可获得直接贷款。对于大型项目，银行有能力与世界银行等多边机构合作，提供共同融资服务或国际银团贷款。第二，如果项目需要战略投资，蒙古开发银行也可以为其提供股权融资。第三，蒙古开发银行也提供咨询服务，为企业提供融资解决方案，寻找重要的资金来源，规划项目，并为蒙古企业与国际融资机构进行磋商。

治理与监管

蒙古开发银行的董事会有 9 位成员。现任主席为兼任经济发展部秘书长的什聂巴塔（Shinebaatar）。该行 9 位董事会成员均由蒙古国政府任命：其中 6 位来自各部委的官员，另外 3 位成员则从蒙古银行、本土工商部（Department of Local Business and Industries）和蒙古银行业委员会（the Committee of Mongolian Banks）中选拔。银行总经理由董事会提名，并由代表政府的股东大会通过。该行现任总经理为曼赫巴特（N. Munhbat）。总经理负责贷款、投资、资产和负债、风险管理及监管 5 个部门。其中，风险管理部的职责在于甄别、衡量以及管控金融性和非金融性危机，并定期向董事会和总经理汇报工作。董事会负责监管风险并确保银行的合理运营。

马来西亚开发银行

基本信息

马来西亚开发银行（Bank Pembangunan Malaysia Berhad，BPMB）成立于1973年，并自1974年6月8日起正式运营。BPMB依照1965年的《马来西亚公司法》注册成立，注册地位于吉隆坡。

使命与战略

BPMB最初的目标是通过提供融资支持、开展企业家培训以及咨询指导等服务，帮助中小企业发展。

"如今，BPMB的职责是为伊斯兰和传统的资本密集型行业（包括基础设施建设、航海、科技以及石油、天然气等领域）提供中长期融资。"

公司治理

马来西亚政府通过财务部和联邦土地委员会（Federal Lands Commissioner）完全控股BPMB。

资金来源

以往，BPMB的资金主要来自政府支持。现在，BPMB正逐步使其融资方式多样化，现有渠道包括：（1）普通民众存款；（2）来自其他机构拆借、当地发行的债券；（3）政府通过预算转移支付给予的支持，具体形式可以是各种类型的基金、补贴以及票据、贷款担保。例如，2013年，BPMB从政府得到1.2亿马来元（3 660万美元）的补贴。此外，政府还对BPMB的多种债务进行了担保，包括基础设施票据以及从雇员公积金局（Employees Provident Fund，EPF）获得的全部贷款。BPMB的五大融资渠道，即客户存款、实收资本、政府转移支付、向其他金融机构借款以及可赎回票据的比例关系为 7 430∶3 039∶120∶311∶3 025。

经营数据

BPMB 只对终端消费者提供直接贷款。截至 2013 年年底，BPMB 集团的总资产为 292.5 亿马来元（89.2 亿美元）。得益于 2013 财年的净利润，当年总股本大幅提升至 75.9 亿马来元（23.1 亿美元）。集团净贷款、预付款及融资总额达到 242.1 亿马币（73.8 亿美元）。BPMB 还通过两家子公司进行战略投资。2013 财年，BPMB 的资产收益率为 1.74%，净资产收益率为 6.65%。截至 2013 年年底，总减值贷款比率（gross impaired loan ratio）为 10.17%，净减值贷款比率（net impaired loan ratio）为 4.19%。马来西亚中央银行对 BPMB 提出了以下几项资本金要求：BPMB 必须保证 3 亿马来元（8 358 万美元）的绝对最低资本金，同时还要求任何时候的风险加权资本比率不得低于 8%。此外，BPMB 还被要求通过逐步的、系统性的准备金积累，进一步巩固资本金状况，正常情况和特殊情形下最低风险加权资本比率分别不得低于 20% 和 12%。贷款利率的浮动在 6.8%~10% 之间，最长贷款期限为 20 年。

商业模式与产品

BPMB 的信贷主要投向以下几个领域：农业、建筑业、工业/制造业、服务业、基础设施、能源、教育、卫生和海事。得到投资最多的行业包括：（1）建筑；（2）电力、燃气及供水；（3）运输、仓储及通信。除此之外，为支持政府振兴发展旅游产业的规划，BPMB 还专门设立了旅游基础设施基金（Tourism Infrastructure Fund，TIF）和旅游基础设施发展基金（Tourism Infrastructure Development Fund，TIDF），用于支持旅游基础设施建设。同时，海事基金（Maritime Fund）和海事发展基金（Maritime Development Fund，MDF）则主要用于扶持新成立或是已经成立的从事航运、造船、海洋—石油—天然气相关活动和服务的企业。BPMB 的目标群体包括政府、小微企业等所有单位。BPMB 通过传统证券或伊斯兰证券来提供运营资金、过桥资金、短期贷款、长期贷款以及银团贷款（Susuk 发行以及伊斯兰 CP&MTN 计划）。

治理与监督

政府部门，尤其是财政部，一直给予 BPMB 大力支持。同时，BPMB 也得到了马来西亚中央银行的指导和关注。BPMB 的公司治理主要依据马来西亚中央银行对金融机构的指导条例以及其他主要法规。BPMB 的伊斯兰银行业务主要是参照马来西亚中央银行于 2011 年制定的针对伊斯兰机构的《伊斯兰教法治理框架》（Shariah Governance Framework，SGF）。BPMB 对审慎限制的规定与审慎规则是一致的。法律规定，BPMB 由安永会计师事务所进行审计。

菲律宾开发银行

基本信息

菲律宾开发银行（Development Bank of the Philippines，DBP）的总部位于马加地（Makati），是一家以支持可持续发展为主要任务的国有开发性金融机构。起初，DBP 只从事开发性金融业务，但从 1995 年起，DBP 获得许可，扩大了经营范围，可以从事普通商业银行业务。

DBP 的董事局由 9 名成员组成，包括 2 名独立董事，所有成员均由菲律宾总统任命。现任主席是乔斯·A·努涅斯（Jose A. Nuñez, Jr.），比娜文图拉（Buenaventura）任副主席、总裁兼首席执行官。

使命与战略

DBP 的使命是以政策为导向的："提升经济竞争力以促进可持续发展；支持基础设施建设，帮助有责任感的企业，提升社会服务水平，加强环境保护；提升并维持忠实客户的合作水平以及银行的服务水平。"DBP 的主要目标是提供融资服务，满足农业和工业企业的中长期资金需求，重点支持中小企业。

公司治理

DBP 由菲律宾政府全额出资，并受政府控制，是一家具有较强实力的国有金融机构。

DBP 享受准政府信用，评级与国家债务评级相同，这反映出 DBP 在支持菲律宾经济社会发展方面扮演的重要角色，并且表明，如果 DBP 遭遇严重的财务困难，菲律宾政府将会给予有力且及时的财务帮助。

资金来源

DBP 的主要资金来源是存款，占其总资产的 61.75%，注册资本只占其资金来源的 2.82% 左右。

经营数据

DBP 披露的 2014 年主要运营数据如下：总资产为 4 753.6 亿菲律宾比索（106.16 亿美元），净收入为 51.8 亿菲律宾比索（1.16 亿美元）。2013 年的 ROA 与 ROE 分别为 1.33%、12.73%，明显低于菲律宾银行业的平均水平（2.0%、15.4%）。不良贷款率为 3.34%，与平均水平接近。

商业模式与产品

DBP 提供多种金融产品：投资、存款、贸易融资、债券、汇兑、信托和电子银行服务。2013 年，DBP 的贷款投向主要分为两大部分：第一优先级（first priority）领域（45.37%）以及其他优先级（other priority）领域（54.63%）。其中第一优先级领域又分为四大子领域：基础设施建设和物流（63.36%）、环境保护（17.77%）、中小微企业（MSMEs，14.31%）以及公共社会服务（4.57%）。其他优先级领域包括制造业（39.44%）、批发及零售贸易（28.44%）、公共管理及国防（18.91%）。

治理与监管

DBP 的董事会由独立董事、执行委员会和各职能委员会组成（包括审计与执行、风险监督、信托、IT 管理、政府治理、人力资源、发展规划）。管理委员会、信贷委员会以及资产负债管理委员会共同负责管理经营事务。

DBP 受菲律宾共和国第 7353 号法案，又称《1992 年农村法案》（*Rural Act of 1992*）所管理。依据该法案第三章内容，"菲律宾中央银行的货币局应当制定相应的规则与条例……并且监管 DBP 等银行的运营。"由于 DBP 在 1995 年后取得了普通银行的执照，因此也须接受其他私人商业银行相同的法规管理。

总体而言，没有政府保护的情况下，DBP 成功地参与到市场竞争中，这使得它能够为中小企业以及其他相关领域的企业提供更好的贷款服务。除此之外，DBP 在与小额信贷机构（Microfinance Institutions）的合作中，获利颇丰，这也表明政府在收集中小企业借贷信息方面做得不及私营部门。DBP 的成功之处在于综合运用了政府与市场、国有与私营合作的独特优势。

印度工业开发银行

基本信息

印度工业开发银行（Industrial Development Bank of India，IDBI）成立于 1964 年。IDBI 成立之初，印度就颁布了《印度工业开发银行法》，将 IDBI 的性质定义为开发性金融机构，总部位于孟买。2004 年，印度工业开发银行变更为商业银行，目前是一家提供个人银行服务和金融解决方案的综合性银行，在印度各大商业中心设有分行，并在迪拜设有分支结构。董事会有 9 名成员，包括 5 名独立董事。董事会主要负责 IDBI 的重大发展领域。作为一家由董事会管辖的机构，IDBI 的日常管理工作由董事长、总经理和副总经理负责。

使命与战略

IDBI 担负多方面的使命，包括：用优质的服务和全面的金融方案回馈客户；提供企业和基础设施方面的资金，同时开展更多小额业务帮助解决更多民生问题；坚持公正、透明、负责任的工作方式；成为公司治理方面的领导者；运用世界先进的技术、系统和流程提升商业效率；鼓励积极、有活力的企业文化，鼓励员工发展，帮助员工树立热情、高效的工作态度；增强国际影响力；不断追求成为绿色银行。

公司治理

IDBI 的主要持股人是印度政府，持有 76.5% 的股份。其他股东包括保险公司（9.65%）、个人持股者（6.47%）和外国投资机构（2.9%）。总体而言，没有证据表明 IDBI 拥有政府特殊预算。然而，在过去 5 年，银行 3 次接受了来自政府的资金，政府的持股比例从 52.67% 上升至 76.5%。但政府不为 IDBI 的债务偿还提供担保或为坏账注资。

资金来源

IDBI 的主要资金来源是存款，占总资产的 71.7%。大多数存款为定期存款（77.4%），以保证资产的稳定性。标准普尔对 IDBI 的评级为 BB+，对印度主权债务评级为 BBB-，说明 IDBI 债务能够获得政府支持。

经营数据

2014 财年 IDBI 的主要经营数据如下：总资产约为 3.29 万亿印度卢比（547.79 亿美元），净收益为 0.12 万亿印度卢比（1.87 亿美元）。资产收益率和净资产收益率分别为 0.41% 和 5.57%，明显低于印度银行业平均水平（平均值分别为 0.80% 和 11.70%）。净利息收益率为 2.17%，不良资产率为

4.9%，比印度平均4.0%的水平略高。

商业模式与产品

IDBI业务包括企业银行和零售银行两部分，下设零售银行业务、优先发展行业业务（中小企业和农业）、基础设施建设业务和企业银行业务4个部门。银行总贷款余额为2.03万亿印度卢比（338.45亿美元），其中包含企业银行服务（47.81%）、基础设施借贷（24.73%）、零售银行业务（18.68%）以及优先发展行业业务（8.48%）。

最近，IDBI做出了多项关键性的商业决策，其中一项为拓展银行网点，2014年，IDBI新增网点309家，支行总数增加到1388家。同时，IDBI深化并扩展企业银行业务以及与投资银行的合作。此外，IDBI更加关注优先行业的借贷业务（priority sector lending，PSL），如农业、中小微企业（MSMEs）、房地产和教育的贷款。

治理与监管

IDBI的治理原则是服务于IDBI股东的最高利益。保持高水准的治理水平是董事会和各级董事的职责。IDBI有13个负责不同工作的董事：审计、商业审核、执行、股东、欺诈监控、风险管理、企业社会责任、客户服务、信息技术、酬劳、人力资源、人事提名和恢复审查（recovery review）。

IDBI主要受两部法律直接管辖：《1956年公司法》和《1949年银行监管法》。IDBI和正常商业银行一样接受监管，遵守政府制定的规定。IDBI根据《巴塞尔协议III》每季度提交监管报告。

IDBI尽可能地使业务多元化，优化资产投资组合，而不是单纯依赖经济增长。IDBI和政府的合作降低了信息成本，实现资金有效支付。IDBI让银行业不发达地区和农村地区能够及时获得资金，支援了经济发展。

土耳其工业发展银行

基本信息

土耳其工业发展银行（Turkiye Sınai KalkınmaBankasıA. Ş. TSKB）是土耳其首家私人开发和投资银行。1950 年，TSKB 在世界银行、土耳其共和国（T. R.）政府、土耳其中央银行和商业银行的支持下，依据第 3/11203 内阁部长决议成立。TSKB 历史悠久，延续至今，以支持经济社会可持续发展为目标，提供贷款和项目融资。

该行的董事会由阿德南·巴利（AdnanBali）任命。高级管理机构由以下部分组成：项目评估、估价和金融机构协调、企业银行业务和项目融资、金融控制、预算计划和投资者关系、财政和人力资源、贷款、信息技术和操作、企业架构、公司金融和经济研究、秘书处和内部系统。

该行总部位于伊斯坦布尔，同时在伊兹密尔和安卡拉设有 4 个子公司和 6 个分支机构。根据银行法第 5411 条分类设定，TSKB 的定位是"开发和投资银行"，TSKB 没有开展存款业务的许可。

使命与战略

TSKB 的使命是"为企业提供中长期融资、经纪和咨询支持，在土耳其资本市场的发展中发挥作用，为股东、客户、员工和其他利益相关者创造更多附加价值"，以实现土耳其的可持续发展。

其战略是：（1）支持不同领域企业的可持续发展（可持续性融资）；（2）为创业者提供资金、资本市场经纪和咨询支持；（3）确保可持续的盈利能力和增长；（4）加强公司结构；（5）与股东保持有效沟通。

公司治理

TSKB 不使用政府补贴，没有通过政府拨款获得的资产。t. İŞBankası A. Ş.（İş 银行）集团拥有 50% 的股份，直接或间接控制着该行的股权；T. VakıflarBankasıT. A. O. 拥有 8.38% 的股份，其他机构和个人拥有其余的 41.62%。

资金来源

作为开发和投资银行，TSKB 获得的大部分资金来自土耳其以外，该行从资本市场获得融资，其评级是 Baa3（穆迪）和 BBB－（惠誉），它从土耳其国内外金融机构获得拆借资金，在货币市场借款或在国内外市场发行证券。

在过去的 5 年里，土耳其政府没有给 TSKB 的不良贷款以豁免特权，但土耳其财政部为一些多边基金提供担保。

经营数据

2014 年，TSKB 的总资产达 67 亿美元，总贷款达 47 亿美元，年增长率分别为 21.6% 和 19.7%。2014 年，银行的股本为 9.8 亿美元，同比增长 21.4%，年平均股本回报率为 17.7%。TSKB 的资产回报率为 2.6%，其贷款的平均年利率是 4.33%，不良贷款率是 0.15%。

TSKB 在 2014 年的净利润达到了 1.583 亿美元，同比增长 13.3%。此外，2014 年，TSKB 在国际市场获得的融资超过 14 亿美元。其母行与国际金融公司也签署了一项 5 000 万美元的次级贷款协议。

截至 2014 年年底，TSKB 为可持续发展项目融资共计 21.5 亿美元，占贷款组合的 52%。其中，13 亿美元支持可再生能源领域，4.19 亿美元投入能源、资源效率和环境领域，2.3 亿美元投入旅游业。

商业模式与产品

TSKB 的业务主要分为 3 个部分：企业银行业务、投资银行业务和咨询业务。

企业银行业务包括：（1）企业贷款（工业投资、能源和资源效率、环境保护投资、可再生能源、旅游、教育、健康投资和多边基金）；（2）其他信贷产品（批发银行业务和中小企业融资、对外贸易金融、国家 ECA 信用、资本运营、租赁）。

投资银行业务包括：（1）企业融资（IPO 准备和执行，债券发行承销、并购，资产购买和销售，私有化咨询）；（2）资金和资本市场（股票经纪服务、固定收益证券经纪、外汇交易、回购交易、授权和认证交易、衍生品市场、外汇杠杆交易、针对证券的贷款、资产管理、投资咨询）；（3）衍生品和结构化产品（期货、期权、利率上下限、互换、互换期权）；（4）经济研究（每日公报和分类研究）。

咨询业务包括：（1）战略金融咨询；（2）房地产评估；（3）可持续发展和环境保护咨询。

治理与监管

TSKB 审计委员会由两个非执行董事组成。审计委员会的职责是依据法律和内部规定建立内部审计和风险管理体系。TSKB 的风险管理是通过提供持续的系统性信息来辅助银行管理层的决策过程，通过使用先进的分析方法科学运营 TSKB。TSKB 完全遵守土耳其现行的有关防止洗钱和恐怖主义融资的法律法规，其业务流程已经包含所有必要的控制、预警和其他机制。

公司治理委员会由两个非执行董事组成，职责是确保公司的治理完全符合有关法律的规定，实现 TSKB 的可持续发展，建设道德和公平的竞争环境，维护不同利益相关者的权益。

TSKB 符合大通曼哈顿银行 2014 年修订的公司治理原则，其公司治理评级得分 9.44，被授予"BIST 公司治理指数评级得分最高公司"的评价。

专栏 4-4 作为可持续发展银行的 TSKB

TSKB 具有全球性视野，高度关注环境保护和可持续发展。基于可持续发展的理念，TSKB 将气候变化、环境保护和可持续发展都纳入到公司战略和业务原则中。TSKB 关注可持续发展始于 1980 年，而且已深入其员工内心。

TSKB 在以下 4 个方面实践可持续发展理念：

- 减少贷款支持项目中出现的环境风险：关注 TSKB 外部的环境影响。
- 控制和减少 TSKB 因运营出现的内部环境影响：关注电力、水资源、天然气使用，纸张消耗和二氧化碳排放的系统化管理。
- 重点将 TSKB 可持续发展银行业务的产品和服务用于可再生能源、能源效率和环境保护等融资服务。
- 告知所有 TSKB 员工和利益相关方，鼓励他们积极参与并提高环境意识，鼓励他们参与应对气候变化并推动低碳经济。

TSKB 为土耳其私营部门开展低碳生活和高效率生产提供金融支持和咨询服务。TSKB 在土耳其的银行业发挥了先锋、先导作用，并将继续为土耳其的可持续发展而努力。

土耳其农业银行

基本信息

土耳其农业银行（TÜRKİYE CUMHURİYETİ ZİRAAT BANKASI，TCZB）是土耳其一家具有商业性质的银行，由土耳其财政部副部长主管。1863 年，这家国家银行在政府的资助下开始其银行业务。土耳其农业银行是土耳其实力最强、根基最深厚的银行。1888 年，根据议会制定的第 444 条预算法，该行从国家机构转变为福利基金的股份制公司。该行的唯一股东代表是财政部副部长，董事长由马哈瑞姆·卡斯利（Muharrem KARSLI）担任。总行设在安卡拉，旗下总计有 1 708 家分行（包括国内和国外），这些分行形成了土耳其最大的分行网络。截至 2014 年年底，它已经占据 12.4% 的市场份额——这是土耳其银行业最大的市场份额，并且在土耳其银行排名中独占鳌头。土耳其农业银行是政府所有的银行。不过，该行并没有利用政府激励措施来平衡资产负债表。

使命与战略

土耳其农业银行的使命是：成为一家了解客户需求和期望，以最合适的渠道提供最佳解决方案和价值的银行；成为一家为社会各界提供丰富的产品和服务，以广泛的分支机构和分销网络开展高效服务的银行；成为一家履行全球标准的社会责任，开展盈利和高效经营的银行；成为一家以客户满意为核心的银行。

该行的发展战略是：（1）为每个客户提供银行服务，包括成为让客户满意、愉快合作的"志在高远"的银行；提供全面、无处不在、优质、高水平的服务；更高效地管理农业融资，尤其是农业工业化融资，以确保本国和全球分销网络的有机增长。（2）有效开展银行业务，确保客户投资组合最优化，通过积极的信贷流程管理确保信贷质量，有效开展业务和支出管理。（3）成为一个全球参与者，包括迅速提高对外贸易交易的市场份额，为客户提供全球价值，更有效地整合国际金融体系，成为一家遍及北非、中东、海湾地区和远东市场的银行。

资金来源

土耳其农业银行的主要资金来源包括：土耳其新里拉存款（deposits）、

回购协议（repurchase agreements）、发行债券（issued securities）、股东权益（shareholders' equity）和政府基金的预算（budget）转移。银行通过立法和行政决定获得来自部长办公室的资源和其他公共资源。存款、非存款、股权分别占土耳其农业银行负债的62%、23%、12%。

经营数据

截至2014年年底，土耳其农业银行的总资产增长到1 061.7亿美元，其贷款总额增长到608.5亿美元。该行的股本达到122.4亿美元，年平均净资产收益率为19.0%，资产收益率为1.8%，贷款的平均年利率为5.17%，不良贷款率为1.9%。

排名前一百和前两百的现金贷款分别占现金贷款总额的22%和27%。排名前一百和前两百的非现金贷款分别占非现金贷款总额的61%和73%。排名前一百和前两百的现金贷款与非现金贷款分别占贷款总额的27%和33%。最近，TCZB公布的净利润为14.1亿美元，成为最盈利的银行。

商业模式与产品

由于该行在土耳其主要满足农业部门金融机构的需求，因此它依据自身资源直接向生产商和农业信贷企业联盟调配农业和工业贷款、基金贷款等资金，以资助蔬菜、动物、渔产等农业部门的个人和企业。

TCZB的业务主要分为3个部分：零售、中小企业（SME）和商业。零售部分包括：储蓄产品、投资产品、贷款、信用卡、缴费、服务、保险、养老金以及直销银行。中小企业部分包括：储蓄产品、投资产品、贷款、外贸、信用卡、现金管理和POS服务。商业部分包括：储蓄产品、投资产品、现金贷款、非现金贷款、国外贷款来源、外贸、信用卡和现金管理。

治理与监管

TCZB的高级管理部门由内部系统、首席执行官、信息技术管理、零售银行、金融协调、财政管理部、国际银行业务、人力资源、贷款分配和管理、贷款政策、业务交易、市场营销等组成。

为防止由于过失或舞弊导致错误报告，银行董事会负责建立和维护对财务的有效内控。为选择和运用恰当的会计政策，该行遵守2006年11月1日官方公报第26333号公告《关于银行会计应用和维护规范性文件》、《土耳其会计标准》、《土耳其财务报告准则》等其他法规，以及银行监管机构公布的会计和财务报告准则。

专栏4-5　第一产业的专业优势

土耳其经济的主要挑战是经济失衡，在第一产业中，农作物生产比例太高，而林业、渔业、牧业的发展缓慢，这表明第一产业的产业结构不合理，管理不完善，需要进一步改善。

作为一家国有的、为支持土耳其第一产业发展而设立的银行，TCZB优先募集农业资金，启动"以农工业贷款打造高端价值链"的新战略。2014年，TCZB把非零售贷款的27%发放给农业，不仅涉及养殖业，还涉及林业、渔业、牧业（见图4.1）。

在对农业的各种支持中，该行还提供由国家支持的农业保险。由国家支持的农业保险的主要特点如下：

● 对于农作物生产的保险，保费的25%由投保人预缴，其余部分最迟在农忙丰收结束时缴纳。

● 对于温室效应的保险，保费的10%由投保人预缴，其余部分在指定期限结束时缴纳。

● 对于动物、家禽和水产养殖生产的保险，保费的25%由投保人预缴，其余部分最多按5次分期付款缴纳。

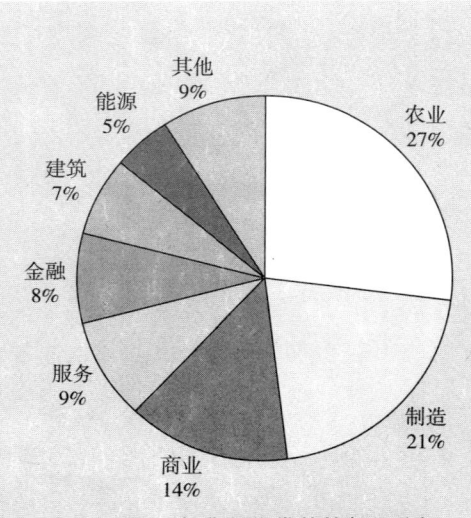

图4.1　2014年非零售贷款的部门分解

资料来源:"投资者手册2014年第四季度,TCZB",第11页

这说明,发挥专业知识优势,开发性金融机构具有依据国家发展战略推动产业升级的作用。

巴西开发银行

基本信息

根据1628号法令,巴西开发银行(The Brazilian Development Bank,BNDES)作为政府机构成立于1952年6月20日,负责制定、实施国家经济开发政策。1971年6月21日,按照第5662号法令,其转型为国有企业。该行位于巴西里约热内卢,主要有3家子公司:FINAME公司(负责融资租赁、销售业务、巴西制造机械设备的出口以及海外制造商品的进口);位于巴西的BNDESPAR公司(由民营集团主导资金业务,同时遵守巴西开发银行的规划和政策）以及位于伦敦的 BNDES PLC 公司（负责提高该行在国际金融组织中的知名度，充分支持巴西国内公司的国际化、寻找国际市场商机）。该行董事会有 9 名成员：董事会主席、副主席和 7 名董事，所有成员最终由巴西共和国总统任命，总统有权撤销任命。图 4.2 是该行的组织结构图。由于在非洲、拉丁美洲、加勒比地区拥有大规模的国际业务，世界各地的经济学家认为巴西开发银行是巴西非常重要的金融机构。

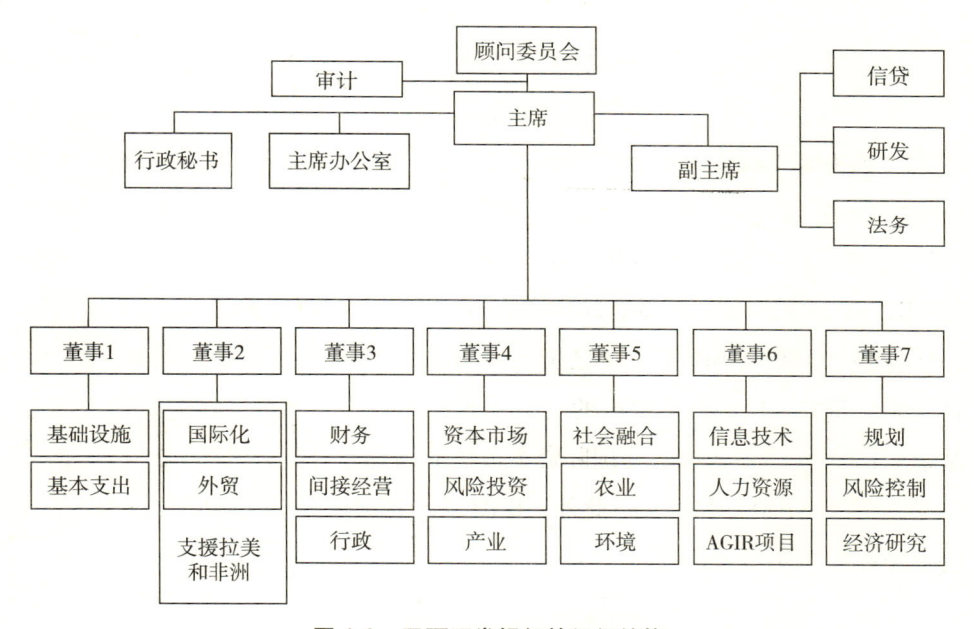

```
                    顾问委员会
           审计          │
             └─────── 主席 ───────┐           信贷
                        │                    研发
    行政秘书   主席办公室      副主席         法务

  ┌────────┬────────┬────────┬────────┬────────┬────────┐
 董事1    董事2    董事3    董事4    董事5    董事6    董事7
 基础设施  国际化   财务    资本市场  社会融合  信息技术  规划
 基本支出  外贸    间接经营  风险投资   农业    人力资源  风险控制
          支援拉美  行政     产业     环境    AGIR项目  经济研究
          和非洲
```

图 4.2　巴西开发银行的组织结构

使命与战略

该行的宗旨："促进巴西经济的可持续性和竞争性发展，创造就业机会，同时减少社会和地区不平等。"为巴西各种规模的公司和公共管理机构提供多种融资支持，并向所有经济领域提供投资，强调 3 个战略因素：创新、本土发展和社会环境发展。

政府支持

巴西开发银行是一家国有银行，是与巴西国家开发部、工业部和贸易部紧密相关的联邦公共公司。巴西政府通过巴西国库来支持巴西开发银行的低成本融资。

资金来源

在巴西，本地的信贷主要是短期贷款，所以巴西开发银行必须寻求可替代的融资解决方案来支持长期投资项目。融资业务收益是其主要创收来源，2009 年以来，巴西国库成为其资金最主要的来源。2014 年，在第 13000/14 法令的范围内，国家财政部向巴西开发银行注资 600 亿巴西雷亚尔（BRL）（226 亿美元）。为支持巴西开发银行，巴西国家财政部在 2009 年拨出 1 050 亿 BRL（603 亿美元）贷款；2010 年拨出 1 070 亿 BRL（637 亿美元）贷款；2011 年拨出 500 亿 BRL（266 亿美元）贷款；2012 年拨出 550 亿 BRL（268 亿美元）贷款。巴西开发银行的资金来源还包括其他多边实体，如工人援助基金（FAT）、企业股权、在国际资本市场的国外筹款，以及多边机构，如美洲开发银行（IDB）和世行。此外，BNDES 也通过其子公司 BNDES PAR 在国内市场筹款（见图 4.3）。

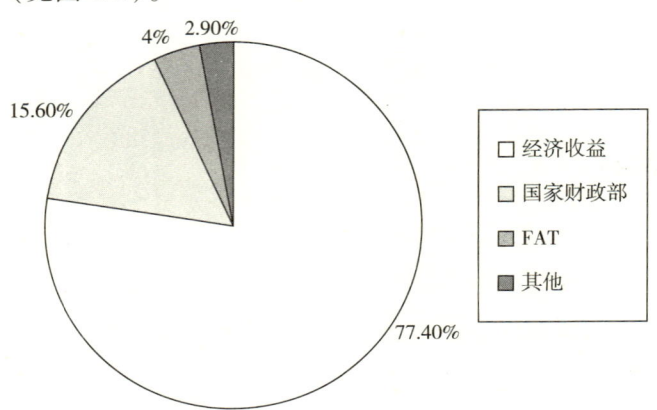

图 4.3 2012 年年底巴西开发银行资金来源

经营数据

截至 2014 年 12 月，巴西开发银行的股东权益为 663 亿 BRL（249.16 亿美元）。2014 年巴西开发银行的净利润从 2013 年的 81.5 亿 BRL（34.51 亿美元）增加到 85.84 亿 BRL（32.31 亿美元）。资产收益率为 1.03%，净资产收益率为 13.05%；不良贷款率为 0.01%，与 2013 年同期相同。表 4.1 和表 4.2 是 2014 年 12 月巴西开发银行的部分财务数据。

表 4.1　2013 年 12 月与 2014 年 12 月巴西开发银行资产负债表金融指标

资产负债表比率	2014 年 12 月	2013 年 12 月
总资产（100 万 BRL）	877 219	782 043
股东权益（100 万 BRL）	66 276	60 626
股东权益/总资产	7.56%	7.75%
贷款、净补贴/总资产	74.24%	72.28%
不良贷款/总贷款*	0.01%	0.01%
贷款损失准备/总贷款*	0.49%	0.56%
重新协商贷款/总贷款	0.66%	1.17%
贷款损失准备/不良贷款*	45.76	46.42

注：* 表示包括贷款和银行间贷款。

表 4.2　2013 年 12 月与 2014 年 12 月巴西开发银行利润表金融指标

收入表比率	2014 年	2013 年
净收入（100 万 BRL）	8 594	8 150
ROA（净收入/平均总资产）	1.03%	1.10%
ROE（净收入/平均股东权益）	13.05%	16.51%
股权投资回报率	3.53%	2.96%

商业模式与监管

巴西开发银行优先对能够促进社会和谐、增加就业机会和提高收入的项目提供融资支持。该行业务覆盖大部分的经济领域。巴西开发银行支持的主要项目类型包括：

（1）为工业投资和基础设施建设提供长期融资。"以投资着重支持巴西工业部门（包括畜牧业和农业部门）的发展壮大。巴西开发银行努力实现3个重要目标：扩大产能、增加出口和发展创新能力，这也是全球化、一体化中重要的成长因素。巴西开发银行依据联邦政府的生产发展政策制定自身发展政策。"

（2）巴西开发银行为以下领域提供金融服务：畜牧业和农业、贸易、服务、旅游、文化、社会和城市发展、创新、环保和保护特殊群体，包括对巴西土著社区的保护。

（3）巴西开发银行将依据政府政策投资大型企业。

（4）从事债券和证券承销商业务，例如为公开上市的公司或中期可能进入资本市场的公司，国际化重组业务的竞争公司、并购公司提供债券和股票业务。在此背景下，巴西开发银行优先考虑中小型创新公司，通过直接或封闭方式参与基金投资。受益于其涉足地区和领域广泛，该行可以提供更广泛的业务范围，从而引领社会资金参与这些公司的融资活动。

（5）作为南美最大国家的主要融资提供者，巴西开发银行尤其重视国际贸易，对巴西产品和服务的出口提供融资支持。它还致力于促进海外巴西企业的国际参与。巴西开发银行同样对国外贸易和巴西企业的国际化进程提供支持。

巴西开发银行旨在支持企业的现代化和业务拓展，涉及所有经济领域，包括创新、环境、文化、基础设施、工业、巴西机械设备出口和服务等。无论企业规模大小，都有机会获得巴西开发银行的资金支持。"通过遍布全国的分支机构与其他金融机构开展合作，充分利用了巴西开发银行的资源，扩大了信贷的覆盖和传播范围。"图4.4显示了巴西开发银行对主要领域的支持情况。

巴西开发银行的支出遍布巴西，图4.5为分区域支出图。

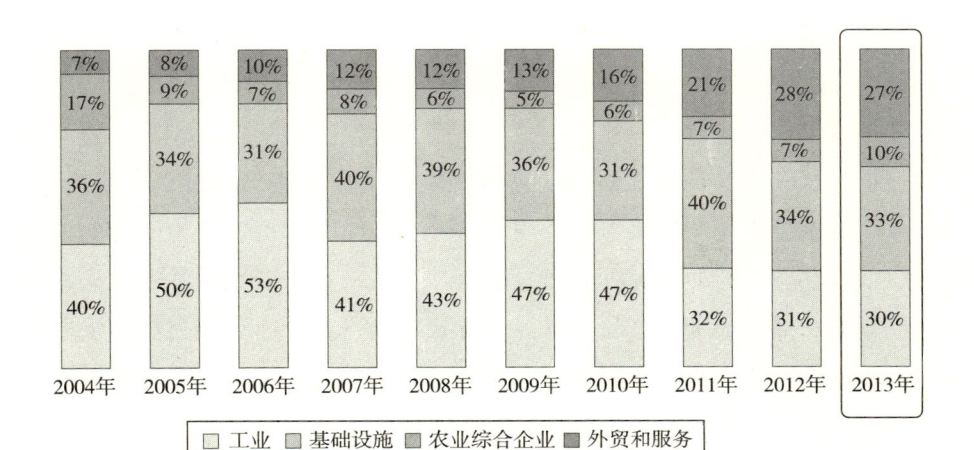

图 4.4　2004～2013 年按业务领域的支出统计

图例：工业　基础设施　农业综合企业　外贸和服务

（地图标注）北方 13.8；东北 25.7；中东 20.9；东南 87.0；南方 43.1

图 4.5　2013 年分区域支出统计（单位：10 亿 BRL）

为进行项目的分析和挑选，该行制定了一系列融资申请程序，包括预先磋商、分类、项目介绍、项目分析和付款。预先磋商是企业家融资的第一步，即为了项目的实施，需要对该公司的规模进行预评估。如果融资获批，批准文件中将会列明由巴西开发银行哪个业务部门负责分析和开展业务，该部门也会指导相关公司提供信息和其他必要文件。提出的项目由主管业务部门分析，并将分析鉴定报告发送给该业务部门的领导。之后由他提交至巴西开发银行董事会，在每周会议召开时实施考核。一旦所有条件都满足，第一笔支付资金将按照合同施行。在融资合同的存续期间,将对公司的金融运行状况和经济表现进行持续跟进。

巴西开发银行通过以下几种方式解决长期客户的投资需求,如融资、无偿资源的配置和证券认购。该行的项目融资由所投资项目的融资结构决定,并且依据该项目的现金流来签订合同。资产和应收账款可以作为同样的承诺保证。而在某些特定的情况下,通过融资项目获得部分资金,并通过认购证券来获得另一部分资金,也就是以混合方式获取资金。申请贷款可以采取直接、间接或混合的方式,这取决于所使用的载体类型:实行直接方式操作可以直接或通过代理与巴西开发银行联系;间接方式操作通过有资质的金融机构,或者通过使用巴西开发银行发行的银行卡进行操作;混合操作方式混合了直接和间接两种方式。

巴西开发银行的内部审计师与咨询委员会直接联系,负责协调巴西开发银行系统的外部控制与监管机构的所有沟通,如与总审计长办公室和巴西中央银行的沟通。

公司治理

巴西开发银行的高级管理机构是顾问委员会,包括:(1)巴西共和国总统任命的 10 名成员。规划部部长、预算和管理部部长、劳动和就业部部长、财政部部长和外交部部长分别提名一名成员。其余提名来自发展部部长以及工业和外贸部部长。这 10 名成员任期为 3 年,董事会主席从这些成员中选出;(2)巴西开发银行的员工代表,以及其空缺情况下的代理;(3)巴西开发银行的主席,同时担任顾问委员会副主席。

审计委员会负责审计相关事宜,财政委员会负责审查并对资产负债表和其他财务报表签发意见。财政委员会还要负责向巴西开发银行理事会递交年度账目,并实施公司法以外的职权。

委内瑞拉经济与社会发展银行

基本信息

委内瑞拉经济与社会发展银行（Banco de Desarrollo Económico y Social de Venezuela，BANDES）是委内瑞拉国有控股的开发银行。其前身是原委内瑞拉投资基金（西班牙语称为 FIV），2011 年成为现在的委内瑞拉经济与社会发展银行，总部位于委内瑞拉首都加拉加斯。BANDES 依据相关法律注册成立，包括关于该银行的法令——《委内瑞拉经济与社会发展银行法》。

BANDES 由该国财政部部长领导，董事会由 7 名成员组成：一位董事长兼主席、6 名董事和候补，7 名成员全部由财政部长任免。董事会每月至少召开两次会议，会议的召开要由主席召集或最少两名成员提出。主席是该行的法人代表，负责该行的管理。2014 年 2 月 7 日，西蒙·塞尔帕（Simon Zerpa）被任命为 BANDES 的主席。

2006 年以来，BANDES 已经在厄瓜多尔和尼加拉瓜共和国设立代表处。2007 年 3 月 24 日，中国—委内瑞拉联合基金（FCCV）成立，并归该行管理，该行在乌拉圭设有分支机构。

使命与战略

根据法律，该行旨在"遵循国家经济和社会发展的规划纲要，通过对国内外的生产性投资提供技术和资金支持，促进国家经济开发和社会发展"。BANDES 重视公正、平等和团结。

公司治理

该行是国有独资金融机构。

资金来源

该行主要资金来源是其他金融机构的借款。2013 年，该行与国内金融机构之间的债务是 25.1 亿玻利瓦尔（4 亿美元），与外国机构之间的债务是 1 409.3 亿玻利瓦尔（224.3 亿美元），占总负债的比例分别为 1.61% 和 90.4%。2009 年和 2010 年，BANDES 实现实收资本的增长，2013 年达到近 88.7 亿玻利瓦尔（14.1 亿美元）。委内瑞拉没有明确的规定表明，政府将帮助该行降低不良贷款比率或提供债务担保。

经营数据

BANDES 兼有批发贷款和零售贷款两种业务。2013 年，该行贷款利率近 15%。最长的国内贷款期限为 10 年，然而，对于国际资金的偿还期限可达 20 年。2013 年 6 月，BANDES 的总资产为 1 827.9 亿玻利瓦尔（290.9 亿美元），总股本为 269.4 亿玻利瓦尔（42.9 亿美元），资产收益率和净资产收益率分别为 2.61%、17.82%。同年 6 月，不良贷款率为 10.88%。

商业模式与产品

根据法律规定，该行可以开展多种常规业务以及优惠业务。根据《委内瑞拉经济与社会发展银行法》第 6~9 条，BANDES 被授予以下权利：

（1）利用自有资金为具体目标创设基金。用于创建基金的资金不能超过银行预算的 25%。BANDES 直接或间接地为项目提供短期、中期、长期的融资服务。用于融资操作的资金额度由执行董事会确定。

（2）与公共或私人机构签订咨询合同。

（3）提供优惠业务：可使用本行资金实行优惠，但不能超过税前净利润的 5%。

（4）参股公司或风险投资基金的金额不得超过改行税前净利润的 20%，投资比例将由董事会确定。

(5) 开展国际合作业务。

(6) 向区域性重点项目提供专项资金贷款。

(7) 提供直接或间接的技术和资金援助，改善中小微企业以及其他类型企业的生存环境；同时，也援助各种机构以及公共和私营机构。

(8) 提出并签署国内和国际融资合同。

(9) 在法律规定的债务限度内，以本国货币或外汇形式发行证券。

(10) 提供的各类担保均不能超过银行流动资产的10%。

(11) 保管物质化和非物质化证券。

BANDES宣布，优先考虑支持制造业和旅游业。在国际化经营方面，主要集中在拉美，尤其是南美洲。BANDES所提供的贷款与业务本身的特性相关。根据生产方式的所有权，制造业的利率是6%~10%，旅游业的利率是5%~9%。固定资产投资（不含运输）的最长期限为10年，银行为这些贷款提供担保，在贷款第一次发放之前，至少占贷款总额的一半。

治理与监管

在未投资的流动资金和资金限制方面，该行不受一般银行和金融机构法律的约束。它的信贷业务仅仅受到具有一定等级、价值、效力和融资政策的法律的限制。该行和其他商业银行一样，受该国银行与金融机构监管局的监督。

专栏4-6 在经济冲击中为制造业部门融资

2014年6月以来，由于国际市场石油价格大幅下降，委内瑞拉经济也遭受了挫折。该国已采取一切手段确保其经济稳定，促进社会发展。为了达到上述目的，BANDES为制造业部门的公司提供融资，增加其生产能力，促进经济增长。

2014年10月9日,BANDES拨出5 000万玻利瓦尔(800万美元)支持制造业公司,期望其通过购买机器设备、原材料、物资和人力来提高盈利能力。

其中,受益公司包括:苏克雷州的板和变压器公司(Tableros y Transformadores CA),接受资助大约1 700万玻利瓦尔(271万美元);卡拉沃沃的美味包公司,接受资助2 100万玻利瓦尔(334万美元)以上;猎影州的一家酒店(ProcesadoraLos Pirineos),接受资助1 400万玻利瓦尔(223万美元)以上。

Tablerosy y Transformadores CA

据该公司总裁马克·米伦(Mark Millan)说,这些资金将被用于购置新的大楼以及原料。他说,产量的50%交付给Corpoelec公司,作为一项协议以提高全国电力系统。由于新的资金支持,在不久的将来,该公司的变压器产能将从2 000台增至6 000台。公司还预计增加人力资源,将员工从14名增至22名。

美味包公司

据该公司董事胡安·卡洛斯·马丁内斯(Juan Carlos Martinez)说,由于资金支持,他们增加了生产线,并购买了能够提高产能(从65%提高至95%)的自动化设备。他说:"我们渴望开始一个新的阶段,希望生产低成本的面包、玉米饼、皮塔饼等产品。"

最近公司增加了人力,创造了40多个直接就业机会和130多个间接就业机会,并对社区产生积极影响。与其主要贸易伙伴,如Industrias Diana,共同促进了国家食品的安全。

综上所述,在经济冲击情况下,开发性金融机构可以作为刺激增长和创造就业机会的缓冲力量。

埃及工业发展与工人银行

基本信息

埃及工业发展与工人银行（Industrial Development & Workers Bank of Egypt，IDWBE）成立于1947年，为私营企业提供专业化融资。1971年，该银行的前身与亚历山大银行合并成为一个专门的微型贷款部门。1976年，该行重建为埃及工业发展银行，成为一个独立的专业金融机构，致力于为新兴民营工业项目提供结构性融资。2008年11月，该行并购了埃及工人银行并更名为埃及工业发展与工人银行，目标是成为一家能够对埃及工业提供强大金融支持的金融机构。该行的股权结构是：财政部占84.4%、公共部门占3.3%、私营部门占12.3%。IDWBE的总部设在开罗，全国设有19个分支机构，董事长是赛义德·穆罕默德·卡萨耶（El-Sayed Mohamed-Kosayer），另有8名董事会成员。

使命与战略

该行的使命是"促进、增强、服务埃及私营工业部门，特别是对中小型工业企业的发展支持"。工业部门的重要性意识逐渐凸显，而中小工业企业则成为盘活国民经济的催化剂，IDWBE一直是资助中小工业企业领域的先行者，通过拓展各种技术、市场和金融服务来扶持企业。该行的战略是促进、提高、服务埃及私营工业部门，特别是埃及中小型工业企业。基于稳定的中长期资金基础和业务、产品开发团队的支持，IDWBE致力于拓展多元化量身定制的产品和服务，以满足存款人、企业家和商业类的要求和需要。该行的愿景是成为一家在专业领域内具有一定经营活力，在经济和行业变革中保持一定积极性，具有客户导向、先进技术、资金雄厚且可盈利的领头人。此外，该行的目标是为现存新型中小规模的工业项目提供持续不断的资金、技术和市场支持。因此，在一个活跃市场中，须确保这些企业项目持续的增长与竞争。

政府支持

埃及财政部拥有 IDWBE 84.4% 的股权，这意味着，该行可以从埃及政府获得相当程度的支持，同时也有一定增信效果。2006 年，IDWBE 的唯一股东承诺注资以帮助该行整顿资产负债表和增加必要准备金。该行可随时使用来自埃及中央银行（CBE）5 亿埃镑（0.88 亿美元）的信用额度，并且相较于埃及的其他银行（包括其他公共部门银行）来讲，该行在赎回资产或处置抵押时具有一定优先权（CBE 授权）。

资金来源

该行的资金主要来源于存款和同业拆借。

经营数据

截至 2009 年年底，IDWBE 的总资产不断增加并达到 35.247 36 亿埃镑（6.426 亿美元）。2009 年，资产中大部分是贷款及垫款，合计占资产总额的 76.48%。截至 2009 年年底，该行的股东权益总额为 8.58 亿埃镑（1.562 3 亿美元）。在 2008 年，资产收益率和净资产收益率并不令人满意，分别为 -2.25%、-7.44%，到 2009 年，资产收益率和净资产收益率有所改善，分别达到 0.01% 和 0.02%。该行的不良贷款率很高，通过努力，不良贷款率由 2008 年的 74% 降至 2009 年的 63%，但比例仍然很高，使得该行无法获取大额利润。该行的资本充足率（CAR）为 44.86%。

商业模式与产品

IDWBE 主要有三大产品线，分别是储蓄工具、信贷及零售银行业务。储蓄工具：1~12 个月的定期存款利率是 5.875%~7.25%；储蓄账户年利率为

7.5%，半年利率为 7%。信贷：该行的信贷业务涉及各种项目，例如根据《环境法》援助工业项目的利率为 2.5%。零售银行业务：该行为个人提供多种产品服务，例如该行向政府、公共业务部门和专业领域员工提供教育贷款的利率是 9%；最低贷款金额为 2 000 埃镑，最高贷款金额为 30 000 埃镑。

IDWBE 的目标市场包括建筑、制造、能源、卫生等。除上述一些核心的专项银行业务外，该行向客户提供的额外服务包括：项目评估、金融工程、可行性研究，同时还可以代表客户处置资产。

治理与监管

IDWBE 并未在其官方网站详细说明其治理结构及发布年度报告。但在 2009 年，该行不断提升 IT 系统，同时加强管理信息系统的管理，用以监管和衡量该行整体以及不同业务线的执行状况和执行效率。此外，为更好地满足客户需求，该行着重改善、重新定位并扩大了其分行网络，涵盖了埃及大多数工业城市。新分支机构将设在赫勒万、奥博、马哈拉、考波拉和库斯纳地区。

南非开发银行

基本信息

南非开发银行（Development Bank of Southern Africa，DBSA）始建于 1983 年，系国有独资金融机构。1997 年，根据《南非开发银行法》（1997 年第 13 号法案）注册成立，其他相关法令包括 1999 年的《公共财政管理法》（1999 年 1 号法令）和 2008 年的《南非公司法》（2008 年第 71 号法令）。该行总部设在南非约翰内斯堡，共计 425 名员工。该行在董事会和执行管理委员会系统下运营，委员会主席是贾布·莫莱凯蒂（Jabu Moleketi），首席执行官是帕特里克·德拉米尼（Patrick Dlamini）。

使命与战略

DBSA 旨在通过对基础设施进行金融与非金融投资,加速社会经济的可持续发展,提高南非人民的生活质量。

该行的整体议程以愿景、使命及价值为前提。

愿景:繁荣一体化区域,逐步摆脱贫困和依赖。

使命:通过扩展开发性金融、有效整合与实施可持续发展来推动该地区发展。

价值:高性能、共同愿景、诚信、创新、以服务为导向。

根据《南非开发银行法》(1997 年 13 号法案)的规定,DBSA 的任务是:"促进该地区的经济发展和增长、开发人力资源和提升机构能力;支持该地区的可持续发展项目与计划;注重基础设施建设,并为私营机构提供融资服务。"

公司治理

DBSA 的唯一股东是南非共和国政府,尤指财政部。

资金来源

作为一家非吸储机构,DBSA 采用新的融资战略,并于 2013 年 6 月开始致力于寻求多种资金来源,其中包括发行债券(2 921 680 万兰特)、信贷额度融资(1 360 610 万兰特)、利用回购协议、股本(100 亿兰特)和政府永久资助(619 234 万兰特)进行融资。这种多样性的资金来源显著降低了融资成本。同时,银行总共发行的债券从 2012~2013 年的 260 亿兰特在 2013~2014 年增加到了 290 亿兰特。

2013~2014 年是新一轮政府资本结构调整(240 亿兰特)。该行在 2012~2013 年的处境较为困难,但并无直接证据表明这次资本结构调整解决了其不良贷款问题。

DBSA 的信用评级受南非共和国主权评级的直接影响,2014 年年底,标准普尔下调该国的主权信用评级至 BBB−，惠誉国际对该国展望从稳定下调为负面。如前所述，DBSA 受到上述主权评级的影响。2014 年 6 月，标准普尔对 DBSA 的评分在长期外币项降为 BBB−，长期本币项降为 BBB+。

经营数据

在南撒哈拉地区飞速发展及呈现新挑战的背景之下，2014 年，DBSA 的跨领域业务取得令人瞩目的成绩，总支出增加了 39%，从 92 亿兰特（10 亿美元）增至 127 亿兰特（12 亿美元），这使得该行当年总资产从 2013 年的 540 亿兰特（58.5 亿美元）增至 638 亿兰特（60.6 亿美元），总负债和总权益也分别从 2013 年的 373 亿兰特（40.4 亿美元）、168 亿兰特（18.1 亿美元）分别增至 429 亿兰特（40.7 亿美元）、199 亿兰特（18.9 亿美元）。

与此同时，相较于 2012/2013 年亏损的 8.26 亿兰特（8 900 万美元），该行在 2014 年盈利能力有所回升，净收入达到 7.87 亿兰特（7 500 万美元）。同年，该行资产收益率从 2013 年的 1.3% 上升到 1.6%；净资产收益率从 2013 年的 −4.8% 上升到 4.3%。此外，银行的资产质量已经得到改善，不良贷款率由 2013 年的 7.3% 降至 5.8%。

2014 年，DBSA 的贷款年均利率约为 7.69%，开发建设贷款的期限为 1 年以内到 14 年以上。期限超过 14 年的贷款占总贷款的 8.35%（43.80 亿兰特/524.50 亿兰特）。表 4.3 显示了不同期限的贷款量。

表 4.3　开发建设贷款额和期限　　　　　　　　　　　　　（单位：百万美元）

期限	2014 年	2013 年
<1 年	651.87	664.49
1~2 年	420.62	425.78
2~3 年	433.90	420.30
3~4 年	360.90	434.09

(续表)

期限	2014 年	2013 年
4~9 年	1 601.49	1 599.09
9~14 年	1 087.94	647.21
>14 年	415.90	676.37

商业模式与产品

DBSA 涉及批发和零售业务,以开发性金融机构、政府和私人实体为目标客户。根据可持续性金融概念,该行实行业务循环经营,经营始于可靠的资金来源,继而实施发展投资项目,运用反馈的主要财务指标进行重估,如利息收入和非利息收入。最后,该行将利用返回的利润开展新一轮业务。

总体而言,该行在 2013~2014 年的贷款刷新了纪录,从 2008~2009 年涵盖 116 个项目和 13 个国家的 93 亿兰特(9.77 亿美元)增至 127 亿兰特(12.1 亿美元)。DBSA 致力于 4 个关键领域:能源[67 亿兰特(6.36 亿美元),53%]、运输[23 亿兰特(2.18 亿美元),18%]、水力[9.89 亿兰特(9 400 元美元),8%]和通信[6.52 亿兰特(6 200 万美元),5%](见图 4.6)。确切来讲,该行在国内融资领域的总支出为 92 亿兰特(8.74 亿美元),其余 36 亿兰特(3.42 亿美元)支出在国际项目上。有关国际融资业务,在未来 3 年,该行有望在地域范围上向北拓展,即从南撒哈拉拓展到非洲其他地区。在此之前,该行的国际投资主要流向南部非洲发展共同体(南共体)成员国:即安哥拉、博茨瓦纳、刚果、莱索托、马拉维、毛里求斯、莫桑比克、纳米比亚、斯威士兰、坦桑尼亚、赞比亚和津巴布韦的民主共和国。2014 年,DBSA 在安哥拉的支出占总支出的 16%,其次是津巴布韦(5%)(见图 4.7)。

图 4.6　DBSA 在各领域的支出

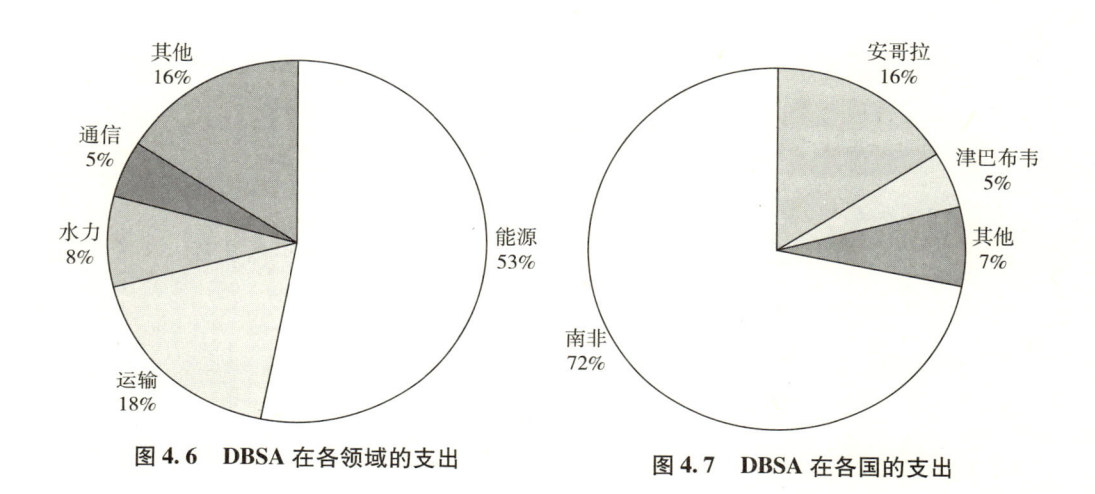

- 其他 16%
- 通信 5%
- 水力 8%
- 运输 18%
- 能源 53%

图 4.7　DBSA 在各国的支出

- 安哥拉 16%
- 津巴布韦 5%
- 其他 7%
- 南非 72%

治理与监管

DBSA 由南非财政部监管，而南非的商业银行由南非储备银行监管。此外，作为公共财政实体，该行遵循《公共财政管理法》和《公司法》第 27~31 章，以及该行和商业银行都应遵守的法律和规则。

专栏 4-7　绿色基金

在 21 世纪，当环境问题和气候变化成为突出问题时，向绿色经济转型成为世界范围内所有国家的一项紧迫挑战。所谓绿色经济是指改善人类福祉和社会公平，同时显著降低环境风险和生态资源稀缺问题。

绿色基金是一个刚成立不久的国家基金，可带来环境效益与社会效益，旨在支持绿色计划，帮助南非过渡到低碳、资源高效和适应气候变化发展的道路上，从而提供高效经济。而 DBSA 代表南非环境事务部门对该基金进行管理。

该基金成立于 2012 年 4 月，目标是通过提供各种金融和非金融服务以实现三大领域的改善：绿色城市、低碳经济以及自然资源的管理。由绿色基金提供的财政支持主要表现为可回收和不可回收的补助金以及在利率、期限和权益方面的贷款优惠。

2013/2014 年度，该基金批准了 27 个项目，价值 3.398 亿兰特（3 200 万美元）；至今，该基金引进的所有批准项目价值共计 6.711 亿兰特（6 400 万美元）。该基金承诺全年项目达到 2.326 亿兰特（2 200 万美元），支出增加至 1.893 亿兰特（1 800 万美元），同比增长 539.3%。

自绿色基金成立以来共批准了 49 个项目，其中 26 个属于投资项目，16 个属于研发项目，7 个属于能力开发项目（见图 4.8）。

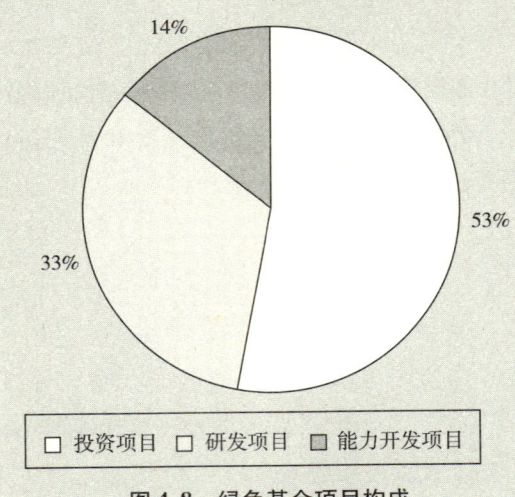

图 4.8 绿色基金项目构成

最近，南非开发银行的绿色基金赞助了一个由尤丹赫皮—德士帕奇发展倡议（Uitenhage-Despatch Development Initiative，UDDI）和南非气候创新中心（Climate Innovation Centre of South Africa，CIC）共同开发的项目。随着低碳技术在东开普省和纳尔逊·曼德拉湾地区的发展，该项目旨在为一些企业家或小型公司提供资金、培育和商业支持服务。合格的小型公司和企业家将在公司招聘、技术、业务支持等方面获利，UDDI 和 CIC 将为中小型、微型企业提供办公空间、训练、资助、商业化以及法律和知识产权服务。为此，中小型企业在埃滕哈赫（Uitenhage）和东开普省地区的发展继而将推动绿色经济。

绿色基金项目报告是基于 14 个核准项目的现场考察编写而成的，该报告显示这些项目对经济、社会和环境效益均有所贡献。例如，预期带来超过 3 500 万兰特（330 万美元）的经济利润，创造 14 957 个就业机会，碳排放量将减少 100 693 吨。

上述案例证明了国家基金的力量，该基金使得政府与 DBSA 通力合作以援助发展中国家的环境项目融资。

第五章 与中国相关的开发性金融机构

中国共产党和中国政府高度重视开发性金融服务国家战略、支持经济社会发展的作用，并且自2013年以来为促进开发性金融发展提出了一系列重要理念和部署，进行了必要的制度安排，标志着中国的开发性金融进入了全新的发展阶段：

2013年11月，中共十八届三中全会提出，"建立开发性金融机构，加快同周边国家和区域基础设施互联互通建设，推进丝绸之路经济带、海上丝绸之路建设，形成全方位开放新格局。"

2014年4月2日，国务院常务会议要求，发挥好依托国家信用、服务国家战略、资金运用保本微利的开发性金融的"供血"作用，更大规模推进棚改。

2014年4月25日，中央政治局会议提出，更好地运用开发性金融支持棚户区改造。

2014年11月4日，中央财经领导小组第八次会议研究丝绸之路经济带和21世纪海上丝绸之路规划，要求发挥好开发性金融、政策性金融的独特优势和作用。

2015年3月5日，国务院总理李克强在《2015年政府工作报告》中强调，发挥好开发性金融、政策性金融在增加公共产品供给中的作用。

2015年3月，国务院批复国家开发银行深化改革方案，强调国家开发银行要坚持开发性金融机构定位，适应市场化、国际化新形势，充分利用服务国家战略、依托信用支持、市场运作、保本微利的优势，进一步完善开发性金融运作模式，积极发挥在稳增长、调结构等方面的重要作用，加大对重点领域和薄弱环节的支持。

国家开发银行

基本信息

国家开发银行成立于1994年，总部设在中国北京。2008年12月11日，其改制为国家开发银行股份有限公司。2015年3月，中国国务院批准了国家开发银行深化改革的方案。根据改革方案，要将国家开发银行建设成为资本充足、治理规范、内控严密、运营安全、服务优质、资产优良的开发性金融机构。

国家开发银行的股东包括：中国财政部、中国中央汇金投资有限责任公司和中国全国社会保障基金理事会。2014年年底，财政部持股50.18%，汇金公司持股47.63%，社保基金持股2.19%。目前，国家开发银行董事会由11名董事组成。其中，董事长由胡怀邦担任，副董事长由郑之杰担任。国家开发银行受中国人民银行和中国银行业监督管理委员会监管。与其他中国国内商业银行相同，国家开发银行需要遵守相关法律法规约束，并由外部专业审计机构审计（由德勤审计）。

截至2014年年底，国家开发银行拥有办公厅、政策研究室、业务发展局、资金局、风险管理局、信贷管理局、国际合作业务局等31个厅局，以及37家分行、5家境外机构。

使命与战略

国家开发银行主要通过开展中长期信贷与投资等金融业务，为国民经济重大中长期发展战略服务。

国家开发银行贯彻国家宏观经济政策，筹集和引导社会资金，缓解经济社会发展的瓶颈制约和薄弱环节，致力于以融资推动市场建设和规划先行，支持国家基础设施、基础产业、支柱产业以及战略性新兴产业等领域发展和国家重点项目建设，促进区域协调发展和城镇化建设，支持保障性安居工程、中小企业、"三农"、教育、医疗卫生以及环境保护等领域的发展，支持国家"走出去"战略，拓展国际合作业务。以此，增强国力，改善民生，促进科学发展。

国家开发银行坚持以开发性方法和市场化运作服务经济社会发展，努力保持强有力的发展能力、创新能力和先进的市场业绩。

2014年发展战略

2014年年初，国家开发银行董事长胡怀邦提出，2014年国家开发银行将把握稳中求进的工作总基调，坚持开发性金融发展方向，围绕服务国家改革、深化国家开发银行改革和推进内部改革，大力支持新型城镇化基础设施、保障性安居工程、产业结构调整和国际合作等国家重点领域，同时不断完善管理架构，全面加强风险管理，提高经营发展质效，进一步增强服务国家战略的能力。行长郑之杰对2014年工作做出部署，要求国家开发银行发挥综合金融服务优势，积极引导社会资金，加大对新型城镇化等重点领域的支持力度；大力支持农、林、水利建设，促进教育、医疗、养老等社会事业发展，开创服务民生新局面；稳步推进国际合作业务，服务于"丝绸之路经济带"、"21世纪海上丝绸之路"等建设，实现中国和合作国互利互惠，共同发展。

经营数据

截至2014年年底，国家开发银行的资产总额已突破10万亿元，增长率26%；贷款余额达到7.94万亿元，净利润稳步增长，全年实现净利润977亿元；风险管控全面深化，2014年年底不良资产率为0.65%，连续39个季度保持在1%以内，资产质量保持同业领先水平。截至2014年年底，ROA为1.06%，ROE为15.63%，资本充足率为11.88%。

按照年初提出的发展目标，2014 年国家开发银行支持经济社会发展取得以下成绩：

（1）支持新型城镇化建设，全年发放城镇化贷款 1.11 万亿元，占当年人民币贷款发放的 60%。

（2）支持区域协调发展，新增中西部贷款人民币 4 629 亿元，占比 66%；新增东北老工业基地贷款人民币 796 亿元，占比 11%；新增西藏和 4 个省份藏区贷款人民币 147 亿元；新增新疆贷款人民币 218 亿元。

（3）支持重大基础设施项目建设，发放铁路贷款 1 195 亿元，水利贷款 814 亿元，支持了高速公路、铁路客运专线、油气基础设施、煤炭深加工、新能源发电、水利工程等国家重点项目建设。

（4）促进产业结构调整，参与发起设立国家集成电路资金，发放战略性新兴产业贷款 2 182 亿元，文化产业贷款 425 亿元，环保及节能减排贷款余额 9 585 亿元，同比增长 7.2%。

（5）成立住宅金融事业部，当年发放棚户区改造贷款人民币 4 086 亿元，同比增长近 3 倍，同业占比 80% 以上，累计支持棚户区改造总面积 9 亿平方米，惠及 916 万户、2 857 万人。被中国《金融时报》和中国社会科学院金融研究所授予"年度最佳棚户区改造贡献银行"。

（6）截至 2014 年年底，累计发放助学贷款 692 亿元，支持家庭经济困难学生 1 239 万人次，覆盖 26 个省（自治区、直辖市）、2 732 所高校，占全国助学贷款市场份额的 80% 以上。截至 2014 年年底，中小企业贷款余额达 2.47 万亿元，其中小微企业贷款余额 1.03 万亿元，惠及中小型企业、微型企业、个体工商户、农户、创业青年、城市下岗职工等各类社会群体，覆盖制造业、农林牧渔业等近 20 个行业。

（7）截至 2014 年年底，外币贷款余额 2 670 亿美元，跨境人民币贷款余额 564 亿元，继续保持中国对外投融资主力银行地位。

（8）围绕着支持"一带一路"建设和周边互联互通建设，推动开展"一带一路"的国别规划、区域规划、专项规划、战略规划等工作，推动能源资源开发、通信、核电、高铁等产业走出国门，累计向沿线国家发放贷款超过1 200亿美元。

资金来源

国家开发银行依靠国家信用在市场上发债，通过国家信用证券化，把短期的、零散的资金转化为长期的大额资金，支持国家重点领域和薄弱环节的发展。国家开发银行通过市场化方式发债筹资始于1998年，主要在银行间市场发行金融债，如今已经成为中国境内债券市场仅次于财政部的第二大发债主体。

2014年，国家开发银行在发债方面取得两项重要突破：一是在伦敦首发20亿元离岸人民币债券，是首只登陆伦敦市场的中国准主权人民币债券。二是首次向个人发售金融债券。2014年5月6~8日，国家开发银行首只柜台金融债券通过中国工商银行成功发行，该债券期限1年，票面利率为4.5%，通过工商银行的电子银行渠道及境内营业网点向社会公众发行20亿元，单笔交易起点及最小递增单位均为100元。据统计，个人投资者和非金融机构投资者分别认购15.45亿元和4.55亿元，个人投资者最大认购额达2 500万元。该债券也是中国首只银行柜台金融债，为社会公众投资金融债券开辟了一条新的渠道。

中国开发性金融促进会

2013年4月，由国家开发银行发起的中国开发性金融促进会正式成立，这是中国开发性金融唯一的全国性社团组织，其主要宗旨是总结中国开发性金融的发展经验，推动开发性金融的理论研究和制度建设，运用开发性金融的原理和方法促进市场建设、信用建设和制度建设，促进各国开发性金融机构之间的交流与合作等。经会员代表大会选举，全国政协副主席、国家开发银行原董事长陈元担任首任会长，胡怀邦、郑之杰等国家开发银行的主要领导担任副会长。

中国开发性金融促进会的会员主要是在开发性领域开展投融资活动的大型企业和科研机构，截至 2014 年年末，共有会员 8 000 余家。中国开发性金融促进会积极整合会员资源，创办开发性金融大讲堂，已举办 18 期，成立"文化金融俱乐部"和"能源金融俱乐部"，促进国有企业和民营企业之间的产业链合作，通过引入优质企业的方式支持贫困地区的基础设施建设、产业发展、居民就业等扶贫开发事业，积极推动国际开发性金融机构的联系与合作。

2014 年，国家开发银行做出了如下新尝试：成立住宅金融事业部（见专栏 5 – 1）；在伦敦首发 20 亿元离岸人民币债券（见专栏 5 – 2）；参与设立国家集成电路产业基金（见专栏 5 – 3）；支持中国武陵山地区的扶贫开发（见专栏 5 – 4）；推动信贷资产证券化业务（见专栏 5 – 5）。

专栏 5 – 1　成立住宅金融事业部

2014 年 7 月底，国家开发银行按照中国国务院要求，成立住宅金融事业部。成立该事业部是为了充分发挥开发性金融的市场建设、制度建设和"融资、融智"（指提供融资支持和提供规划等发展理念支持）的功能，实现住宅金融业务的集约化、专业化管理和长期可持续发展。业务范围包括：办理纳入全国棚户区改造规划的棚户区改造及相关城市基础设施工程建设贷款业务；在经批准的额度内办理软贷款回收再贷业务，专项用于支持纳入全国棚户区改造规划的棚户区改造及相关城市基础设施建设项目。

国家开发银行支持棚户区改造始于 2004 年的辽宁省。主要做法是，首先推动政府整合资源、构建市场化的借款人，再由国家开发银行向借款人贷款启动项目，形成早期成效和示范效应，进而带动社会资金投入，在 21 个月内实现了辽宁省 14 个城市约 120 万户棚户区居民从低矮、破败的棚户房迁入宽敞明亮新楼房的目标。2013年，中国政府提出5年内改造1 000万户棚户区的计划。国家开发银行住房金融事业部的成立，将为保障性安居工程提供长期稳定的建设资金，缓解棚户区改造相关工程建设的资金瓶颈，对解决中国中低收入家庭困难、健全住房保障和供应体系具有重要意义，是中国住房金融领域的重大改革，被列入"2014中国银行业十大新闻"。

专栏5-2 在伦敦首发20亿元离岸人民币债券

2014年9月12日，第六次中英经济财金对话在伦敦举行，双方就支持国家开发银行在英国开展业务、在伦敦设立代表处达成共识。双方一致认为，在英国发行以人民币计价的政府债和准政府债有利于支持人民币离岸市场的发展，双方同意探索支持人民币离岸债券市场流动性和有效性的途径。作为第一步，中国国家开发银行在伦敦成功发行20亿元离岸人民币债券；英方宣布有意向发行以人民币计价的英国国债，发行国债的收入将作为英国政府外汇储备。英国因此成为首个发行海外人民币债券的西方国家。

当天，国家开发银行成功在伦敦发行总值人民币20亿元的3种离岸人民币债券，包括：3年期固息债6亿元，利率为3.35%；5年期固息债5亿元，利率为3.6%；10年期固息债9亿元，利率为4.35%。本次发行吸引了全球投资者的踊跃认购，认购倍数约两倍，其中欧洲地区投资者认购金额占比约30%。这是首只登陆伦敦市场的中国准主权人民币债券，是中英两国深化金融合作的重要成果，是离岸人民币市场发展的又一个里程碑。

国家开发银行是以发债为主要筹资手段的债券银行，累计在中国国内市场发债超过10万亿元，债券余额占国内债市总额的1/5。从2007年开始作为境内首家机构赴香港发行人民币债券,到本次在伦敦发行人民币债券,国家开发银行已经累计在境外发行人民币债券208亿元,在支持离岸人民币市场建设方面发挥了重要作用。

专栏5-3 参与设立国家集成电路产业基金

2014年,中国政府发布《国家集成电路产业发展推进纲要》(以下简称《纲要》)。《纲要》认为,集成电路产业是信息技术产业的核心,是支撑经济社会发展的战略性、基础性和先导性产业,并提出设立国家产业投资基金,吸引大型企业、金融机构以及社会资金,重点支持集成电路等产业发展,促进工业转型升级。9月24日,国开金融有限责任公司(国家开发银行的全资子公司)、中国烟草总公司、北京亦庄国际投资发展有限公司、中国移动通信集团公司等共同签署协议,正式设立集成电路产业投资基金。据媒体报道,基金一期总规模1 200亿元,其中国家财政360亿元,国开金融320亿元,亦庄国投100亿元,其余420亿元面向市场募集。参与设立该基金,是开发性金融支持国家新型工业化和信息化的重要体现。

专栏5-4 支持中国武陵山地区的扶贫开发

武陵山区域跨湖北、湖南、重庆、贵州四省,是跨省交界面大、少数民族聚集多、贫困人口分布广的连片特困地区。国家开发银行运用产业扶贫、基础设施扶贫和教育扶贫等多种方式,推动该地区扶贫开发工作由"输血"向"造血"的转变。

在武陵山区域的贵州省印江县，国家开发银行通过"四台一会"模式开展农业产业扶贫。"四台一会"模式是指构建融资平台，作为借款人承接开行信贷资金，再批量支持符合条件的用款的中小企业等；成立担保平台，负责中小企业或农户的贷款申请材料审核、保前调查和保后监管；搭建管理平台，指导合格贷款对象申请贷款、用好贷款；组建公示平台，公示用款人姓名、额度、用途等；成立信用协会，建立信用体系。截至2014年年底，国家开发银行共向印江发放农业产业贷款1.314亿元，支持当地的茶叶、绿壳蛋鸡、食用菌、乡村旅游四项支柱产业。其中2011年，国家开发银行与贵州省扶贫办合作，通过给该县板溪镇的食用菌合作社贷款100万元，由扶贫办在贷款基准利率上贴息5个点，农民只需支付1%的利息，使菇农人均增收2.5万元。为支持湖南省花垣县的旅游产业基础设施建设，国家开发银行采取公私合营模式（PPP）与地方政府合作，打造特殊目的公司（SPV），以该公司作为承贷主体贷款2.6亿元，用于旅游基础设施建设，以门票收益、服务收益、地产收益作为还款来源。截至2014年年底，国家开发银行湖南省分行为武陵山片区累计提供贷款845.7亿元，包括支持高速公路、农村干线公路、水利、电力、城市路网、保障性住房、土地综合开发等城市基础设施建设192.7亿元，支持产业龙头企业及中小微企业19.5亿元，同时，还为困难家庭发放生源地助学贷款15.3亿元。

武陵山区的扶贫开发是国家开发银行支持各省扶贫开发的一个缩影。2014年5月，国家开发银行与国务院扶贫办签署《开发性金融扶贫合作协议》，从4个方面加大扶贫资金的支持，即特色产业扶贫、基础设施改善、发展教育和重大项目建设。截至2014年年底，国家开发银行先后向贫困地区发放基础设施贷款超过1.3万亿元，向405个国家级贫困县发放助学贷款149.8亿元，支持贫困学生266.9万人次。减贫是世界各国面临的共同任务和挑战，国家开发银行通过自己的方式对此做出了不懈努力。

> **专栏 5-5　推动信贷资产证券化业务**
>
> 　　信贷资产证券化是指把欠流动性但有未来现金流的信贷资产重组成资产池，以此为基础发行证券，盘活存量资金，更好地支持实体经济发展。
>
> 　　2013年8月，中国政府决定进一步扩大信贷资产证券化试点，盘活存量信贷资产，将有效信贷向经济发展的薄弱环节和重点领域倾斜。国家开发银行是中国信贷资产证券化市场的先行者和最主要的参与者之一，发行期数、规模、种类均居国内银行业首位。截至目前，在本轮试点中，国家开发银行共发行10单，多次刷新单笔发行规模最高纪录，总规模1 013亿元，同期市场占有率34.2%，已经兑付完毕的产品均实现了"资产零违约、管理零差错"。盘活存量资产所释放的信贷规模主要投向了棚户区改造、铁路等经济发展的薄弱环节和重点领域建设项目，其中盘活铁路资产510亿元，为金融支持铁路投融资体制改革做出了有益探索。

亚洲基础设施投资银行

基本信息

　　2013年10月，中国国家主席习近平和总理李克强在先后出访东南亚时提出了筹建亚洲基础设施投资银行（简称"亚投行"）的重要倡议。

　　2014年10月21日，包括孟加拉国、文莱、中国、印度、巴基斯坦等在内的21个国家正式签署《筹建亚投行备忘录》，共同决定成立亚投行。根据《筹建亚投行备忘录》，亚投行法定资本为1 000亿美元，总部设在中国北京。随后，印度尼西亚签署备忘录，成为亚投行第22个意向创始成员国。

　　2015年3月12日，英国正式宣布将加入亚投行。法国、意大利和德国也相继宣布将加入亚投行。截至 2015 年 4 月 15 日，已有 57 个国家正式成为亚投行意向创始成员国，分别为：奥地利、澳大利亚、阿塞拜疆、孟加拉国、巴西、文莱、柬埔寨、中国、丹麦、埃及、法国、芬兰、格鲁吉亚、德国、冰岛、印度、印度尼西亚、伊朗、以色列、意大利、约旦、哈萨克斯坦、韩国、科威特、吉尔吉斯斯坦、老挝、卢森堡、马来西亚、马尔代夫、马耳他、蒙古、缅甸、尼泊尔、荷兰、新西兰、挪威、阿曼、巴基斯坦、菲律宾、波兰、葡萄牙、卡塔尔、俄罗斯、沙特阿拉伯、新加坡、南非、西班牙、斯里兰卡、瑞典、瑞士、塔吉克斯坦、泰国、土耳其、阿联酋、英国、乌兹别克斯坦和越南。

截至目前，美国政府表示，只要亚投行与现有机构形成互补，并采取严格的治理标准，美国将对亚投行持欢迎的态度。但就是否最终加入亚投行，美国政府仍未明确表态。

迄今为止，创始成员国已就筹建亚投行分别在中国昆明、印度孟买、哈萨克斯坦阿拉木图、中国北京和新加坡举行了五次谈判代表会议。在第五次谈判代表会议期间，各方就《亚投行章程》文本达成一致，并商定将于 2015 年 6 月底在北京举行《亚投行章程》签署仪式。而在章程经合法的创始成员国批准生效后，亚投行将于 2015 年年底正式成立。

使命与战略

根据《筹建亚投行备忘录》，亚投行系"一个旨在向亚洲地区在发展基础设施、推进互联互通方面提供融资支持的多边开发银行"。

为实现这一目标，亚投行将"专注于亚洲地区的基础设施及其他生产性行业的发展，这将涉及能源、电力、交通、通信、农村基础设施、农业发展、城市发展及物流等。亚投行所有投资将遵照董事会批准的经济战略和政策执行"。另外，亚投行还将重点加强与其他多边、双边开发机构（如世界银行、亚洲开发银行）之间的相互协作。

在亚投行正式成立之前，董事会将有权根据具体情况就亚投行的具体运行策略及重点支持领域进行修改或调整。

亚投行大事记

- 2013年10月：中国国家主席习近平和总理李克强在先后出访东南亚时提出了筹建亚投行的重要倡议。
- 2014年10月：21个亚洲国家正式签署《筹建亚投行备忘录》，共同决定成立亚洲基础设施投资银行。
- 2015年3月：英国正式宣布将加入亚投行。随后，法国、意大利和德国纷纷宣布将加入亚投行。
- 2015年4月：已有57个国家正式成为亚投行意向创始成员国。
- 截至2015年5月底：创始成员国已就亚投行的筹建分别在昆明、孟买、阿拉木图、北京和新加坡举行了五次谈判代表会议。
- 2015年6月：有关各方商定《亚投行章程》的终稿并完成签署。
- 2015年12月：预期章程将经意向创始成员国批准后生效，亚投行正式宣布成立。

股权结构与资金来源

《筹建亚投行备忘录》明确，亚投行法定资本为1 000亿美元。鉴于亚投行的区域性定位，区域内成员国将是多数股东，而区域外成员国则为少数股东。根据亚投行官网，亚投行的"股权分配一方面要反映出区域内成员国的权利义务与所有权，另一方面还要为鼓励区域外国家的积极参与提供机会"。

除了各成员国认缴的资本外，亚投行还将"通过在金融市场发行债券、银行间市场交易及其他金融工具筹措资金。与此同时，亚投行还将可能创立和管理信托基金和专项基金"。

商业模式与产品

根据亚投行官网资料，其融资支持方式主要包括贷款、股权投资以及提供担保等。同时，亚投行将具备向有关国家提供技术援助的能力。

亚投行的建立将充分吸取多边开发银行及民营金融机构的经验。因此，其将秉承"精干"、"廉洁"、"绿色"的治理理念："精干"意味着亚投行将维持一个小而精的管理团队和业务娴熟的员工队伍；"廉洁"则为亚投行确保廉洁透明，对腐败实行零容忍；而"绿色"则是指亚投行将会高度重视生态环境的保护和改善。

金砖国家开发银行

基本信息

金砖国家开发银行（简称"金砖银行"）是由金砖五国（巴西、俄罗斯、印度、中国和南非）共同管理的一家多边开发性金融机构。

2012年，在印度新德里举行的金砖国家领导人第四次峰会期间首次提出了建立金砖银行的倡议；2013年，在南非德班召开的金砖国家第五次峰会上，该倡议正式公之于众。后来，在巴西福塔莱萨和巴西利亚两地举行的金砖国家领导人第六次峰会期间，金砖五国一致表示，金砖国家及其他新兴市场和发展中国家在解决基础设施缺口和满足可持续发展需求方面仍面临极大的融资困难。有鉴于此，各国宣布签署协议成立金砖银行。

根据福塔莱萨宣言，金砖银行总部将落户中国上海，而首个区域办公室则将设在南非约翰内斯堡。

金砖银行大事记

- 2012年3月：金砖银行的倡议在新德里金砖国家领导人第四次峰会期间正式提出。
- 2013年3月：筹建金砖银行的倡议在德班金砖国家第五次峰会上正式公布。

- 2014年7月：在巴西福塔莱萨和巴西利亚两地举行的金砖国家领导人第六次峰会期间，金砖五国宣布签署协议成立金砖银行。
- 2016年：金砖银行开始运营。

使命与战略

根据《金砖银行章程协议》，金砖银行"将为金砖国家和其他新兴经济体和发展中国家的基础设施和可持续发展项目筹集资金，并对现有多边和区域金融机构促进全球增长和发展的努力做出有益补充"。

以该宗旨为指引，金砖银行将重点做好以下几项工作：

- 通过贷款、担保、股权投资及其他金融工具等支持公共事业及私营企业的发展。
- 在支持基础设施、可持续发展项目的同时为其提供技术性援助。
- 支持跨国性基础设施、可持续发展项目。
- 创设或委托管理专项基金。
- 与其他国际性组织、金融机构展开合作。

股权结构

根据《金砖银行章程协议》，其初始核定资本为1 000亿美元，而初始认缴资本为500亿美元，由各创始成员国均摊。

《金砖银行章程协议》第六条规定，各成员国的投票权与其认缴资本份额挂钩。由于金砖银行的初始认缴资本由金砖五国均摊，故金砖国家各个成员国具有相同的投票权。与世界银行采取的按基金份额多少来分配投票权的方式截然不同的是，金砖银行的任何成员国都将不会拥有一票否决权。章程协议中还规定，金砖银行将定期发布年度报告，而报告中将包含一份经审计的财务报表。

金砖银行将采取理事会、董事会、行长会的三层架构。行长由理事会从创始成员国中选举产生，其余各创始成员国各推选一名副行长。副行长由行长提名、理事会聘任。行长、副行长每届任期 5 年。

丝路基金

基本信息

2014 年 11 月 4 日,中国国家主席习近平在中央财经领导小组第八次会议上首次提出"丝路基金"(The Silkroad Fund)的概念。同年 11 月 8 日,习近平主席正式宣布中国将出资 400 亿美元成立丝路基金。

依照《中华人民共和国公司法》有关规定,丝路基金有限责任公司于 2014 年 12 月 29 日在中国北京注册成立。中国国家工商总局公布的丝路基金工商公示信息显示,丝路基金的初期资本由中国外汇储备、中国投资有限责任公司、中国进出口银行、国家开发银行共同出资。

由于丝路基金有限责任公司并非国际性组织,故该基金不会吸纳其他成员国。然而,作为一个公司,丝路基金将会向国内外的投资者开放。

丝路基金大事记

- 2014 年 11 月 4 日:中国国家主席习近平在中央财经领导小组第八次会议上首次提出"丝路基金"。
- 2014 年 11 月 8 日:中国国家主席习近平正式宣布中国将出资 400 亿美元成立丝路基金。
- 2014 年 12 月 29 日:丝路基金有限责任公司在北京注册成立。
- 2015 年 4 月 21 日:中国国家主席习近平访问巴基斯坦期间,丝路基金、三峡集团与巴基斯坦签署协议,决定共同开发该国卡洛特水电项目。

使命与战略

中国国家主席习近平表示,丝路基金将与亚投行一道支持"一带一路"

战略构想。习主席还特别指出，设立丝路基金是为了凭借中国资金实力直接支持"一带一路"。

股权结构与资金来源

丝路基金的初期资本由中国外汇储备、中国投资有限责任公司、中国进出口银行、国家开发银行共同出资。各方出资额分别为：6.5亿美元、1.5亿美元、1.5亿美元和0.5亿美元（见图5.1）。

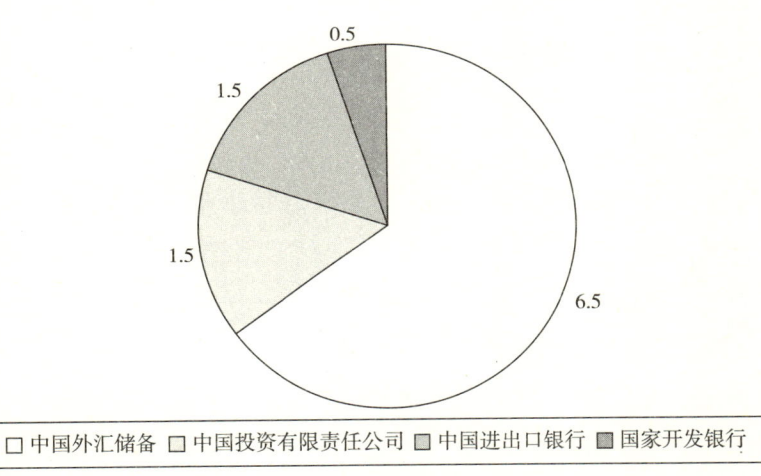

图5.1 丝路基金的初期资本来源（单位：亿美元）

商业模式与产品

为实现合理的财务收益和中长期可持续发展，丝路基金将以股权为主的多种市场化方式，投资于基础设施、资源开发、产业合作、金融合作等领域。

丝路基金的经营范围将主要集中于：
- 进行股权、债权、基金贷款等投资。
- 与国际开发机构、金融机构等发起设立共同投资基金。
- 进行资产受托管理、对外委托投资等。

- 中国国务院批准的其他业务。

公司治理

丝路基金有限责任公司已经于2014年年底在中国北京注册成立，首任董事长由中国人民银行（央行）前行长助理金琦担任。

该公司股东有4位，分别为中国进出口银行、梧桐树投资平台有限责任公司、赛里斯投资有限责任公司和国开金融有限公司。董事会由10名董事组成，分别为：金琦（董事长）、王燕之（执行董事、总经理）、刘劲松、樊海斌、刘薇、郭婷婷、张勃、田锦尘、袁兴永、胡学好。

专栏5-6　巴基斯坦卡洛特水电项目

在巴基斯坦，电力短缺的状况较为严峻。据巴基斯坦国家计划委员会2013年估计，电力能源的短缺使得该国经济的年增长率至少降低了两个百分点。而巴基斯坦并没有足够的财政力量来支持电力基础设施的发展。

正因如此，巴基斯坦计划发展和改革部表示，改善电力供应状况并进一步促进经济发展是巴基斯坦政府工作的重点。另外，以水电开发促经济发展也是《水资源开发指导原则之年度规划》的重要内容。

早在1984年11月，巴基斯坦水利电力开发署便将卡洛特地区一带选定为潜在的水电站的站址。直到2014年，该项目才出现重大转机：来自中国、巴基斯坦的投资商最终决定为该水电项目提供融资支持。

2014年3月，该项目的可行性报告出炉。紧接着，由于"这一项目将可能促进该干旱地区的农业发展，且不会产生重大负面影响"，旁遮普省环境保护署于2015年3月正式批准卡洛特水电项目。

2015年4月21日，在中国国家主席习近平对巴基斯坦进行国事访问期间，丝路基金、三峡集团与巴基斯坦签署协议决定共同开发卡洛特水电项目。

该项目总投资额约16.5亿美元，建成之后将改善巴基斯坦的电力供应，推动该国经济发展。丝路基金将入股由三峡集团控股的中国三峡南亚投资有限公司，并以此向该项目提供资金支持。另外，中国进出口银行也将为该项目提供较大的融资支持。

随着该项目的发展，世界银行集团下属的国际金融公司也于2015年4月22日与中国三峡南亚投资有限公司签署股东协议。自此，丝路基金和世界银行国际金融公司均成为三峡南亚公司的股东。恰如新华网评论所言，国际金融公司的参与将增强合作各方的信心，并将吸引更多的额外投资。

该项目的预期效果如下：

第一，据新华社报道，该项目将于2015年年底开工，2020年投入运营，规划装机容量72万千瓦，年发电32.13亿度。另据《华尔街日报》消息，该项目将首先由中方运营30年，到期后将转让给巴方。

第二，丝路基金还将继续投资该地区的其他水电项目，以实现3 350兆瓦的水电项目开发目标。这些水电项目的建设将有助于缓解巴基斯坦电力供应瓶颈，推动巴经济发展、民生改善和社会稳定。

第三，正如丝路基金董事长金琦所说，该项目及后续项目还将帮助国内企业走出去，从而推动中国高科技设备制造业的发展。

第四，该项目亦是北起中国西北部的新疆喀什、南至巴基斯坦瓜达尔港的"中巴经济走廊"的优先项目之一。正如中巴两国共同声明指出，丝路基金将积极地在"中巴经济走廊"的大框架下为更多项目提供融资支持。该项目及后续投资一方面将推动巴基斯坦的经济发展，另一方面将可能为中国从中东进口石油开辟新的通道。

第五，丝路基金亦是中国"一带一路"倡议的重要组成部分。作为丝路基金2014年12月成立以来的首个海外投资项目，卡洛特项目从长远上推动了"一带一路"倡议的实施。

国际金融公司与丝路基金在巴基斯坦的合作标志着中国与世行集团在"一带一路"战略上合作的开始。同时，二者间的合作势必会吸引更多的国际开发性金融机构加强与丝路基金的合作，同时也将吸引更多资本涌入亚洲国家的基础设施领域。

第六章 开发性金融机构协会

本章将介绍三家开发性金融机构协会。这些协会不是开发性银行,但是由开发性银行组建。它们的主要功能包括:为开发性银行构建社会网络,共享成员的实践经验,甄别并开发合资商业机会,共享实践知识和经验来共同学习,促进对开发性银行的研究,协助开发性银行与政府、行业进行沟通,并促进成员之间的相互交流。同时,它们还组织会议,出版数据和研究报告。这些协会是国际开发性银行体系的一部分。

长期投资者俱乐部

俱乐部成员

当前,长期投资者俱乐部(Long-Term Investors Club, LTIC)共有18个成员,包括:波兰国家经济银行(Bank Gospodarstwa Krajowego, BGK)、中国国家开发银行、巴塞罗那储蓄银行(La Caixa Bank)、法国储蓄托管机构、魁北克储蓄投资机构(Caisse de dépôt et placement du Québec)、意大利储蓄信贷银行(Cassa Depositi e Prestiti, CDP)、摩洛哥储蓄和管理银行(Caisse de Dépôt et de Gestion, CDG)、巴西联邦储蓄银行(Caixa Econômica Federal, CEF)、日本政策投资银行、欧洲投资银行(European Investment Bank, EBI)、西班牙官方信贷局(Instituto de Crédito Oficial, ICO)、印度基础建设发展金融公司(Infrastructure Development Finance Company Ltd, IDFC)、日本国际协力

银行（Japan Bank For International Cooperation，JBIC）、德国复兴信贷银行、加拿大安大略省市政雇员退休金计划（Ontario Municipal Employees Retirement System，OMERS）、美国教师退休基金会（Teachers Insurance and Annuity Association-College Retirement Equities Fund，TIAA CREF）、土耳其工业发展银行、俄罗斯开发与对外经济事务银行（The Bank for Development and Foreign Economic Affairs，Vnesheconombank，VEB）。

俱乐部的成员可以分为两类，第一类是创始成员，包括：法国储蓄托管机构、意大利储蓄信贷银行、德国复兴信贷银行、欧洲投资银行；第二类是普通成员。该俱乐部的成员都是长期金融机构，经俱乐部同意加入并遵守俱乐部的相关章程规定。

除了俱乐部内部的关系网之外，长期投资者俱乐部还与其他组织机构建立了合作关系，包括：经济合作与发展组织、世界经济论坛（World Economic Forum）、欧洲金融界智囊团（Eurofi）、长期基础设施投资者协会（Long-Term Infrastructure Investors Association，LTIIA）、欧洲长期投资者（European Long-Term Investors，ELTI）。

使命与战略

俱乐部的目标如下：

- 成员之间共享实践经验，增强相互之间的社交网络，通过成员关系提升长期投资者的非金融价值。
- 促进对长期投资的学术研究，为公众和专业讨论做出贡献。
- 协助成员和政治利益相关者彼此沟通，帮助成员实现其投资政策。
- 为合作投资提供便利，促进形成合作开发。

历史和治理

2009年，法国储蓄托管机构、意大利储蓄信贷银行、欧洲投资银行、德国复兴信贷银行发起创建了长期投资者俱乐部。它们的目标是联合世界范围内的长期机构投资者，鼓励合作，培育长期投资的良好环境，以此促进经济增长。现在，长期投资者俱乐部已经吸引了世界范围内的 18 家主要金融机构和机构投资者，这 18 家俱乐部成员主要来自 G20 国家，它们管理的资产达 5.4 万亿美元。俱乐部位于法国巴黎里尔街 67 号 Pomereu 酒店。

俱乐部主要由指导委员会、主席、副主席、秘书长管理和指导：（1）指导委员会由 4 家创始成员和 4 家被选举出来的普通成员组成，指导委员会的 4 家普通成员每两年选举一次。指导委员会成员应派出代表或者候补代表出席指导委员会会议，候补代表的身份应在会议开始之前向秘书长申请确认。指导委员会是俱乐部唯一的决策机构。（2）俱乐部的主席由指导委员会选举产生，创始成员轮流担任主席一职，任期两年。主席在副主席的协助下领导指导委员会的工作，副主席可以是一个或者多个，代表着俱乐部成员的多样性。（3）秘书长由指导委员会任命，任期三年。秘书长的主要职责是：组织和管理俱乐部的日常工作；编制俱乐部年报，包括资产负债表及注解；为主席和副主席提供秘书服务；执行指导委员会做出的决策。

信息交流活动

"欧洲长期投资会议：重启固定的、网络化的社会基础设施"（罗马，**2014 年 12 月 12～13 日**）

这次会议由意大利银行保险和金融联合会（Italian Banking Insurance and Finance Federation）、经合组织、长期投资者俱乐部、意大利储蓄信贷银行联合组织召开。会议的合办方包括：时任欧盟轮值主席国意大利（Italian EU presidency）、欧洲长期投资者协会（European Long-Term Investors Association）、货币金融机构官方论坛（Official Monetary and Financial Institutions Forum）、Integrate 智库、欧洲统合运动意大利理事会（the Italian Council of the European Movement）。

会议为期两天，共包括 4 项议题和三轮讨论：

议题1：欧洲的长期投资。目前我们身处何处？我们取得的进步和下一步的方向。与会者讨论的话题有"欧洲的长期投资"、"如何在欧盟内部构建一个更适合长期投资的金融和非金融监管架构"等。

议题2：社会机构、产业和国内社会的应对。与会者讨论的话题有"在长期投资中，机构投资者扮演的角色"、"全球资产层面的基础设施投资"等。

议题3：重新调整欧洲公营部门与私营机构合作议程（European Public-Private Partnership Agenda）。与会者讨论的话题包括"欧洲交通基础设施融资"和"欧洲能源基础设施融资"。

议题4：尚未涉足的社会基础设施领域。共展开三轮讨论，讨论内容包括需求面、供给面和机构投资者的作用。

第四届长期投资者俱乐部国际会议"增长与就业——长期投资者的作用"（卢森堡，2012年10月8日）

卢森堡会议在欧洲投资银行召开，会议的主题主要是关于增长和就业，解决与公共政策相关的问题，会议还重点关注具体部门长期金融供给的问题，这些问题对经济增长和就业有很重要的作用。

会议期间，主要讨论了两个话题"增长和长期融资"、"能源、气候变化和长期投资"。

国际开发性金融俱乐部

俱乐部成员

截至2015年，国际开发性金融俱乐部（International Development Finance Club，IDFC）共有23名成员，2010年俱乐部成员总共管理的资产规模约为3 900亿美元。成员的地理位置分布广泛：

欧洲：黑海贸易和发展银行（Black Sea Trade and Development Bank，BSTDB）、法国开发署（Agence Française de Développement，AFD）、克罗地亚

复兴开发银行（Croatian Bank for Reconstruction and Development，HBOR）、德国复兴信贷银行集团（KfW Bankengruppe）、土耳其工业发展银行、俄罗斯开发与对外经济银行。

中南美地区： 墨西哥国家金融公司（Nacional Financiera，NAFIN）、拉丁美洲开发银行（Development Bank of Latin America，CAF）、中美洲经济一体化银行（Central American Bank for Economic Integration，BCIE/CABEI）、哥伦比亚企业发展与外贸银行（Bancoldex S. A.）、秘鲁开发金融公司（Corporación Financiera de Desarrollo S. A.，COFIDE）、巴西国家经济与社会开发银行（Banco Nacional de Desenvolvimento Econômico e Social，BNDES）、智利国家银行（Banco Estado，BE）。

非洲： 摩洛哥储蓄和管理银行、南非开发银行（Development Bank of Southern Africa，DBSA）、多哥西非开发银行（Banque Ouest Africaine de Développement，BOAD）、布隆迪东非及南非贸易与发展银行（the Eastern and Southern Africa Trade and Development Bank，PTA）。

亚洲、中东和北非： 印度小型企业发展银行（Small Industries Development Bank of India，SIDBI）、印度尼西亚进出口银行（Indonesia Exim Bank）、中国国家开发银行、沙特阿拉伯伊斯兰私营部门发展集团（Islamic Corporation for the Development of the Private Sector，ICD）、韩国金融公司（Korea Finance Corporation，KoFC）、日本国际协力机构。

2010年IDFC成立时，19个成员国的承诺总额约为3 900亿美元。2010年在IDFC中，最高的承诺额来自KfW（德国，1 080亿美元）和BNDES（巴西，1 050亿美元）。

使命与战略

国际开发性金融俱乐部的目标是：

- 团结一心共同制定章程，追求共同利益。

- 甄别和开发合资商业机会。
- 共享知识和实践经验，相互学习。

历史与治理

国际开发性金融俱乐部是一个于2010年成立的非常年轻的组织。2010年开发性银行首席执行官（CEO）首次会晤之后，几家参与机构提议建立合作组织。他们认为，CEO级别的常规交流和决策论坛能够帮助国家开发性银行和次区域开发性银行发出它们的声音，特别是在整个国际金融被多边金融机构掌控的情况下。因此，国际发展性金融俱乐部就成立了，这是一家志同道合的开发性银行组成的联合体。成员之间的法人资格迥然不同，除章程中的规定外，俱乐部会员之间无法律债务约束。各个俱乐部成员都在本国的发展政策框架下运作，在宪法规定范围内帮助本国政府完成相应的国际国内事务。

国际开发性金融俱乐部的组织结构有意保持简洁精益：

（1）所有俱乐部成员均需派出CEO或指定代表出席年会。

（2）指导委员会由主席和副主席组成，指导委员会由全体成员选举产生，任期两年。他们主要负责准备年会的召开以及相关后续事务。指导委员会每年至少应召开两次会议。

（3）秘书处人员由主席任命，秘书处的日常办公场地和资金来源由主席所代表的俱乐部成员负责。秘书处的主要工作是在指导委员会的要求下代表俱乐部进行日常接洽，组织和管理俱乐部的日常工作，负责执行年会做出的决策。

（4）各国代表由各成员任命，主要负责秘书处和成员之间的沟通。

（5）工作组由年会特别任命，负责准备和研究俱乐部目前关注的话题，并发布相应的信息和文件。

信息交流活动

气候金融论坛（巴黎，2015年3月31日）

国际开发性金融俱乐部的成员参加了这次论坛。通过参加这次论坛，国际开发性金融俱乐部在促使金融机构抗争气候变化的实践方面取得了重大进展。

国际开发性金融俱乐部第一次年会（东京，2012年10月14日）

参加年会的成员就俱乐部成员、使命和工作方式达成了一致意见。俱乐部2012年工作进展顺利，期间出版了《国际开发性金融俱乐部绿色金融地图报告》、《私募和公募基金影响报告》，会议通过了2013年新的工作计划。俱乐部将在工作中重视发展的可持续性，重点关注绿色发展和社会发展。绿色发展包括但不限于（环保）基础设施部门、可再生能源和能源利用效率；社会发展主要关注中小企业的发展以及与消除贫困相关的社会融入问题。

世界开发性金融机构联盟

机构成员

世界开发性金融机构联盟（World Federation of Development Financing Institutions，WFDFI）是全球范围内开发性银行的协会，联盟具有以下几种类别的成员：

地区成员：（1）传统地区成员，共有4个具有法人资格的传统地区成员——非洲开发性金融机构协会（African Association of Development Finance Institutions，AADFI）、亚洲及太平洋开发性金融机构协会（Association of Development Financing Institutions in Asia and the Pacific，ADFIAP）、伊斯兰开发银行成员国开发性金融机构协会（Association of National Development Finance Institutions in Member Countries of the Islamic Development Bank，ADFIMI）、拉丁美洲开发性金融机构协会（Latin American Association of Development Financing Institutions，ALIDE）；（2）临时地区成员，即尚未成立地区协会的国家开发性金融机构集团。

特殊成员：对开发性金融感兴趣的国际组织机构（世界的、地区的或者亚地区的），国家层面的开发性金融机构协会，帮助联盟实现目标的其他非开发性金融机构。

独立成员：社会著名人士，他们的参与能够支持完成联盟的目标和活动。

荣誉成员：在开发性银行或相关经济发展领域做出杰出贡献的个人，经管理委员会同意，可被选举为联盟的荣誉成员。

地区成员详细介绍如下：

非洲开发性金融机构协会：1975年3月，在阿比让会议上，非洲开发银行提议组建非洲开发性金融机构协会。会议任命AfDB的一位多哥（Togo）高级官员乔治（George Aithnard）担任非洲开发性金融机构协会的秘书长，并为他提供办公场地和员工专门负责非洲开发性金融机构协会的组建工作。1975年5月，在达喀尔（Dakar）举行了协会的第一次全体会议，协会第一任主席是象牙海岸（Ivory Coast）的多布雷（August Daubrey）。此后，非洲开发性金融机构协会经历了几任秘书长，目前由2000年上任的塞内加尔的韦德（Magatte Wade）主持工作。

亚洲及太平洋开发性金融机构协会：对亚太地区所有关注可持续发展项目融资的开发性银行及其他机构来说，亚洲及太平洋开发性金融机构协会是一家重要的机构。该协会成立于1976年，目前拥有来自42个国家和地区的117家组织成员，亚洲开发银行是该协会的特殊成员。亚洲及太平洋开发性金融机构协会是世界开发性金融机构联合会（World Federation of Development Financing Institutions，WFDFI）的创始成员，是联合国经济和社会理事会的咨询机构，为非政府、非商业、非盈利的国际组织，总部位于菲律宾的马尼拉。2008年，该协会获得了由美国协会领导组织（American Society of Association Executives）和协会领导中心所授予的"让世界更美好协会奖"（发展中国家的评选范畴）。

伊斯兰开发银行成员国开发性金融机构协会：伊斯兰开发银行成员国开发性金融机构协会是一个地区性金融机构协会，协会特点是自治、独立和国际化。在第11届伊斯兰开发银行理事会会议（安曼，1986年3月）上，选举了开发性金融机构代表并举行临时成立会议，建立了伊斯兰开发银行成员国开发性金融机构协会。该协会于 1987 年 9 月开始正式运转，总部设在土耳其伊斯坦布尔，土耳其政府给予了该组织国际组织的地位。

拉丁美洲开发性金融机构协会：拉丁美洲开发性金融机构协会是拉丁美洲和加勒比海地区开发性银行的代表性国际组织。该协会于 1968 年成立，总部位于秘鲁利马。协会的目标是促进该地区开发性银行和金融机构的合作，加强相互交流，提高参与度。协会的成员身份广泛，包括致力于为地区发展提供金融服务的机构、活跃协会和合作成员。拉丁美洲开发性金融机构协会拥有来自 31 个国家（地区和非地区）的 80 个成员，以及国家金融组织和多边开发性银行。该协会也是世界开发性金融机构联盟的发起方。

历史与治理

1979 年 6 月，在苏黎世举行的联合国工业发展组织开发性银行会议上，非洲开发性金融机构协会、亚洲及太平洋开发性金融机构协会和拉丁美洲开发性金融机构协会联合德国复兴开发银行签订协议共同组建世界开发性金融机构联盟。第一任理事包括：德国复兴开发银行的恩格尔（Willi F. L. Engel）；非洲开发性金融机构协会的阿米起亚（René Amichia）；拉丁美洲开发性金融机构协会的帕斯托里萨（Tomás Pastoriza）；非洲开发金融机构协会的雅伊梅（Vicente R. Jayme）。1979 年年底，世界开发性金融机构联盟在位于马德里的西班牙官方信贷局设立秘书处，由拉斐尔（Rafael Bermejo Blanco）主持工作。

加列戈斯（José Elías Gallegos）是该协会的第一任秘书长，协会历史上共有 11 位秘书长。1979~1994 年，世界开发性金融机构联盟的总部位于马德里，在此期间，世界开发性金融机构联盟决定秘书处采取轮流制，每个协会成员有 3 年的轮值期。1995~1998 年，秘书处位于马尼拉的亚洲及太平洋开发性金融机构协会；1999~2002 年位于伊斯坦布尔的伊斯兰开发银行成员国开发性金融机构协会，期间由土耳其的奥汉·塞西（Orhan Sagci）担任秘书长。2002 年 5 月，拉丁美洲开发性金融机构协会的秘书长阿塞韦多（Rommel

Acevedo）担任世界开发性金融机构联盟秘书长，并一直履职到2009年。2009年在伊斯坦布尔，任命非洲开发性金融机构协会的佩拉尔塔（Octavio B. Peralta）为秘书长，2010年1月上任，任期3年。原伊斯兰开发银行成员国开发性金融机构协会秘书长努里·伯特克（Nuri Birtek）为现任秘书长。他于2012年10月11日在东京的一次理事会上被选举为秘书长，2013年1月1日上任，任期3年。

联合大会

联合大会是世界开发性金融机构联盟的最高机构，由传统成员机构的主席或CEO构成，拥有完成联盟目标的最高权威，具体权力如下：

- 检查并批准理事会的年度报告。
- 决定成员的吸纳、暂停及开除。
- 如果联合会解散，决定联合会资产的分配。
- 负责检查任何理事会提交的其他事项。

理事会

管理团队包括各家传统成员机构的秘书长，具体的责任和权力如下：

- 召开联合大会。
- 选举、任命秘书长。
- 审议、批准秘书长提交的计划、方案和联合会的预算。
- 决定理事会官员和秘书长的权利。
- 负责全面监督秘书处和秘书长。
- 委派机构或者个人执行具体任务以促进联合会的工作。
- 执行联合大会传达的指令或制定其行动方案。

管理机构

联盟的管理主要由秘书处负责，秘书处在联合会秘书长（联合会CEO）的指导下开展工作。秘书处应按照程序执行任务，遵守相应政策，符合理事会规定的预算约束。

信息交流活动

国际联合发展论坛："企业协同发展：挑战性商业环境下的决定性因素"（马来西亚吉隆坡，2014年10月20~21日）

伊斯兰开发银行成员国开发性金融机构协会—中小企业银行联合发展论坛2014，会议为期一天半，主要有以下4个议题：

- 议题一：融资之外的问题——对创造和维持高速增长的企业家来说，游戏规则有所改变。会议讨论了一些重要的战略性问题，同时也讨论了金融机构和其他企业遇到的问题。

- 议题二：创新——在多变的商业环境中有价值地创造工具。这一部分讨论了在价值增值过程中新的创新方法。不仅保证了金融机构在市场的相对地位，也鼓励企业去创造价值，通过结构性合作进行混合投资。

- 议题三：风险管理——在协作创业环境下的替代模型。这一部分讨论了已有的经验，提供了可用模型——做出行动前的知识准备及其含义，这些经验都是一些主要金融机构和企业在管理投资过程中可能遇到的内生性商业风险。

- 议题四：跨境合作——可持续发展下，金融机构和中小企业合作遇到的挑战。这一部分讨论了相关的挑战并探索了解决挑战的方法，所有的讨论都是基于金融机构和中小企业协同合作的背景。

非洲开发性金融机构协会/亚洲开发银行联合讨论会：提升国家开发性金融机构的效率（2013年5月28日，马拉喀什，摩洛哥）

非洲开发性金融机构协会/亚洲开发银行联合讨论会试图探讨如何扩大非洲开发性金融机构对促进当地经济社会发展的贡献。会议主要关注非洲开发性金融机构的原理及使命，讨论了国际上审慎监管、企业的风险管理（社会风险和环境风险）、成果的测量和监测等领域的最佳解决方案。

第二篇　开发性金融机构的
　　　　分析与展望

第二篇将在开发性金融综述的基础上，进一步分析并展望开发性金融机构。第七章为读者提供样本开发性金融机构的结构特征与发展趋势。第八章将通过案例研究，对开发性金融机构在实现转型发展的进程中所承担的三大战略角色做详细阐释。这三大战略角色分别是：长期规划、市场培育，以及聚合各方力量，促成政府与社会部门的合作。

第七章 全球开发性金融机构的结构与发展趋势

第二章到第六章我们详细介绍了样本选取的每一家开发性金融机构。第七章将介绍这些机构的总体结构和发展趋势。

如前所述,我们的样本涵盖了 30 家开发性金融机构,其中包括 8 家多边开发银行、18 家国家开发银行、4 家有中国因素的开发性金融机构。这一样本包括了世界上重要的开发性金融机构,特别是本报告最感兴趣的亚洲地区的机构。但是由于样本不是随机抽取的,并且样本量不足以进行更详尽的分析,因此以下统计分析的结果只代表样本内开发性金融机构的一般特征。

结构

本节将通过机构间的横向比较来描述样本中的开发性金融机构,分析使用的大多数统计数据来自 2014 年。

开发性金融机构的成立

样本中的开发性金融机构分布在世界各地。8 家多边开发银行中,一家为世界性开发银行,其余 7 家为区域性开发银行,为非洲、亚洲、北美和拉丁美洲、欧洲、欧亚地区、加勒比地区和伊斯兰国家提供服务。18 家国家开发银行中,3 家来自欧洲,3 家来自俄罗斯和前苏联国家,8 家来自亚洲,两家来自拉丁美洲,两家来自非洲。4 家有中国因素的开发性金融机构的总部都位于中国。

本研究一个有趣的发现是开发性金融机构的成立时间分布。大量开发性金融机构成立于1945~1985年和2000~2014年。这表明，世界经历了创建开发性金融机构的两个主要浪潮，一次出现在第二次世界大战后，另一次出现在21世纪初（见图7.1）。

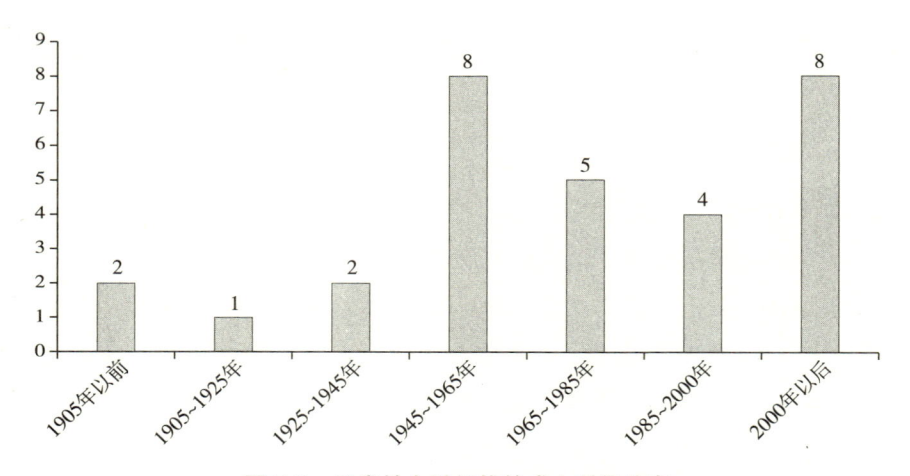

图 7.1　开发性金融机构的成立时间分布

注：数据包括30家开发银行。

成立时间分布表明：首先，大量的开发性金融机构成立于30多年前并持续经营至今；其次，尽管在一些国家出现了国有金融机构私有化浪潮，但仍有大批新的开发性金融机构成立于21世纪初。

开发性金融机构的规模

开发性金融机构的规模可以通过资产、股权和贷款的规模来衡量，这些指标反映了开发性金融机构的规模和全球地位。

数据表明，大多数开发性金融机构的资产在2006~2013年实现增长。样本中，总资产增幅最大的是中国国家开发银行（无论从增量还是从增速来衡量），其次是德国复兴信贷银行。目前，中国国家开发银行和德国复兴信贷银行是世界上排名在前两位的大型开发性金融机构。图7.2显示了样本中各开发性金融机构的总资产，小框放大了图中资产规模较小的开发性金融机构的资产。

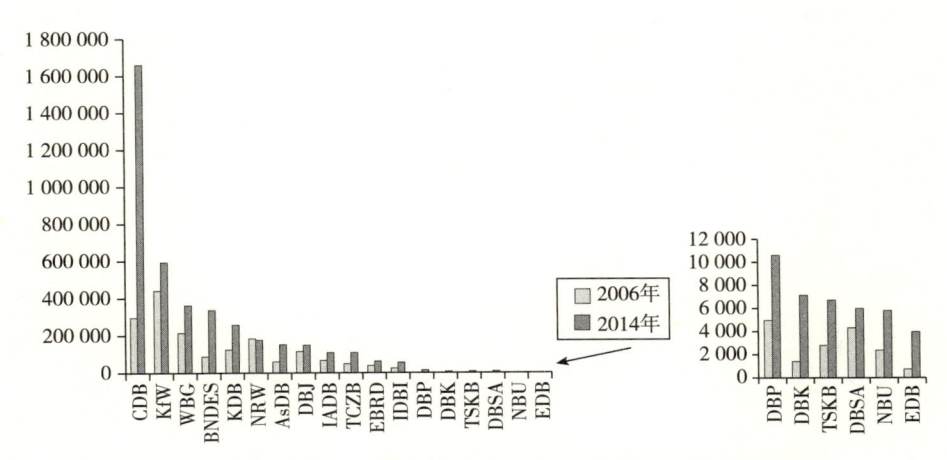

图 7.2　2006 年和 2014 年各开发性金融机构的资产（单位：百万美元）

2014 年年底，样本中开发性金融机构的总资产达到 4.25 万亿美元。其中，中国国家开发银行的总资产在 2014 年达到 1.66 万亿美元。我们将开发性金融机构按资产分成 4 组：小规模（小于 10 亿美元）、中等规模（10 亿~99 亿美元）、大规模（100 亿~999 亿美元）和超大规模（超过 1 000 亿美元）。超大规模开发性金融机构的份额从 2006 年年底的 27% 上升到 2013 年年底的 38%（见图 7.3）。

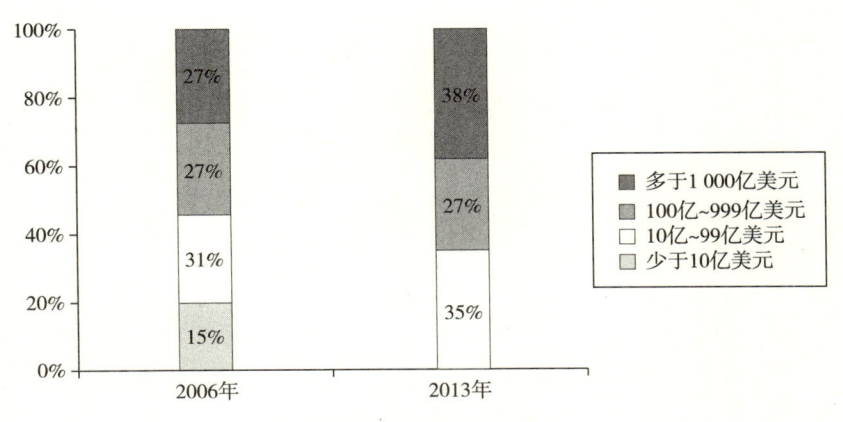

图 7.3　资产分组（2013 年）

注：包括 26 家可以得到数据的开发性金融机构。

样本中开发性金融机构的总权益同样在2006～2014年经历了高速增长。其中，中国国家开发银行总权益的增速最为强劲（见图7.4）。

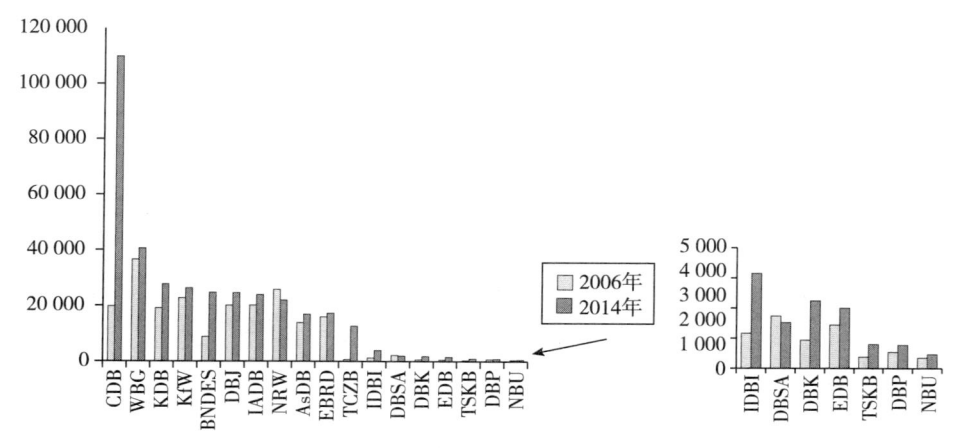

图7.4 各开发性金融机构的权益（单位：百万美元）

从可得到的数据（包含大多数开发性金融机构）来看，开发性金融机构的贷款总额在2006～2014年实现了大幅增长。就单个机构而言，CDB拥有最大贷款组合规模和2006～2014年的最高增速（见图7.5）。

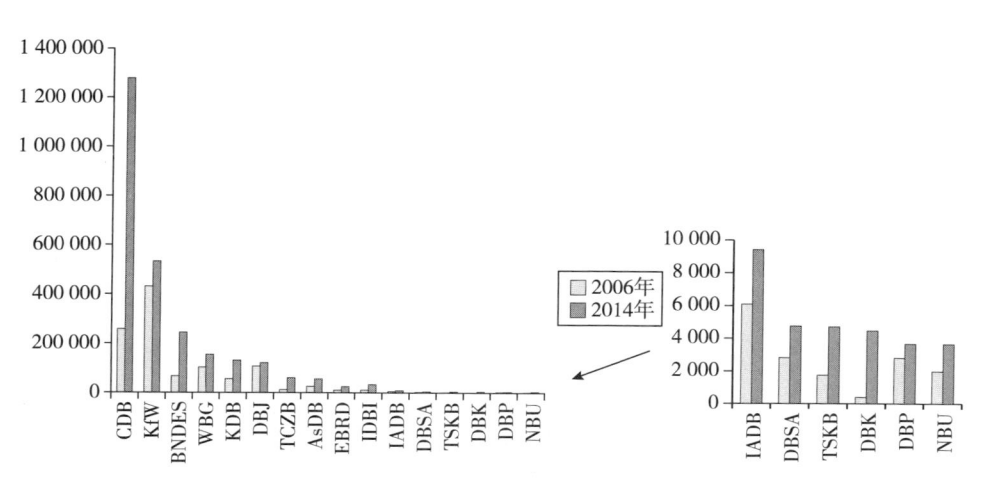

图7.5 2006年和2014年各开发性金融机构的总贷款（单位：百万美元）

总体而言，开发性金融机构的总资产、总权益和总贷款在过去几年里出现了显著的增长。一些开发性金融机构已成长为超大型金融机构，并在世界金融市场中扮演重要角色。

股权结构和政府支持

样本中的大多数国家开发性金融机构由政府所有或支持。大多数情况下，政府为其确定战略方向和任命高级管理人员。不过，政府所有权仍然有多种形式，并且不是样本中所有的开发性金融机构都完全归政府所有。

政府给予开发性金融机构大力支持。在我们的样本中，82%的开发性金融机构得到了来自政府的直接预算拨款（见图7.6）。

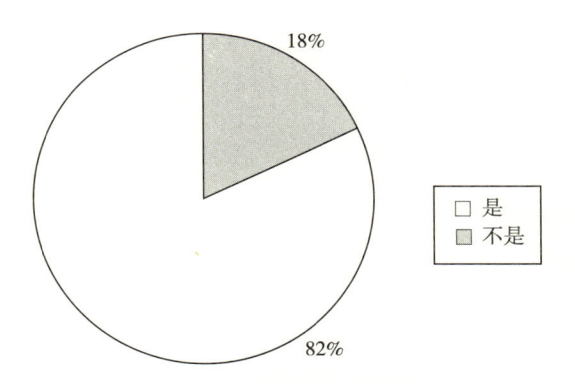

图7.6　政府是否直接拨款

注：包括17家可以得到数据的国家开发性金融机构。

但是，如果没有政府拨款，大部分开发性金融机构仍能依靠自身创造的收入维持运营（见图7.7）。

数据表明，19家国家开发金融机构中有16家的债务由政府担保。另外，在过去5年里，样本中85%的开发性金融机构得到了政府资金、补贴或转移支付，以弥补亏损和改善财务状况。

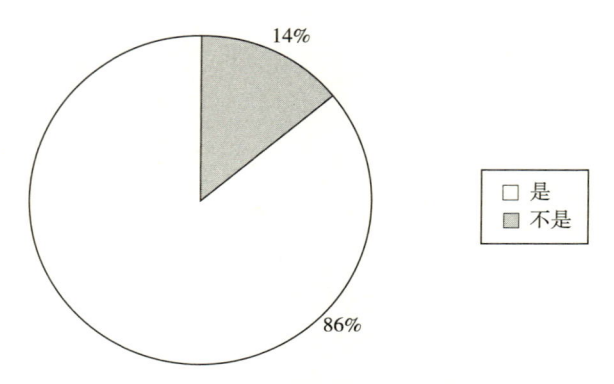

图 7.7　是否依靠自身收入经营

注：包括可以得到数据的 14 家国家开发性金融机构。

资金

开发性金融机构有多样化的资金来源，包括吸收公众存款、从其他金融机构借款、在国内和国际资本市场上发行债券、取得政府预算拨款和使用自身股本。

样本中的大多数开发性金融机构可以向其他金融机构借款或在本地资本市场发行债券。大多数开发性金融机构得到过政府的直接拨款。一些开发性金融机构接受政府的资金、补贴或转移支付，以弥补亏损或改善财务状况。

不同于一般商业金融机构，半数以上的开发性金融机构不将吸收公众存款作为资金来源（见图 7.8）。这将使开发性金融机构专注于贷款业务，并避免与商业银行的竞争。

商业模式

开发性金融机构开创和采取了一系列商业模式，为不同类型的客户服务，并通过这些商业模式实现其使命。

开发性金融机构的贷款业务包括零售（直接放贷给最终客户）、批发（贷

31%

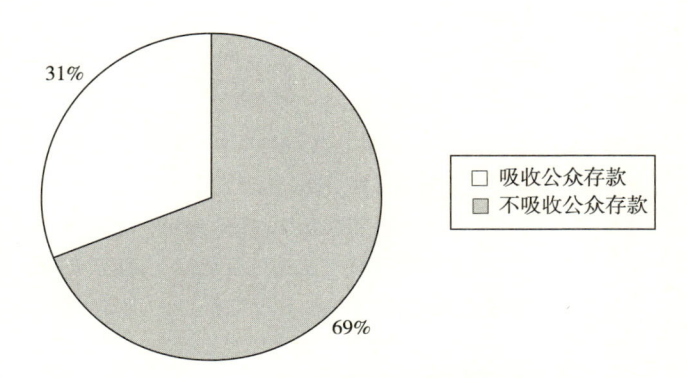

69%

☐ 吸收公众存款
■ 不吸收公众存款

图 7.8　向公众吸收存款的开发性金融机构比例

注：包括 26 家开发性金融机构。

款给其他金融机构，这些金融机构再贷款给最终客户），或两者兼具。在样本中，8%的开发性金融机构仅开展批发贷款，23%仅开展零售贷款，69%二者兼具（见图 7.9）。

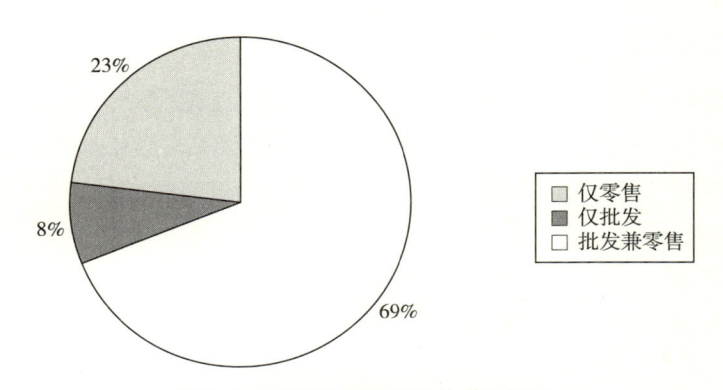

23%

8%

69%

☐ 仅零售
■ 仅批发
☐ 批发兼零售

图 7.9　开发性金融机构的商业模式

注：包括可以得到数据的 26 家开发性金融机构。

　　开发性金融机构贷款覆盖众多领域。大多数开发性金融机构贷款的主要覆盖领域包括建筑（100%）、能源（96%）和基础设施（96%）。其他覆盖领域包括工业/制造业、服务业、农业综合经营和医疗保健（见图 7.10）。

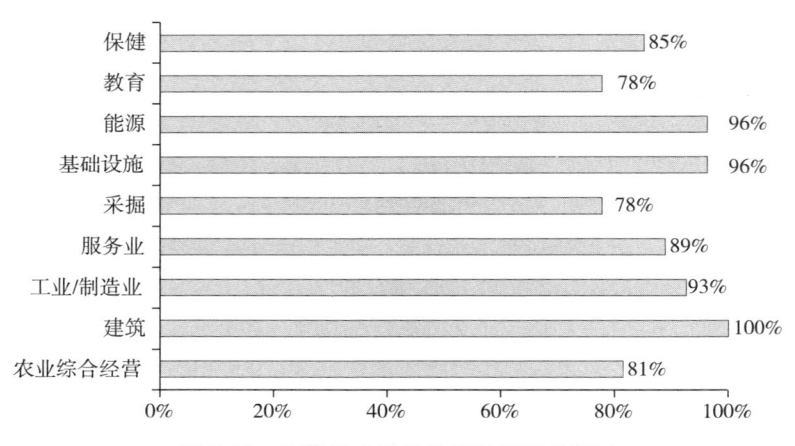

图 7.10 开发性金融机构贷款的覆盖领域

保健 85%
教育 78%
能源 96%
基础设施 96%
采掘 78%
服务业 89%
工业/制造业 93%
建筑 100%
农业综合经营 81%

注：包括 27 家开发性金融机构。

大多数开发性金融机构选择中小微企业、大型民营企业和国家作为目标市场，其次是其他金融机构、其他国有企业、个人和家庭以及新创企业（见图 7.11）。

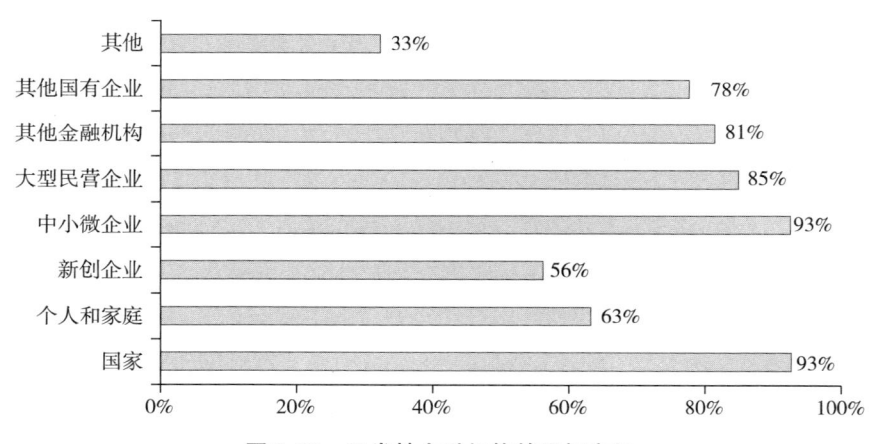

图 7.11 开发性金融机构的目标市场

其他 33%
其他国有企业 78%
其他金融机构 81%
大型民营企业 85%
中小微企业 93%
新创企业 56%
个人和家庭 63%
国家 93%

注：包括 27 家开发性金融机构的数据。

开发性金融机构向客户提供多样化的贷款产品。最常见的贷款类型包括长期贷款、过桥贷款或短期贷款以及银团贷款，样本中分别有 89%、81% 和 81% 的开发性金融机构提供上述 3 种贷款（见图 7.12）。其他常用的贷款方式有运营资本贷款和创业贷款。

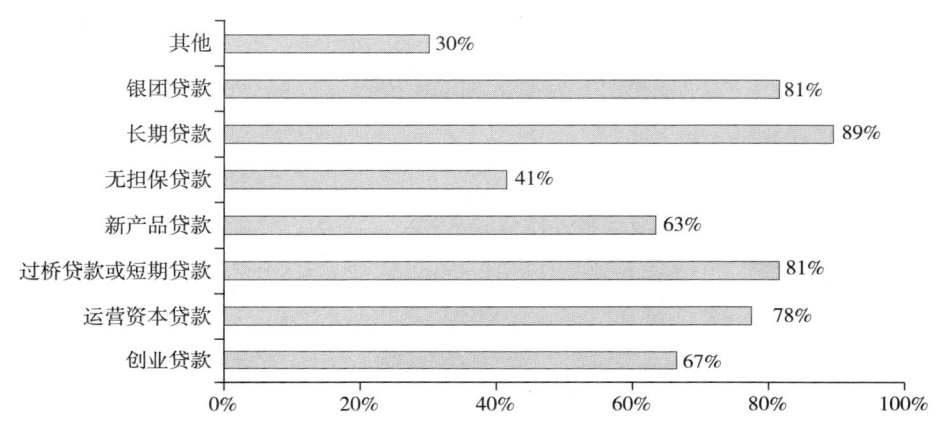

图 7.12 开发性金融机构的贷款产品

- 其他：30%
- 银团贷款：81%
- 长期贷款：89%
- 无担保贷款：41%
- 新产品贷款：63%
- 过桥贷款或短期贷款：81%
- 运营资本贷款：78%
- 创业贷款：67%

注：包括 27 家开发性金融机构的数据。

开发性金融机构提供给客户的平均年利率通常低于普通商业银行。样本中开发性金融机构的平均年利率为 5.1%。根据我们的数据，15 家开发性金融机构提供利率补贴（低于市场利率）。

样本中的开发性金融机构还提供其他金融产品，包括贷款担保、信托服务、现金转账、小额保险、储蓄账户和存款账户（见图 7.13）。

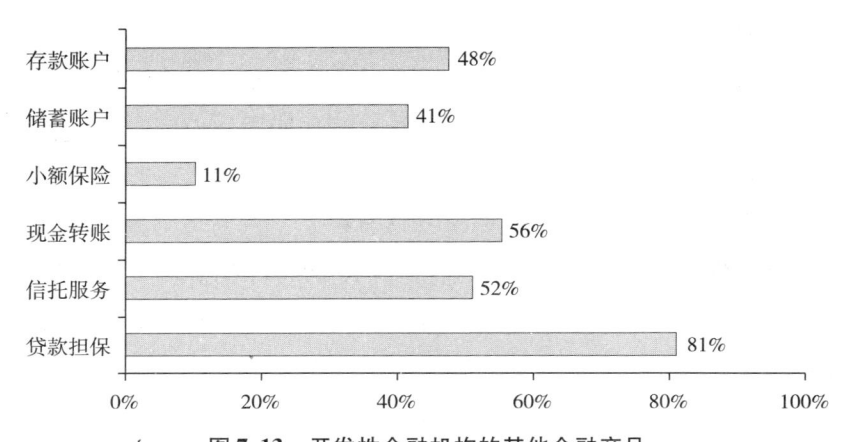

图 7.13 开发性金融机构的其他金融产品

- 存款账户：48%
- 储蓄账户：41%
- 小额保险：11%
- 现金转账：56%
- 信托服务：52%
- 贷款担保：81%

注：包括 27 家开发性金融机构的数据。

开发性金融机构向客户提供长期贷款。图7.14显示了样本中的开发性金融机构对其客户提供的最长贷款期限。在19家披露贷款最长期限信息的开发性金融机构中，约42%的开发性金融机构的贷款期限超过21年，有42%的贷款期限为11~20年。

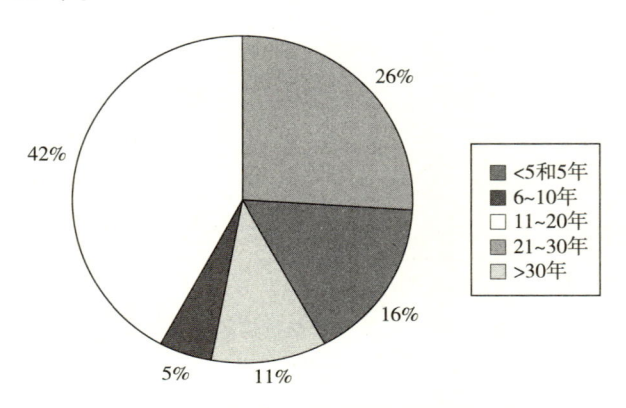

图7.14 开发性金融机构最长贷款期限按年限分布
注：包括可以得到数据的19家开发性金融机构。

盈利能力和资产质量

虽然开发性金融机构不以利润最大化为经营目标，但许多机构仍致力于提高自身的盈利能力和资产质量。

资产收益率衡量的是投资资本（资产）产生的收入，是反映公司总资产盈利水平的一项指标。ROA给出了测量资产管理使用效率的一种方法。ROA为百分比形式，通过公司年收益除以总资产计算得出。上市公司的资产收益率通常有较大差异，与所在行业和国家高度相关。为了避免测量误差，我们比较了各开发性金融机构的ROA与其所在国家的行业平均资产收益率。图7.15显示了这一差别。尽管有一些例外，但大多数开发性金融机构的资产收益率都高于其所在国家的行业平均值（说明样本中的多数开发性金融机构比其他金融机构表现更好）。这反映了这些开发性金融机构在2014年的优良绩效。

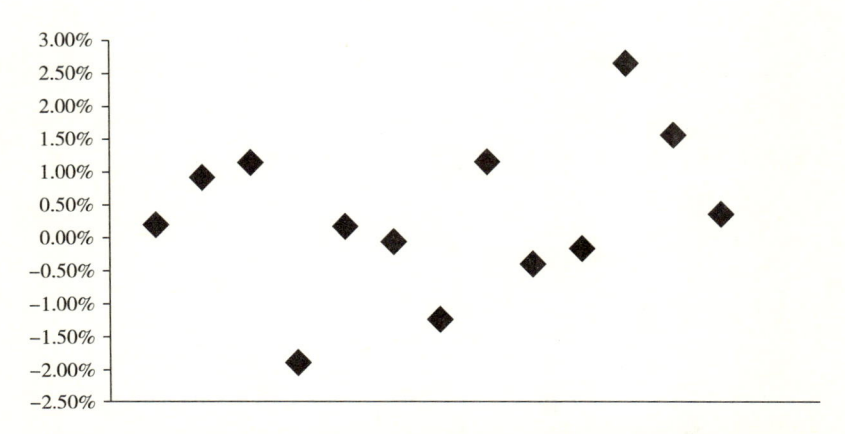

图 7.15 2014 年各开发性金融机构的 ROA 与所在国所有银行的平均值比较

资料来源：本图特定国家资产收益率和图 7.16、图 7.17 的净资产收益率均来自 http：//www.helgilibrary.com/sectors/index/banking, and Bankscope Country Reports, The Economist Intelligence Unit, May 9, 2015, retrieved at https://bankscope.bvdinfo.com/version－201556/Search.EIUCountry-Reports.serv?_CID=4&context=2X88BC5YQBB3M2Q

净资产收益率衡量的是普通股的所有者权益（或股东权益）的回报率，反映了企业每一单位权益创造利润的效率。ROE 显示的是公司如何利用投资来创造盈利增长。对净资产收益率的分析表明，较多开发性金融机构的 ROE 低于其所在国行业平均值（见图 7.16）。

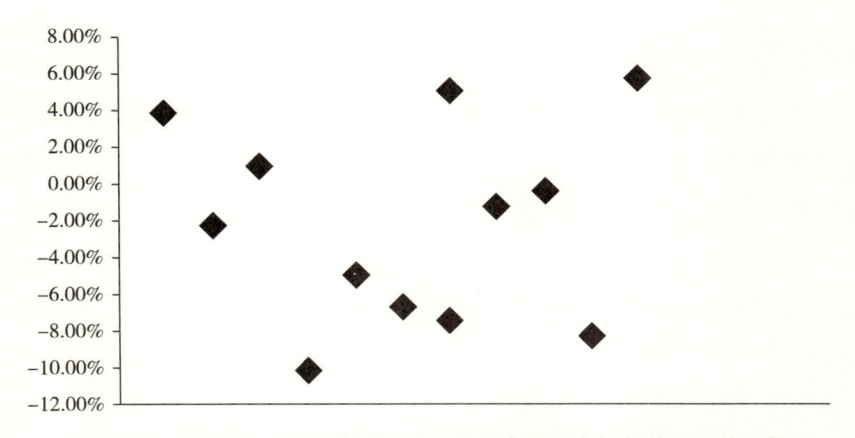

图 7.16 各开发性金融机构的 ROE 与所在国所有银行的平均值比较

我们收集了开发性金融机构的不良贷款率。不良贷款率是衡量资产质量的一个指标。我们计算了开发性金融机构的不良贷款率与其所在国家的银行业平均值的差异。结果显示，在 11 家开发性金融机构中，7 家的不良贷款率低于本国的行业平均值，这与世行 2012 年的调查结果一致（见图 7.17）。

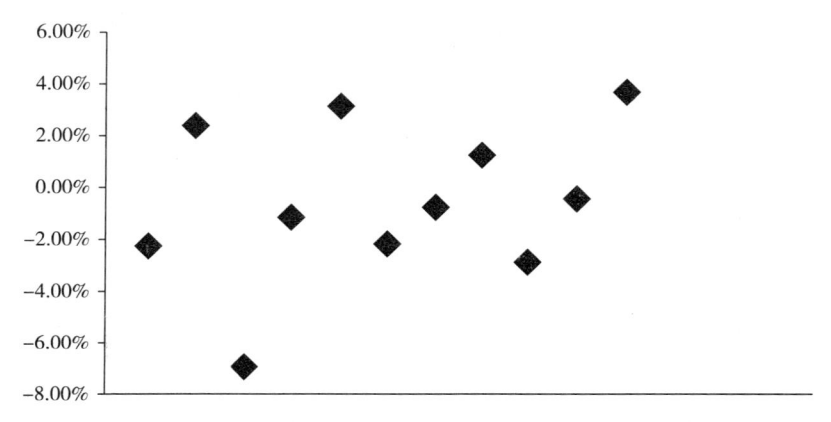

图 7.17　各开发性金融机构的不良贷款率与所在国的银行业平均值比较

通过上述几种指标的对比可以看出，虽然开发性金融机构不追求利润最大化，但大多数处于盈利状态，其中大部分开发性金融机构的表现要好于本国平均水平。

公司治理与监督

提升公司治理对于开发性金融机构来说至关重要。开发性金融机构的公司治理所面临的挑战源于其特征。因为大多数开发性金融机构由政府所有和控制，它们的公司治理较一般商业银行更为复杂。非利润最大化目标和良好的经济表现也可能互相冲突。数据显示，许多开发性金融机构正在通过提高信息披露的透明度和建立有效的监督管理结构来努力完善公司治理。

样本中所有的开发性金融机构都有一个风险管理（或起同等作用的）部门，负责机构运营中的风险识别、风险监控和风险管理。

在样本中，大多数开发性金融机构每年至少披露一次公司治理和监管信息。所有开发性金融机构都披露经审计的财务报告。然而，并不是所有机构都披露关于公司治理、风险管理框架、表外项目和资本充足率的信息（见图7.18）。

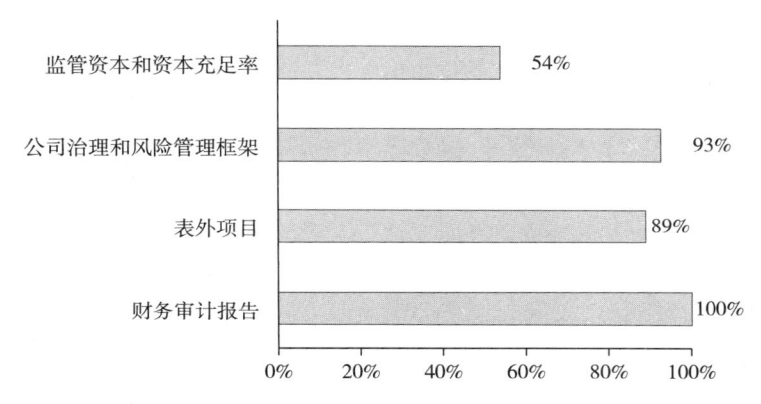

图7.18　开发性金融机构的公开披露情况

注：包括27家开发性金融机构。

作为样本的开发性金融机构中，58.3%遵守与私人商业金融机构相同的审慎监管标准。而其余的41.7%遵守其他标准（见图7.19）。

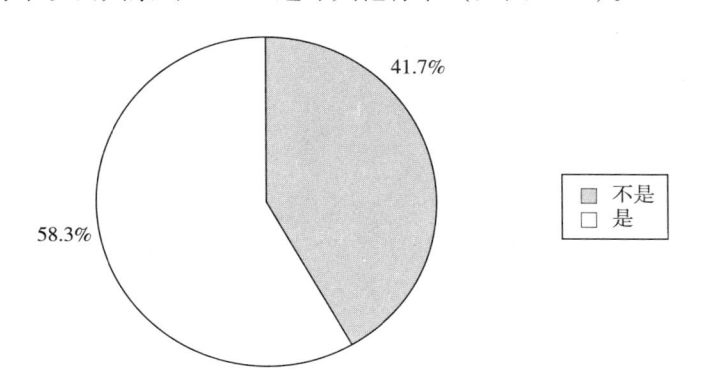

图7.19　是否遵守同样的审慎监管标准

注：包括可以得到数据的24家开发性金融机构。

样本中有77%的开发性金融机构按法律规定进行专业外部审计。

发展趋势

在21世纪的前15年中,世界经济经历了繁荣与衰退,特别是2007~2009年的金融危机。在此期间,开发性金融机构取得了显著增长,在许多领域的表现也明显提升。本节我们将使用样本数据指出世界开发性金融业的一些发展趋势。

规模大幅提高

2014年,样本中的开发性金融机构的资产总额从2006年的2.03万亿美元显著增至4.27万亿美元。8年间,总资产保持持续增长,仅在2009年的金融危机期间增速略有放缓(见图7.20)。

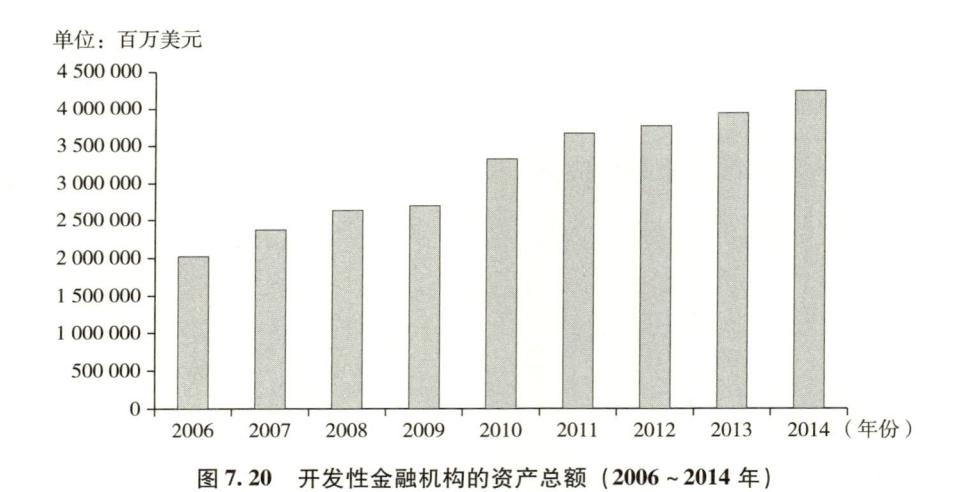

单位:百万美元

图7.20 开发性金融机构的资产总额(2006~2014年)

平均而言,开发性金融机构在整个金融系统中占有显著的比重。分析表明,2012年样本中的开发性金融机构的资产总和约占全球银行业资产总和的6.27%(见图7.21)。

开发性金融机构的总权益和总贷款在2006~2014年的发展情况与总资产类似(见图7.22)。

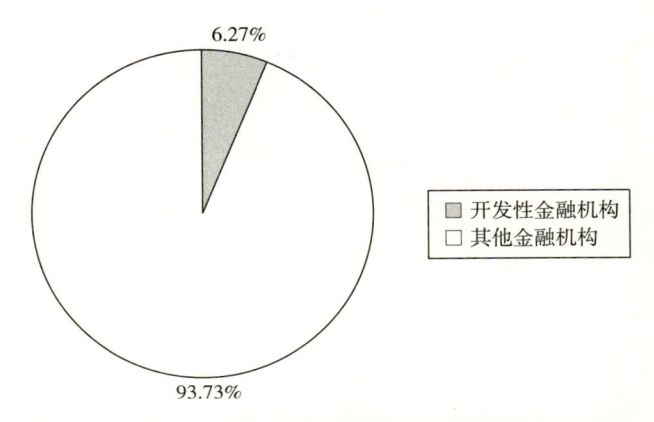

图 7.21 开发性金融机构占所有银行业机构的资产比重

资料来源：Helgilibrary, Banking Asset, retrieved May 12, 2015, http://www.helgilibrary.com/indicators/index/bank-assets-usd

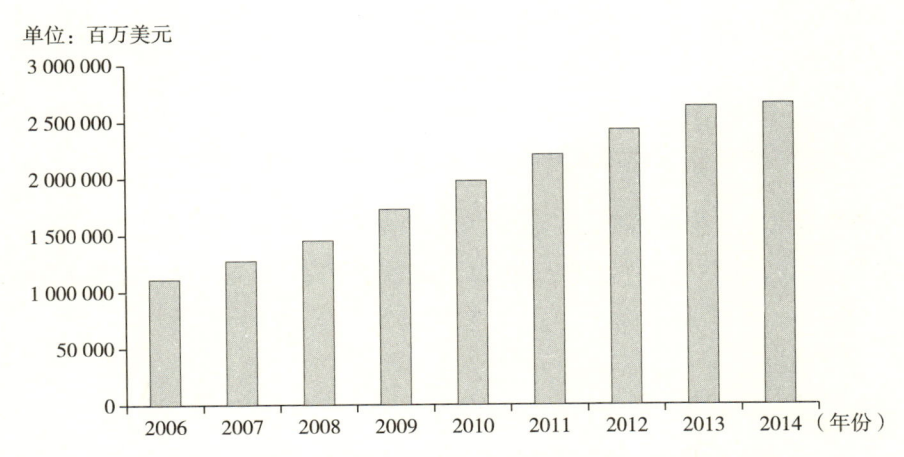

图 7.22 开发性金融机构的总贷款（2006 年年底～2014 年年底）

总体而言，样本中的开发性金融机构的总资产、总权益和总贷款在 2006～2014 年经历了持续增长。2007～2009 年的全球金融危机并没有减缓世界主要开发性金融机构的强劲发展。相反，开发性金融机构的活动呈现明显的反周期特性。

运营改善

在快速增长的同时，开发性金融机构在 2006～2014 年改善了经营业绩。样本中开发性金融机构的 ROE 的平均值在 2008 年和 2011～2012 年有所下降之后回归较高水平。不过，2014 年 ROA 的平均值仍略低于金融危机前的峰值水平（见图 7.23）。

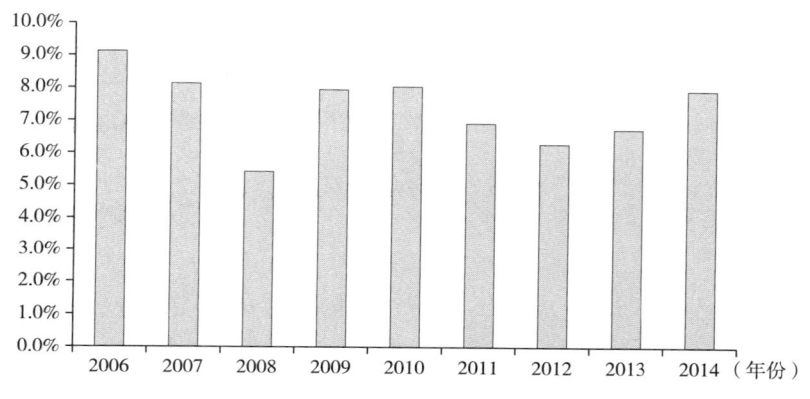

图 7.23 开发性金融机构的 ROA 平均值（2006～2014 年）

不良贷款率的平均值在金融危机之前和金融危机期间达到峰值，此后下降。在危机结束后，大多数开发性金融机构的不良贷款率下降到正常水平（见图 7.24）。

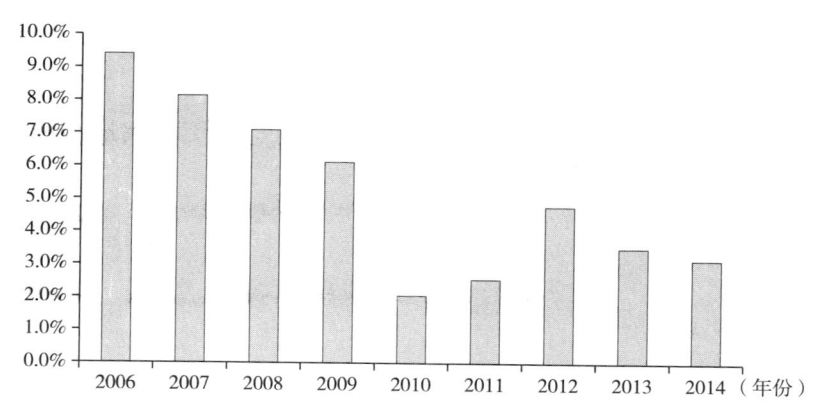

图 7.24 开发性金融机构的不良贷款率平均值（2006～2014 年）

结论

尽管特点多样，但我们样本中的开发性金融机构仍呈现出某些共同特点：

- 在过去几年里，不管是以总资产、总权益衡量，还是以总贷款衡量，开发性金融机构都经历了显著增长。单一开发性金融机构的总权益和总贷款在此期间均出现快速增长。无论就数量还是增长速度而言，中国国家开发银行的总资产和总权益都增长最快。

- 样本中的大多数开发性金融机构完全由国家所有。政府给予开发性金融机构大力支持。然而，政府的支持采取了多种形式。

- 开发性金融机构有多样化的资金来源，包括吸收公众存款、从其他金融机构借款、在国内和国际市场上发行债券、接受政府预算拨款和使用自身权益。

- 开发性金融机构开创并采取了一系列商业模式，为不同类型的客户提供服务。开发性金融机构的贷款业务通过零售、批发，或两者兼具的方式开展。目前，开发性金融机构聚焦于一些商业银行无法提供融资的战略投资领域。通过这些商业模式，开发性金融机构帮助政府重新配置资源，并突破经济发展的瓶颈制约。

- 完善治理结构对于开发性金融机构来说至关重要。在过去的几年中，开发性金融机构致力于在不断变化的全球经济环境中改善业务，并改革内部管理和监督结构。

- 全球金融危机期间，开发性金融机构发挥了稳定金融市场和宏观经济的重要作用。金融危机之后，开发性金融机构的绩效进一步改善，尽管有些指标仍未回到金融危机前的高点。

第八章　转型进程中开发性金融机构的作用

这一章将通过案例研究，详细阐释开发性金融机构在实现转型发展的进程中所承担的三大战略角色。这三大战略角色分别是：长期规划，市场培育，以及聚合各方力量，促成政府与社会部门的合作。这样做的目的并不是要定义"最优"做法，而是旨在促成各开发性金融机构间的相互学习，从而更好地以创新思维应对发展挑战。

长期规划

长期且全面的规划对实现经济转型来说至关重要。与传统计划型经济中的国家计划不同，开发性金融机构制定长期规划的出发点是该经济体的要素禀赋（这些要素禀赋"在某一特定时期是给定的，且随着时间推移是可变的"），由此识别出它的比较优势和主要的发展瓶颈，从而持续推动产业升级和经济多元化进程。在一个宏大愿景的引导下，长期规划可以帮助制定中期战略和短期工作计划，建设"硬件"和"软件"的基础设施，实现经济转型，攀上增长阶梯。

本节将首先引入中国国家开发银行的案例，研究它如何以制定规划为首要着力点，促进本国经济转型，并将成功经验向海外推广。随后，我们将探讨非洲开发银行如何通过制定规划，帮助非洲各国驶上经济发展快车道，从而逐步实现《非洲联盟转型规划》（the African Union Transformation Plan）所确定的长期目标，即到 2063 年，非洲整体达到中等收入水平。

中国国家开发银行案例

早在2003年,国家开发银行就提出了"规划先行"的理念。2006年以来,以参与中国"十一五"规划实施为契机,国家开发银行创造性地与有关各方开展密切的规划合作。2009年,国家开发银行正式成立规划局,各分行设立规划发展处,此后又设立规划院、科学发展规划委员会,系统推动区域、行业、战略客户等国内规划工作,探索国家规划咨询合作、国家规划编制、双边合作规划等国际规划形式,搭建起业务发展规划编制与实施的初步框架,逐步形成涵盖国际国内、行外行内的规划体系。

规划先行是开发性金融的重要组成部分,是促使中长期投融资提高前瞻性、把握主动性的重要手段。在实践中,国家开发银行紧密围绕国家经济外交战略、区域协调发展、产业转型升级、重点领域建设,坚持以各级政府、重大客户的长远发展需求为出发点,集思广益,通过规划共谋发展思路,提供高水平融智服务,以规划合作推动银政、银企合作,拓宽国开行服务国家战略的实现路径。同时,国家开发银行立足于发挥自身融资优势,运用开发性金融的原理和方法,注重市场、信用、制度建设,统筹设计融资模式、路径、产品、方案,批量开发重大项目,推动规划开发与下游业务有效衔接,树立了特有的系统性融资规划品牌,丰富和完善了国家规划的内容。规划先行已经成为开发性金融区别于商业性金融的重要特征,是国开行密切与外部合作、防范风险的核心竞争力。规划先行在开发性金融服务国家战略中承担着越来越重要的使命,发挥着越来越大的作用。

在具体方法上,国家开发银行将规划视为一项跨领域、多学科的系统工程。首先是区域和城镇规划,在测算人口、土地、资源、环境等承载力的基础上,倒算城镇的建设规模、功能分区、产业布局以及基础设施的配置;其次是产业规划,根据当地资源禀赋进行产业布局,以技术研发为龙头,关注产业链及背后的融资体系和信用体系;再次是社会规划,以人口数量和人的全面发展为中心,根据区域和产业的发展配置学校、医院、文化等社会基础设施;然后是市场规划，发展中国家需要经过艰苦努力，从无到有建设充满活力、富有效率的市场机制；再然后是融资规划，动员社会资金保障发展的融资需要；最后是富民规划，设计普通百姓都能致富、共同富裕的路径。这其中，区域规划是核心，能带动产业和社会发展，市场规划是基础性的和贯穿始终的。

专栏8-1、8-2、8-3将介绍国家开发银行的三个典型案例，分别阐述其在国内和海外制定和实施发展规划的具体做法。

专栏8-1 国家开发银行国内规划案例：辽宁沿海经济带

辽宁省是中国东北部唯一既沿海又沿边的省份，是中国重要的老工业基地，被誉为"东方鲁尔"。2005年，辽宁省政府提出重点发展由长兴岛、营口、锦州湾组成的"三点一线"环渤海经济带，并希望国家开发银行支持。经过调查，国家开发银行认为，基于辽宁省的港口、土地资源和区位优势，如果辽宁沿海能够发展起来，那么对促进辽宁省老工业基地转型和中国东北振兴有积极意义，应该在"三点一线"的基础上，将丹东产业园区、大连花园口产业园区和葫芦岛、盘锦两市纳入辽宁沿海经济带的整体规划，形成"五点一线"的整体概念（见图8.1）。

国家开发银行与辽宁省达成共识，共同成立领导小组，推动辽宁沿海"五点一线"的编制工作，国家开发银行专门向辽宁省发放60万元技术援助贷款，用于整体规划编制。2007年3月，辽宁沿海经济带发展规划编制工作完成，2009年，规划经中国国务院批准上升为国家发展战略。为支撑规划实施，国家开发银行对整体项目进行系统性融资规划，设计用3~5年时间融资300亿元支持经济带的基础设施建设，搭建产业投资平台和中小企业融资平台，引导企业进入当地园区。截至2012年年底，300亿元的总体授信已经完成贷款发放，规划的重点项目顺利实施。

图8.1 辽宁"五点一线"沿海经济带规划图

从提出"规划先行"理念到"十二五"规划末，国家开发银行先后推动珠三角、长三角、关中—天水、武汉城市圈、长株潭城市群、图们江、江苏沿海、广西北部湾、浙江海洋经济发展示范区等53项重大区域规划上升为国家战略，参与了"一带一路"、京津冀协同、长江经济带、新型城镇化等国家重大战略规划的编制与实施。

专栏8-2 国家开发银行国际规划案例：委内瑞拉

国家开发银行认为，规划引领改革发展的理念同样适用于其他国家，通过规划咨询合作能够帮助合作国明确发展战略，梳理重大项目并促进规划实施，减少盲目投资和重复建设，促进合作国的经济全面协调可持续发展,增强经济社会发展的内生动力。

2010年,应委内瑞拉政府要求,国家开发银行开始为委内瑞拉提供规划咨询服务。按照工作流程,国家开发银行组织中方联合专家团,深入研讨合作国国情资料,赴合作国考察调研。按照委内瑞拉提出的规划与每届政府6年任期同步的要求,分别提供了2010~2012年、2013~2018年、2019~2030年3个阶段的规划咨询。包括一个经济社会发展总体规划,以及农业、住房与城市、工业、交通、电力、油气石化、矿业、财政金融8个专题规划咨询意见。规划结合委内瑞拉政府的建议多次修改,最终递交给委内瑞拉政府,获得了委内瑞拉政府的高度肯定。随后,委内瑞拉政府派出由多位部长、专家组成的高级代表团来中国就规划工作进行考察调研,国家开发银行邀请中国政府有关部门向委内瑞拉代表团介绍中国"十二五"规划情况,并组织代表团实地考察10多家中国大型企业,进一步丰富双方规划与融资合作的内涵和形式。

专栏8-3 国家开发银行国际规划案例:瑞典

除了与委内瑞拉等发展中国家开展规划咨询合作以外,国家开发银行也与瑞典等发达国家积极开展规划合作。

2010年3月,国家开发银行原董事长陈元随同时任国家副主席的习近平同志访问瑞典期间,与瑞典政府投资促进署签署了《开发性金融合作备忘录》,拉开了中国金融机构与瑞典政府开展开发性金融合作的序幕。为落实备忘录中关于规划合作的要求,2011年3月,国家开发银行与瑞典政府投资促进署在北京签署规划合作协议,使瑞典成为首个与国家开发银行签订规划合作协议的国家。双方合作旨在通过搭建规划合作平台,促进两国经贸合作，为企业和项目对接疏通瓶颈，并确定基础设施、风能及清洁能源、矿产资源、高科技中小企业等中瑞互补性行业作为首批重点合作领域。按照协议约定，双方共同组织了瑞典国情研讨会，组织国内一流规划专家团队赴瑞典进行实地考察调研，通过多种形式与瑞典政府交通署、能源署、创新署、国家地质局等部门以及多家国家基金、重点企业进行深入沟通和对接，提出了中瑞规划合作意见，并梳理出合作项目，初步估计总投资额超过400亿美元。在此基础上，双方在北京和瑞典共同举办了中瑞规划合作投资论坛，进一步探讨了中瑞投融资合作模式，并与中瑞企业交流了有融资需求的项目以及对中资企业有合作需求的项目情况，推动国内多家龙头企业与瑞典合作方达成具体项目合作协议。我国驻瑞典大使和商务参赞对国家开发银行通过规划合作促进与瑞典双边经贸合作的积极态度及高效行动表示高度赞赏，认为通过规划合作平台促进经贸合作是重要的金融创新，为经济全球化背景下加强企业合作提供了科学指引和国际典范。

非洲开发银行案例

与中国一样，非洲各国迫切地希望实现经济起飞和持续发展。目前，整个非洲大陆的经济发展速度位居世界第二。尽管世界经济正在经历震荡，非洲经济却未如悲观论者所料，反而逆势上扬，加速增长。但是，这一积极发展态势同时受到一系列负面因素制约，比如基础设施不健全、新旧冲突频发、青年失业率高企、不公平现象日益凸显等。在这些紧迫的挑战面前，唯有制定长远规划，才有可能实现可持续增长，推动结构改革和经济转型，使非洲大陆参与到全球价值链中来。

非洲开发银行将自己定位为推动非洲转型的核心机构。在他们看来，"转型就是使经济增长的来源和机遇多样化，以此提高劳动生产率，实现经济的可持续包容性增长。转型还意味着支持那些借已有的比较优势来强化自身影响力的产业发展,进而提升非洲的国际竞争地位。"

首先要做的就是明确发展愿景。2006年,在名人小组的指导下,非洲开发银行编写了《向非洲未来投资——21世纪的非洲开发银行》(*Investing in Africa's Future—The African Development Bank in the 21st Century*),为非洲大陆的发展前景和非洲开发银行的成长路径做出远景规划。以此为契机,该行在2008~2012年做出一系列战略决策,据此指导经营活动。按照这一规划,非洲将依靠高质量的经济增长,为全体劳动者尤其是妇女和青年创造更多就业岗位,实现整体繁荣。为实现这一目标,有关方面需要制定合理有效的政策,完善基础设施,从而为私有经济提供更好的发展条件,促进投资,培育企业家精神,助力中小微企业的成长,顺利实现非洲的转型。

下一个关键环节是制定中期发展战略。2013年,非洲开发银行编制了新的十年规划——《非洲转型的核心:2013~2022年发展战略》(*At the Center of Africa's Transformation: Strategy for 2013 – 2022*)。该战略旨在确保非洲的经济增长既是包容性的、也是"绿色"的,从而拓展转型进程的广度和深度。为实现这两个目标,十年规划提出了五大优先发展事项,用以指导日常运营,提高非洲发展质量,五大优先发展事项分别是:(1)基础设施建设;(2)区域经济整合;(3)私营经济的发展;(4)治理与问责机制的建立与完善;(5)技术与科技进步。在推进十年规划的过程中,非洲开发银行还对三方面的问题给予了特别关注:政局动荡、农业和粮食安全受到威胁以及两性不平等。

非洲开发银行认识到,要实现有效干预,政府主导的国家发展战略是必不可少的。因而,该行为每个借款国都制定了一个五年期国家发展战略。

专栏8-4 埃塞俄比亚:2011~2015年国家发展战略

埃塞俄比亚,全称埃塞俄比亚联邦民主共和国,位于非洲东北部的

"非洲之角",是全世界人口最多的内陆国家,也是非洲人口第二大国,首都是第一大城市亚的斯亚贝巴(Addis Ababa)。为实现减贫和经济转型,埃塞俄比亚政府从2010年起开始实施"经济增长与转型规划"(GTP),期望到2025年步入中等收入国家行列。

为实现这一愿景,非洲开发银行与埃塞俄比亚政府合作,共同制定了"2011~2015年国家发展战略"(CSP),该战略和经济增长与转型规划相一致,同时具体说明了非洲开发银行将如何支持该战略的实施。

这一战略首先分析了埃塞俄比亚的现状和未来面临的机遇与挑战,继而针对该国的情况量身订制了支持方案。支持方案将重点放在两个方面:(1)支持该国提升基础设施建设水平;(2)支持该国完善基本服务的供给和问责机制,以营造更好的商业环境。

在设定优先发展事项之后,非洲开发银行进一步细化了其预期成果和具体目标:"我行将综合运用多种方式以求总体规划和具体项目相结合,包括为世行的基本服务保护计划(Protection of Basic Services)提供预算支持。我们还将在可能的情况下使用非洲发展基金的部分风险担保(The African Development Fund Partial Risk Guarantee),以支持私人资本参与基础设施建设。我们也将与世行集团政策保持一致,在各项工作的规划实施中始终关注那些跨领域问题——性别平等、艾滋病防治以及环境保护(包括气候变化)等。"

接下来,非洲开发银行指明了可能妨碍国家发展战略实施和经济增长与转型规划实现的五大风险:(1)面临外部冲击时的高脆弱性;(2)组织机构能力不足;(3)融资和宏观经济风险;(4)治理风险;(5)地区局势动荡风险。

非洲开发银行相信,"埃塞俄比亚的新国家发展战略的提出十分及时;它切合经济增长与转型规划的要求,将有力推进减贫,为埃塞俄比亚成长为中等收入国家打下良好基础。"

> 埃塞俄比亚2011~2015年国家发展战略与该国制定的经济增长与转型规划相契合,支持该国经济在2012~2013年实现了9.7%的增长,成为非洲经济发展最快的国家之一。

市场培育

开发性金融机构的战略定位是增强投资者信心,为大规模转型投资培育市场,以实现包含经济发展、社会进步和环境保护三个维度的可持续发展。开发性金融机构可以担当市场先行者的角色:它们可以承担风险、厘清误解,乃至克服市场低迷的状态,从而为投资者建立信心,以较小规模的投资引致更大规模的私人投资。

本节将介绍3个典型案例,研究开发性金融机构如何以主权信用为依托,在发展不成熟的市场中降低风险、推动前沿市场发展以及培育绿色债券市场。

在发展不成熟的市场中降低风险

20世纪90年代私有化浪潮的巅峰时刻,自由市场的信奉者们预言,多边开发银行(MDBs)必将退出私营基础设施的融资活动,因为他们相信,私有制市场完全可以独力实现这一功能。然而历史证明并非如此。融资需求太大,各种挑战太多,而供需缺口太难填补。在基础设施融资领域,多边开发银行既没有因无所作为而离场,也没有因使命达成而功成身退,相反,多边开发银行在长期融资方面扮演了关键角色,尤其是在那些至关重要的项目上,这些项目往往结构和合同都非常复杂,难以吸引商业银行投资。

专栏8-5将以亚洲开发银行为例,具体说明多边开发银行如何在发展不成熟的市场中降低风险,吸引更多的私人资本投资基础设施建设。

专栏 8-5　亚行在发展不成熟的亚洲项目融资市场上降低风险

亚行的首要职责之一是为那些被忽视的亚洲项目融资市场提供支持。亚洲开发银行的一项研究显示，全亚洲每年基础设施建设大约需要 8 000 亿美元。"当然，亚洲各国都对基础设施建设资金有巨大的需求，但这一需求在那些市场发展不成熟的地区显得特别紧迫。因为当地银行最欠缺融资实力，而国际银行又迟疑不前。"

亚行对政局动荡的风险有特殊的洞察力和应对能力，因而能对很多项目是否具备投资可能做出良好判断。比如，它曾为阿富汗一家电信持牌商、柬埔寨一条输电线路以及乌兹别克斯坦一座数十亿美元资产的化工厂提供融资服务。此外，只要有可能，亚行都尽力吸引商业银行参与融资，用产品和亲身参与来打消它们的顾虑。比如，为阿富汗那家移动电话公司提供的就是 B 类贷款和政治风险担保。

迎接先期挑战

亚行敢于在商业银行不敢涉足的地方投资，这不仅包括政治动荡的地区，也包括在"起初可能被视为技术上或结构上有风险"的领域，从而引领市场发展方向。以下是亚行近期的几个案例：

- 亚行在印度和泰国主导太阳能项目融资市场，协助两国创建首个大型光伏太阳能电厂，最近又在印度建立了世界上最大的线性菲涅尔聚光太阳能发电项目。
- 亚行在印度尼西亚为该国首个私营地热工程提供融资服务，该项目已持续超过十年；这个投资试验项目的成功促使更多地热工程准备上马建设。

推动市场发展

为项目融资是亚行的主营业务之一。然而，虽然亚行已在极力扩展私营基础设施融资规模，但它所提供的直接贷款仍然很少。虽能填补资金缺口、支持项目实施，但"与亚洲工程项目融资需求相比，不过沧海一粟"。亚行越来越关注的不是自有资金的规模，而是能运用多少私人资金进行投资。吸引投资的手段多种多样：亚行对项目的参与本身就是一重保证（由于所谓的"光环效应"，亚行的参与使投资者相信项目风险已显著减小）；亚行的产品也具有吸引力［亚行将资金部署在多种B类贷款、政治和局部风险担保（political and partial risk guarantee）以及风险参贷（risk participation）］；亚行与商业银行的风险取向和风险状况也不同（在项目需要和银行风险审核通过的情况下，采用更长的贷款期限、不同的债务分割方式，以及更早、更广泛地引入股权融资等）。此外，还包括了"超越商业银行市场限制，激发陷入停滞的项目债券市场的活力"。

创建更多优质项目

人们常争论的一个问题是，亚洲究竟是缺乏私营基础设施项目融资，还是缺乏值得投资的优质项目？结论往往是后者。"亚行在这方面做了大量工作，并且将重心放在刺激优质项目融资上。它首先说服各国采取政府与社会部门合作的模式（public private partnerships，PPPs），并帮助各国建立政府与社会部门合作的管理中心，制定和调整有关法律和规定，帮助政府选择可以特许私人经营的基础设施项目，进而精心设计、正式公布并交付实施等。在此过程之后，亚行将与市场各方共同为这些项目融资。"

推动前沿市场的发展

在前沿市场进行创新往往伴随着很高的风险，这使得投资者们不愿开发新产品；而创新的匮乏又反过来进一步削弱投资者信心，抑制创新。要打破这一恶性循环，推动前沿市场蓬勃发展，最关键的就是为这些风险较高的开发项目提供融资支持。

专栏8-6将介绍欧洲复兴开发银行的一个案例，考察该行是如何促进制药行业的创新和生产能力的。

专栏8-6 欧洲复兴开发银行为制药行业生产融资

蓬勃发展的制药行业是创新强度最高的行业之一（见图8.2）。医药领域的研发活动有助于降低人口死亡率（见图8.3）。制药行业不仅能提升人们的生活质量，还能促进经济增长，增强创新生产能力。

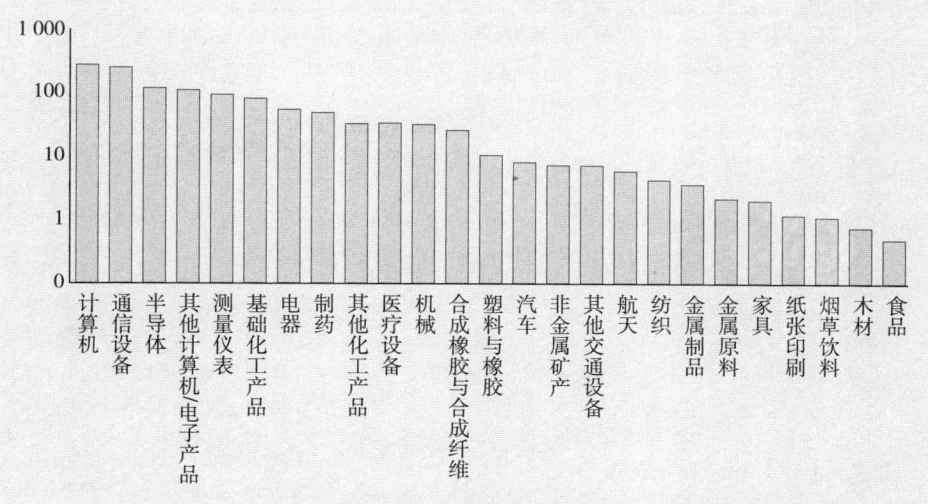

图8.2 各行业创新强度

然而，对大多数制药商而言，资金不足制约着新药的研发。比如，有报道称，在约旦，仅有8%的制药企业能获得充足资金，用于新产品的开发研制。

为推动各成员国制药行业健康发展，欧洲复兴开发银行为医药公司提供资金支持。2014年的新增投资中，有9%投向制药业。该机构还首次

图 8.3　医学研发与死亡率的关系

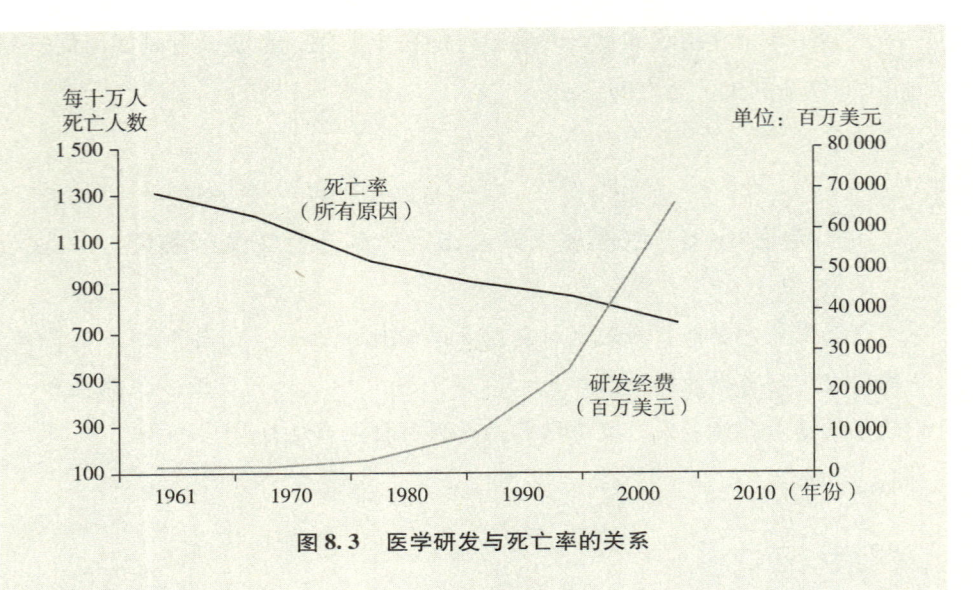

与约旦政府合作，共同向医药公司投资，资助其扩大生产能力、广泛研发新产品。欧洲复兴开发银行还与克罗地亚合作，包括与该国主要制药企业之一 Jadran Galenski Laboratorij 公司开展合作，此外在乌克兰也有投资。

下文将用 3 个实例具体说明欧洲复兴开发银行如何推进制药行业的前沿发展。

约旦 Hikma 制药集团

2014 年 4 月，欧洲复兴开发银行向约旦 Hikma 制药公司提供了 5 000 万美元的贷款，帮助该企业"维持在国内的高效运营，并对地中海东部和南部地区的分公司进行制造标准升级"。

有关各方期待通过这样的方式，促成更多新药的问世，同时健全当地的法律框架，使知识产权得到有效保护。根据欧洲复兴开发银行的说明和设计，这笔贷款主要用于 Hikma 制药公司，资助其发展，主要途径是"支持该公司取得知识产权（IPRs）。业内普遍认为，知识产权收益是激励制药公司持续研发新产品的主要动力"。该计划未来目标是为整个地中海东部和南部地区提供具有最佳疗效的平价药品。

克罗地亚 Jadran Galenski Laboratorij 制药公司

克罗地亚 Jadran Galenski Laboratorij 制药公司（JGL）的努力目标是成为全世界最大的无菌溶液制造商。2014年11月，欧洲复兴开发银行为该公司提供了高达2 000万欧元（2 490万美元）的多币种长期营运资本贷款。

这项投资的目标是使该公司的生产能力提高一倍。为实现这一目标，这家制药公司计划建设一个新的"药谷"，以增加现有设备设施，这将使该公司"无菌溶液产量翻一番，并创造100个新的就业岗位"。此外，克罗地亚开发银行（HBOR）也将为该公司提供3 270万欧元（4 071万美元）的贷款，作为前述贷款的补充。

乌克兰 Farmak 制药公司

在欧洲复兴开发银行的资助下，乌克兰医药市场的巨大潜力得以释放，但行业整体仍面临缺乏更好的融资渠道的问题。为与乌克兰深化该领域合作，欧洲复兴开发银行于2014年12月向该国的一家制药企业——Farmak制药公司发放了第三笔贷款，总额高达850万欧元（1 029万美元）。欧洲复兴开发银行承诺将提供营运资本融资和硬通货兑换服务。

迄今为止，已有超过9 500万欧元（1.150 5亿美元）的制药行业支持资金投向了乌克兰，而该项目整个运营区域投入资金的总数也不过5亿欧元（6.055 2亿美元）。这一融资项目旨在提高医药技术水平、尽最大可能降低药品成本，使更多有需要的人负担得起药费。

总之，欧洲复兴开发银行以投资推动了制药行业前沿市场的发展。由于中东和北非地区（MENA）的药品很少是在当地生产的，因而该地区制药业的发展潜力极大，而市场潜力也相当可观。

培育绿色债券市场

气候变化将给全球带来灾难性后果,没有哪个国家能置身事外,这迫使我们采取强有力的措施,降低温室气体排放总量,从而实现向抗风险能力强的低碳经济的平稳转型。以目前趋势看,如果国际社会不能有效应对气候变化,那么到本世纪末,世界平均气温将提高4摄氏度;随之而来的将是一系列灾难性后果——极端炎热天气频现、全球粮食储备减少以及海平面上升,海平面上升将影响数以亿计沿海居民的生活。人类自身的存亡正遭受严重威胁。因此,我们相信,实现向低碳经济的转型,是人类当下面临的有史以来最严峻的挑战之一,这绝不是危言耸听。

然而,与巨大的需求相比,治理气候问题的资金供应只是杯水车薪。国际气候政策中心(Climate Policy Initiative)的资料显示,2013年全球治理气候问题的融资总额约为3 310亿美元,比2012年减少了280亿美元。资金供需缺口不断累积、日渐扩大。照此趋势,全球气温目标将难以保持,人类将更可能为气候变化付出昂贵代价。

弥合这一融资缺口离不开公共部门的积极作为,只有这样才能带动更大规模的私人投资。很多投资者都对气候变化的后果感到担忧,他们希望通过支持应对气候变化的项目来遏止这一趋势。但是,私人投资者往往因畏惧未知领域的风险,而不敢有所作为。

培育绿色债券市场是打破这一瓶颈的有效手段,在这一方面,开发性金融机构有两大优势:一,由于其一般享有主权信用,因而有效降低了风险,不至于如私人资本一样望而却步;二,其所拥有的专业意见能更好地完成项目管理,积累成功经验和资历。

专栏8-7、8-8给出了开发性金融机构培育绿色债券市场的两个实例。专栏8-7介绍了由一家多边开发银行——世界银行发行的绿色债券,目前发展势头强劲;专栏8-8介绍了由一家开发银行——北莱茵威斯特法伦州银行发行的绿色债券。

专栏8-7 世界银行发起并培育绿色债券市场

应对气候变化需要世界各国以前所未有的力度开展跨境合作。世行的做法是为发展中国家提供帮助，为制定全球解决方案贡献力量。

2008年，世行启动《发展与气候变化战略框架》(Strategic Framework for Development and Climate Change)，旨在鼓励与协调公共部门和社会部门在该领域积极参与、通力合作。世行绿色债券就是世行在该框架下鼓励创新的一个典型成果。

世行绿色债券由世行向固定收益投资者发售，所募集的资金用于向符合要求的项目发放贷款，这些项目有些致力于减缓气候变化，有些用来为受气候变化影响的人们提供帮助。项目的选择由世行环境专家具体执行，主要是看候选项目是否符合低碳发展的某一特定标准。这一标准已经通过位于挪威奥斯陆大学的国际气候与环境研究中心 (the Center for International Climate and Environmental Research，CICERO) 的独立审查。该机构相信，有世行的治理结构和保障措施为依托，这些活动可以确保挑选出适宜的气候友好型项目。

"对投资者来说，世行绿色债券给投资者提供了一个机会：通过投资于3A评级的固定收益产品，支持气候变化解决方案。绿色债券的授信品质与世行发行的其他债券相同。债券的偿付与项目的信用或绩效状况无关，投资者无需承担某具体项目的运营风险。投资者可以得到双重保障：一是世行3A评级的信用保障，二是世行尽职调查的程序保障。"

2014年，世行绿色债券发行创历史新高：2014财年（2013年7月~2014年6月）共融资近30亿美元。随着2015财政年度世行第一只绿色债券的发行（该债券与可持续权益指数有关），世行总计已用17种货币发行了总计68支、总额64亿美元的绿色债券，为20个国家的62个项目提供融资支持。各币种所占比例如图8.4所示。

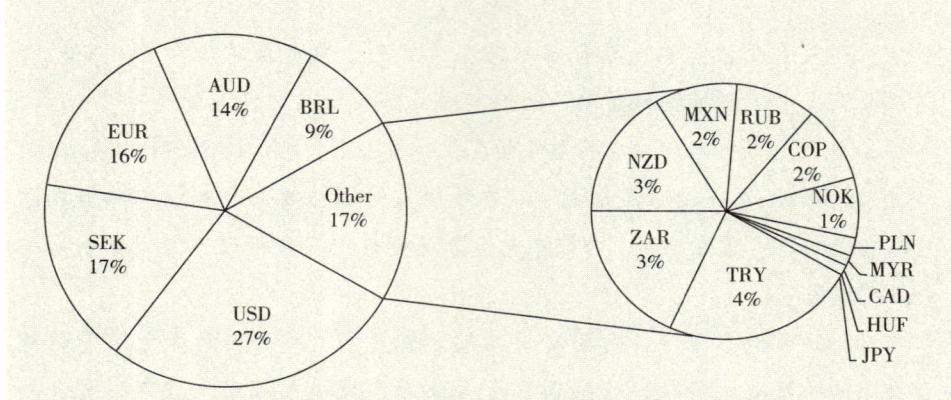

图8.4 世行流通在外的绿色债券比例（各币种，截至2014年7月31日）

注：1. 目前发行的绿色债券总值合640万美元，其中价值530万美元的债券流通在外，共分17个不同币种。

2. USD（美元）；SEK（瑞典克朗）；EUR（欧元）；AUD（澳元）；BRL（巴西里尔）；TRY（土耳其里拉）；ZAR（南非兰特）；NZD（新西兰元）；MXN（墨西哥比索）；RUB（俄罗斯卢布）；COP（哥伦比亚比索）；NOK（挪威克朗）；PLN（波兰兹罗提）；MYR（马来西亚林吉特）；CAD（加拿大元）；HUF（匈牙利福林）；JPY（日元）。

市场对世行绿色债券显示出强烈需求，与此同时，整个绿色债券市场也在快速发展。截至2014年7月，绿色债券年度总发行额已超过200亿美元，是2013年发行额的两倍。

专栏8-8 北莱茵威斯特法伦州银行发行绿色债券

为了以创新手段募集绿色投资，德国北莱茵威斯特法伦州银行采取的是发行绿色债券的方式，通过这种方式筹集的资金专款用于为此前认证的环境改善项目提供再融资服务。

北莱茵威斯特法伦州银行在2013年首次发行绿色债券，随后又在2014年10月成功发行第二支总值5亿欧元（6.055 2亿美元）的四年期绿色债券。这支债券仍选择"水"和"能源"作为重点投资领域，但2014年的重点放在了"能源"上，总计约3.7亿欧元（4.480 8亿美元）的投资将定向投入这一领域。

如果某项目希望获得该行2014年绿色债券的资金支持，则必须满足一整套详细的资格要求，包括到期日应在该自然年内、项目主题必须与该绿色债券指定的主题相关。

北莱茵威斯特法伦州银行向投资者做出保证：通过绿色债券获得的全部收入都将用于发放2014年审批通过的项目贷款，这些项目涉及的领域包括水资源管理、能源效率提升、可再生能源以及电动交通。北莱茵威斯特法伦州银行已通过绿色债券筹集了总计5亿欧元（6.055 2亿美元）的款项，用以支持这些开发项目。

发行绿色债券旨在为降低碳排放、提升水资源品质提供资金支持。北莱茵威斯特法伦州银行利用绿色债券收入，资助建起了20多架风力发电机，推动本地交通系统升级使用更加环保的设施设备，投资建设更高效利用能源和资源的工厂，以及许多类似的项目。2014年发行的绿色债券收入中，有1.3亿欧元（1.574 3亿美元）用来建立一套现代高效的污水系统，该系统将显著提升用水质量，保护生物多样性，从而从总体上改善环境。

这也是北莱茵威斯特法伦州银行首次邀请外部评级机构，对2014绿色债券选择的贷款项目的环境效益和项目质量做出分析和评估。

未来，对绿色债券发展至关重要的一点，就是要制定更为严格的标准。唯有如此，才能发挥这一创新型金融工具的最大效用，引导更大规模的私人资本投资绿色增长领域。

聚合各方力量，促成政府与社会部门的合作

开发性金融机构是连通政府和社会部门的特别理想的桥梁。发展带来的挑战十分复杂，往往不是某一个资金提供者能独力承担的。开发性金融机构能为各国政府、多边开发银行、私营部门投资者和融资人构建合作平台。

专栏8-9、8-10、8-11将用3个案例说明多边和国别的开发性金融机构如何善用多种金融工具，构建知识共享平台，以融汇各方专业智慧。3个案例概况如下：

- 世行创立全球基础设施基金（Global Infrastructure Facility，GIF），为各国政府、多边开发银行、私营部门投资者和融资人提供新平台，在那些单个机构无法独力承担的复杂项目上开展合作（见专栏8-9）；
- 伊斯兰开发银行设计出"三方共赢"机制，与慈善家合作应对紧迫的发展挑战（见专栏8-10）；
- 印度工业开发银行与信用评级机构和小额信贷机构合作，为中小企业提供融资服务（见专栏8-11）。

专栏8-9 世行全球基础设施基金

世行集团创立的全球基础设施基金是一个开放的全球性平台，主要功能是为复杂的公私合营的基础设施（infrastructure PPPs）项目提供筹备和结构设计方面的便利，以吸引私人资本和机构投资者。全球基础设施基金依靠诸多技术和咨询合作伙伴（其中也包括私人投资者）为项目提供全程支持，确保将结构完备、能吸引银行投资的项目投向市场。它独一无二的合作模式已获得机构投资者的有力支持。该项目旨在运用世行集团内部自

有和从公私部门调集的各种技术和资源,加以整合,为新兴市场和发展中经济体源源不断地提供可靠、可行且能获得银行贷款的政府与社会资本合作项目,解决基础设施建设难题。

2014年10月,在全球基础设施基金成立的发布会上,世行行长金墉(Jim Yong Kim)说:"设立全球基础设施基金,是为了将世行内外的专业意见汇聚起来,为复杂的公私合营基础设施项目提供支持,这些项目往往是单个机构无力承担的。"

全球基础设施基金为各资金供应方建立了可靠渠道,填补了发展中国家基础设施建设的资金缺口:到2020年为止,在这方面全球每年需追加投资1万亿美元。最新案例之一是厄瓜多尔首都基多市的地铁建设项目。基多市地处火山环绕之中,拥有160万人口。该项目于2014财年开工建设,全长23公里,日运载能力36万人次。2018年年底该项目建成后,将缓解当地交通拥堵,减少空气污染。

该项目的资金由国际复兴开发银行、安第斯开发公司(the Andean Development Corporation,CAF)、欧洲投资银行(the European Investment Bank,EIB)、泛美开发银行(the Inter-American Development Bank,IDB)以及厄瓜多尔地方和中央政府合作募集。这是4家多边机构和一国各级政府的首次合力融资,这次融资为基多市的第一条地铁线路筹集了15亿美元的建设资金。

世行拉丁美洲和加勒比地区副行长哈桑·塔利(Hasan Tuluy)称:"由项目所在国的政府牵头,世行与安第斯开发公司、欧洲投资银行、泛美开发银行通力合作,共同支持项目建设,这在世行历史上还是第一次。这一成功案例为其他国家和城市做出示范,各国均可从中学习获益。"

拟建地铁项目全长23公里,设15站,其中6站与基多市城市快速公交系统(the Metrobus-Q network)相连。这是该市首条地铁线路,日运载能力达36万人次。项目建成后,基多市将拥有美洲最好的地铁系统,该系统每年将节约价值 1 400 万美元的燃油，创造 1 800 个直接就业岗位，使城市南北贯通，并有力激发当地经济活力。一旦建成通车，当地居民从南向北穿越全城仅需半小时左右。近年来，基多市对高效公共交通的需求日益增长，这一项目将有效提升城市整体交通水平。

专栏 8-10　伊斯兰开发银行的三方共赢机制

近年来的金融危机给各国都带来了冲击，尤其造成了援助规模缩减，对全球公共品的融资需求更为紧迫。因此，关键的一点是促进模式创新，实现对市场资源的有效利用，为发展中国家的农业、营养、教育、能源、基础设施和气候变化等领域的项目提供融资支持。

为实现这一目标，2012 年，伊斯兰开发银行营运副行长组织行内骨干力量，与比尔及梅琳达·盖茨基金会（the Bill and Melinda Gates Foundation，简称"盖茨基金会"）进行了几个月的洽谈交流，设计出"三方共赢"的创新性融资机制。

举一个试点项目为例，作为"全球根除小儿麻痹症计划"（the Global Polio Eradication Initiative，GPEI）的组成部分，巴基斯坦计划在全国范围内消灭小儿麻痹症，但资金存在缺口。为此，"三方共赢"融资机制调集各种必要资源，募集项目资金。盖茨基金会和伊斯兰开发银行还称，将继续向尼日利亚和阿富汗提供支持，帮助两国消灭小儿麻痹症。此外，还将把这一融资机制推广到更多领域，比如根除疟疾和确保粮食安全等。这一机制使银行能将普通资源引入，以拓展优惠资金池，从而为某一成员国募集大量基金，应对紧迫的发展挑战。借款国仅需偿付本金，其余所有费用由盖茨基金会支付。

这一机制看上去与盖茨基金会的另两个合作机制相类似：与世行集团合作的"贷款转赠款"（buy down）机制，以及与日本国际协力机构合作的"贷款转股权"（loan conversion）模式。但这一新的融资机制有所创新："它在巴基斯坦小儿麻痹症项目上的应用，创立了这样一种新的模式，即国际融资机构（IFI）通过普通资金来源筹集大笔资金，然后借由慈善捐赠的资助，将之转换成软贷款，用来资助发展中国家的公益项目/工程。"

"三方共赢"的创新型融资机制最突出的贡献之一，就是为优惠型融资（concessional financing）的未来提供了新思路。这在全球经济形势严峻、援助预算收紧、全球公共品融资需求更为紧迫的今天尤为及时。这一新的融资机制用于提高优惠型融资的规模，比如，世行国际开发协会（International Development Association，IDA）的非洲开发基金（African Development Fund）可以将拟发放的补助金拿来支付利息，由此从市场上获得大量融资，其数额要远比原本的补助金多得多。

总之，这一创新性融资机制符合伊斯兰世界特有的融资模式，使更大规模的优惠型融资得以投向亚非发展中国家，这将为数以百万计的人民带来希望。

专栏8-11 印度工业开发银行助力中小企业融资

中小企业面临的最大挑战是信息不对称。从贷方角度看，由于中小企业规模过小且过于细微，银行很难考察其经营状况与信贷条件，因而不愿提供贷款；此外，因为达不到规模经济，也缺乏管理能力，中小企业往往盈利能力不足。从借方角度看，由于难以跟踪考察经营状况，那些业绩不佳的中小企业的违约风险上升，这相当于让它们搭了便车，对负担一般利率的业绩良好的中小企业不公平。总之，信息不对称问题使银行在处理中小企业贷款业务时面临更大的风险。由于借贷双方都能意识到这个问题，最终后果就是贷款利率奇高，伴随着少量信用品质极差的借款者。

解决中小企业融资难的关键，是降低信息不对称的程度，从而改善中小企业信用，使之更容易取得贷款。下文两个实例将展示印度工业开发银行如何与信用评级机构和小额贷款机构合作，帮助中小企业持续获得信贷支持。

为了更好地了解各个中小企业，识别哪些企业信贷风险较高，印度工业开发银行与印度评级机构开展合作。比如，它与印度第二大评级机构信贷分析与研究公司（Credit Analysis & Research，CARE）合作。截至2015年3月，印度工业开发银行仍是CARE第一大股东。

针对中小企业，CARE专门制定了评级方法，尤其对与偿付能力和盈利能力密切相关的指标予以特别关注。此外，CARE还将资本形式和企业创始人自筹的无担保贷款列入评价指标。根据这些指标可以将中小企业信用分为若干等级，银行可以据此制定贷款计划。CARE建议，有意发展中小企业信贷业务的银行，最好独立建立一套贷款利率比一般贷款低的框架体系服务于中小企业。

除了与评级机构合作外，印度工业开发银行还与小额贷款机构开展合作。双方通过合作取长补短，互利共赢。小额贷款机构对中小企业了解很深，但缺乏资金；印度工业开发银行资金充裕，但无法解决信息不对称问题。因而，双方合作前景广阔。

比如，印度工业开发银行与印度最大的小额贷款机构Bandhan建立伙伴关系，意在将业务拓展到目前没有开设银行的地区。对缺乏融资渠道的小企业来说，小额贷款机构是重要的融资渠道，因而银行为全国几乎所有主要的小额信贷机构都给予了信贷支持。尤其在2012年，印度工业开发银行买入了总值5 000万印度卢比（98万美元）的农户贷款（farm loans），这是当时最大一笔资产证券化交易。印度工业开发银行将贷款汇聚到一起进行证券化，然后出售给投资者。Bandhan因此无需从银行借款就能为穷人提供现金流，从而改善了中小企业的融资条件（见图8.5）。

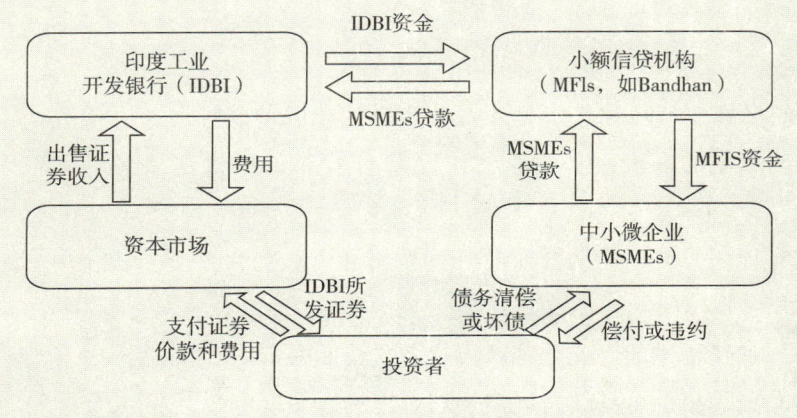

```
              IDBI资金
   ┌──────────┐ ⇄ ┌──────────────────┐
   │印度工业   │   │小额信贷机构      │
   │开发银行   │   │（MFIs，如Bandhan）│
   │（IDBI）   │   │                  │
   └──────────┘   └──────────────────┘
   出售证券 ↑↓ 费用   MSMEs贷款  ↑↓ MFIS资金
   ┌──────────┐        ┌──────────────┐
   │资本市场   │        │中小微企业    │
   │          │        │（MSMEs）     │
   └──────────┘        └──────────────┘
        ↑ IDBI所发证券   债务清偿或坏账 ↑↓ 偿付或违约
        │ 支付证券价款和费用
        └──────────┬──────────┘
              ┌─────────┐
              │ 投资者  │
              └─────────┘
```

图8.5 印度工业开发银行—小额信贷机构合作运营流程

当然，创新之路不会总是一帆风顺。根据印度Nirmal Bang证券公司为印度工业开发银行出具的报告，与上年同期相比，该行2015年第一季度净获得利率下降15%，利润额下降0.42%，这是刻意提高中小企业贷款在整体贷款业务中的比率的后果。

本质上，在为发展融资的诸多挑战面前，开发性金融机构适宜担当三大角色：长期规划制定者，市场培育者，以及聚合各方力量、促成政府与社会资本合作的组织协调者。本章的案例研究证明，尽管创新之路难免有曲折，但在推进转型进程方面仍有巨大潜力。

第九章 结论

我们身处变革的时代。对开发性金融需求的前瞻性分析，使我们清晰地看到日益凸显的三大趋势，这其中既孕育着崭新的机遇，又潜伏着未知的挑战：

（1）地区发展加速融合需要开发性引导资金为大型项目提供融资，并起到示范和引领作用。

（2）加速推进的工业化和城市化需要长期融资。

（3）成规模的可持续发展需要培育市场以实现有效融资。

为了化挑战为机遇，积极推动变革，开发性金融机构需要同时担当三大战略角色：

（1）积极开展富有战略视野的长期规划。

（2）积极依托政府信用建设市场信用。

（3）积极凝聚各方力量，促成政府与社会资本合作。

在全球开发性金融领域，有一种趋势越来越明显：近年来，受到金融危机的冲击，各国政府在推进一系列关键性战略目标上越来越倚重开发性金融机构，包括维持金融体系稳定、产业结构升级、技术创新、筹集中长期融资，以及培育前沿市场、推动经济向绿色增长模式转型。在私有化浪潮高涨的时代，有人曾预言，开发性金融机构终将黯然离场，如今，开发性金融广阔的发展前景使这种悲观论调不攻自破。

开发性金融机构的资金实力和影响力正在不断增强。推动开发性金融机构发挥更大作用，需要以互信与合作为首要原则。唯其如此，才能助推各国、各区域乃至全球各层面更广泛的合作共赢,推进创新发展。历史已经向我们昭示了互信与合作的必要性。20世纪70年代,世界各国都对本国开发性金融机构予以大力支持,各国开发性金融机构纷纷与他国竞争者攀比资金实力,谋求官方信用支持以提升信贷额,却忽视债务人、债权人的经济实力和政治风险。历史经验表明,如果各开发性金融机构间的激烈竞争失控,就很可能走向金融领域的"军备竞赛";在缺乏合作且都不遵守规则的情况下,很可能滑向"竞次"(race-to-bottom)的深渊。为了不重蹈历史的覆辙,我们有必要呼吁开发性金融机构之间加强互信与合作,这是达到良性竞争和共赢伙伴关系的必由之路,只有这样,才有可能充分释放开发性金融机构的巨大潜能,推进变革进程。

展望未来,各开发性金融机构间的合作可以在以下关键领域开展:

第一,在发展理念和实践的创新上鼓励相互学习。各国开发性金融机构的共同目标是在本国、本地区乃至全球范围促进可持续发展和包容性增长。各国开发性金融机构应当定期举办政策论坛,经常开展合作研究,彼此学习先进理念和实践经验,更好地应对重大发展挑战。

第二,在推进长期融资方面加强相互合作。长期融资是一种重要的金融工具,能起到稳定金融市场、缓解经济周期性震荡以及支持公共基础设施的作用。与转型相关的项目往往比较庞大复杂,需要在各种资金提供者间加强协调,合作增效。

第三,在制定和实施发展规划方面促进各方合作。规划工作是发展进程不可或缺的环节,有助于一个国家发现自身要素禀赋和比较优势,有助于根据具体情况有针对性地设计发展战略,也有助于减少盲目投资和重复建设。在发展规划领域提倡合作能增进规划的严谨性和可行性,在不同国家和地区间促进互联互通,为区域内和区域间多种形式的合作奠定良好基础。

第四,动员引导各方资金,建设工业园和跨境经济合作区,领跑技术革新和产业升级。开发性金融机构可以结合实施发展规划,为企业提供稳定而经济的融资,帮助它们在农业、制造业、能源行业、绿色投资、技术进步等方面开展创新活动。

第五，同样重要的是，在国际信用体系建设方面加强合作。各国开发性金融机构可以彼此学习怎样依托主权信用培育市场、建立社会信用体系，还可以通过合作提升风险识别、预警、防范和危机管理能力，创建交流合作机制，解决跨境风险和危机，增强国际金融体系化解风险的能力。

总之，该报告的首次公布，开启了开发性金融机构之间相互学习、相互合作的新篇章，这必将推进共赢伙伴关系的建设，为实现时代的变革目标创造条件。

机构名称简写

英文简写	中文全称
多边开发性金融机构	
WBG	世界银行集团
AsDB	亚洲开发银行
IADB	美洲开发银行
EDB	欧亚开发银行
AfDB	非洲开发银行
EBRD	欧洲复兴开发银行
Caribbean DB	加勒比开发银行
IsDB	伊斯兰开发银行
国别开发性金融机构	
KfW	德国复兴信贷银行
NRW. BANK	北莱茵威斯特法伦州银行
CDC	法国储蓄托管机构
DBJ	日本政策投资银行
KDB	韩国产业银行
DBM	蒙古开发银行
BPMB	马来西亚开发银行
DBP	菲律宾开发银行

英文简写	中文全称
国别开发性金融机构	
IDBI	印度工业开发银行
VEB	俄罗斯发展与对外经济事务银行
DBK	哈萨克斯坦开发银行
NBU	乌兹别克斯坦共和国国家对外经济活动银行
TSKB	土耳其工业发展银行
TCZB	土耳其农业银行
BNDES	巴西开发银行
BANDES	委内瑞拉经济社会发展银行
IDWBE	埃及工业发展与工人银行
DBSA	南非开发银行
有中国因素的开发性金融机构	
CDB	国家开发银行
AIIB	亚洲基础设施投资银行
NDB BRICS	金砖国家开发银行
Silk Road Fund	丝路基金

机构名称简写

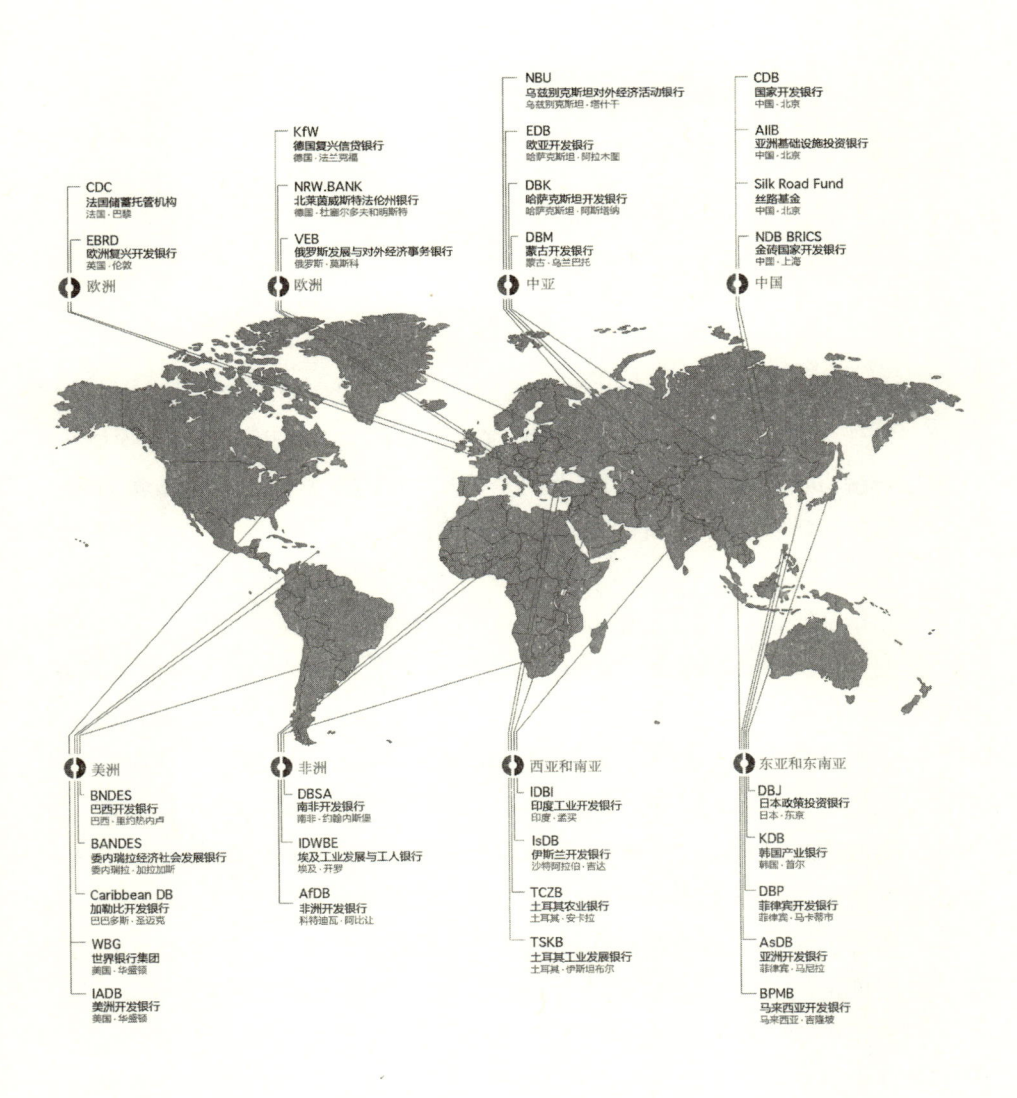

- **CDC** 法国储蓄托管机构 法国·巴黎
- **EBRD** 欧洲复兴开发银行 英国·伦敦

◆ 欧洲

- **KfW** 德国复兴信贷银行 德国·法兰克福
- **NRW.BANK** 北莱茵威斯特法伦州银行 德国·杜塞尔多夫和明斯特
- **VEB** 俄罗斯发展与对外经济事务银行 俄罗斯·莫斯科

◆ 欧洲

- **NBU** 乌兹别克斯坦对外经济活动银行 乌兹别克斯坦·塔什干
- **EDB** 欧亚开发银行 哈萨克斯坦·阿拉木图
- **DBK** 哈萨克斯坦开发银行 哈萨克斯坦·阿斯塔纳
- **DBM** 蒙古开发银行 蒙古·乌兰巴托

◆ 中亚

- **CDB** 国家开发银行 中国·北京
- **AIIB** 亚洲基础设施投资银行 中国·北京
- **Silk Road Fund** 丝路基金 中国·北京
- **NDB BRICS** 金砖国家开发银行 中国·上海

◆ 中国

◆ 美洲

- **BNDES** 巴西开发银行 巴西·里约热内卢
- **BANDES** 委内瑞拉经济社会发展银行 委内瑞拉·加拉加斯
- **Caribbean DB** 加勒比开发银行 巴巴多斯·圣迈克
- **WBG** 世界银行集团 美国·华盛顿
- **IADB** 美洲开发银行 美国·华盛顿

◆ 非洲

- **DBSA** 南非开发银行 南非·约翰内斯堡
- **IDWBE** 埃及工业发展与工人银行 埃及·开罗
- **AfDB** 非洲开发银行 科特迪瓦·阿比让

◆ 西亚和南亚

- **IDBI** 印度工业发展银行 印度·孟买
- **IsDB** 伊斯兰开发银行 沙特阿拉伯·吉达
- **TCZB** 土耳其农业银行 土耳其·安卡拉
- **TSKB** 土耳其工业发展银行 土耳其·伊斯坦布尔

◆ 东亚和东南亚

- **DBJ** 日本政策投资银行 日本·东京
- **KDB** 韩国产业银行 韩国·首尔
- **DBP** 菲律宾开发银行 菲律宾·马卡蒂市
- **AsDB** 亚洲开发银行 菲律宾·马尼拉
- **BPMB** 马来西亚开发银行 马来西亚·吉隆坡

209

致 谢

本报告由中国开发性金融促进会发起,与北京大学国家发展研究院共同编写,得到了国家开发银行、亚投行筹备组、丝路基金等机构的大力支持。

报告编写过程中,北京大学国家发展研究院的同学们承担起收集各开发性金融机构基础数据和资料的重任,他们是程圆佳、楚波、李哲、刘畅、蒋卓、金德弘、刘孟静、刘双城、吕筱萱、马诗琦、屈博雅、沙凡、宋美婧、王龙林、王晓雯、魏李萍、吴克谦、吴石磊、俞婕、钟泱、周雨思、周越等,赵普生老师对团队管理做了大量的细致工作;同时,国家开发银行的潘成龙、杨李梅、左玮、顾阳、尤伟、陈斐、吴良云、陈晓鹏、杨丽华、李百山,亚投行筹备组的孙雪,丝路基金的谢静、冯艳秋、周莹等同志对资料收集工作提供了大量的直接帮助。报告原文由英文写作,北京大学的宫宁、韩璇、侯国栋、李虹达、卢君言、任翊诚、王潘潘、唐诗晨、郑婕、邹静娴,中国开发性金融促进会的李杰丰、任继宁、沈炜、闫杰、唐芬、齐爽、陈迎彗、张榉成等同志担任了中文翻译和校对工作。在报告审核阶段,国家开发银行政策研究室副主任刘进、研究院副院长邹力行为完善报告提出了重要建议。

报告是集体智慧的结晶,融合了上述所有人员的创意和扎实工作,感谢他们展现出的专业精神和团队合作,感谢他们在面对开创性工作时迎战挑战的勇气,感谢他们对开发性金融国际合作的信念和为此做出的所有努力。

由于时间仓促和经验不足,报告难免有不当和错误之处,恳请读者批评指正。对报告中的任何问题,可以联系执笔人:

张帆:zhangfan@nsd.pku.edu.cn 徐佳君:jiajunxu@nsd.pku.edu.cn
王春来:hrb_wangchunlai@cdb.cn

Editorial Board

Director: CHEN Yuan
Deputy Director: HU Huaibang　ZHENG Zhijie
　　　　　　　　LI Jiping　YUAN Li　LIN Yifu
Chief Editors: XING Jun　YAO Yang
Editors: ZHANG Fan　XU Jiajun　WANG Qian
　　　　　JIN Baohua　WANG Chunlai

PREFACE

As this round-table conference on "Development Financing and Asian Development" opens at the Inaugural Annual Non-Governmental Organization Forum of the Conference on Interaction and Confidence Building Measures in Asia (CICA), I salute the formal release of "Global Development Financing Report 2015."

Global Development Financing Report 2015 is a ground-breaking and forward-looking report. It is of great significance for enhancing our knowledge of development financing and its trends. Development financing institutions originated from Europe two hundred years ago, with a long history. With official support, it has been booming since World War II and made great contributions to promoting national economic growth and sustainable development as well as to maintaining economic and financial security. According to rough estimates, the members of the World Federation of Development Financing Institutions (WFDFI) number as many as 328. They play a decisive role in the international financial system. Currently, global development requires that development financing play a more and more important role. Yet our knowledge about development financing is far from comprehensive, and our understanding of its working principles and main functions is insufficient. In this sense, this timely report is of great importance, for it sets out the overall pattern and future trends of development financing institutions.

Meanwhile, this report also provides a great opportunity for mutual exchange and learning. The major purpose of development financing is to help governments achieve their development targets. Through medium-/long-term financing backed by sovereign creditworthiness, development financing can leverage financial market operations to mitigate the bottlenecks in social and economic development and maintain financial stability. Due to differences in political institutions, legal systems, economic policies, and development missions and priorities, development financing institutions differ from each other in many aspects, such as operational models, practical experiences and specialized advantages. These diversities inspire innovations in international development financing. In order to jointly promote the healthy development of global development financing, all development financing institutions need to learn from each other. This report is a step towards mutual learning among development financing institutions.

Enhanced mutual trust and cooperation among development financing institutions have become more and more important, particularly as countries are increasingly inter-connected and interdependent with each other, as regional or inter-regional cooperation is booming, and as the construction of interconnections and intercommunications speeds up. Mutual trust and cooperation are the key pillar for both maintaining regional financial stability and financial security and enhancing the medium-/long-term momentum of economic development. Furthermore, mutual trust and cooperation among development financing institutions are the driving force behind constructive interactions and coordinated development among Asian economies—a community of common destiny. In the past twenty years, development financing institutions in China, represented by the China Development Bank, have provided Chinese experiences and wisdom in an effort to innovate development financing worldwide, by combining international experiences with China-specific circumstances at different development stages. Looking forward, development financing will experience further significant growth, because it will be increasingly emphasized by governments and demanded by capital markets. Meanwhile, the inconsistency of national market rules and incompleteness of market systems call for more integrated cooperation among development financing institutions, in order to jointly incubate markets, respond to risks and challenges, and shape the future. This is the goal pursued by the report, and the ultimate driving force for carrying on further research.

I sincerely hope that all development financing institutions will make new contributions to promoting global sustainable development and improving human well-being.

Vice Chairman of the National
Committee of Chinese People's Political Consultative Conference

Chairman of China Association for the Promotion
of Development Financing

Part One   Overview of Development Financing

In order to catch the new opportunity for transformation via a new wave of green growth, industrialization and urbanization, and to meet the demands of the Sustainable Development Goals (SDGs), the world is calling for the acceleration of large-scale, long-term and sustained development financing. Chapter 1 introduces the demand and supply of development financing and the strategic role of development financing institutions. DFIs throughout the world have adopted diverse forms with different sizes, targets, functions, and business models. Chapter 2 – 5 present an overview of the world's major DFIs, categorizing them by function and geographical area and dividing them into four groups: multilateral DFIs, national DFIs in high-income countries, national DFIs in medium-/low-income countries, and China-related DFIs. Chapter 6 examines three associations of DFIs. In total, the report selects 30 DFIs. It provides a general description of the establishment, mission, ownership and funding, business model and financial products of each of them. We collect the most updated data available from various sources, such as the institutions' official websites and annual reports, and news reports.

Although we attempt to make the case selection as representative as possible, the list here is not intended to be exhaustive. To strike a proper balance between width and depth, we select DFIs that are significantly important with respect to their size, impacts, and/or innovations in operational models. In addition, because the present report is designed to serve as a background paper for a roundtable discussion at the fifth summit of the Conference on Interaction and Confidence Building Measures in Asia (CICA), we select a larger number of Asian DFIs than DFIs in other regions. In brief, there is no intentional bias against any type of DFI or jurisdiction.

Part one Overview of Development Financing

Chapter 1   Introduction[*]

The world is facing a historic opportunity for transformation *via* a new wave of green growth, industrialization and urbanization at an unprecedented scale and pace. This transformative agenda calls for the acceleration of large-scale and long-term development financing on a sustainable basis.

Development finance encompasses a wide range of financial instruments from both public and private sources, including domestic resource mobilization and international finance. The path forward for development finance is now widely held to involve the use of official support for "leveraging" or "catalyzing" vast amounts of finance to meet the demands of the Sustainable Development Goals (SDGs) — a universal development agenda that includes three pillars of economic, social and environmental development to be endorsed by United Nations member states in September 2015.

This report aims to map the strategic role of development banks in addressing the compelling challenge of financing a transformative development agenda.

A Forward-Looking Analysis of Development Financing Needs

Three future major trends in global development entail vast demands for long-term transformative investments. The first major trend is that the deepening regional inte-

---

[*]   The lead authors of the report is ZHANG Fan, XU Jiajun and WANG Chunlai.

gration demands catalytic and development financing to initiate transformative projects. The second major trend is that accelerating industrialization and urbanization calls for long-term finance. Finally, the third major trend is that the scalable sustainable development financing entails market incubation.

Deepening Regional Integration Demands Catalytic and Demonstration Financing

Regional integration is deepening in the 21st century in line with a trend towards a multipolar world, economic globalization, cultural diversity and greater IT application. In the aftermath of the international financial crisis, an open regional cooperation is pivotal to upholding the global free trade regime and the open world economy. In economic terms, regional integration is aimed at promoting orderly and free flow of economic factors, highly efficient allocation of resources and deep integration of markets.

Inspired by the ancient "Silk Road Spirit" — "peace and cooperation, openness and inclusiveness, mutual learning and mutual benefit", the Chinese government has drafted and published the *Vision and Actions on Jointly Building Silk Road Economic Belt and 21st Century Maritime Silk Road* in March 2015. The Belt and Road Initiative is "a systematic project," which aims to "promote the connectivity of Asian, European and African continents and their adjacent seas, establish and strengthen partnerships among the countries along the Belt and Road, set up all-dimensional, multi-tiered and composite connectivity networks, and realize diversified, independent, balanced and sustainable development in these countries."

Driven by the same spirit, the Asia-Pacific Economic Cooperation (APEC) leaders endorsed the "Beijing Agenda for an Integrated, Innovative and Interconnected Asia-Pacific" in November 2014. This Agenda is aimed at "advancing regional economic integration, promoting innovative development, economic reform and growth, and strengthening comprehensive connectivity and infrastructure development with a view to expanding and deepening Asia-Pacific regional economic cooperation, and attaining peace, stability, development and common prosperity of the Asia-Pacific."

Aligned with the goal of further strengthening regional integration, the 2015 Boao Forum for Asia launched "the Year of China-Association of Southeast Asian Nations (ASEAN) Maritime Cooperation" to jointly building the 21st Century Maritime Silk Road by deepening mutual trust and enhancing connectivity between China and Southeast Asian countries. China has already carried out a variety of ocean-related cooperation with Indonesia, Thailand, Malaysia, India and Sri Lanka while steadily pushing multiple projects supported by the China-ASEAN Maritime Cooperation Fund and the China-Indonesia Maritime Cooperation Fund.

Most recently, China and Russia issued a "Joint Declaration on the Connection between China's Silk Road Economic Belt Initiative and Russia's Trans-Eurasia Continent Strategies" on May 8, 2015. Both sides agreed to enhance trade and investment facilitation, strengthen the connectivity in logistics, infrastructure, and production networks, and working together to build industrial parks and cross-border economic cooperation zones.

Beyond Asia and Europe, Africa is accelerating its pace of regional integration. The African Development Bank has formulated the *Regional Integration Strategy Paper*. Cross-border infrastructure is under construction. Recently the African Union envisages a Continental Free Trade Area (CFTA) to be launched in 2017. It aims to create a single market for Africa so that one billion African people, goods, services and skills will move freely, creating a larger, vibrant economic space for trade and investment.

The above deepening regional integration has opened up new cooperation areas including infrastructure connectivity, industrial investment, resource development, economic and trade cooperation, financial cooperation. First, cross-border infrastructure construction entails large-scale long-term finance. Second, building industrial parks and cross-border economic cooperation zones help to promote industrial cluster development across and beyond the region. Third, financial cooperation is an important underpinning for implementing regional integration. Building international creditworthiness systems is crucial to improving the system of risk response and crisis management, establishing a regional financial risk early-warning system, and creating an exchange and cooperation mechanism of addressing cross-border risks and crisis.

Promoting the new cooperation areas is often beyond the reach of commercial capital, since private investors make decisions based on short-term risk-return calculation. Hence, commercial capital is hesitant to participate in large-scale and complex cross-border projects.

Therefore, accelerating the pace of regional integration demands large-scale and long-term financing in order to initiate key strategic projects. Successful initiatives can demonstrate the value of transformative investments so as to catalyze more commercial investments.

Accelerating Industrialization and Urbanization Calls for Long-Term Finance

Driven by the rising tides of industrialization and urbanization, the world is confronting considerable demands for long-term finance. The pace of industrialization is accelerating, thus heightening the need for long-term finance to increase productivity, upgrade industrial structures and climb up along the global value chains. In parallel, a new wave of urbanization is generating growing demand for sustainable and resilient urban infrastructure and social services. In emerging economies, the number of people living in cities is expected to double by 2030 (relative to the 2000 level), adding 2 billion more people. This mass urban migration entails increased demand for basic services such as water, power and transport. A substantial long-term financing gap represents a stumbling block to achieving the transformation agenda. World Bank research shows that a 10% increase in infrastructure investment generates a 1% increase in GDP. Thus, bridging the long-term financing gap is critical for growth, job creation, industrial upgrading and economic transformation.

For example, the estimated financing gap in infrastructure investment is vast. The OECD "Infrastructure to 2030" report concluded that the global infrastructure investment needs across the land transport, telecommunications, electricity, water and sanitation sectors could amount to an estimated USD 53 trillion through 2030. The annual investment requirement would equal approximately 2.5% of world GDP. According to the *Infrastructure Investment Policy Blueprint* published by the World Economic Forum, the estimated shortfall in global infrastructure debt and equity investment is at least USD 1 trillion per year. Asia is confronting particularly extensive infrastructure investment needs. The Asian Development Bank estimates that Asia will need to invest approximately USD 8 trillion in overall national infrastructure for energy, transport, telecommunications, water and sanitation during the 2010 – 2020 period.

Several demanding challenges arise in mobilizing and sustaining long-term finance. First, the long-term investment is vulnerable to cyclical financial crises. During periods of financial distress, the world economy suffers from contraction in international long-term credit flows. Hence, finance providers that act as "shock absorbers" are important contributors to financial stability. For example, World Bank research shows that development financing institutions (DFIs) have assumed "a counter-cyclical role" by scaling up their lending operations precisely when private banks experienced temporary difficulties in granting credit to the private sector. Second, a severe lack of bankable projects has greatly constrained the flow of long-term finance. Hence, improving the capacity for project design and implementation on the ground is crucial. Finally, the driving force for a nation's medium-and-long-term growth is key to sustaining long-term finance. Long-term finance is often closely linked with the dynamics of the real economy. Hence, strategies to identify and facilitate growth are indispensable to promoting industrial upgrading and structural change to create a two-way positive link between long-term finance and sustained growth.

The crux of the massive deficit in long-term finance lies not in the shortage of capital but rather in the lack of effective financial intermediaries that are able to channel capital to complex, longer-term and riskier investments. According to World Bank research, long-term investment financing channels are underdeveloped. Current instruments, institutions and policies must be reformed to allow for the volume of long-term financing necessary to maintain growth. Therefore, stronger bridges between global savings and long-term investment are crucial.

Sustainable Development Financing of Scale Entails Market Incubation

The Sustainable Development Goals (SDGs) encompass three pillars of economic, social and environmental development—a universal development agenda to be endorsed by United Nations member states in September 2015. The path forward for sustainable development financing is now widely held to involve the use of official support for scaling up vast amounts of finance to realize a transformation agenda. This transformation agenda demands a proactive role of the state in incubating frontier markets.

First, sustainable economic growth entails renewed technological innovation and industrial upgrading to foster new driving forces for the medium-/long-term economic development. Industrial policies for economic transformation go well beyond received ideas of protecting infant industries, to cover skills, finance, infrastructure and political economy, in the context of the new global landscape of value chains. A new type of industrial policies needs to proactively generate the technological learning processes that are the core driver for moving up the value chain. Fostering an enterprise sector that can create and capture value is indeed the heart of the catch-up development process. Indeed, many transformative technologies of today have their origins in publically funded research activities. In short, an entrepreneurial state is the key to economic transformation.

An entrepreneurial state is particularly important for economic take-off in transforming low-income countries (LICs). After a decade of steady economic growth, the number of LICs declined dramatically from 63 in 2000 to 34 at the present time. This wave of graduation is expected to continue in the foreseeable future. Yet as this growing tide of LICs begins to emerge from low-income status, they are likely to fall between the two stools of ODA and private market financing. These countries will no longer be eligible for soft loans and grants from multilateral aid agencies. However, they have yet to secure reliable access to global capital markets. This predicted shortage of financing stands in stark contrast to the tremendous demand for investment generated by transforming LICs as they increase their rate of industrialization and urbanization. Hence, the compelling challenge ahead concerns how to help transforming LICs to incubate markets in order to bridge their transition to reliable and substantial market access to enable them to achieve leapfrog economic transformation.

Second, social development demands the provision of public goods, which cannot be provided by private sectors alone. Public goods have positive externalities so that their benefits do not exclusively accrue to providers alone. As a result, profit-oriented private sectors may lack incentives to provide public services such as education, health, poverty reduction and housing for low-income households. In other words, the market for public goods provision are often underdeveloped.

The undersupply of public services can lead to severe repercussions. Social inequality can result in instability and even conflicts. Low-quality education and health can hinder the accumulation of human capital, undermining equal opportunities to pursue a decent life. These problems will be exacerbated as a new wave of urbanization heightened the demand for the provision of public services on a much greater scale.

Hence, mobilizing development finance to provide public goods is pivotal to social stability, high-quality social welfare and long-run economic growth.

Third, green growth is of paramount importance, as unsustainable production would threaten public health, trigger a cascade of cataclysmic environmental degradation and ultimately undermine long-term growth and social welfare. Green growth has been prominent on the agendas of high-level international forums and national development strategies. The OECD established the Green Growth and Sustainable Development Forum to foster green growth in OECD and partner countries. China's rapid industrialization, intensified agricultural production and urbanization have heightened its commitment to achieving a green economy, as embodied in the 12th Five-Year Plan (2011 – 2015). Achieving green growth entails comprehensive efforts in a wide range of areas, including sustainable agriculture, industrial upgrading, innovations in renewable energies and sustainable infrastructure.

The transition to the green growth path demands scalable green investments that often extend beyond the initial reach of the private sector. For instance, the International Energy Agency (IEA) estimates that an additional USD 1.1 trillion in average annual low-carbon investments will be necessary between 2011 and 2050 in the energy sector alone. Investing in uncharted renewable energies often entails high risks at an early stage, which makes it difficult to reap profits in the short term. Private agents follow an investment logic in which profit maximization and risk minimization largely determine their decision-making processes. Active private participation is feasible only when risk-return fundamentals reach a tipping point at which technological breakthroughs reduce costs and thereby enable large-scale production.

In brief, scaling up sustainable development financing requires states to play a proactive role in incubating frontier markets. Given the short time horizon and the risk aversion of private sector actors, it is crucial for the public sector to help to unleash business opportunities by mitigating risks and building investor confidence in incubating frontier markets.

In summary, a transformation agenda ahead demands large-scale and transformative development financing in order to better harness the three major trends as a positive force. A forward-looking analysis of development financing needs highlights the following potential opportunities and challenges: (a) deepening regional integration demands catalytic and demonstrative financing to initiate transformative projects; (b) accelerating industrialization and urbanization calls for long-term finance; and (c) scalable sustainable development financing entails market incubation.

Large-Scale and Long-Term Development Financing Is in Short Supply

Despite the massive demand analyzed above, long-term transformative investments are in short supply. Below is a brief explanation of why official development assistance and private capital have been unable to provide as much long-term development finance as needed.

Official Development Assistance Is Small and Piecemeal

Development finance is often associated with ODA, which is funded by taxpayers in wealthy countries and disbursed to poor countries. The aid policies of major donor countries are coordinated by the OECD's Development Assistance Committee (DAC).

The scale of ODA is too small to meet the vast demand for funding by itself. In 2013, gross disbursements of ODA amounted to approximately USD 150 billion. Even if DAC donors are able to honor their commitments of providing 0.7% of their GNI as ODA—an international reference point for aid commitment endorsed by most developed countries (except the US) at the United Nations in 1970 and repeatedly re-endorsed at the highest level at international aid and development conferences—reaching this target would require an amount on the order of USD 400 billion. Hence, even such an ODA effort would fall considerably short of the external financing required to support the infrastructure involved in the urbanization and green growth agendas that are central to transformative growth.

Furthermore, the current international aid system has not been successfully geared toward generating large-scale, long-term transformative investments as a result of a set of pathologies. First, aid agencies confront the need to meet short-term performance targets. Second, aid agencies suffer from disincentives to foster the mindsets and mandates to engage in scaling up projects and building systemic capacities. Finally and fundamentally, the development model in vogue over the last three decades has downplayed the role of the state as a creator of economic landscapes and as a coordinator of interlinked investments.

In brief, ODA is too meager to meet the demand for large-scale development finance and too piecemeal to achieve a long-term vision for transformation.

Private Capital Markets Are Afflicted with Short-Termism

The prevailing short-termism in capital markets means that their supply of long-term financing falls short of investment demands. Recent history shows that private capital has not automatically flown into developing countries to finance their infrastructure projects. The myth of private markets in the 1990s led to the belief that private investors would usher in infrastructure investment. However, this expectation was not fulfilled: With the dwindling of official support, private capital did not flow in as expected. Misperceptions of risks create the first-mover problem on the ground (Roland Berger, 2012).

To address the inherent problem of prevailing short-termism in private capital markets, intensive efforts have been made to unleash the potential of institutional investors to provide long-term finance. Institutional investors such as pension funds, insurers and sovereign wealth funds typically have long-term liabilities and are thus expected to have a long-term investment horizon. Launched in February 2012, the OECD project involving institutional investors and long-term investment is a case in point. The OECD prepared the *High-Level Principles of Long-Term Investment Financing by Institutional Investors* endorsed by G20 leaders in September 2013. Subsequently, approaches to implement these principles have been identified. Despite the tremendous potential possessed by institutional investors, interventions by target governments are believed to be indispensable in effectively using policy levers and risk mitigants to surmount barriers to investment.

In brief, the prevailing short-termism in private capital markets hinders the flow of long-term finance.

The Strategic Role of Development Financing Institutions

DFIs are strategically positioned to fill the vast gap in long-term transformative investments. This section begins with a working definition of DFIs and then elaborates on their three strategic roles in promoting long-term transformative investments.

What Are Development Financing Institutions?

DFIs are financial institutions that rely on sovereign creditworthiness and deploy market mechanisms in an effort to achieve the public mandates or strategic objectives of a given national state or a group of national states. DFIs can be national, regional or global, depending on the number of countries involved and their geographical distribution.

DFIs differ from traditional policy banks in the following respects:

First, traditional banks primarily depend on governmental transfers or subsidies, paying little attention to their own performance. By comparison, DFIs emphasize asset quality, risk management and financial sustainability and diversity of their funding sources, including bonds issued on capital markets, deposits from the public, paid-in capital and contributions from governments, and borrowing from or co-financing with other financial institutions.

Second, traditional policy banks rely on administrative command to allocate resources and are financially dependent on the government to subsidize their operations. By contrast, DFIs typically exercise considerable discretion in using market mechanisms to attain the goals of public (or international development) policies.

Finally, DFIs are more effective in generating scalable, sustainable and high-impact operational outcomes than traditional policy banks are. Hence, DFIs are more proactive in promoting public mandates and strategic objectives.

In essence, despite their shared common goal of materializing public mandates, DFIs have outperformed traditional policy banks with respect to risk management, financial sustainability, and the creation of scalable and high-impact development outcomes.

DFIs are also distinct from commercial banks in the following ways:

First, regarding corporate goals, commercial banks seek to maximize profits and shareholder interests, whereas DFIs primarily seek to comply with the public mandates and strategic objectives of their governments. Hence, commercial banks follow the principles of safety, liquidity and profitability, whereas DFIs desire only to break even or make marginal profits to achieve their own sustainable operations while achieving public goals.

Second, regarding financial instruments, commercial banks primarily provide retail and short-term financing that is constrained by maturity mismatch. By contrast, because DFIs rely on sovereign creditworthiness to raise bonds on capital markets, they are effective in providing long-term and large-scale financing to support infrastructure, core industries, public projects, and international development cooperation.

Finally, regarding their role in the market, commercial banks focus on expanding their market shares in a mature market environment; thus, they are reluctant or unable to fill the financing gap when it is difficult to make profits within a relatively short time horizon, such as in cases of slum renovations. By contrast, DFIs fill the gap in cases of market failure and create market creditworthiness and institutions to provide a foundation for private participation.

Three Strategic Roles of DFIs

The primary role of DFIs is to mobilize medium-/long-term finance in an effort to achieve economic and social development in a sustainable way. This role is of significant importance given the prevailing short-termism in capital markets. This section builds on the fundamental role of mobilizing medium-/long-term finance to explore three understudied strategic roles of DFIs in realizing a transformation agenda.

Conventionally, the role of DFIs is confined to redressing market failures. In areas where profits are too meager to attract private capital, DFIs can provide financing to improve social welfare, including health and education investment.

However, the perspective above neglects three important strategic roles that DFIs can play in realizing a transformative development agenda. These strategic roles include long-term planning, market incubation and convening power to facilitate public-private cooperation.

Long-Term Planning

A comprehensive long-term plan is crucial to achieving leapfrog development. The starting point is a grand vision that aims to achieve long-term strategic development goals. Such a vision is particularly important for developing countries because it can unleash the tremendous potential of the latecomer advantage to catch up with advanced economies. Targeted planning can also help to identify and resolve bottlenecks in the areas of resources, technology, and institutions. Removing these bottlenecks is critical to scaling up, industrial and technological upgrading, and leapfrog development. Furthermore, institutionalized planning can help to mitigate the abuse of political power and to ensure rigorous implementation of a comprehensive long-term plan. Finally, good planning must maintain pace with change by adapting strategies and approaches to meet new challenges.

DFIs can be knowledge banks endowed with strong expertise in comprehensive and long-term planning. DFIs can work with governments at different levels to establish long-term development goals, to identify major bottlenecks and to develop a wide range of innovative strategies for implementing development plans. From this perspective, DFIs are not simply sources of development financing but also providers of highly specialized knowledge.

Given the tremendous number of catching-up developing countries, long-term planning has become much more significant. The transformation process involves shifting from a largely traditional economy with relatively low productivity to a largely modern economy with relatively high productivity. Today, the transformation process is operating at a historically fast pace, taking only a generation. Unleashing the latecomer advantage demands that the public sector assume a proactive role in creating necessary "soft" and "hard" infrastructure to enable economic takeoff. The Asian economic miracles are a prime example, as exemplified by the Asian "Four Dragons" (Korea, Taiwan, Hong Kong, and Singapore) since the 1970s and, more recently, by China. Economic transformation is now high on the agenda in Africa, where more than three-quarters of LICs are currently located. The African Union Transformation Plan targets the year 2063 for achieving middle-income status for the entire continent. Planning under a grand vision is crucial to marshaling public resources in concert with private resources to fulfill this vision.

Yet it is worth noting that state capacity is the key to effective long-term planning. While a grand vision can unleash the tremendous potential of the latecomer advantage to catch up with advanced economies, capable states are a precondition for garnering the national support for this shared vision. In reality, fragile states have the "weak capacity to carry out basic governance functions," and lack "the ability to develop mutually constructive relations with society." In fragile situations, if the legitimacy of governments is under question, it is unreasonable to expect that there governments can establish a shared vision and formulate the long-term planning necessary to achieve it.

In brief, DFIs can offer expertise to assist governments, especially those in catching-up developing economies, in developing comprehensive long-term planning to achieve leapfrog development.

Market Incubation

A binding constraint in developing countries is that the market is underdeveloped, flawed, or even nonexistent. This constraint would severely hinder the pace of the transformation agenda. Large-scale transformation investments often entail an order of unprecedented complexity and magnitude with a long-term horizon. Transformative investments are usually perceived as technically or structurally risky; hence, they are often beyond the reach of private players, whose range of action is typically constrained by short-or-medium-term performance criteria. This problem is particularly severe when the market remains at an embryonic or even dormant stage in many developing countries. Hence, developing countries need to build markets in a proactive manner in order to lay the foundation for transformative investments.

At the core of market incubation is to cultivate creditworthiness. Because of the lack of proven track record, risk is often excessively overestimated in developing countries. Such errors in risk assessment lead to the first-mover problem, in which few investors are willing or able to assume risks and to bear the losses of failure in experimentation. Thus, creating conditions that enable takeoff and scaling-up value creation is crucial to overcoming *diffidence* and *inaction*.

For developing countries, sovereign creditworthiness is valuable reputation capital, enabling them to play a proactive role in building up market and social creditworthiness. DFIs rely on sovereign creditworthiness and deploy market mechanisms in an effort to initiate and scale up transformative investments. DFIs can act as first-movers in assuming risks, overcoming misperceptions or even disillusionment, and developing investor confidence to leverage private financing. Such pioneering efforts can help to move beyond commercial banking to incubate markets by improving the credit standing of borrowers and the governance structure of project companies and by designing different models of market participation.

In summary, DFIs are strategically positioned to drive forward the green investment, to develop investor confidence and to incubate the market for large-scale sustainable transformative investments.

Convening Power in Creating Public-Private Synergies

DFIs serve as a bridge between the public and private sectors. DFIs are quasi-public corporations, as their aim is to achieve the public mandates and strategic objectives defined by governments, and they typically rely on sovereign creditworthiness to raise capital in the capital markets at a relatively lower cost. Moreover, DFIs primarily follow the market principles of risk management, project management and financial performance. Because of their dual identities, DFIs have the credibility to establish productive working relationships with both the public and private sectors. Hence, DFIs are ideal candidates to forge synergies between the public and private sectors.

Creating public-private synergies is indispensable in mobilizing long-term finance. For example, consider infrastructure investment: no single institution can undertake such investment on its own because of the diverse risks at the various stages of the investment cycle. DFIs can provide a platform that provides governments, multilateral development banks, private sector investors and financiers with opportunities to collaborate. Such collaboration can not only help to utilize a wide range of financial instruments encompassing (but not limited to) grants, loans, equity, guarantee, and insurance but also contribute to a knowledge-sharing platform to bring together diverse expertise.

In summary, at the interface between the public and private sectors, DFIs are well positioned to forge partnerships among different finance providers in an effort to address complex long-term investments.

Roadmap for the Report

The present report proceeds as follows: Chapter 2 – 5 introduce selected multilateral, national and China-related DFIs by tracing their history, presenting basic information on their operation, and highlighting their most recent and significant projects and innovations. Chapter 6 introduces associations that aim to foster peer learning and cooperation among DFIs. Chapter 7 examines the patterns of selected DFIs in terms of ownership, size, funding sources, asset quality and other features. Chapter 8 explores case studies with a particular focus on how DFIs address major development challenges by engaging in long-term planning to achieve leapfrog development, by taking advantage of sovereign creditworthiness to incubate markets, and by utilizing convening power to create public-private synergies. Chapter 9 concludes by presenting a positive agenda for harnessing the growing financial power of DFIs as a positive force and for promoting trust and cooperation among DFIs.

Chapter 2   Multilateral DFIs

Multilateral development banks (MDBs) are development banks that have been established by multiple nations and hence are subject to international law, but not subject to any particular sovereign jurisdiction. Their owners or shareholders are generally national governments, although other international institutions and organizations occasionally serve as shareholders. The typical missions of MDBs are to reduce the level of poverty in the world or in a large geographical area. These institutions provide low-interest credits to support a wide array of investments, most of which are long-term investments. Currently, the best-known MDBs are the World Bank and regional MDBs with continental scope, most of which were established after World War II to assist the reconstruction of the world economy and to provide mechanisms for international cooperation on long-term development.

The World Bank Group (WBG)

General Information

The World Bank is a United Nations international financial institution that provides loans to developing countries for capital programs. The World Bank is part of the World Bank Group and a member of the United Nations Development Group. The World Bank Group consists of five international organizations: the International Bank for Reconstruction and Development (IBRD), the International Development Association (IDA), the International Finance Corporation (IFC), the Multilateral Investment Guarantee Agency (MIGA), and the International Centre for Settlement of Investment Disputes (ICSID). The current president of the World Bank Group is Jim Yong Kim. The World Bank was created at the 1944 Bretton Woods Conference, along with three other international institutions located in Washington, D.C., in the United States, with 131 representative branches in the world and 17,139 employees at the end of 2014. In 2010, based on the contributions of the member countries, voting powers at the World Bank were revised to increase the voice of developing countries. The countries with the most voting power are currently the U.S. (15.85%), Japan (6.84%), China (4.42%), Germany (4.00%), the U.K. (3.75%), France (3.75%), India (2.91%), Russia (2.77%), Saudi Arabia (2.77%) and Italy (2.64%).

Mission and Strategy

The official goal of the World Bank is to reduce poverty. The World Bank Group has established two goals for the world to achieve by 2030: (i) to end extreme poverty by decreasing the percentage of people living on less than USD 1.25 a day to no more than 3%, with an intermediate target of reducing the percentage of extremely poor people to 9% before 2020, and (ii) to promote shared prosperity by fostering income growth of the bottom 40% people in every country. To realize these goals, the World Bank is undertaking a large-scale institutional readjustment emphasizing cooperation with the IBRD, IDA, IFC, MIGA and ICSID.

Ownership and Governance

The World Bank is owned by its member countries and regions. The IBRD has 188 member countries and regions, and the IDA has 172 members. These member countries and regions, or shareholders, are represented by a Board of Governors, which is the ultimate decision maker at the World Bank. Generally, the governors are member countries' and regions' ministers of finance or ministers of development. The governors meet once per year at the Annual Meetings of the Boards of Governors of the World Bank Group and the International Monetary Fund. The governors delegate specific duties to 25 executive directors who work on-site at the World Bank. The Board of Directors consists of the World Bank Group president and 25 executive directors. The five largest shareholders (the U. S., Japan, China, Germany, and the U. K.) appoint an executive director, while other member countries and regions are represented by elected executive directors. The Board of Directors elects the president every two years. The president of the World Bank is the president of the entire World Bank Group. The president is responsible for chairing the meetings of the Board of Directors and for overall management of the bank. The Board of Directors is responsible for daily operations of the Bank and policy making.

Funding Sources

The World Bank's funds come from four major sources: member countries' paid-in capital, funds raised in international financial markets, grants from member countries, and business revenues. The IBRD issues bonds in international capital markets and provides loans, guarantees and other risk management products, as well as technical assistance for economic reform projects and programs in middle-income countries and creditworthy LICs. In fiscal year 2014, the World Bank raised the equivalent of USD 51,000 million by issuing bonds in 22 currencies. The IBRD's standing in the capital markets and its financial strength allowed it to borrow these large volumes on highly favorable terms despite volatile market conditions. The IBRD's financial strength is based on its robust capital position and shareholder support as well as on prudent financial policies and practices that help to maintain its triple-A credit rating. The IBRD's equity primarily comprises paid-in capital and reserves. Under the terms of the general and selective capital increase resolutions approved by the Board of Governors on March 16, 2011, subscribed capital is expected to increase by USD 87,000 million, of which USD 5,100 million will be paid over a five-year period. In fiscal year 2014, the IBRD's subscribed capital totaled USD 232 million, its usable paid-in capital reached USD 14 million and the equity-to-loans ratio was 25.7%. As of June 30, 2014, the cumulative increase in subscribed capital totaled USD 42,600 million, in which the paid-in amounts were USD 2,500 million. The IDA is largely financed by contributions from partner governments. Additional financing is obtained from transfers from the IBRD's net income, grants from the IFC, and borrowers' repayments of earlier IDA credits. During the Sixteenth IDA Replenishment (IDA16), which covered fiscal year 2012 – 14, total resources, which reflected updates subsequent to the replenishment discussions, amounted to 33,800 million in special drawing rights (SDR) (equivalent to USD 50,800 million).

Operational Data

In fiscal year 2014, total assets reached USD 358,883 million, and total equity reached USD 40,467 million. Each year, the IBRD earns income from the return on its equity and from the small margin that it makes on lending. This income pays for the IBRD's operating expenses and provides for an annual transfer of funds to the IDA, the fund for the poorest countries. The IBRD had a net loss of USD 978 million in fiscal year 2014. The World Bank Group committed USD 65,600 million in loans, grants, equity investments, and guarantees to its members and private businesses. Commitments from the IBRD totaled USD 18,600 million, while the IDA made commitments of USD 22,240 million for the poorest countries. The IFC provided more than USD 22,000 million in financing for private sector development, approximately USD 5,000 million of which was mobilized from investment partners. The MIGA issued USD 3,200 million in political risk and credit enhancement guarantees to support investments, including those in transformational projects. Standard & Poor's rated the World Bank AAA, and Moody's issued a rating of Aaa.

Business Models and Products

The World Bank engages in wholesale and retail lending. The China-Large City Congestion and Carbon Reduction Project is an example of the World Bank's wholesale project, which is intended to help establish a policy framework to alleviate traffic congestion and reduce greenhouse gas emissions in large cities in China, primarily through public transport development and travel demand management. Two major business models are used to allocate funds: issuing loans and providing grants. The World Bank Group provides low-interest loans, zero-to-low-interest credits and grants to developing countries. This assistance supports a wide array of investments in such areas as education, health, public administration, infrastructure, financial and private sector development, agriculture, and environmental and natural resource management. In particular, 22% of the IBRD and IDA loans are invested in public administration, and justice; 17% in transportation; and 16% in energy and mining. Some projects are co-financed with governments, other multilateral institutions, commercial banks, export credit agencies and private sector investors.

The primary target regions for IBRD investment are Europe and the Middle East, Latin America, East Asia and Pacific regions, whereas the IDA covers the Africa, South Asia, East Asia and Pacific regions. The World Bank Group also provides or facilitates financing through trust fund partnerships with bilateral and multilateral donors. Many partners have asked the World Bank to help manage initiatives that address needs across a wide range of sectors and developing regions. Grantmaking is another important task of the World Bank group through the IDA. The IBRD also supplies financial derivatives to customers. In addition, the World Bank Group offers support to developing countries in the form of policy advice, research and analysis, and technical assistance.

Box 2 – 1 Forging Synergies within the World Bank Group to Undertake Transformative Projects

To increase the pool and types of funding available to developing countries, particularly for transformative projects, the World Bank has adopted a new approach geared toward leveraging the financial resources and instruments of the entire World Bank Group to create synergies among the IBRD, IDA, IFC, and MIGA.

One innovation is that the Bank Group's political risk insurance arm, the Multilateral Investment Guarantee Agency (MIGA), is entering into an innovative MIGA/IBRD exposure exchange agreement to improve the diversification of each organization's portfolios, thereby creating the capacity to support additional business. One early example of collaboration is an innovative exposure swap between IBRD and MIGA of up to USD 100 million of principal that will enable each institution to conduct more business in Brazil and Panama. MIGA's mission is to avoid the political risk of investors' direct investment in developing countries as well as to provide guidance and advice, share investment information through online information services, and better settle disputes between government and investors. MIGA guarantee the effectiveness of loans from IBRD and other World Bank Group members by eliminating the potential political risk of investing in the country. In 2014, MIGA was planning to increase its new guarantee extension by nearly 50% over the next four years.

The IBRD/IDA, IFC and MIGA teams have gathered to discuss joint initiatives to design and implement high-impact transformative projects: "A truly successful partnership would be a result of the teams being honest, candid and real. Building and leveraging on each other's strengths will be key."

The Asian Development Bank (AsDB)

General Information

The Asian Development Bank (AsDB) was established in 1966 under the Agreement on Establishing the Asian Development Bank. Currently, the AsDB has 67 members, 48 of which come from the Asia and Pacific region. The bank headquarters is in Manila, the Philippines. The largest shareholders of the AsDB are Japan (15.7%), the U.S. (15.6%), the People's Republic of China (6.5%), India (6.4%) and Australia (5.8%). The AsDB is headquartered in Manila, the Philippines, and has offices worldwide, including representative offices in North America (Washington, D.C.), Europe (Frankfurt) and Japan (Tokyo). As of December 31, 2014, the AsDB's staff totaled 3,051 from 61 of its 67 members.

The highest policy-making body of the bank is the Board of Governors, which is composed of one representative from each member state. The Board of Governors in turn elects 12 members from its own Governors to compose the Board of Directors and their deputies. Eight of the 12 members come from regional (Asia-Pacific) members, and the others come from non-regional members. The Board of Governors also elects the bank's president, who is the chairperson of the Board of Directors and manages the AsDB. The president has a five-year term of office and may be reelected. Traditionally, because Japan is one of the bank's largest shareholders, the president has always been a Japanese. The current president is Takehiko Nakao, who succeeded Haruhiko Kuroda in 2013. The AsDB has permanent delegations in 11 Asian cities and representative offices in Tokyo, Washington, D.C., and Frankfurt.

Mission and Strategy

The AsDB's vision is "an Asia and Pacific region free of poverty." Its mission is to help its developing member countries reduce poverty and improve living conditions and quality of life. The AsDB aims to make substantive contributions to this vision by focusing its support on three strategic agendas: inclusive economic growth, environmentally sustainable growth, and regional integration.

In the AsDB's long-term strategic framework adopted in 2008, the bank defined its role and strategic directions to guide operations through 2020 and increased its relevance and effectiveness in assisting developing member countries. The AsDB promotes the economic growth and social development of its developing member countries through a wide range of activities and initiatives. Under the AsDB's Strategy 2020, the bank will focus on five key areas: developing the private sector; encouraging good governance; supporting gender equity; helping developing countries gain knowledge; and expanding partnerships with other development institutions, the private sector and community-based organizations. These areas are tightly linked to the AsDB's three strategic development agendas of achieving inclusive economic growth, environmentally sustainable growth and regional integration.

Ownership Structure

The AsDB's shareholders consist of 48 developing and developed member states in the Asia and Pacific region and 19 members from outside the region. Each shareholder is represented on the Board of Governors, in which all of the AsDB's powers are vested.

Funding Sources

The AsDB's funding sources are divided into those from ordinary capital resources (OCR) and a special fund. Funding sources from OCR include paid-in capital, retained earnings, and proceeds from issuance of bonds. To finance its OCR lending operations, the AsDB issues bonds in the international and domestic capital markets. The AsDB's bonds carry the highest possible investment ratings from major international credit rating agencies. The special fund is financed by contributors to the

AsDB's Special Funds, such as the Asian Development Fund, the AsDB Institute, and the Japan Special Fund. In 2014, the AsDB raised a total of USD 11,975 million in long-and-medium-term funds and USD 2,518 million in short-term funds. The AsDB's estimated borrowing requirement over the next three years ranges from USD 13,000 million to USD 15,000 million per annum.

Operational Data

At the end of 2014, the AsDB's total assets reached USD 154,092 million and its total equity was USD 16,938 million. In 2014, the AsDB's operations totaled USD 22,930 million, of which USD 13,690 million was financed by the AsDB and USD 9,240 million by co-financing partners. Sovereign operations totaled USD 15,990 million and non-sovereign operations totaled USD 6,940 million. Authorized and subscribed capital stock amounted to USD 154,090 million and USD 153,060 million. Disbursements in 2014 totaled USD 7,368 million (USD 6,280 million for sovereign loans and USD 1,088 million for non-sovereign loans), an increase of 23.1% from the USD 5,985 million disbursed in 2013 (USD 5,178 million for sovereign loans and USD 807 million for non-sovereign loans).

From its establishment through December 31, 2013, the AsDB had approved loans (excluding terminated projects), amounting to USD 155,491 million in its ordinary operations. As of December 31, 2013, the total of the AsDB's loans outstanding, undisbursed balances of effective loans, and loans not yet effective in its ordinary operations amounted to USD 85,185 million. Of this total, 92.7% represented sovereign loans, which were loans to the public sector (member countries and, with the guarantee of the respective member, government agencies or other public entities). Approximately 7.3% of this amount represented non-sovereign loans, including loans to private enterprises, financial institutions and selected non-sovereign public entities.

Business Models and Products

The AsDB's business models include: (i) loans, (ii) equity investment, (iii) technical support, and (iv) joint financing with other agencies. The AsDB offers "hard" loans from OCR on commercial terms, whereas the Asian Development Fund (ADF) affiliated with the AsDB extends "soft" loans from special fund resources with concessional conditions. The AsDB lends through wholesale and retail operations. The top five recipients including co-financing are India (USD 2,660 million), Pakistan (USD 2,580 million), the People's Republic of China (USD 2,360 million), Vietnam (USD 2,060 million) and Indonesia (USD 2,050 million). When co-financing is excluded, the top five recipients are as follows: India (USD 2,450 million), the People's Republic of China (USD 2,050 million), Pakistan (USD 1,540 million), Indonesia (USD 1,020 million) and the Philippines (USD 880 million). The AsDB will continue to operate in providing health, agriculture, and disaster and emergency assistance but will do so on a more selective basis. The AsDB also facilitates policy dialogues, provides advisory services and mobilizes financial resources through co-financing operations that tap official, commercial, and export credit sources. Such activities maximize the development impact of its assistance. Operations are financed through OCR and special funds. The AsDB's charter requires OCR and special funds to be held and used separately at all times.

Box 2 – 2 Cross-Border Hydropower Project between Georgia and Turkey in 2014

AsDB is collaborating with the International Finance Corporation (IFC), a member of the World Bank Group, and the European Bank for Reconstruction and

Development (EBRD) to help Georgia tap its hydropower potential and achieve energy self-sufficiency by investing in the construction and operation of the Shuakhevi hydropower plant in September 2014.

The USD 250 million debt financing arranged by IFC represents the largest-ever private hydropower investment in Georgia, consisting of two USD 90 million long-term senior loans, one each from AsDB and EBRD, and USD 70 million from IFC. IFC's total investment in this project is USD 104 million, which includes a USD 34 million equity investment in the project company Adjaristsqali Georgia, a joint venture among India's Tata Power, Norway's Clean Energy Invest (40% each), and IFC (20%).

The Shuakhevi plant will satisfy Georgia's electricity demand in the winter, reducing dependence on imported fuel and increasing renewable energy output. This plant will also foster cross-border electricity trading during other seasons of the year by exporting electricity to Turkey through a transmission line financed by EBRD. The project will benefit local communities by helping to create jobs, boosting municipal incomes, and upgrading area roads. This project demonstrates that non-recourse cross-border financing is feasible for green field hydro-projects in Georgia, and it will be important for the development of the sector and for Georgia. The project will promote regional cooperation and generate additional revenues for Georgia through energy trade. This groundbreaking renewable energy investment highlights the important role of AsDB in leveraging support for energy security and environmentally sustainable growth in the region.

Some USD 15 million of AsDB's USD 90 million in financing will be provided by the Canadian Climate Fund for the Private Sector in Asia, funded by Canada's government and administered by AsDB. Private investment in energy generation projects stimulated by EBRD's initial investment in the Georgia-Turkey cross-border transmission line is a prime example of how the bank facilitates private sector investment as part of its mandate to help countries transition to open market economies. The Shuakhevi project is expected to strengthen investor confidence in Georgia and to stimulate more private sector investment in the sector.

The project is the first hydropower project in Georgia certified by the United Nations Framework Convention on Climate Change for carbon emission reductions. The project is expected to produce approximately 450 gigawatt hours of power annually and to reduce greenhouse gas emissions by more than 200,000 tons per year. The project will develop the 187-megawatt Shuakhevi hydropower scheme, consisting of the Shuakhevi and Skhalta hydropower plants located in the Adjara region in southwest Georgia. Work on the plant began in September 2013 with the target to begin producing electricity in 2016.

Inter-American Development Bank (IADB)

General Information

The Inter-American Development Bank (IADB) is a main source of development financing for Latin America and the Caribbean. Established under the Agreement Establishing the Inter-American Development Bank in 1959, the IADB supports Latin American and Caribbean economic development, social development and regional integration by lending to governments and government agencies, including state-owned corporations. The IADB is owned by its shareholders, comprising 48 countries, including 22 that are non-borrowing members. At the end of 2013, the bank's top five shareholders were the U.S. (29.34%), Argentina (10.77%), Brazil (10.77%), Mexico (6.92%), and Canada (6.29%). With 2,000 staff and branch offices in its 26 borrowing countries, the IADB's headquarters is located in

Washington, D. C., in the United States. The Board of Directors of the IADB includes 14 executive directors, and each has an alternate executive director. Luis Alberto Moreno, the current IADB president, chairs the Board of Directors.

Mission and Strategy

The IADB has five goals: reducing poverty and social inequalities; addressing the needs of small and vulnerable countries; fostering development through the private sector; addressing climate change, renewable energy and environmental sustainability; and promoting regional cooperation and integration. Since 2012, the bank has been engaged in the reformulation of its strategic and normative sector instruments to achieve the mandates established under the Ninth General Increase in the Resources of the Inter-American Development Bank (IADB-9). In that same year, Sector Framework Documents were established to provide, in a given sector: (i) a flexible framework that can accommodate the range of challenges and institutional contexts encountered by the bank's 26 borrowing member countries, and (ii) meaningful strategic guidance for project teams to provide a clear sense of the bank's goals in each sector.

Ownership Structure

The bank is owned by its member countries. These members include 26 borrowing member countries and 22 non-borrowing member countries. The bank's top five shareholders are the U. S. (29.34%), Argentina (10.77%), Brazil (10.77%), Mexico (6.92%), and Canada (6.29%); the five largest members based on their share of total voting power are the U. S. (30.0%), Argentina (11.0%), Brazil (11.0%), Mexico (7.1%) and Japan (5.0%).

Funding Sources

The IADB obtains its own financial resources from its 48 member countries, borrowing on the financial markets and trust funds that it administers as well as through co-financing ventures. The IADB's debt rating is triple-A, the highest possible rating. The callable capital pledged by the 22 non-borrowing members, which include the world's wealthiest developed countries, therefore functions as a guarantee for the bonds that the IADB sells. This arrangement ensures that the IADB maintains a triple-A credit rating and can therefore provide loans to its borrowing member countries at interest rates similar to those that commercial banks charge their largest corporate borrowers. Moreover, the 22 non-borrowing countries are only offering guarantees—not actual funds—and, hence, their support for the IADB's lending operations has a minimal impact on their national budgets. The funds that the IADB lends are raised by selling bonds to institutional investors at standard commercial interest rates. The bonds are backed by the sum of the capital subscriptions actually paid in by the bank's 48 member countries plus the sum of the callable capital subscriptions pledged by the bank's 22 non-borrowing member countries. Together, these sums constitute the bank's ordinary capital, totaling USD 101,000 million. Of this amount, 4.3% is paid in, and the remaining 95.7% is callable. In addition to its lending activities for member countries, the IADB also has lending operations with private companies, both directly through its Structured Corporate Finance Department and Opportunities for the Majority Initiative and through the Inter-American Investment Corporation (IIC), a multilateral lender created by the IADB member countries to help develop small and medium-sized companies in Latin America and the Caribbean.

Operational Data

The total assets of the IADB at the end of 2014 were USD 106,299 million, compared with USD 97,007 million at the end of 2013. The IADB's total equity was USD 23,697 million at the end of 2014 and USD 23,550 million at the end of 2013. The institution's return on assets (ROA) was 0.52% in 2014 and 1.36% in 2013. The mandate of the bank's Capital Adequacy Policy reconfirms the objective established by the Board of Governors regarding the preservation of the bank's AAA rating. The bank treats non-performing sovereign-guaranteed loan differently depending on the number of days after the loan's due date.

Business Models and Products

The IADB operates through retail. The bank finances development projects in 26 borrowing countries in Latin America and the Caribbean, generating between 20,000 and 30,000 contract opportunities for businesses and consultants from all member countries each year. The IADB Group promotes development in Latin America and the Caribbean through the private sector. With financing and technical assistance to companies engaging in projects that have a positive impact on social and economic development in the region, the IADB supports a wide range of players, from microenterprises to large companies and financial institutions.

Loan approvals in 2014 were concentrated in the five priority areas under the Ninth General Increase in the Resources of the Inter-American Development Bank (IADB-9), contributing to the objectives established in the Results Framework. In terms of sectors, 42% of approved financing was allocated to institutional support for development, 38% to the infrastructure and environment sectors, 16% to social sector programs, and 5% to integration and trade programs. Furthermore, 35% of newly approved operations were in the area of institutional support for development, 34% in the infrastructure and environment sectors, 17% in integration and trade, and 14% in the social sectors.

Supervision and Regulation

The use of loan proceeds is supervised. Bank employees monitor and supervise the ongoing progress with respect to the development objectives of each operation through the bank's country offices in each of its 26 borrowing member countries, and fiduciary arrangements are in place to ensure the proper use of bank resources to achieve the operational objectives. The Board of Executive Directors has the right to make amendments to the liquidity policy, which would increase the policy band ceiling, to provide additional funding flexibility to strengthen liquidity. The policy allows management to dynamically manage liquidity based on the bank's expected future cash flow needs.

Box 2-3 Expansion of Financial Services for Women Entrepreneurs in Ecuador

Ecuadorian enterprises have identified access to finance as one of the greatest obstacles to business, as it prevents small businesses from reaching their full potential. In addition, World Bank data indicate that only 28.5% of small businesses in Ecuador are owned by women. With regard to access to finance, only 15% of loans are granted to enterprises headed by women. The gap between loans to businesses owned/led by women and those owned/led by men can be reduced by providing access to specialized financial products.

The "Expansion of Financial Services for Women Entrepreneurs in Ecuador" project was approved in 2013 and contracted in 2014. Through this project, the Multilateral Investment Fund of the IADB Group (MIF), the leading provider of technical assistance for the private sector in Latin America and the Caribbean, will support Banco Pichincha in Ecuador with non-reimbursable technical cooperation funding to increase access to finance for small businesses owned/led by women. This support will boost the capacity of Banco Pichincha to serve this segment by improving its risk analysis tools and developing specialized products and services for women. In addition, Banco Pichincha will join the Global Banking Alliance for Women (GBA), a global platform for sharing lessons learned from and best practices related to financing for female entrepreneurs. The project's sustainability is primarily based on the unequal access to finance confronted by small businesses led by women; given the wide gap with respect to those led by men, the number of unserved potential clients represents an opportunity for Banco Pichincha.

This project is the continuation of a partnership initiated by the MIF with Banco Pichincha in 2008. At the first stage, the MIF helped Banco Pichincha to successfully downscale by conducting the operation "Non-reimbursable technical cooperation funding to expand financial services for small enterprises through Banco Pichincha." As a result, the bank expanded its small business portfolio to 32,465 active small business clients, greatly exceeding the project's original target. After this success, however, an imbalance was detected in terms of access to credit on the part of small businesses owned/led by women compared with those owned/led by men—an imbalance that this project intends to correct.

This project will also coordinate efforts with another MIF project known as "Rolling out a Psychometric Tool for Expanding Small Business Finance," as Banco Pichincha will implement a risk analysis model using psychometric parameters developed by the Entrepreneurial Financial Lab. This model will be included as a supplementary risk analysis methodology to enable the bank to help enterprises that do not currently meet its minimum requirements to qualify as borrowers.

Eurasian Development Bank (EDB)

General Information

The Eurasian Development Bank (EDB) was established in 2006 by Russia and Kazakhstan. The headquarters of EDB is located in Almaty, Kazakhstan. It was incorporated under the Agreement on the Establishment of the Eurasian Development Bank initially signed by Russia and Kazakhstan. The EDB currently has six members: Russia (2006), Kazakhstan (2006), Tajikistan (2006), Armenia (2009), Belarus (2010) and the Kyrgyz Republic (2011). The current chairman of the EDB is Dmitry Pankin.

The EDB is the manager of the EurAsEC Anti-Crisis Fund (EAF or ACF), which was established in 2009 by Armenia, Belarus, Kazakhstan, the Kyrgyz Republic, Russia and Tajikistan. The EAF's primary goals are to assist member countries in overcoming the consequences of global financial crises, to ensure their long-term economic stability and to foster economic integration. EAF interventions assume the form of loans to support the budget, the balance of payments and national currency, and the investment credit to finance international projects.

The ownership shares in the EDB at the end of 2014 were as follows: Russia (65.97%), Kazakhstan (32.99%), Armenia (0.01%), Tajikistan (0.03%), Belarus (0.99%), and Republic of Kyrgyz (0.01%). This ownership structure reveals that the EDB is primarily controlled by Russia and Kazakhstan, serving the economic development in the CIS (Commonwealth of Independent States) area. The bank's charter capital totals USD 7,000 million, including USD 1,500 million of paid-in capital and USD 5,500 million of callable capital. At the end of 2014, the EDB had 294 employees. The EDB has a branch in Saint Petersburg and six representative offices in the capitals of its members.

Mission and Strategy

The bank's mission, as defined in Article 1 of the Agreement on Establishing the Eurasian Development Bank, is to contribute to strengthening and developing market economies in the member states of this agreement and to enhance trade and economic integration among them by engaging in investment activities. The bank promotes international financial and economic cooperation by participating in the activities of other international financial and banking institutions and unions. The bank's mission is to facilitate, through its investment activity, the development of market economies, the economic growth and the expansion of trade and other economic ties in its member states. The objectives of the EDB's investment activity include: the technical assistance to facilitate interstate relations and promote regional integration initiatives in

Eurasia; the establishment of financial and investment support mechanisms for regional integration processes and developing financial markets; and the environmental management, conservation enhancement and improvement of the environmental situation. According to the Strategy for 2013 – 2017 approved by the council on July 2014, the EDB will focus on the following areas: financing projects to develop power generation, transport and municipal infrastructure in its member states; promoting improved energy efficiency of member economies through financing projects to reduce the energy intensity of enterprises and to improve resource-saving indicators; further financing of projects facilitating trade and economic ties; and the attraction of mutual investment to deepen the economic integration between member states. However, the EDB does not finance social projects such as the construction of schools and hospitals.

Ownership Structure

In accordance with the Agreement on Incorporation, the EDB has immunity against any legal proceedings under the jurisdiction of its member states. The property and assets of the bank have the same immunities from search, requisition, arrest, confiscation, expropriation or any other form of withdrawal or alienation prior to final judgment in relation to the bank. The bank is exempted on the territory of the member states from any taxes, levies, duties, income taxes and other payments, except for those representing a payment for specific types of service.

According to Article 9 of the charter, the bank shall operate using its own or borrowed funds, although the EDB is likely to receive direct financial support from member governments in the event of need. The EDB issues local bonds and Eurobonds under the Euro Medium Term Notes (EMTN) Program in local and foreign markets, raises funds from Euro Commercial Paper (ECP) Program securities and borrows from other financial institutions through bilateral bank loans. The EDB's debt is likely to be guaranteed by member governments should the need arise. The EDB's credit rating is independent from those of its member states. For example, Moody's current rating of the EDB is Baa1/(P)Baa1, whereas its rating for Russia is Ba1.

Funding Sources

The bank's charter capital totals USD 7,000 million, including USD 1,500 million of paid-in capital and USD 5,500 million of callable capital.

Operational Data

The EDB's total assets at the end of 2014 were USD 3,915.50 million, compared with USD 4,593.66 million at the end of 2013. The EDB's total equity was USD 1,638.27 million at the end of 2014 and USD 1,632.16 million at the end of 2013. The EDB's total liabilities at the end of 2014 were USD 2,277.20 million, while the corresponding figure for the end of 2013 was USD 2,961.50 million. The net profit in 2014 was USD 17.78 million, whereas the year of 2013 experienced a loss of USD 72.51 million. The average loan rate to customers in 2014 was 8.58%. The EDB's ROA was -1.8% at the end of 2013. The EDB's return on equity (ROE) was -4.3% at the end of 2013. The non-performing loan (NPL) ratio was 4.5% at the end of 2014, according to an estimate from Moody's.

Business Models and Products

The EDB lends through wholesale and retail operations. EDB lending may assume the form of a one-off loan, non-revolving and revolving credit facilities, and syndicated loans. The maximum loan term is 15 years. Businesses in the real sector can be granted credits between USD 30 million and USD 100 million. The EDB's average investment amount is approximately USD 50 million. The EDB offers consulting and technical assistance and is active in research and analytical activities and in international cooperation.

The EDB has established the following project-financing procedure: preliminary project evaluation; adoption of a resolution for project financing; preparation to disburse funds for the project; commencement of project financing; and project monitoring, implementation and repayment. Special procedures have been established for those projects involving selection procedures for investors (competitive tendering and projects involving public-private partnerships) and the organization of syndicated (club) financing. Nearly all projects financed by EDB are located in the territories of its member states. The following is the distribution of the EDB's current investment portfolio by country: Russia, 45.18%; Kazakhstan, 36.76%; Belarus, 12.58%; Armenia, 1.57%; Tajikistan, 0.38%; Kyrgyzstan, 0.9%; and other EurAsEC countries, 2.63%.

Organization and Regulation

According to Article 2 of the Agreement on Establishing, the EDB shall be governed by the generally adopted principles and standards of international law, applicable international treaties, the Agreement on Establishing the EDB and the charter of the bank. The agreement and other agreements made between the EDB and members supersede the members' domestic laws. According to Article 5 of the charter, the members' right to vote is determined by the shares that they have contributed. The authorized capital of EDB is divided into 1.5 million shares with a par value of USD 1,000 each. Each paid share shall confer the right to cast one vote. Nine members constitute the EDB's management board, whose chairman is Dmitry Pankin. The EDB Council, the members of which are ministers and deputy ministers of finance or equivalent ministers and deputy ministers of member countries, appoints the board and the chairman of the management board. The EDB is required to be audited by external auditors on an annual basis according to Article 7.3 of the Corporate Governance Regulations. According to Article 4.5 of the Corporate Governance Regulations, the EDB has two supervisory bodies accountable to the council: the Revision Committee, which is the supervisory body of the council that supervises the bank's finance and business, and the Internal Audit Service, which is the bank's independent structural department that assists the council and the executive body in achieving the bank's strategic goals by applying a systematic and consistent approach to risk assessment and enhancing the efficiency of risk management, internal control and corporate governance.

> ### Box 2-4 Financing Projects in Kazakhstan's Rail Sector
>
> Kazakhstan is a landlocked country with a flourishing export-oriented economy. Oil and oil products, metals, hundreds of other raw materials and semi-finished products and grain are its most significant export products. However, Kazakhstan is located thousands of kilometers away from the ocean and from its many target markets.
>
> In April 2013, EDB and Trans-telecom JSC, a subsidiary of KTZ (Kazakhstan National Railway Company), signed an agreement under which EDB would finance investment to develop the Automated Traction Power Dispatch Control System. Accordingly, EDB opened a credit line of KZT 17,500 million (USD 113 million) for Trans-telecom JSC for a period of 7.5 years. The project costs a total of KZT 25,500 million (USD 165 million) and involves the development of an automated rail traffic control system in Kazakhstan. KTZ is installing precision devices to measure diesel and electricity consumption by its locomotives. A system is being installed to collect and analyze real-time data. Analysts predict that the automated control system, when implemented, will result in reductions of up to 13% of diesel consumption and up to 7% of electricity consumption.
>
> The project is expected to have a positive effect on the country's sustainable economic development. According to EDB's analysts, the project will provide an annual boost of more than USD 40 million to the Kazakh economy. Because of the long-term construction of projects in the rail sector, it is too early to assess the effect of these financial projects.

In October 2014, EDB increased its share in the financing of this project, lending an additional KZT 7,500 million (USD 44 million) to Trans-telecom JSC in addition to the KZT 17,500 million (USD 1,020 million) that the bank provided in 2013.

This case shows how DFIs can help to resolve the binding constraints of developing countries by investing in transformative infrastructure.

The African Development Bank (AfDB)

General Information

The African Development Bank (AfDB) effectively began operations on July 1, 1966. Its major role is to contribute to the economic and social progress of its regional member countries—both individually and collectively. The Agreement on Establishing the African Development Bank was adopted and presented for signature in Khartoum, Sudan, on August 4, 1963. The AfDB's authorized capital is subscribed to by 79 member countries comprising 53 independent African countries (regional members) and 26 non-African countries (non-regional members).

The Board of Directors of the AfDB includes 20 executive directors, and each has an alternate executive director. Donald Kaberuka, president of the AfDB Group, chairs the Board of Directors. At the end of 2014, the bank's top five shareholders were Nigeria (9.3%), the U.S. (6.6%), Japan (5.5%), Egypt (5.4%), and South Africa (4.8%). The Board of Executive Directors makes day-to-day decisions regarding which loans and grants should be approved and what policies should guide the AfDB's work. Each member country is represented on the board, but their voting power and influence differ depending on the amount of money that they contribute to the AfDB. The bank has 13 branch offices, and its headquarters is located in Abidjan, Côte d'Ivoire.

Under Article 8 of the Agreement on Establishing the AfDB, the bank is also authorized to establish or be entrusted with administering and managing special funds that are consistent with its purposes and functions. In line with this provision, the African Development Fund (ADF) was established with non-African states in 1972 and the Nigeria Trust Fund (NTF) by the Nigerian government in 1976.

Mission and Strategy

The mission of the AfDB is to promote sustainable economic growth and reduce poverty in Africa. The bank has developed a Ten-Year Strategy (2013 – 2022) that highlights the importance of global value chains (GVCs) in linking Africa to the global economy. The bank's policies and strategies in the private sector, regional integration, agriculture and human development are consistent with the above aims.

Ownership Structure

The AfDB's authorized capital is subscribed by 79 member countries comprising 53 African countries (regional members) and 26 non-African countries (non-regional members). Non-African countries constitute 40% of the total shareholding, whereas African countries constitute 60%.

Funding Sources

The boards of the AfDB approve the group's annual borrowing program, which has the aim of raising cost-effective resources to finance the group's clients and to meet its liquidity requirements. In contrast to commercial banks, which have the central bank as a lender of last resort, the AfDB must fully rely on its liquid resources to meet its obligations. The bank issues medium-and-long-term debt securities, and such debt securities are issued following a strategy of combining large global benchmark bonds with smaller transactions targeted to particular segments of demand.

Standard & Poor's rated all senior debt issued under the Global Debt Issuance Facility as AAA. The bank's strong equity base is buttressed by its callable capital, and there has never been a call on the capital of the AfDB. The bank is not involved in deposit or government transfer activity. AfDB has co-financing operations with multilateral partners, bilateral institutions, governments and local firms.

Operational Data

The AfDB's total assets were UA 22,951 million (USD 33,252 million) at the end of 2014 and UA 20,997 million (USD 32,335 million) at the end of 2013. Its total equity UA 6,080 (USD 8,809 million) was at the end of 2014 and UA 5,831 million (USD 8,980 million) at the end of 2013. The institution's ROA was 0.14% in 2014 and 0.35% in 2013. The institution's ROE was 0.52% in 2014 and 1.25% in 2013. Of the bank's Outstanding Non-Sovereign Loan and Equity Portfolio, 2% is at very high risk. With a lending spread specific to each project, the longest loan maturity period is 50 years.

Business Models and Products

The institution lends through retail operations. Sector-level bank group operations indicate that the selectivity and the focus on results have continued to guide the bank group's operations. Infrastructure approvals represented the largest proportion of AfDB approvals. Transport was the dominant subsector, followed by energy and water and sanitation. Finance operations comprising lines of credit, trade finance, and support for small and medium-sized enterprises (SMEs) were significant in the AfDB window but not in the (African Development Fund) ADF window. The bank provides the following products: the Enhanced Variable Spread Loan (EVSL) Product for sovereign-guaranteed borrowers, single currency loans, guarantees and a range of risk management products, including interest rate and currency swaps, caps, collars, commodity hedges and indexed loans. The AfDB offers its borrowers flexibility to customize their debt repayment profile with access to annuities, step-up or step-down amortization of principal, or bullet repayment.

Supervision and Regulation

The policies, processes and procedures by which the bank manages its risk profile continually evolve in response to market, credit, product, and other developments. The guiding principles by which the bank manages its risks are governed by the bank's Capital Adequacy Policy, the General Authority on Asset Liability Management, the General Authority on the Bank's Financial Products and Services, and the Bank's Credit Risk Management Guidelines.

European Bank for Reconstruction and Development (EBRD)

General Information

The European Bank for Reconstruction and Development (EBRD), founded in 1990 after the Cold War, is a multilateral DFI with its headquarters in London. The EBRD's leadership is composed of five parts: the president, the Board of Governors, the Board of Directors, the Executive Committee and the Senior Leadership Group. By the end of 2014, EBRD membership had expanded to Central Asia and to the Southern and Eastern Mediterranean (SEMED) countries. To date, 64 countries and regions, the European Union and the European Investment Bank have joined the EBRD.

Mission and Strategy

The EBRD's mission is defined as follows: "Uniquely for a development bank, the EBRD has a political mandate in that it assists only those countries 'committed to and applying the principles of multi-party democracy (and) pluralism'. Safeguarding the environment and a commitment to sustainable energy are also central to the EBRD's activity."

Ownership Structure

The EBRD is owned by all member countries and regions, and the largest five shareholders are the U. S.(10.1%), France(8.6%), Germany(8.6%), Italy(8.6%), Japan(8.6%) and the U. K.(8.6%).

Funding Sources

The EBRD receives and borrows financial resources from governments, international institutions (bilateral donors) and a wide range of funds (multilateral funds). Major donors and funds include sovereign governments, international financial institutions, the European Union, the EBRD shareholder special fund (SSF), and concessional financing (climate change).

Over the past five years, the EBRD has maintained its performance stable. Its debt has received a triple-A rating from all three major rating agencies—Standard & Poor's, Moody's and Fitch—since 2011. Thus, a reasonable conclusion can be adequately made that over the past five years, the EBRD has not suffered from loan impairment or past and overdue loans, nor have its member governments assisted in solving the problems. Because the EBRD is funded by its member governments, its debt is guaranteed by member governments' sovereign credit. Apart from governments, the EBRD also has access to funding in capital markets via its global medium-term note program and commercial paper facilities based on member countries' sovereign credit.

Operational Data

The EBRD's total assets were USD 63,563 million at the end of 2014, representing a decline of 5.76% compared with USD 67,445 million in total assets at the end of 2013. Its total shareholders' equity decreased to USD 17,135 million at the end of 2014, representing a 16.4% decline compared with the corresponding figure of USD

20,493 million at the end of 2013. Its total gross loan portfolio was USD 25,063 million at the end of 2014, representing a 7.56% decline compared with the corresponding figure of USD 27,113 million at the end of 2013. The EBRD's ROA was −0.9% in 2014 and 1.8% in 2013. Its ROE was −3.8% (on net profit basis) in 2014 compared with 7.2% in 2013. The EBRD's gross non-performing portfolio ratio was 5.6% in 2014, which increased significantly compared with the level of 3.3% in 2013. The interest rates on the EBRD's loans are based on the current market rate. Both fixed and flexible rates are offered. The longest maturity period for loans is 15 years.

Business Models and Products

The EBRD is not a retail bank, and it offers no deposit or savings accounts or commercial products such as mortgages. Subsectors funded by the EBRD include agribusiness, financial institutions, information and communication technologies, manufacturing and services, municipal infrastructure, natural resources, nuclear safety, real estate, tourism, sustainable resources and climate change and transport. The EBRD's projects are primarily intended to promote the economic development of member countries. The EBRD also offers financial support for large private corporations, such as its 2013 support for the Turkish firms Evim. net and TurkNet, which are Internet and telephony companies, respectively. The EBRD emphasizes the following operational areas in policy making: financing early transition countries (ETCs) and newly enrolled member countries, such as those in the SEMED region; promoting sustainable development both environmentally and socially; narrowing the gender gap in the countries in which the institution invests and fostering gender equality; and promoting local currency loans and strengthening capital market development.

Box 2 – 5 Sustainable Resource and Energy Projects in Central and Western Asia

The EBRD regards environment safeguarding and energy sustainability as its central issues. Rapid economic growth results in much greater demand for energy and resources and, hence, increasing concerns regarding environmental sustainability and climate change. Thus, creating and implementing policies and operations devoted to resource issues are critical in EBRD member countries.

EBRD has been exerting great efforts to increase the priority of resource efficiency for all members. Following the *Sustainable Energy Initiative* (SEI) launched in 2006, EBRD started the *Sustainable Resource Initiative* in 2013 as the extension of SEI. The year 2014 witnessed several important projects related to sustainable resources and energy operating in Central and Western Asia, where the concept of sustainability has yet to be given greater attention in the face of vast infrastructure financing demands.

Below, several key projects initiated in 2014 are described.

1. Energy efficiency projects in Kyrgyz Republic

The Kyrgyz Investment and Credit Bank (KICB), having cooperated with EBRD since 2001 as one of the leading banks in Kyrgyz Republic, received a loan of USD 5 million that was financed by EBRD via local banks in July 2014. The loan would be used in enterprises and households for improvements and modernization of energy-efficient equipment.

This project was designed to promote energy efficiency, invoke awareness of energy security and decrease energy consumption. Future plans included the promotion of a structural transition to renewable and efficient energy in the private sectors.

KICB would reportedly receive a loan of USD 2 million from EBRD, which would be spent on purchasing energy efficiency equipment and installing insulation for households and private enterprises.

2. Expansion of hydropower generation in Georgia

In Dariali in northeastern Georgia, a new hydroelectric power plant (HPP) was under construction in November 2014. This project was one major way in which EBRD assisted in the development of renewable energy in Georgia, which is believed to be one of the countries with the most hydropower resources throughout the world.

The hydropower project was financed by EBRD in the form of an USD 80 million syndicated loan to JSC Dariali Energy, which is one of the privately owned hydropower plants in Georgia. After completion, the hydropower plant is estimated to play a crucial role in utilizing the potential of hydropower in Georgia and reducing carbon emissions.

3. Solar power plants in Jordan

In November 2014, EBRD, in cooperation with the French Development Finance Institution PROPARCO, provided Jordan a USD 100 million loan (USD 50 million each) to build three solar photovoltaic generation plants located in southern Jordan.

This program aimed to boost the production of renewable energy in Jordan, where new and sustainable forms of energy such as solar power have not been fully developed. These plants were expected to result in approximately 40 MW of generating capacity to reduce Jordan's reliance on energy imports.

4. Wind farm in Kazakhstan

One remarkable project implemented in Kazakhstan's renewable energy sector was its first large-scale wind farm, financed by EBRD. EBRD, with the Clean Technology Fund (CTF), provided a KZT 14,000 million (USD 71.7 million) loan to Wind Power Yereymentau (one special-purpose vehicle in Kazakhstan) in November 2014. The loan was guaranteed by JSC Samruk-Energo, a national energy company in Kazakhstan.

Through this operation, Kazakhstan's wind power capacity was expected to increase from 45 MW to 95 MW. The wind power plant was expected to offset 120,000 tons of CO_2 per annum and to contribute to the transition of energy forms in Kazakhstan, where more than 70% of electricity is still generated by coal.

5. Biomass boiler plant in Bosnia and Herzegovina (BiH)

In December 2014, a sovereign loan of up to EUR 7 million (USD 8.5 million) offered by EBRD was distributed to BiH to assist in the construction of a biomass boiler plant in Prijedor. This project was further supported by grant funding of up to EUR 2 million (USD 2.4 million) from the Swedish International Development Cooperation Agency (Sida).

This project was the first operated in the BiH municipality, and it aimed to increase heat service through the installation of individual heat substations. More than 13,000 individuals were estimated to benefit from the program.

In recognition of its contribution to sustainable resources and energy, the EBRD was awarded US Treasury Development Impact Honors in 2014. The EBRD's sustainable resource and energy projects in Central and Western Asia have led to more vigorous and sustainable regional economies.

Caribbean Development Bank (Caribbean DB)

General Information

The Caribbean Development Bank (Caribbean DB), incorporated in 1969, is a regional financial institution with its headquarters in Barbados. The leadership group of the Caribbean DB is composed of the president, the Board of Governors, and the Board of Directors. At the end of 2014, the Caribbean DB had 19 regional borrowing member countries (BMCs), three regional non-borrowing members and five non-regional non-borrowing members.

Mission and Strategy

The Caribbean DB's mission is as follows: "CDB intends to be the leading catalyst for development resources into the Region, working in an efficient, responsive and collaborative manner with our BMCs and other development partners, towards the systematic reduction of poverty in their countries through social and economic development."

Ownership Structure

The Caribbean DB is owned by its member countries. The six largest shareholders are Jamaica (18.62%), Trinidad and Tobago (18.62%), Canada (10.02%), the U.K. (10.02%), Germany (6.00%) and China (6.00%).

Funding Sources

As a development financial institution, the Caribbean DB does not have banking accounts as those offered by commercial banks. The Caribbean DB issues debt securities in international capital markets and receives lines of credit from multilateral institutions. Its primary sources of funding include Ordinary Capital Resources (OCR) and Special Funds Resources (SFR). OCR includes subscription to the capital and debt from European Investment Bank (EIB), Inter-American Development Bank, the World Bank and international capital market. SFR includes two categories: Special Development Fund (SDF) and Other Special Funds. Funding for SDF is provided in four-year replenishments by members. Contributors to the SDF negotiate with the Caribbean DB on the priority areas which should be addressed by the Caribbean DB over the next four-year cycle. Over the past five years, the Caribbean DB has maintained stable performance in the management of impaired loans. The highest NPL ratio from 2009 to 2013 was the 4.0% level experienced in 2012, and the lowest was 0.1% in 2013. In 2013, Moody's Investors Service rated the bank's long-term issues as Aa1. Thus, the Caribbean DB has not faced the situation in which member governments need to help solve problems related to impaired loans. Because the Caribbean DB is funded by its member governments, the latter's sovereign credit guarantees its debt. Apart from governments, the Caribbean DB also has access to funding in international capital markets based on its member countries' sovereign credit.

Operational Data

The Caribbean DB's total assets were USD 1,452.30 million at the end of 2013, representing an 11.5% decrease from USD 1,640.80 million at the end of 2012. The total shareholders' equity amounted to USD 743.60 million at the end of 2013, which represents a 5.2% increase from USD 706.90 million at the end of 2012. The bank's total gross loan portfolio reached USD 972.70 million at the end of 2013, which is a slight decrease (0.73%) over the USD 979.90 million figure at the end of 2012. In 2013, The Caribbean DB's ROA was 1.17%, whereas in 2012, its ROA was 1.52%. Its ROE was 0.39% in 2013 compared with 2.17% in 2012. The gross non-performing portfolio ratio was 0.1% in 2013 compared with 4.0% in 2012. The interest rates on its loans are specific to the bank's various funds. In 2013, the average interest rate for the Special Development Fund (SDF) was

2.44%, and the rate for other Special Funds was 2.23%. The maximum maturity period for loans is 22 years.

Business Models and Products

The Caribbean DB is not a retail bank and hence does not offer deposit or savings accounts or commercial products. Subsectors in which the Caribbean DB invests include agriculture and rural development, manufacturing and industry, transportation and communication, power, energy, water and sanitation, social infrastructure and services, environmental sustainability and disaster risk reduction, and financial and business. The Caribbean DB assists regional development through several hierarchies. The Caribbean DB's borrowing member countries enjoy the right to borrow financial resources directly. The bank emphasizes the following operational fields: fostering production and trade in agriculture; promoting private and public investment and facilitating business start-ups and development; providing technical assistance; supporting regional and local financial and capital market development; and supporting education, training and human resource development.

Box 2-6 The Caribbean Development Bank as a Bridge in Mobilizing External Resources

The Caribbean region is composed of more than twenty countries and political entities. The economies of most countries in the Caribbean region are small in scale and not sufficiently robust. Some countries, such as Haiti, still suffer from an insufficient supply of living necessities. Financial activities in most countries are relatively small-scale, and funding shortages are common.

Realizing insufficiency by solely depending on internal members' endeavors, the Caribbean DB has made great efforts in recent years to build a robust financing support system by welcoming cooperation with multilateral international institutions and other regions throughout the world. A number of projects are provided under the agreements signed with entities outside of the Caribbean region and supported by external financial sources.

Some major programs were implemented in 2014, including the following:

- In January 2014, the Caribbean DB and IFC, a member of the World Bank Group, signed a Memorandum of Understanding to "support public-private partnerships that are crucial to building better infrastructure in the Caribbean." This memorandum was expected to encourage a wider participation of private sectors in infrastructure development.

- In April 2014, the Caribbean DB and the Caribbean Disaster Emergency Management Agency received EUR 20 million (USD 24.2 million) for disaster management. This grant funding was expected to strengthen the ability of the Caribbean region to defend against natural disasters and improve disaster risk management.

- In July 2014, the Caribbean DB, IADB and JICA signed a Memorandum of Cooperation to promote renewable energy and energy efficiency in the eastern Caribbean region. This program aimed to address issues related to high energy costs and to reduce dependency on traditional fuels.

- In September 2014, the European Union, Spain, and the Inter-America Development Bank promised to help the Caribbean DB develop renewable energy, aiming to accelerate development, mitigate the effects of climate change and achieve greater energy security.

- In October 2014, the Caribbean DB discussed regional development issues with Canada in terms of how to deepen the Caribbean DB's relevance and capacity to provide solutions to the challenges encountered by the bank's borrowing members.

Among all cooperative projects, the projects in energy and resources fields are the most remarkable. Following the trend of advocating sustainable energy and considering the current situation of energy utilization in the Caribbean region, the Caribbean DB has recently attached great importance to "Sustainable Energy Initiatives." In August 2014, the Caribbean DB developed a blueprint in which the bank would serve as the executive agency for sustainable energy and resource projects, while the IADB, JICA and EU, among others, would act as funding donors.

Interregional cooperation is expected to generate not only more secured financial resources but also advanced management tools and ideas to increase efficiency in the Caribbean DB's operations. DFIs should follow and take advantage of the future trends and opportunities associated with financial globalization. Resorting to external funding sources and management instruments is particularly vital for small multilateral development institutions. It is expected that the world will witness a new Caribbean region embracing cooperation with other regions and increasing participation and voices in regional and global affairs.

Islamic Development Bank (IsDB)

General Information

The Islamic Development Bank (IsDB) is an international financial institution established in pursuance of the Declaration of Intent issued by the Conference of Finance Ministers of Muslim Countries held in Jeddah in December 1973. The bank was formally opened on October 20, 1975. Its principal office is in Jeddah, the Kingdom of Saudi Arabia. Four regional offices were subsequently opened in Rabat, Morocco; Kuala Lumpur, Malaysia; Almaty, Kazakhstan; and Dakar, Senegal. The IsDB also has two country gateway offices in Ankara (Turkey) and Jakarta (Indonesia) as well as field representatives in 14 member countries. The largest shareholders are Saudi Arabia (23.52%), Libya (9.43%), Iran (8.25%), Nigeria (7.66%), and the United Arab Emirates (7.51%). The president of the IsDB is H. E. Dr. Ahmad Mohamed Ali, who has served in this capacity since 1975. The Board of Executive Directors is composed of 18 members in the current term: nine appointed by their countries, which are the main shareholders, and nine others elected by the governors of other countries. According to its charter, the IsDB is mandated to foster the socioeconomic development of its member countries and Muslim communities in non-member countries in accordance with the principles of Shari'ah (Islamic law) (see Box 2 – 7 for the essence of Islamic finance).

Box 2 – 7 Essence of Islamic Finance

Islamic finance is subject to Shari'ah law, which is a system of beliefs revealed in the Qur'an and the Sunnah; Shari'ah is a generic term. Although scholars agree on the main principles, different interpretations exist among the various schools of Islamic religious scholarship and different jurisdictions. In many countries, Islamic and conventional financial institutions operate side by side. At its heart, Islamic finance is a moral system of finance.

- Islamic finance is a moral system of finance.

- Zakat is an obligatory charity that requires payment once per year. Among other things, a charge of 2.5% on an idle balance of money must be donated to the poor and the needy annually.

- Interest on loans or usury (Riba) is subject to various forms of regulations and restrictions. All divine religions strictly prohibit taking interest on loans.

- The parties must share the risks and rewards of a business transaction.

- The transaction should have a real economic purpose without undue speculation and should not involve the exploitation of either party or any activities that are considered sinful.

- Islamic transactions tend to be asset based, although the underlying assets do not necessarily constitute collateral.

Mission and Strategy

The IsDB's mission is to promote comprehensive human development by focusing on the priority areas of alleviating poverty, improving governance and promoting prosperity among the people. The IsDB Group Vision Journey comprises several phases: the Medium Term Business Strategy (MTBS 1.0: 2009 – 2012), or the Foundation Phase and the MTBS 2.0 (2013 – 2015). The MTBS 2.0 was approved in 2012. The IsDB also formulated a 10-Year Detailed Strategy in 2013. The 10-Year Strategic Framework is based on three strategic objectives, five strategic pillars or priority areas, and one crosscutting theme. The three strategic objectives are anchored in inclusive solidarity, connectivity for growth and promotion of Islamic financial sector development. The five strategic pillars are economic and social infrastructure, private sector growth, inclusive social development, Islamic financial sector development, and cooperation between Muslim countries and with Muslim communities in non-Muslim countries.

Ownership Structure

The IsDB is owned by its member countries. The present membership of the bank consists of 56 countries. The basic condition for membership is that the prospective member country should be a member of the Organization of Islamic Cooperation (OIC).

Similar to other multilateral development banks, the IsDB is governed solely by international law and is not subject to any particular sovereign jurisdiction. The majority of the IsDB's operational assets, which are equivalent to the development loans offered by other MDBs, benefit from sovereign guarantees; the remaining assets are supported by the undertakings of government-owned entities or highly rated bank and commercial guarantees. In addition, as a supranational body, the IsDB is exempt from taxation.

Funding Sources

The IsDB's capital comes from the contributions paid by member countries. Saudi Arabia is the largest member state, with 23.9% of callable capital. At the end of 2013, the subscribed capital was ID18,000 million (USD 27,560 million), of which ID 17,800 million (USD 27,260 million) was fully subscribed. Initially, the IsDB's financing operations were funded primarily by its shareholders' equity. The proportion of the IsDB's subscribed capital held by Aaa-, Aa- and A-rated countries was approximately 46.3%, which is lower than most other Aaa-rated multilateral development banks (MDBs). The member countries have consistently demonstrated a propensity to support the bank through regular injections of fresh capital. However, with the member countries' increased demand for resources to finance projects, the IsDB has turned to market resources by issuing Sukuk to complement its shareholders' equity (see Box 2 – 8 for more information). Another source of funds is co-financing with development partners, such as the Abu Dhabi Fund for Development, the Kuwait Fund and the Saudi Fund for Development.

Box 2-8 IsDB's Sukuk (Islamic Bonds)

Initially, the IsDB's operations were funded primarily by its shareholders' equity. However, in the face of increasing demands for resources to finance projects from member countries, the IsDB decided to mobilize funds from capital markets. In August 2003, IsDB issued USD 400 million worth of trust certificates due in 2008. The emergence of Sukuk has provided IsDB with a novel means of resource mobilization. Apart from complementing its internal resources, Sukuk issuance is also aimed at promoting the development of Sukuk industry in the global capital market.

Although Sukuk (Islamic bonds) has characteristics similar to those of a conventional bond, it is structured to be compliant with Shari'ah law and to be sold to Islamic investors who are prohibited by Shari'ah law from investing in conventional debt securities. The following are the key differences between Sukuk and conventional bonds:

- Sukuk indicates asset ownership. Conventional bonds indicate a debt obligation.
- The assets that back Sukuk are compliant with Shari'ah. Assets backing conventional bonds may include products or services that are opposed to Islam.
- Sukuk are priced according to the value of the assets backing them. Conventional bond pricing is based on credit rating.
- Sukuk can increase in value when the assets increase in value. Profits from bonds correspond to fixed interest, making them Riba.
- When one sells Sukuk, one is selling ownership in the assets backing them. The sale of conventional bonds is the sale of debt.

- Rather than charging interest, which is unacceptable under Shari'ah law, an Islamic bond investor receives a share of the profits generated by the underlying assets being financed.

Although the issuance of Sukuk remains small compared with the issuance of conventional bonds, this instrument is experiencing rapid growth (see Figure 2.1). To date, Sukuk bonds have primarily been issued by sovereigns (notably Bahrain, Malaysia, Qatar and Pakistan), corporations, supranational organizations and, to a lesser extent, Islamic banks.

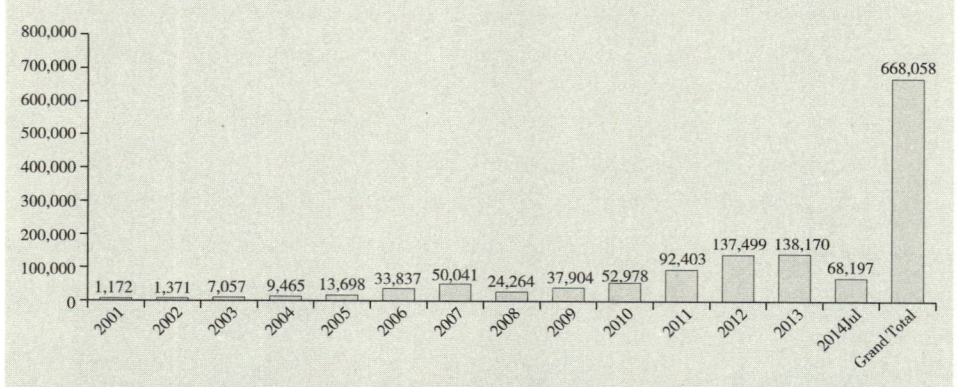

Figure 2.1 Total Global Sukuk Issuances (Jan. 2001 – Jul. 2014, USD Millions)

In 2005, IsDB established a USD 1,000 million Medium Term Note (MTN) Program to tap global capital market resources on a more regular and organized basis. The program allows IsDB to issue Sukuk in various currency denominations. The Sukuk program was increased from USD 1,000 million to USD 3,500 million in September 2010 and further increased to USD 10,000 million in November 2013 in tandem with IsDB funding requirements to support its operational growth. Under the MTN program, through November 2012, the IsDB had issued 13 series of Sukuk, of which five series were issued in 2012 via four private placements and one public Sukuk.

In 2014, IsDB issued two Sukuk in USD worth USD 1,500 million, respectively, with five tenure years and 1.8% coupons issued. The two Sukuk issued in 2014 were the largest-ever privately placed transactions from the supranational institution. IsDB has demonstrated its commitment to the Sukuk market by regularly tapping into the public markets for the past 10 years; as of June 2014, the bank has issued approximately USD 7,000 million Sukuk.

With Sukuk, IsDB can seek beyond its initial reliance on its equity to fund its operations. The bank is now more capable of financing the development projects in its member countries and Muslim communities in non-member countries. Furthermore, the issuance of Sukuk is compliant with Shari'ah, which helps to promote Islamic finance in the global capital market.

Operational Data

Despite the continuing effects of the global economic crisis and political uncertainty in several member countries, the IsDB's financial performance has remained robust. However, as in most MDBs, the IsDB is not profit oriented and does not distribute dividends. Profits are moderate compared with those of commercial banks, but they have been steady in line with their peers. The bank's ROA in 2012 and 2013 was 1.19% and 1.44%, respectively, while its ROE values for the same years were 1.91% and 2.51%. However, the IsDB's net income averaged ID 143 million per year (1.7% of earning assets) over the past five years. The IsDB is one of the best-capitalized and least-leveraged MDBs, with an equity-to-assets ratio of 54% and a debt-to-equity ratio of 79.5%. The IsDB's capital adequacy ratio was 43.3% relative to a minimum requirment of 35%. Despite the risky operating environment that is inherent to its role as a development bank, the IsDB's operational assets continue to perform well with a low level of impairment. The NPL ratio remains low at 1% as of 2013. Its loan tenures differ for high-income, middle-income and low-income countries. The longest loan maturity period is 30 years, including a grace period of 10 years for the poorest countries.

Business Models and Products

The IsDB operates according to Islamic Shari'ah principles. Thus, the IsDB does not receive deposits and its operations are sustained by shareholder capital, retained earnings and funds generated internally through its foreign trade and project financing operations. The bank offers various Shari'ah-compliant financial products to support developmental projects in its member countries. Through these financial products, the IsDB finances a variety of projects in the agricultural, industrial, agro-industrial, infrastructural and various other sectors. The IsDB does not charge interest on its loans, although it does charge a 0.75% to 2.0% service fee per annum to cover administrative costs. The IsDB provides loan approvals and financial assistance for its member countries and Muslim communities in non-member countries across Asia, Africa and the Middle East through its member countries, with a focus on energy, transportation and other infrastructure sectors.

Supervision and Regulation

The IsDB's governance can be explained by the activities of the IsDB Board of Governors and the Board of Executive Directors and by the reports of the bank group's evaluation, risk management, internal audit and integrity functions, which are aimed at achieving institutional efficiency and development effectiveness.

Part one Overview of Development Financing

Chapter 3　National DFIs in High Income Countries

The second group of development institutions is a group of national development banks. This type of bank is a financial institution that is typically created by a country's government to provide financing for the economic, social and environmental development of the country. National development banks play an important role in long-term economic development in its own countries and have positive effects on the world economy. Currently, a large number of national development banks are operating in a vast geographical area worldwide, with various organizational structures, funding sources and business models. We identify 18 important development banks in Asia, Africa, Europe, and Latin America and divides them into high, medium and low income countries according to the World Bank's definition. This Chapter will present an overview of the DFIs in high income countries.

Reconstruction Credit Institute (KfW)

General Information

KfW (Kreditanstalt für Wiederaufbau, "Reconstruction Credit Institute") is a government-owned development bank in Germany formed in 1948 after World War II under KFW law as part of the Marshall Plan. The KfW headquarters is located in Frankfurt, Germany, with more than 80 offices globally. The Federal Republic of Germany participates in the nominal capital of KfW in the amount of EUR 3 billion

(USD 3.63 billion, 80%), and the Federal states participate in the amount of EUR 750 million (USD 908.25 million, 20%). No individuals or private institutions are shareholders.

KfW Group consists of KfW and five consolidated subsidiaries: (i) **IPEX-Bank GmbH** provides project and corporate finance and offers trade and export finance in Germany and abroad; it has been run as a legally dependent bank within KFW Group since January 1, 2004, and it separated on January 1, 2008, into a legally independent subsidiary. (ii) **DEG** promotes private-sector initiatives in developing and transition countries. (iii) **Tbg** focuses solely on bank commitments left over by history. (iv) **FuB** handles special tasks associated with the currency conversion in eastern Germany and the performance of agency business for the former Staatliche Versicherung der DDR in Abwicklung. (v) **Dena** promotes the efficient and environmentally friendly production and use of energy, including renewable energies.

Mission and Strategy

KfW is "a public law institution." The missions of KfW can be summarized in four parts: (i) domestic promotion, namely, the promotion of investments by citizens, small and medium-sized enterprises (SMEs), and the municipal and social infrastructure; (ii) export and project finance, which supports German and European companies on the global market; (iii) development finance, which supports economic and social progress in developing and transitioning countries; and (iv) special tasks conducted on behalf of the German Federal Government.

KfW supports sustainable development of the economy, ecology and society. The focal points of its work include: (i) the promotion of SMEs and startups; (ii) the provision of equity capital; (iii) programs devoted to the energy-efficient refurbishment of residential buildings; (iv) support for measures to protect the environment; (v) educational finance for retail customers; (vi) funding programs for municipalities and regional development banks; and (vii) export and project finance, including the promotion of developing and emerging market countries.

The concrete missions vary according to the needs of the times. After World War II, KfW was sponsored by the Marshall Plan and promoted reconstruction, which contributed greatly to the economic miracles in BRD (Die Bundesrepublik Deutschland, Federal Republic of Germany). In the 1970s, when BRD stepped onto a stage of stable development, KFW began to support SMEs, particularly those in high-tech and environmental protection areas, providing SME-friendly long-term loans and thus helping to create jobs for two-thirds of the population. After the integration of West Germany and East Germany, KFW helped develop the former East Germany. KfW also played an important role in the process of the privatization of Lufthansa, Deutsche Telecom and other large enterprises. In the 2000s, the KfW Group emerged from the former KfW. Currently, the working focuses of KfW have been broadened: climate and environmental protection projects have as much emphasis as the funding of education and SMEs. Notably, in 2014, KfW provided a promotional volume of EUR 74.1 billion (USD 89.74 billion). Of this total, 36% was spent on climate and environmental protection measures (see Table 3.1).

Table 3.1 Commitment by KfW, 2013 – 2014

Commitments by KfW Development Bank from 2013 – 2014, by OECD/DAC development sector[1]

	2014		2013	
	EUR in mil.	%	EUR in mil.	%
Social Infrastructure & Services	1,589	22	1,609	31
Education	325	4	257	5
Health	267	4	297	6
Population Policy/Programmes & Reproductive Health	58	1	110	2
Water Suply & Sanitation/ Waste Disposal	588	8	726	14

(continued)

	2014		2013	
	EUR in mil.	%	EUR in mil.	%
Government & Civil Society	324	4	176	3
Other Social Infrastructure & Services	27	0	43	1
Economic Infrastructure & Services	4,358	59	2,906	55
Transport & Storage	107	1	202	4
Energy Generation / Distribution	2,837	39	1,461	28
Finance	1,408	19	1,243	24
Business & Other Services	5	0	0	0
Production Sectors	396	5	161	3
Agriculture, Forestry, Fishing	380	5	160	3
Industry, Construction, Mineral Resources & Mining	16	0	1	0
Humanitarian aid	142	2	68	1
Other	872	12	524	10
Total	7,356	100	5,268	100

Note: Differences in the totals are due to rounding.

1) Consistent with CRS (Creditor Reporting System) sector names of the OECD's (Organisation for Economic Cooperation and Development) DAC (Development Assistance Committee).

Governmental Support

The original capital of KfW came from the Federal Republic and federal states' budget. The government provides budget funds to KfW, which works to promote development, primarily in developing countries, and follows certain themes such as environmental protection on behalf of the federal government.

In terms of refinancing, the capital market is KfW's most important funding source, in which it raises more than 90% of its funds. As a state-owned institution, KFW enjoys government guarantee and thus has the advantage of better credibility on the capital market. KfW also receives budget transfers from the federal government. Budget transfers are typically incorporated into loans provided in economically or developmentally important areas, but they are also given in the form of non-repayable grants.

The Federal Republic guarantees all obligations of KfW with respect to loans extended to and debt securities issued by KfW, fixed forward transactions or options entered into by KfW, and other credits extended to KfW as well as credits extended to third parties in as much as they are expressly guaranteed by KfW.

KfW is exempt from income tax. For the construction, accommodation and rent of buildings, KfW has the same rights as the German Central Bank (Deutsche Bundesbank).

Funding Sources

The refinancing process of KfW is conducted on the international capital market. KfW is one of the largest and most active bond issuers in the world, funding its business activities almost exclusively via international money and capital markets. With its first-class credit rating, KfW is able to borrow at a low interest rate and ensure sustainable funding.

KfW Group's funding strategy in the international capital markets rests on the three pillars of "benchmark bonds in euros and US dollars", "publicly placed bonds outside the benchmark programs" and "private placements". Funds raised in the form of certificated liabilities continued to play a critical role, at 83% of total assets, unchanged from the previous year. In view of the persistent low interest rate, KfW expects to raise its share of foreign currencies in the total funding volume and plans to expand its green bond offerings in 2015.

KfW raised EUR 57.4 billion (USD 69.5 billion) in long-term funds to fund its promotional business on the international capital markets in 2014 [2013: EUR 65.4 billion (USD 90.1 billion)], issuing 250 bonds in 13 different currencies and benefitting from the continued demand for high-volume liquid bonds (benchmark bonds) among investors. At 57%, these bonds account for one of the key pillars of KfW's overall funding concept. KfW's capital market activities were primarily shaped by two product innovations in 2014—the issuance of KfW's first renminbi bond listed on the Frankfurt stock exchange and its issuance of KfW's first two Green Bonds in EUR and USD. KfW thus set market standards and contributed to the establishment of this still new market segment.

Operation at Data

At the end of 2014, the total assets of KfW amounted to EUR 489.1 billion (USD 592.3 billion) and its total equity amounted to EUR 21.6 billion (USD 26.2 billion). The ROA and ROE in 2014 were 0.31% and 7.01%, respectively. As part of risk reporting, the credit quality is presented into four categories: investment grade, non-investment grade, watch list and default. The latter two accounted for 7% of the total credit at the end of 2014 (see Figure 3.1). KFW holds the tier 1 capital of 14.1%. Long-term credit ratings from Fitch, Moody's and Standard & Poor's all reach superlative levels.

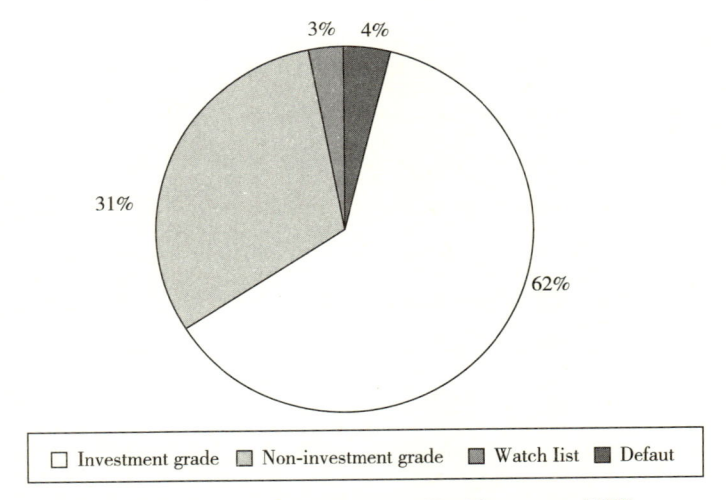

Figure 3.1 Credit Quality by Net Exposure, KfW

Business Models and Products

The business of KfW can be divided into domestic and international business. The domestic business includes: (i) KfW Mittelstandbank, which provides loans and investments to SMEs; (ii) KfW Kommunal-und Privatkundenbank/Kreditinstitute, which provide services in housing, environment, and education to private customers and provide services for governments; and (iii) governments' special purpose programs and strategic stock holdings of large companies. The international business includes: (i) international investment by KfW Entwicklungsbank; and (ii) international trade by KfW IPEX-Bank.

As a development bank, KfW's fund for promoting development increased to EUR 74.1 billion (USD 89.7 billion) in 2014, which included EUR 47.6 billion (USD 57.6 billion) spent in domestic promotional business and EUR 25.5 billion (USD 32.1 billion) spent in international finance. SMEs accounted for 44% of all domestic promotion. KfW's target markets include private customers, companies, public institutions and international customers.

KfW provides individuals with loans for the purchase and construction of houses, education and business startups. The energy-efficient modification of existing properties is encouraged. KfW provides companies with funds to found, expand and consolidate their business, thus covering all stages of a company's life span. Energy efficiency, corporate environmental protection and renewable energies are particularly encouraged (see Box 3 – 1 for the KfW's Financing of the World's Largest Solar Energy Farm in Morocco). For example, KfW's Environmental Protection Program fund investments that contribute to the environment at protection with loans that are repayment-free for up to 3 years. Particularly favorable interest rates are offered to small enterprises. Another SME-friendly program is the ERP Startup Loan. In addition to loans, KfW also supports businesses through an advisory program.

Loans from KfW are typically lent through regular banks. Savings banks, cooperative banks and commercial banks are KfW's main distribution partners. Currently, grants are available for energy-saving projects are disbursed to recipients directly by KfW. In general, KfW provides loans directly to public borrowers such as cities and municipalities.

Box 3 – 1 The KfW's Financing of the World's Largest Solar Energy Farm in Morocco

As the largest energy importer in North Africa, Morocco is making concerted efforts to reduce its reliance on imported fossil fuels. In 2013, Morocco achieved economic growth in excess of 4%; it is a country experiencing great progress. Demand for energy is driven by investments in infrastructure and by the establishment of industrial companies. To date, the country has largely relied on importing fossil fuels at high prices.

The Moroccan government is pursuing an ambitious energy strategy. The aim is to develop solar, wind and hydropower generation capacities to 2,000 megawatts each by 2020. Moreover, Morocco is the region's pioneer in renewable energy. This shift to renewable energy sources will contribute to global climate protection and to the security of the country's electricity supply.

As part of the financial cooperation with Morocco, the KfW Development Bank is working on behalf of the Federal Ministry for Economic Cooperation and Development (BMZ) and the Federal Ministry for the Environment, Nature Conservation, Building and Nuclear Safety (BMUB), which, along with other international donors, are financing the power complexes in Ouarzazate, Morocco.

Ouarzazate is on the edge of the Sahara. The radiation intensity of the sun reaches 2,500 kilowatt hours per m^2 and year, making it a favorable location for the first large-scale solar complex in North Africa. It will be one of the world's largest power plants, with an output of up to 560 megawatts generated through four individual power plants covering an area that measures 3,000 hectares.

The building work for the first power plant "Noor I" (Arabic for "light") began in June 2013. A highlight of the system is the molten salt energy storage facility that stores heat efficiently for three hours, enabling electricity to be produced even after the sunset. If the project proceeds according to plan, Noor I will begin operation in October 2015 (see Figure 3.2).

The investment costs for Noor I amount to approximately EUR 633 million (USD 766.6 million). Morocco is not in a position to manage such a large-scale project alone. Among various finance providers, Germany's contribution represents EUR 115 million (USD 139.3 million). The Noor II and Noor III power plants are estimated to involve overall investment costs of EUR1.8 billion (USD 2.18 billion), of which EUR 654 million (USD 792.0 million) will be financed by the KfW Development Bank.

Figure 3.2   Noor I construction site: erection of the parabolic reflector
Source: KfW/Jesús Vazquez Serrano, ARIES INGENIERA Y SISTEMAS, S. A.

> "The project in Ouarzazate is a reference project aimed at making a breakthrough in a low-carbon and environmentally-friendly future technology—not only for Morocco but also for other North African countries. Although the electricity generated is initially intended to cover the requirements in Morocco, this project will inspire a dream of future exporting solar power to supply energy to Europe. This idea is currently a vision, although Morocco is one of the countries wishing to press ahead with this vision, since it is seen as offering great opportunities for the country's own development."

Corporate Governance

Because KfW is a state-owned long-term financial institution, the supervisory system for KfW is completely different from that of commercial banks. The governing body of KfW consists of the executive board and the board of supervisory directors. The executive board conducts KFW's business and administers its assets according to the law concerning KfW and the KfW by-laws. The board is responsible for duly performing its duties and overseeing the implementation of resolutions taken by the board of supervisory directors. The board of supervisory directors and its members supervise the conduct of the bank's business and the administration of its assets. The primary tasks for which it is responsible are the appointment and dismissal of executive board members, the approval of financial statements and the selection of the auditor to be appointed by the supervisory authority.

North Rhine-Westphalia Bank (NRWB)

General Information

NRWB was established on August 1, 2002, with dual head offices in Düsseldorf and

Münster. As of the end of 2014, the bank had no branches performing banking activities outside of the Federal Republic of Germany, and it had 30 subsidiaries in Germany and 1,283 staff. Klaus Neuhaus has been chairman of the managing board since May 1, 2014.

NRWB pools the public-mission activities of the former Westdeutsche Landesbank Girozentrale—a bank whose origins date to the mid-19th century. In 2002, Westdeutsche Landesbank Girozentrale was divided into WestLB AG, a private-law bank, and Landesbank Nordrhein-Westfalen, a bank under public law. Landesbank Nordrhein-Westfalen was established on August 1, 2002, on the basis of the "Act for the Reorganisation of the Legal Relations of the Public-Law Banks in North Rhine-Westphalia." When the "Act on the Reorganisation of Landesbank Nordrhein-Westfalen into the Development Bank of the State of North Rhine-Westphalia and on the Amendment of Other Laws" took effect on March 31, 2004, Landesbank NRW became NRWB—the development bank of the State of North Rhine-Westphalia.

The members of the managing board, the supervisory board and the board of guarantors of NRWB constitute the bank's leadership. The executive and controlling bodies of the bank obtain advice from the Advisory Board for Housing Promotion and the Advisory Board of NRWB on specific topics and issues. Following the resignation of regional associations of the Rhineland and of Westphalia-Lippe as guarantors in 2011, the State of North Rhine-Westphalia became the sole guarantor and owner of NRWB.

Mission and Strategy

NRWB has a public mission aiming to "support its sole guarantor, the state of North Rhine-Westphalia, and its municipal corporations in meeting their public tasks, particularly in the fields of structural, economic, social and housing policy, and carry out and administer development measures in line with the regulations of the European Union." In accordance with its sustainability strategy, NRWB specifically promotes and funds projects and programs designed to improve living conditions, social development and environmental and climate protection in North Rhine-Westphalia.

Funding Sources and Government Support

Funding transactions with domestic investors are dominated by bearer bonds, promissory loans and registered bonds. NRWB also has used its international funding programs. NRWB's equity holdings comprise investments that are primarily held on behalf of the federal state of North Rhine-Westphalia and that were transferred to the bank upon its inception. Moreover, in 2010, the state granted a non-interest-bearing subordinated loan in the amount of EUR 2,413.9 million (USD 3,162.2 million), which must be repaid by 2044. The state is directly liable for loans taken up and bonds issued by the bank, futures and forward transactions, rights arising from options and other loans to NRWB and loans expressly granted by the bank. In the case of eight participation funds in the promotion business with a total exposure of EUR 138.6 million (USD 167.8 million) in 2014 [EUR 120.5 million (USD 166.0 million) in 2013)], the credit risk is reduced by a guarantee from the federal state of North Rhine-Westphalia, which covers 49% of the respective fund's total investment. As a result of its good credit worthiness and active investor service, in conjunction with low interest rates, NRWB was able to issue its bonds in favorable conditions, thus further strengthening its long-term funding base. NRWB was rated as AAA by Fitch Ratings in 2014.

Operational Data

With total assets of EUR 143.8 billion (USD 174.2 billion), NRWB is the second-largest development institution in Germany. The NPL ratio at the end of 2013 was approximately 0.5%. The maximum loan maturity of NRWB is 30 years. Total equity reached EUR 17.9 billion (USD 21.7 billion) in 2014 compared with EUR 19.5 billion (USD 25.7 billion) in 2006. The ROA and ROE in 2014 were 0.01% and 0.09%, respectively.

Business Models and Products

The bank lends both wholesale and retail. The business model of NRWB is that of a largely budget-independent development bank with an integrated promotion and development policy. The bank uses the anticipated profit possibilities for funding in the international capital market. NRWB generates its own income within the parameters of its conservative investment strategy. This income is used to finance the bank's development and promotion activities; to secure its own long-term viability, including the creation of its own non-interest-bearing provisions and reserves; and to finance banking operations. To fulfill its public mission, the bank primarily grants loans, underwrites guarantees and makes equity investments. The use of its own resources (e.g., to reduce interest rates on promotion loans) is a key aspect of the bank's business model.

NRWB's promotional offerings are divided into three fields: "Seed & Growth", "Development & Protection" and "Housing & Living" (see Figure 3.3). A total of nine promotion themes represent three fields of promotion while simultaneously outlining the focal promotion points of the bank. With regard to new promotion business, NRWB committed promotion funds totaling EUR 8.9 billion (USD 10.8 billion) in 2014, which was 3.7% below the 2013 level [EUR 9.2 billion (USD 12.7 billion)]. The bank expects to participate in a growing number of long-term high-volume financings (e.g., investments to support growth of scaled up SMEs and infrastructure projects in North Rhine-Westphalia). The bank also focuses on contributing to the transition toward green energy.

Supervision and Regulation

NRWB has legal capacity based on law and it is a credit institution in the legal form of an institution under public law. The bank also complies with the same prudential rules (e.g., the capital adequacy ratio, loan classification, loan provisioning) as

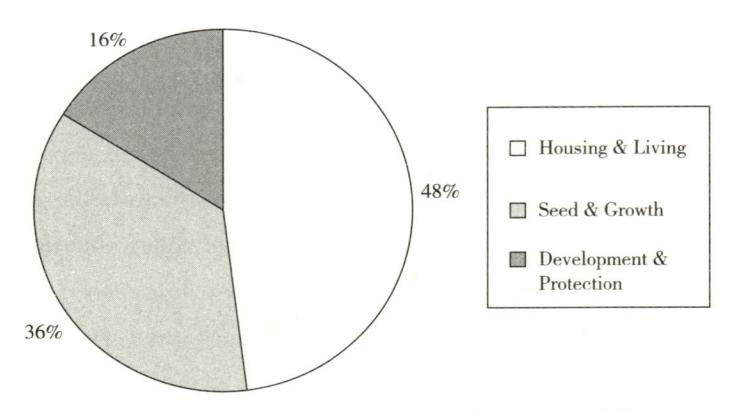

Figure 3.3 Fields of Promotional Offerings, NRWB

(Pie chart: Housing & Living 48%, Seed & Growth 36%, Development & Protection 16%)

commercial banks. The bank was founded on the basis of the "Act for the Reorganization of the Legal Relations of the Public-Law Banks in North Rhine-Westphalia". Governmental control over NRWB is exercised by the Ministry of the Interior of the State of North Rhine-Westphalia. Governmental control over social housing promotion is exercised in agreement with the ministry responsible for housing.

Caisses des Dépôts et Consignations (CDC)

General Information

Caisse des Dépôts et Consignation (CDC), or simply Caisse des Dépôts, was established in 1816 under the ordinance of Louis XVIII and under the first Finance Law in the history of France, in the hope of re-establishing citizens' confidence in state credit. CDC is defined by law as being "a long-term investor and contributes, in adherence with its patrimonial interests, to the development of companies." Acting as an extension of the state, CDC is a fully state-controlled group that centralizes deposit accounts and invests in development projects under the supervision and guarantee of the French Parliament via a supervisory board. CDC plays an important role in serving state strategy and public interest and in facilitating innovation and sustainable growth. The CDC headquarters is located at 56 rue de Lilles in Paris, France. This public institution consists of ten branches and ten subsidiaries, including Bpifrance Group, CNP Assurances, Transdev and La Poste, which operate within competitive sectors such as insurance, banking, real estate, transportation and leisure. CDC operates through its regional institutions, which work with French local authorities and promote the group's management and financing. CDC also invests its deposits in long-term "public projects including subsidized housing and semi-public companies formed with local governments for urban development."

After its creation in 1816, CDC released the first local development loan in 1822. In 1868, CDC created the first life insurance funds. In 1890, it initiated the management of solicitors' deposits. In 1910, CDC began managing the first compulsory pension scheme. In 1945, the institution engaged in financing post-war reconstruction. Between 1950 and 1980, CDC supported the implementation of "Les Trente Glorieuses" (The Glorious Thirty Years) project in France. In 2007, CDC launched its "ELAN 2020 strategic plan" to expand its domains of activity from infrastructure construction to SMEs, social housing, education, sustainable development, and other public interest and strategic priority areas.

Mission and Strategy

CDC is now "a long-term investor serving the general interest and the economic development of the country", as defined by the institution itself. The group "manages funds entrusted to it by the State through certain entities of the public institution, as well as its own funds generated by the businesses of the Group as a whole". CDC's domains of activity include "protecting popular savings, providing reliable banking services, managing retirement pension schemes, insuring individuals, supporting local authorities, developing real estate, financing businesses, long-term investment and fighting against climate change".

Governmental Support and Supervision

CDC is placed under "the supervision and the guarantee of the French Parliament. " It benefits from the French public sector's highly protected status and enjoys French state support as a result of its unique legal status. The law establishes its immunity to liquidation and bankruptcy and protects its solvency. Rating agencies assess CDC as a government-related issuer benefiting from the Republic of France's rating. "Fitch considers that the French state is bound to provide support to CDC and that it has the legal and financial means to enable it to meet its debt service obligations pursuant to Law 80-539 on French public establishments in a timely manner. Consequently, its IDRs are aligned and move in tandem with those of the French sovereign. "

Funding Sources

"CDC mainly finances its long-term investments from accumulated reserves and deposits from the legal professions, although it does access term debt markets to diversify its liabilities. " At the end of fiscal year 2013, customer deposits constituted 44% of total liabilities. Interbank funding accounted for 18.2%, and debt securities constituted 24.7%. "CDC maintains a EUR 18.5 billion (USD 25.5 billion) EMTN program, under which it plans issuance of around EUR 3 – 4 billion (USD 4.2 – 5.7 billion) per year in maturities from 2 to 30 years. "

With respect to the funding pattern of CDC, the institution is state supported, and it uses legal reserves, hedging instruments and pensions as its primary funding sources. In particular, CDC's consolidated businesses and entrusted businesses are dispensed with different legal funding.

CDC's funding of consolidated business includes: (i) legal reserves and public sector deposits—CDC is a bank appointed by French legislation that provides banking services and managing reserves for French social security cash management institutions, local NGOs, social housing construction institutions, donated funds and other public sectors; reserve deposits and other deposits are the primary funding sources for CDC. (ii) the issuance of bonds—as a long-term investment institution, CDC issues bonds to improve the balance sheet structure apart from receiving stable saving deposits.

For the funding of consolidated businesses, CDC's total liabilities consist of legal reserves and other public sector deposits (37.5%), accumulated retained earnings (22.5%) and debt securities derived from legal deposits (40%); for the latter, long-term issued debt represented 7.5%, and short-term debt constituted 22.5%. Repo funding accounted for 10% (see Table 3.2).

Table 3.2 CDC Group (Consolidated) Balance Sheet Structure

Assets		Liabilities and Equity	
Subsidiaries and Strategic Shareholding	20%	Accumulated Retained Earnings	22.5%
Local Development Projects	2.5%	Legal Reserve Deposits	37.5%
Equity Investment	12.5%	Long-term Funding	7.5%
Investment Property	5%	Repo	10%
Portfolios of Securities	60%	Short-term Funding	22.5%

CDC also engages in entrusted business, such as government-regulated savings accounts and pension business.

Operational Data

CDC lends in a wholesale manner. The institution had a net income of EUR 1,793 million (USD 2,171 million) at the end of 2014 compared with EUR 2,137 million (USD 2,944 million) of attributable profits in 2013. Its consolidated assets reached EUR 143.09 billion (USD 197.12 billion) in 2013, compared with EUR 286.65 billion (USD 377.94 billion) in 2012. CDC's total equity was EUR 31.09 billion

(USD 42.84 billion) at the end of 2013, with ROA of 1.49% and ROE equity of 6.87%. According to *Fitch's full rating report of CDC* published in early January 2015, the rates of impaired loans over total loans in 2013 and 2014 were 9.13% and 6.84%, respectively. The average annual interest rate on loans was 2.18% in 2013. The rating of the CDC by S&P, Fitch and Moody's are AA/A1 +, AA/F1 + 1 and Aa/P1 + 1, respectively.

Business Models

CDC's domains of activity primarily include protecting popular savings, providing reliable banking services, managing retirement pension schemes, insuring individuals, supporting local authorities, developing real estate, financing businesses, promoting long-term investment and fighting against climate change.

(i) Protecting popular savings. CDC centralizes and manages a large part of the French people's regulated savings. The funds collected and managed centrally by CDC constitute the "savings funds". Because of this resource, CDC grants loans to sectors of primary importance for the country, such as social housing and urban renewal. In return, part of the deposited money is thus used to finance sectors that benefit the country as a whole. The primary role of CDC is to ensure the security and liquidity of this large quantity of savings. CDC fulfills the double role of managing savings funds and financing public interest programs.

(ii) Promoting long-term investment. Every year, CDC devotes one-third of its profits to public service investments. These investments made with equity capital support the development policies launched by local authorities and public sector actors. CDC adopts a financial approach to its public service investments, which differentiates it from other investors. CDC is one of the largest long-term investors on the financial markets. The prime objective assigned to the management of its securities portfolios each year is to release a lasting profit that allows it both to boost financial stability and to make public interested in investments.

(iii) Financing businesses. Through equity capital financing, CDC has assisted in the establishment of Bpifrance, France's new public investment bank, to spur business and regional growth. CDC invests in SMEs to consolidate their equity capital, to promote innovation, to support the investment capital market and to provide loans to SME via OSEO. The institution supports business startups and the social economy.

(iv) Supporting regional authorities. CDC supports local authorities and inter-municipal institutions in their projects and accomplishments. CDC is a partner in the areas of housing, transportation, engineering, renewable energy and digital technologies.

(v) Managing retirement pension schemes. CDC is a widely recognized fund manager responsible for managing 47% pension schemes and social welfare funds. These funds cover a total of 7.3 million people in active employment and 3.5 million pensioners, representing one in five of all pensioners in France. CDC provides high-value-added services over the long term, acting as a partner of choice to 75,000 public sector employers: the central government, local and regional authorities, and the hospital service.

(vi) Insuring individuals. CNP Assurances, a subsidiary of CDC that has been insuring individuals for 150 years, is the leader in the French insurance market. To help its clients protect themselves against the vagaries of life, the institution offers a large range of products: life insurance savings, retirement, contingency funds and loan coverage. A total of 23 million people are insured for savings and contingency funds and 17 million for loan coverage.

(vii) Developing real estate. In partnership with local authorities, CDC is committed to housing for all and sustainable real estate.

(viii) Offering banking services. Since its establishment, CDC has been the trusted manager of private funds protected by law. Today, the institution is the banker of choice not only for the legal professions but also for social security and public interest bodies. CDC provides services suited to the specific needs of its clients and conforms to the highest security and quality standards.

Corporate Governance

The Caisse des Dépoôts group is run by a chief executive officer (Pierre-René LE-MAS, as of May 21, 2014). The chief executive officer of Caisse des Dépôts is appointed through a decree by the president of the Republic within the Council of Ministers for a five-year term of office. The management committee of CDC also includes 14 other members.

The supervisory board monitors the management of CDC, offering guidance to the chairman and chief executive officer to inspire his management, although he is not obliged to accept such advice. Once a year, the board chairman delivers a report to Parliament that is drawn up and approved by representatives of the nation. "The role of the supervisory board is to monitor Caisse des Dépôts' major decisions, strategic directions, shareholding initiatives, savings fund management and audit accounts."

The supervisory board consists of a chairman, Henri Emmanuelli, and 12 other board members, including three who are not affiliated with government agencies. The supervisory board has thirteen members, including three deputies and three qualified figures, of whom two are nominated by the president of the Chamber of Deputies and one nominated by the president of the Senate.

The French Parliament supervises CDC via the supervisory board. "Although CDC is not a bank, ACPR, France's bank regulator, gives its opinion on CDC's capital adequacy in banking regulation terms as well as on CDC's internal solvency ratio."

Development Bank of Japan (DBJ)

General Information

Japan Development Bank (JDB) was established in 1951 and was the predecessor of

Development Bank of Japan (DBJ). In the 1950s, the primary function of JDB was to provide loans for the rationalization, modernization and cultivation of important industries such as coal and steel. After several reformations, in June 1999, the Development Bank of Japan Act was established. In October of the same year, JDB and the Hokkaido-Tohoku Development Finance Public Corporation, an organization to furnish funds for the effective promotion of community development projects, were completely transferred to DBJ. After the transfer, under the terms of the Development Bank of Japan Inc. Act (Act No. 85, 2007; the "New DBJ Act"), the Development Bank of Japan Inc. was established in Tokyo on October 1, 2008.

Under the New DBJ Act, the DBJ was expected to achieve full privatization within five to seven years after its establishment. With the Act's revision, the target date was extended. Because of the global financial shocks in 2007 – 2008, the new DBJ found it necessary to release money from the government to the public to re-energize the Japanese economy. Recently, DBJ decided to achieve full privatization within five to seven years from the date of April 1, 2015. However, for certain reasons, the Ministry of Finance currently retains full control of DBJ.

The bank has 10 branches; 8 representative offices in Japan; one overseas representative office (New York); and three overseas subsidiaries in Singapore, London and Beijing.

Mission and Strategy

Based on its corporate philosophy of "applying financial expertise to design the future", the DBJ's new mission is "to build customer trust and realize an affluent society by problem-solving through creative financial activities". Based on the New DBJ Act, the bank will provide integrated investment and loan services.

Government Support

DBJ (and its 100% share) currently belongs to the country of Japan, and it is under full control by the Ministry of Finance.

Funding Sources

DBJ issues domestic and international bonds with or without the Japanese government's guarantee and borrows money directly from the government and lenders, such as regional banks. The JPY 150 billion (USD 1,456 million) budget of the Japanese government guaranteed foreign bonds in fiscal year 2014. As for bond issuance, approximately 70% is in the domestic capital market and 30% is in the international market. Most bonds are denominated in JPY, but DBJ aims to increase its USD issuance along with an expected increase in USD assets.

The credit ratings of DBJ are A1 (Moody's Investors Service, Inc.), A + (Standard & Poor's Corp.), AA (Rating and Investment Information, Inc.) and AAA (Japan Credit Rating Agency, Ltd.). DBJ has been maintaining a low level of impaired loans. Its loan portfolio consists primarily of lending to private-sector firms in Japan with a focus on infrastructure business.

Operational Data

The total assets of DBJ as of the March 31, 2014 and September 30, 2014 were JPY 16,310.7 billion (consolidated) (USD 158,479 million) and JPY 16,210.9 billion (consolidated) (USD 147,794 million). The ROE and ROA for the fiscal year 2014 were 2.02% and 0.33%, respectively. The NPL ratio was 0.93%. The amounts of trust funds and stock funds were JPY 134,215.0 billion (USD 1,302,729 million) and JPY 1,640.0 billion (USD 15,918 million), respectively. Gross liabilities were JPY 13,680.0 billion (USD 132,782 million). The amounts of borrowing and bonds were JPY 9,180.0 billion (USD 89,104 million) and JPY 4,240.0 billion (USD 41,155 million), respectively. The amount of net profit was JPY 124.3 billion (USD 1,206 million), and the capital adequacy ratio was 15.23% (Basel III, BIS Guidelines) (as of March 2014).

Business Models and Products

DBJ aims to operate with the business model of a highly specialized financial institution that provides integrated investment and loan services.

The main financial resources of DBJ are from the government and the issuance of bonds. As a result of the financial crisis and the 2011 earthquake, the DBJ has completed its crisis response network. Under the Japan Public Finance Corporation Act, certain financial institutions are designated to provide credit in the event of natural disaster and other crises, and DBJ is designated as such. Such institutions receive credit from the Japan Public Finance Corporation, which employs institutions to provide loans. As a designated financial institution, DBJ plans to continue providing such loans by applying its expertise in this area to crisis response operations (see Box 3-2 for the Role of DBJ in Crisis Management in Japan).

DBJ has recently begun to implement a change in its financing model. Although government support remains the primary financing resource, DBJ is attempting to reduce its reliance on the government. Instead, DBJ is diligently striving to diversify resources and increase the proportion of financial sources from private institutions.

Governance and Supervision

Under the terms of the Development Bank of Japan Inc. Act (the "New DBJ Act") approved by the Japanese Diet on June 6, 2007, as part of the Act on the Promotion of Administrative Reform to Bring About a Simple and Efficient Government (Act No. 47, 2006; the "Administrative Reform Promotion Act") and the fundamental reform of policy-based finance, DBJ, upon its establishment, took over all assets of the Development Bank of Japan (the "predecessor") as investment in kind, with the exception of assets transferred to the government under the provisions of Article 15, Paragraph 2, of the Appendix to the New DBJ Act. Under Article 15, Paragraph 1, of the same Act, DBJ also assumed all rights and obligations of the predecessor, with the exception of assets transferred to the government under Article 15, Paragraph 2, of the Appendix to the New DBJ Act.

The minister of finance has supervisory powers in DBJ's key matters, such as its annual business plan, annual basic policy regarding the issuance of bonds and borrowing, and the amendment of DBJ's articles of incorporation.

Box 3-2　The Role of DBJ in Crisis Management in Japan

Because Japan frequently suffers from natural disasters, crisis management must always be of primary importance to the country. Particularly after the 2008 financial crisis and the 2011 earthquake, crisis management has been given high priority in Japan.

DBJ helps businesses to create countermeasures to hedge against disaster and to provide contingency financing to help recover operations in the event that they are affected by disaster. DBJ assists with a full range of disaster preparedness, from the formulation of business continuity plans to the earthquake-proofing of facilities and the preparation of IT backup systems. In addition, DBJ provides new financing methods to assist in the recovery of disaster-struck businesses.

In the fiscal year 2006, DBJ initiated a financing management system employing a comprehensive method of rating post-disaster reconstruction preparedness. The system involves a combined disaster rating and financing plan. Under this system, clients self-assess corporate plans to manage disasters. Preferential interest rates on financing are established based on rating results. In addition to documentation, the assignment of ratings is based on interviews conducted directly between DBJ and the client in discussing post-disaster reconstruction. Through an objective third-party evaluation of a company's disaster preparedness to do the post-disaster reconstruction, the system is designed to reduce internal barriers to implementing post-disaster countermeasures. Companies can also use the results of their evaluations in corporate publicity, such as in news releases and on websites, to outline their disaster preparedness initiatives.

Since 2011, DBJ has been exerting great effort to provide financial support to help the country recover from the earthquake.

In April 2014, DBJ provided loans for two enterprises in eastern Japan with the Bank of Iwate to help regional enterprises recover from the earthquake crisis. DBJ established the Fund of Eastern Japan in 2011 with the Bank of Iwate. This fund provided financial assistance for enterprises that sustained damage as a result of the 2011 earthquake.

This case illustrates the particular type of support that can be provided by the policy bank. In today's environment, both financial crises and natural crises occur frequently, and ensuring rapid and efficient crisis responses and management is becoming increasingly important. The policy bank, which functions as part of the government in some manner, is responsible for providing further crisis management services and the establishment of a direct and efficient response system to address emergency situations and problems is crucial.

Korea Development Bank (KDB)

General Information

The Korea Development Bank (KDB) was founded on April 1, 1954, in accordance with "The Korea Development Bank Act" in order to finance and manage major industrial projects to expedite industrial development and improve the national economy. Following a national policy, KDB facilitates the normalization of management for troubled companies through corporate restructuring and consulting services and provides capital for strategic regional development projects. Through a network of 82 domestic branches, 8 overseas branches (Tokyo, Beijing, Shanghai, Guangzhou, Shenyang, Singapore, London and New York), 5 overseas subsidiaries (KDB Asia Ltd, KDB Ireland Ltd, KDB Bank Europe Ltd, Banco KDB do Brasil S. A, and KDB Bank Uzbekistan) and 6 representative offices worldwide, KDB provides a full range of financial services. The bank has 3,398 employees. Its head office is in Seoul, Korea. The KDB board has 11 members and the chairman of KDB is Kyttack Hong.

During the early years of KDB, the bank focused on supplying policy financing for infrastructure, including electricity, coal mines, and harbor building, as well as providing domestic enterprises with large-scale facility loans. In 1955, the bank issued industrial financial bonds for the first time. In the 1960s and 1970s, KDB focused on nurturing the heavy and chemical industries to advance the nation's industrial structure, increased its level of statutory capital and became the first institution in Korea to issue foreign currency bonds. In the 1980s and 1990s, KDB began to expand its international and investment banking businesses dramatically, establishing the foundation for becoming a globally competitive investment bank by offering support to high-tech industries. During the financial crises at the end of the 1990s and 2008, KDB took a series of steps to stabilize the country's financial market, to dispel market anxiety and to foster industry growth (see Box 3-3 for the KDB's Preemptive Contribution to National Economic Recovery in the Recent Financial Crisis).

In 2007, the government decided to reform KDB and divided KDB into Korea Finance Corporation (KoFC) and KDB Financial Group (KDBFG). KoFC was responsible for policy-related business, while KDBFG focused on commercial banking. In 2013, the new government halted the commercialization of KDB and reaffirmed its status as an indispensable, wholly state-owned policy finance bank in Korea, and the ownership of KDB is now therefore the Republic of Korea (ROK) government (100%). The Ministry of Strategy and Finance of the ROK supervises KDB. The bank will further solidify its financial stability by improving its profitability and asset quality through profit-oriented qualitative growth. After the amendment of the KDB Act in May 2014, "KDB merged with KDB Financial Group and Korea Finance Corporation (KoFC) to become more competitive, more sustainable" on December 31, 2014.

Box 3-3 KDB's Preemptive Contribution to National Economic Recovery in the Recent Financial Crisis

Korea responded to the 2008 global financial crisis with certain policy measures that helped the Korean financial and real sectors to weather the immediate effects of the global crisis. These measures included policy and financial support to stabilize the money, securities and bonds markets; to extend financial support to corporate and financial entities; and to support SMEs and the microfinance sectors.

Among the above policy measures, KDB played a significant role in stabilizing the financial market. KDB's extensive experience in helping stabilize the financial markets in the 1998 Asian financial crisis proved indispensable in 2009. As corporate loans became increasingly delinquent across the board in the face of the sweeping global financial crisis, KDB bolstered its corporate restructuring operations by relying on various time-tested measures to preempt loan default as well as to manage loans in arrears. KDB carried out various preemptive restructuring operations since 2008 and employed a Fast-Track program to provide liquidity to the SME sector and is a signatory to the Creditor Bank Group Agreement to prevent insolvencies and serial bankruptcies in the domestic construction industry. Additionally, the Bank worked hard to proactively provide assistance to liquidity-strapped small and mid-sized shipbuilders. Moreover, through loan modifications and business reorganizations, the Bank helped normalize corporations being restructured or under workout programs while conducting post-bankruptcy operations such as bad credit liquidation, asset-backed securities issuance, M&A and auctions.

Mission and Strategy

The defined mission of KDB is to "contribute to the development of Korea's financial industry and economy by carrying out advanced policy with a self-sustaining model." In August 2013, KDB established its new vision as the "Financial Engine of Korea's Growth, Global KDB." To bring this vision to fruition, the bank selected five core values: "Trust", "Passion", "Collaboration", "Client Orientation" and "Market Leadership" (see Box 3-4 for the KDB's New Mission to Boost the Creative Economy).

The bank also established five mid-to long-term business strategies according to market conditions, policy finance demand and private financing conditions: (i) foster a creative economy by promoting the growth of innovative high-risk businesses such as venture firms and startups, (ii) lead in the advancement of financial services as a breakthrough in the saturated financial market, (iii) reinforce its role as a market safety net in times of financial crisis to consistently cope with financial turbulence in the future, (iv) solidify the foundation for sustainable policy finance by enhancing its profitability, and (v) prepare for the reunification of the two Koreas and use it as a springboard for pursuing greater economic opportunities.

Box 3-4 A New Mission to Boost the Creative Economy

After its reemergence in 2013, the KDB's new mission is to boost a creative economy. Specifically, KDB will provide financing to industries bearing relatively high risks and will reinforce its partnership with promising SMEs possessing cutting-edge technology through innovative financial products.

> To make 2015 a boom year for its creative economy initiative, the KDB will supply as much as 180 trillion won (USD 164.83 billion) for new growth engine businesses and startups.
>
> Under the government policy, KDB will offer the largest portion of the fund to establish Creative Economy Innovation Centers in as many as 17 cities during the first half of 2015; in such centers, entrepreneurs aspire to launch startups and receive one-stop services to enable the formation of a startup-friendly ecosystem.
>
> The KDB will also offer financial support for the "Manufacturing Innovation Plan 3.0" outlined by the Ministry of Science. Its aim is to merge information technology (IT) with the manufacturing process. The goal of the plan is to encourage approximately 10,000 manufacturers to have "smart" factories that can integrate design, production and distribution with ICT technologies to reduce costs.

Governmental Support

Since its establishment in 1954, KDB as the country's top policy bank has been a strong performer with governmental support and has been issuing policies that support Korea's economic growth. KDB's budget and operation plan must be approved by the government, whereas the government credit provides support for KDB's bond issuance. The government offers loss compensation and credit support for KDB. For example, the government guarantees the credit of industry financial bonds and foreign currency bonds. If KDB cannot cover its deficit with yearly reserves—which has not occurred during the past 5 years—the government will cover the gap.

Funding Sources

KDB acquires necessary funds through the following methods: (i) receiving deposits and installment deposits; (ii) issuing industrial finance bonds, other securities and debt instruments; (iii) borrowing from the government, the Bank of Korea, and other financial institutions, provided that the KDB's obligations to the government are subordinated to other debts incurred by the KDB in conducting its operations; and (ⅳ) borrowing foreign capital. The most important fund comes from issuing industrial finance bonds. After returning to policy banking, KDB reduced the size of the retail bank business.

Operational Data

The total assets of KDB at the end 2013 were KRW 258,802 billion (USD 245,125 million), whereas at the end of June, 2014, total assess KRW 277,278 billion (USD 253,912 million). The total equity of KDB at the end 2013 was KRW 28,812 billion (USD 27,289 million), whereas the total equity at the end of June, 2014 was KRW 30,204 billion (USD 127,659 million).

The ROA of KDB was −0.01 at the end of 2013. The ROE of KDB was 0.054 at the end 2012. The NPL ratio was 0.025 at the end of 2014. The longest loan maturity period was 10 years.

Business Models and Products

KDB's primary areas of business expertise are policy financing, which includes solidifying the foundation for the creative economy, serving the funding needs of ventures and enhancing the competitiveness of techno-banking; corporate banking and restructuring, which involves providing corporate loans and investment guarantees while serving as the market safety net and offering refinancing of corporate bonds; investment banking, which covers products ranging from M&A to venture capital, bond underwriting and project finance; international banking, including syndication, structured finance, trade finance and other financial services; pensions and trusts, retirement allowances and trust business; and retail banking, research and consulting.

In recent years, KDB has been supporting SMEs, startups and the construction of infrastructures. More than half of the credit funds have been provided to SMEs and startups during the past four years. The share of loans for financial services, shipbuilding, transportation, iron and steel, wholesale and retail accounted for 26.5%, 6.9%, 5.1%, 5.0% and 4.8% of the total, respectively (see Table 3.3).

Table 3.3 Industry distribution of KDB loans (5 largest industries)

Industry	Financial service	Ship building	Transportation	Iron and steel	Wholesale and retail	Total
Percentage	26.5%	6.9%	5.1%	5.0%	4.8%	48.3%

Organization

In October 2009, KDB split into Korea Finance Corporation (KoFC) and KDB Financial Group (KDBFG), with the latter focusing on commercial services. In Feburary 2013, President Park geun-hye terminated the commercialization reform of KDB after her inauguration, and thus merged KDB, KDBFG, KoFG. In May 2014, newest edition of KDB Act was passed by National Assembly of South Korea, and a new KDB, with its subsidiaries including KDB Infrastructure, KDB Deawoo Securities, KDB Asset Managent, KDB Capital and KDB life insurance is operating according to the new act since 2015. Figure 3.4 shows the current organizational chart.

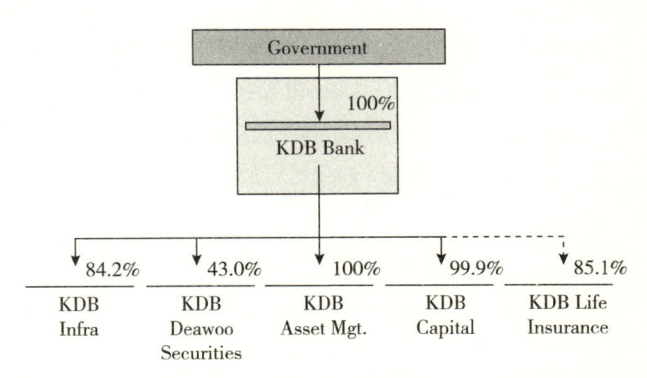

Figure 3.4 Organization Chart, KDB (After Dec. 31st 2014)

An overview of the subsidiaries is provided below:

(i) Daewoo Securities. Daewoo Securities was No. 1 in the market share for brokerage in 2010, posting performance in investment banking by completing high-value-added deals such as IPO arrangements and rights offerings, and it strengthened Korea's market presence in the bond and derivative segments.

(ii) KDB Capital. KDB Capital seeks to be a venture capitalist and the strategic partner most favored by domestic venture companies. The subsidiary has developed strong sales capabilities in green and new growth industries and has broadened its deal-sourcing networks for venture investments.

(iii) KDB Asset Management. Since 1996, KDB Asset Management has been delivering superb performance in collective investment management, investment advisory and discretionary investment services. The subsidiary has expanded sales channels to attract pension funds and funds from major corporations to develop stable assets under management (AUM) and has been developing effective sales capabilities.

(iv) KIAMCO (KDB Infrastructure). KIAMCO is Korea's first and largest asset manager specializing in infrastructure funds. The subsidiary has accumulated an abundance of experience and developed close relationships with investors over its many years of participation in road, rail, port and other infrastructure projects.

(v) KDB Life Insurance. KDB Life Insurance's insurance products consist of survival insurance, death insurance, life and death mixed insurance, group insurance and other types. The company changed its name to KDB Life Insurance Co., Ltd., from Kumho Life Insurance Co., Ltd, after KDB Bank took over Kumho Life Insurance in June 2010.

Part one　Overview of Development Financing

Chapter 4　National DFIs in Medium-/ Low-Income Countries

The stage of development has significant impacts on the organization, strategy and business models of DFIs. The DFIs play an important role in developing countries, where the financial markets need to be developed and the demand for financial services is tremendous. This section presents an overview of the DFIs in medium and low income countries.

Bank for Development and Foreign Economic Affairs (VEB)

General Information

The State Corporation "Bank for Development and Foreign Economic Affairs" (Vnesheconombank, VEB) exists to diversify and enhance the competitiveness of the Russian economy and to stimulate investment activities. The VEB is a state-owned specialized bank. The bank's activity is governed by the Federal Law "Bank for Development and Foreign Economic Affairs" (Vnesheconombank) ("the Law" will be used in the remaining part of the section), which was enacted on June 4, 2007. The chairman of the VEB's supervisory board is Dmitry Medvedev, who is the Premier of the government of the Russian Federation. The chairman of the VEB's management board is Vladimir Dmitriev.

The VEB's main activity is financing long-term and capital-intensive projects that commercial banks cannot afford. The VEB does not compete with commercial credit institutions and participates only in those projects that cannot receive funding from private investors. Under the Memorandum on Financial Policies, the VEB is to extend credits, guarantees and sureties to projects with a payback period of less than 5 years and with a total value of more than RUB 2 billion (USD 60 million).

The Vnesheconombank Group has been established to encompass the VEB's subsidiary institutions whose activities are designed to implement various provisions of the Law.

The VEB performs the functions of an agent for the government of the Russian Federation by maintaining records; servicing and redeeming Russia's sovereign foreign debt and state loans extended to foreign borrowers; and securing repayment of monetary obligations owed to the Russian Federation by legal entities, constituent entities of the Russian Federation and municipalities. The bank also performs functions related to extending and executing state guarantees of the Russian Federation by maintaining analytical records of the state guarantees issued.

The VEB headquarters is located at Vnesheconombank, Akademika Sakharova Prospekt, 9, Moscow, 107996, Russian Federation.

Mission and Strategy

The VEB is a national development bank that is instrumental in pursuing the government's socioeconomic policy by increasing the competitiveness of the national economy and modernizing it in an innovative manner. The bank's mission is to be a driving force for Russia's development through funding investment projects of national significance. The implementation of such projects helps to diversify Russia's economy and enhance its efficiency.

As defined by Article 3.1 of the Law, the VEB shall act to promote the competitiveness of the Russian Federation's economy and its diversification and to encourage investment activity through investments, insurance, consultancies and other activities for implementing projects in the Russian Federation and abroad, including projects involving foreign capital and projects aimed at developing infrastructure, innovations, special economic zones, environmental protections and exports of Russian goods, works and services, as well as to support SMEs.

The current sectorial structure of the VEB development loan portfolio is as follows: the share of projects in industrial sectors is 49.2%, the share of projects in infrastructure sectors is 41.5%, and the share of projects in the agro-industrial complex is 9.3%.

As a development institution, the VEB is in a position to meet the real economy's needs for long-term financial resources under the conditions of closed foreign capital markets, accelerated capital outflows from Russia and the banking sector's reduced level of liquidity. Its activity has a pronounced countercyclical effect. As a result of implementing a modernization scenario, the bank's role is anticipated to substantially increase in terms of implementing large-scale investment projects as well as innovations, import substitutions and infrastructure development, among other activities.

The VEB anticipates that by 2020, the amount of support that it will supply to the national economy, including subordinated credits, the development of leasing transactions and credits for subsidiary banks, will reach 4.5% of Russia's GDP. In addition, its contribution to the aggregate amount of investments in fixed capital will be 2.3%. The VEB's share of the aggregate amount of bank lending will reach 6%, and its share of the amount of long-term bank lending will reach 14%. The VEB's loan portfolio will reach RUB 3,000,000 million (USD 90,000 million), and the amount of financial support for SMEs through the SME Bank (a subsidiary of the VEB) will reach RUB 750,000 million (USD 22,500 million).

Governmental Support

As defined in Article 4 of the Law, "the legal status of VEB is regulated by this Law, other Russian Federation federal laws and regulatory legal acts adopted on the basis thereof. Laws on banks and banking shall apply to VEB activity to the extent that it does not contradict hereto and with due regard to specific features established hereby. Provisions of legislation on banks and banking with regard to the following procedures shall not apply to VEB: (i) state registration of credit institutions and issuance of banking licenses to such institutions; (ii) credit institution liquidation or reorganization; (iii) provision of information on credit institutions' activity; (iv) performance of certain banking operations and transactions contradictory to the procedures contemplated by this Law and laws on banks and banking; and (v) application of credit institution stability and financial soundness standards, and compliance with other mandatory requirements and regulations."

Funding Sources

The VEB's funding comes from the federal budget, the central bank and the National Wealth Fund. These state bodies hold deposits with the VEB, which is the only Russian organization eligible for this type of funding.

According to Article 5 of the Law, the VEB shall not be liable for obligations of the Russian Federation and, in reverse order, the Russian Federation shall not be liable for obligations of the VEB. The VEB shall use its properties solely to satisfy the objectives for which it was created.

At the end of 2013, the total amount of resources raised in capital markets by the VEB was RUB 813,400 million (USD 24,402 million), in which the amount of credits obtained from banks in that year was RUB 342,700 million (USD 10,281 million) and the amount of resources raised through the placement of the VEB's debt securities was RUB 470,700 million (USD 14,121 million), which included Eurobonds of RUB 311,800 million (USD 9,354 million) domestic ruble-denominated bonds of RUB 142,500 million (USD 4,275 million), and domestic foreign currency denominated bonds of RUB 16,400 million (USD 492 million).

Operational Data

At the end of 2013, the VEB's total assets were RUB 3,313,958 million (USD 100,744 million) and the VEB's total equity was RUB 576,859 million (USD 17,537 million). The charter capital of the VEB was RUB 388,069 million (USD 11,797 million).

At the end of 2013, the gross loan portfolio of the VEB was RUB 329,177 million (USD 10,073 million). On February 24, 2015, Moody's downgraded the ratings of seven primary Russian financial organizations: the VEB's Long-term LC and FC Issuer ratings were downgraded to Ba1 from Baa3, its outlook was revised to negative, and the Short-term LC and FC Issuer ratings were downgraded to NP from P-3. These actions followed the weakening of Russia's credit profile, as reflected by Moody's downgrade of Russia's government debt rating to Ba1 from Baa3 on February 20, 2015. As a government-related institution, the supported issuer ratings of the VEB with policy mandates were downgraded in line with Russia's government debt ratings.

Business Model and Products

As defined by Article 3.3 of the Law, VEB shall exercise the following basic functions: (i) Financing of investment projects aimed at the development of infrastructure and implementation of innovative projects, including financing in the form of loans or interest rate in business organizations' capital; (ii) Issuance of bonds or other securities in accordance with Russian Federation laws; (iii) Making arrangements for loans and attracting loans and borrowings, including those in the financial markets; (iv) Purchasing stakes in the charter capital of business entities as well as in the investment and the mutual investment funds; (v) Exercise of rights and performance of obligations of a currency control agent as well as set forth examples for authorized banks; (vi) Issuance of guarantees to legal entities for third parties; (vii) Purchase of rights to demand fulfillment of monetary obligations from third parties and issuance of equity securities secured by such rights to demand; (viii) Arrangement of export credit loans and investment insurance against business and/or political risks in accordance with items 6-9 hereof; (ix) Participation in transactions contemplating payment by the parties thereto of sums depending on changes in the prices of goods and securities, the exchange rate of a specific currency, interest rates and inflation levels in order to minimize the risks on operations carried out; (x) Participation in implementation of federal target programs and government investment projects; (xi) Participation in investment projects of national significance implemented on a public-private basis as well as projects to create infrastructure and other facilities to secure functioning of special economic zones; (xii) Leasing operations; (xiii) Provision of budgetary loans when such loans are extended to support Russian industrial product exports, including construction of facilities abroad and supply of complete installations, issuance of bank guarantees for Russian companies taking part in international bidding and performance of signed export contracts; (xiv) Arranging and carrying out expert examination of investment projects and drafting export contracts of Russian exporters; (xv) Participation in small and medium business support schemes by way of financing credit organizations and legal entities to support small and medium business; (xvi) Monitoring of compliance by legal entities with the regulations of projects implemented in association with VEB; (xvii) Cooperation with international organizations, foreign corporations and institutions for development and participation in implementation by international associations for development of projects in the Russian Federation; (xviiii) Participation in associations, unions and other non-profit organizations being or having been established in the Russian Federation and abroad to promote economic development and investment; (xix) Establishment of branches and opening of representative offices as well as registration of legal entities in the Russian Federation and abroad; (xx) Participation in financial and guarantee support of exports of Russian-made goods; (xxi) Participation in carrying out operations on registration and utilization, servicing and repayment of state credits extended by the Russian Federation to foreign countries; and (xxii) Performance in accordance with the established procedures of works related to the use of information comprising State secrets and other types of confidential information and ensuring its protection.

As defined by Article 4 of the Law, VEB shall carry out the following banking operations: (i) Attraction of monetary funds of legal entities taking part in implementation of VEB's projects in the form of deposits; (ii) Opening of and maintaining bank accounts of legal entities taking part in implementation of VEB's projects as well as correspondent accounts with the Russian Federation Central Bank, credit institutions in the Russian Federation, foreign banks and international settlement and clearing centers; (iii) Investment of attracted funds; (iv) Clearing payments ordered by legal entities; (v) Purchase and sale of foreign currency in cash and non-cash forms; (vi) Collection of cash, bills and payment documents for legal entities taking part in implementation of VEB's projects; (vii) Provision of bank guarantees to legal entities taking part in implementation of VEB's projects.

The VEB is required to invest in a number of priority sectors: aircraft construction, the space industry, shipbuilding, electronics, the atomic energy industry, defense, agro-industry, computer technology, communications systems and medicine.

The bank's participation in conducting its investment projects and support for industrial exports assumes the form of credits, guarantees and sureties, participation in economic entities' authorized capital, leasing transactions, insurance of export credits, and financial and guarantee support for exports.

The VEB participates in investment activities, extends export credit facilities and provides guarantee support for Russian exporters upon exporting Russian industrial products, works and services. The VEB activities that support exporting include subsidizing interest rates as an instrument for export support, lending, export guarantee support, and funding for projects abroad and non-financial instruments such as information services (consulting).

The VEB also participates in innovation activities. Currently, the VEB is participating in the implementation of 66 projects designed to develop innovations. These projects are being implemented in industrial sectors such as the defense industrial complex, aircraft construction, medical equipment and pharmaceuticals, rocket and space industry, electronics industry and engine construction. Currently, innovation projects account for 34.5% of the bank's total loan portfolio. As of July 2014, the VEB's corporate governance bodies had made decisions to fund 26 innovation projects in the total amount of approximately RUB 199 billion (USD 5,731 million), with VEB's participation share at more than RUB 169.9 billion (USD 4,893 million).

The VEB has played an important role in Russia's economic development. The VEB has made investments in diversified infrastructure sectors, including transportation (Brunswick Rail), power (OGK-5 and GSR Energy) and telecommunications (Russian Towers).

Since 2007, the VEB's subsidiary SME Bank (Russian Development Bank, until 2011) has been an agent of the VEB in implementing a program to support SMEs. Through a network of regional partner banks and infrastructure organizations (leasing, factoring companies, microfinance institutions and others), the bank extends loans and other forms of support to SMEs in all of Russia's regions. Credits are extended for a tenure of up to 7 years and in an amount of up to RUB 150 million (USD 4.5 million). The average weighted rate with regard to the portfolio of credits extended by partner banks under the SME Bank's program is 12.6%.

Corporate Governance

According to Article 13 of the Law, the VEB's management board is a collegial executive body that consists of a chairman and eight other members. The chairman directs the board's work. The members are appointed and relieved by the VEB's supervisory board, as recommended by the VEB's chairman. The management board members must be regular employees of the VEB; that is, every board member is an executive.

The VEB's board has the following powers: (i) Prepare and submit for approval by VEB's supervisory board proposals on principal directions of VEB's activity as well as VEB's investment and financial operations parameters; (ii) Approve decisions on investment project financing within amounts contemplated by the provision on VEB's governing bodies; (iii) Draft and submit for approval by VEB's supervisory board financial income and expense plan (budget) of VEB; (iv) Review VEB's annual report and submit the same for approval by VEB's supervisory board; (v) Submit to VEB's supervisory board proposals on appropriation of VEB's profits; (vi) Approve VEB's staff list, set employment and dismissal terms and conditions, social security, office rights and obligations, disciplinary punishment system, size and form of payment of salary to VEB's employees in accordance with Russian Federation laws; (vii) Approve VEB's organizational structure; and (viii) Exercise other powers contemplated hereby, if not within the competence of other VEB governing bodies.

According to Article 15 of the Law, the VEB's chairman is the sole executive body and manages day-to-day operations. The chairman shall be appointed and relieved by the Russian president. The chairman shall be appointed as recommended by the premier of the Russian government for a term not exceeding five years. New chairman candidates shall be presented to the president one month prior to the expiration of powers of the incumbent chairman. If the president rejects the candidate, then the chairman of the VEB's supervisory board shall present to the president another candidate within 15 days.

According to Article 16 of the Law, VEB's chairman has the following powers: (i) Act on behalf of VEB and represent VEB's interests without proxy in its relations with governmental authorities, local authorities, foreign and international organizations, and other organizations; (ii) Head VEB's board and arrange for implementation of resolutions adopted by VEB's board; (iii) Issue orders and instructions covering VEB's activity; (iv) Assign duties among its deputies; (v) Submit to VEB's supervisory board proposals on appointment or dismissal of VEB's board members; (vi) Appoint and dismiss VEB's staff; and (vii) Make other decisions within VEB's competence save for issues within the competence of VEB's supervisory board and VEB's management board.

According to Article 10 of the Law, the VEB's supervisory board is its supreme governing body and shall consist of 8 members and the VEB's chairman. The chairman of the Russian government (the Premier) shall be the chairman of the VEB's supervisory board. The VEB's supervisory board members shall be appointed by the Russian government for a term of five years. The members of the supervisory board, except for the VEB's chairman, shall not be regular employees of the VEB. The Russian government has the power to remove a member of the VEB's supervisory board before the end of the member's term. If such a removal occurs, the government shall appoint a new member within two months.

According to Article 11 of the Law, the VEB's supervisory board shall be convened by its chairman or by any member duly authorized by the chairman at least once per quarter. To pass resolutions, at least half of the board's members must be present in a session. Resolutions shall be passed by a simple majority of votes of those present. In cases of tie votes, the vote of the supervisory board session chair shall be decisive. Supervisory board sessions shall be presided over by the VEB's supervisory board chairman or, if the chairman is absent, by a supervisory board member duly authorized by the chairman.

According to Article 12 of the Law, the VEB's supervisory board has the following powers: (i) Identify principal directions of VEB's activity based on the Memorandum approved by the Russian Federation Government; (ii) Approve the provision on VEB's governing bodies; (iii) Approve the provision on VEB's branches and representative offices; (iv) Approve VEB's annual report; (v) Approve VEB's financial income and expense plan (budget), formation of reserves and funds as well as income, reserve and fund disposition procedures; (vi) Resolve on the establishment of branches, the opening of representative offices and the registration of legal entities; (vii) Approve the auditing firm selected on a tender basis to perform the annual audit of VEB's annual financial statements; (viii) Hear the reports by VEB's chairman on the VEB's activities; (ix) Decide on appointment of VEB's Internal Control head and premature terminations of its powers; (x) Resolve on issue of VEB's bonds and set the securities issuance procedures in accordance with Russian Federation laws; (xi) Specify VEB's investment and financial activity parameters within the powers granted to it by the Memorandum; (xii) Approve transactions or a series of related transactions with respect to the purchase, alienation or possible alienation of VEB's property with a book value of 10 or more percent of VEB's equity (capital) as of the latest reporting date immediately preceding the date of approving such transactions; and (xiii) Exercise other powers contemplated hereby.

Development Bank of Kazakhstan (DBK)

General Information

The Development Bank of Kazakhstan was incorporated with exclusive legal status by the Government Decree of the Republic of Kazakhstan No. 659, "On the Incorporation of the Development Bank of Kazakhstan (DBK) Closed-up Joint Stock Company," dated May 18, 2001. The DBK has a special legal status as an investment institution of the government of the Republic of Kazakhstan, which funds the non-primary sector of the economy. This special status gives the bank advantages, such as (i) the lack of regulation of bank activities by the national regulator on certain issues and (ii) the use of the authorized capital of the development bank for lending. The headquarters of the bank is located in Astana, Kazakhstan. The DBK's 100% ownership by the state also ensures strong implicit sovereign support. With Baiterek National Management Holding JSC as a new shareholder, the bank has concentrated on improving the efficiency of its asset management and optimizing its credit procedures. In 2005, the 100% participation of the DBK subsidiary leasing company DBK Leasing JSC was established. The company aims to provide lease financing for infrastructure projects under construction in the industrial manufaturing and transportational sectors. Legislation on the DBK is based on the Constitution of the Republic of Kazakhstan, the Law of the Republic of Kazakhstan about the Development Bank of Kazakhstan and other regulatory acts.

Mission and Strategy

The bank's mission is "to promote sustainable development of the national economy through investment in the non-energy sectors of the country". The goal defined by DBK is to improve the efficiency of public investment activities, to develop the country's industrial infrastructure and the processing industry and to facilitate external and internal investments in the country's economy. The long-term development strategy of the DBK was approved by a decision of the bank's board of directors on July 14, 2014 (Minutes No. 156); it defines the strategic goals and key trends in the bank's development until 2023. The strategic goal is the transformation of the bank, as a financially stable and dynamic bank organization, into a modern and independent national development establishment that can play a significant role in the creation of a competitive non-energy sector in the country's economy. The bank's strategic directions are lending, financial resource management and corporate management. The bank's activities are intended to provide financial aid for three priorities: the direct financing for enterprises, the promotion of the development of territories/clusters through infrastructure investments and the provision of financing through inter-bank lending for priority branches. According to the DBK's long term development strategy through 2020, at the first-stage strategy, priority will be to provide loans for strategic investment projects implemented under government programs and the development of trade financing. The second stage strategy focus attracting private capital for non-governmental projects, organizing financing transactions and advising clients on entering the capital market and acting as a fiscal agent to attract "cheap" loans for the government's industrial projects.

Government Support

The government of Kazakhstan would provide timely and extraordinary support to the DBK if it encountered financial difficulties. The DBK's integral link with the government would allow the bank to receive direct budget transfers from the government. The DBK received a KZT 50 billion (USD 276 million) loan from the government in October 2014, and before the end of 2014, the bank expected to receive an additional KZT 50 billion (USD 276 million) loan and a KZT 25 billion (USD 138 million) equity injection. The DBK's public policy role has increasingly focused on funding the government's industrialization program. As one of the key operators of the state program FIID (Forced Industrial-Innovative Development), 80% of the bank's loan portfolio covers projects in industrial and innovative development. Approximately 60% of the loans issued by the DBK are for projects in the spheres of oil processing and metallurgy. The transfer of the DBK's shares to Baiterek from Samruk-Kazyna in 2013 with the government retaining indirect ownership improved the bank's governance. In 2013, Baiterek was established by the government as a joint stock company that provides financial and investment support to non-commodity sectors and manages 10 development institutions. The DBK is by far the largest of these institutions, accounting for 58% of the holding's total assets. Baiterek was specifically established to enable the government to increase its focus on development institutions and to help the government improve their efficiency and corporate governance.

The DBK's standalone creditworthiness reflects the bank's public policy role as a national development bank regulated by the respective law and its favorable funding maturity schedule, ample liquidity cushion and acceptable capital adequacy. The

DBK's close links with the government provide the bank with regular access to capital and liquidity resources. The bank is exempt from regulatory oversight by the National Bank of Kazakhstan (NBK). However, the probability of the DBK requiring support is relatively high, given the bank's reliance on non-government wholesale funding sources and its moderate capitalization. The cost of supporting the bank, if needed, is currently modest relative to sovereign financial resources.

Funding Source

Because of the specifics and limitations on the DBK's activities determined by the existing legislation, borrowed funds are the bank's only funding source to provide credit for investment projects. The funding base of the bank's credit operations determines the basic conditions for providing credit for investment projects and export operations. To ensure the necessary base for funding, the bank uses different borrowing instruments in domestic and international capital markets, including the issuance and placement of bonds, the attraction of inter-bank and public budget credits, syndicated loans and the utilization of credit lines. According to the bank's results from 2013, the bank's volume of debt owed to creditors was USD 5.7 billion.

In addition, the bank has reached agreements with existing creditors for early repayments or changes in conditions on "expensive" sources, which were earlier agreed upon under less favorable market conditions. For example, for the first half of 2013, the bank engaged in a number of liability management transactions worth more than USD 770 million, which allowed the bank to noticeably reduce its average cost of funding.

In 2013, the bank's debt structure in terms of finacial instruments consisted of Euro EUROBONDS (34%), inter-bank loans (43%), junior bonds (13%), budget loans and FSA funds (9%), and Islamic bonds (1%).

Operational Data

The DBK's total assets at the end of 2014 were KZT 1,306,686 million (USD 7,160 million), its total equity was KZT 312,968 million (USD 1,715 million), the total gross loan portfolio was KZT 815,187 million (USD 4,467 million), the net profit for the year was KZT 11,262 million (USD 62 million), the ROA was 0.86%, and the ROE was 3.60%. The average weighted interest rate of the bank's investment projects was 6.6% at the end of 2013. The transfer of troubled projects to the Investment Fund of Kazakhstan JSC in late 2013 and the first half of 2014 resulted in a decrease in the portion of non-performing assets in the bank's loan portfolio to 12.5% as of December 31, 2013, compared with 41.9% one year earlier. Non-performing loans decreased to 7.8% in mid-2014. Over 13 years of the bank's activity, it has attracted USD 8.6 billion to the country's economy through the DBK's investments. A total of 75 projects have been commissioned, and 18.9 thousand permanent jobs have been created.

The DBK's management body includes: (i) the supreme authority, which is the sole shareholder; (ii) the management body, which is the board of directors; (iii) the executive body, which is the management board; and (iv) the supervisory body, which is the Internal Audit Service. The board of directors consists of 6 members, 3 of whom are independent directors. Asset Issekeshev has been the chairman of the board of directors of the DBK since May 2009.

The bank also has a risk management committee that plays an important role in making strategic decisions. The primary purpose of the risk management committee is to assist the board of directors in fulfilling its responsibility to ensure the availability and functioning of an adequate system of risk management at the bank and to improve and strengthen the risk management system.

Business Models and Products

The bank finances projects from point zero—including such projects as startup and greenfield projects in processing sectors and infrastructure. The bank also finances projects aimed at the modernization and reconstruction of industrial facilities. As a financial institution of the state tasked with developing the country's infrastructure and non-energy sector, the bank lends to enterprises in sub-sectors such as agribusiness, construction, industry, and infrastructure.

The bank's services include: " (i) Financing of large investment projects (no less than USD 30 million) for the medium term (5 years and longer) and long term (from 10 to 20 years). There is also interim financing for the purposes of provision and implementation of investment projects. (ii) Financing of exports (pre-export operations). (iii) Mezzanine financing, project financing, financing of current operations of borrowers under the implementation of projects. (iv) Issuance of guarantees on loans provided by other lending institutions as well as providing services in co-financing on the issuance of loans by other financial organizations. (v) Inter-bank lending. " The bank also lends through other financial institutions and directly to customers.

In 2013, the projects under the bank's service were in the following sectors: financial activities (22%), energy (40%), space sector (12%), and transport and communication (26%). Regarding the regional structure of projects served by the DBK, a significant share is represented by inter-regional projects (56%) and projects in Almaty City and the Almaty Region (21%).

Box 4-1 Cooperation between the DBK and China

The bilateral relationship between the Republic of Kazakhstan and the People's Republic of China has assumed an important strategic role with the expanding commercial and strategic cooperation between the two nations. In 2013, Mr. Xi Jinping, president of the People's Republic of China, proposed in a speech that China and the Central Asian countries should build an "economic belt along the Silk Road. " The "One Belt and One Road" initiative involves 65 countries and

4.4 billion people. Kazakhstan plans to become a key transit country in Central Asia between China and Europe. In fact, the volume of container traffic traveling from China to the EU through Kazakhstan grew by 4.5 times from 2012 to 2014. In addition, the Chinese government is dedicated to the construction and management of the second and third stages of a China-Kazakhstan logistics project.

The DBK has strengthened cooperation with banks in China.

The chairman of the board of the DBK, Bolat Zhamishev, and the chairman of the China Development Bank (CDB), Zheng Zhijie, discussed the most promising areas of cooperation between the two financial institutions during talks in Astana, according to the DBK's press service, and the two development banks identified areas for further cooperation. The head of the DBK informed his Chinese counterpart about opportunities for funding infrastructure projects and projects in non-resource sectors of the economy in Kazakhstan. Currently, the DBK's portfolio of potential projects (pipeline) exceeds KZT 1 trillion (USD 36 billion). The DBK has previously signed three loan contracts with the CDB totaling USD 300 million (in 2008 and 2009). All loan facilities were fully realized; in particular, projects in the fields of electricity, metallurgy, transportation and textile industry were funded. Moreover, in May 2014, the DBK and CDB signed a general agreement on the opening of a credit line amounting to USD 500 million. Bolat Zhamishev and Zheng Zhijie expressed mutual interest in the implementation of this agreement.

The Export-Import Bank of China provided a loan worth USD 1 billion to the DBK on May 19 – 21, 2014, to be spent on modernizing and reconstructing the Shymkent refinery. The loan agreement was signed in the presence of the heads of state of Kazakhstan and China during President Nursultan Nazarbayev's state visit to China. The loan is allocated to the member state of the Shanghai Cooperation Organization on preferential terms.

National Bank for Foreign Economic Activity of the Republic of Uzbekistan (NBU)

General Information

The National Bank for Foreign Economic Activity of the Republic of Uzbekistan was formed by a Presidential Decree of the Republic of Uzbekistan on September 7, 1991, and was registered on October 25, 1991, as a closed stock company with limited liability under the laws of the Republic of Uzbekistan. The bank's headquarters is located at 101 Amir Temur Street, Tashkent. The bank's council is the representative of the government responsible for the approval and revision of the charter and other important decisions. The chairman of the council of the bank is appointed by the Cabinet of Ministers and the executive agent is the board. The board members include the chairman of the board, Rakhimov Saidakhmat Borievich; the first deputy chairman of the board, Azim Akhmedkhadjaev; the deputy chairman of the board, Alisher Mirsoatov; and people from other departments.

Mission and Strategy

The bank's primary mission is "to service foreign trade operations, to increase the export potential of the republic and to attract foreign investments." Its major goals include attracting external financing to facilitate its role in supporting state-directed economic development and reforms. The most important strategic development in the bank's immediate future will be the privatization of 49% of the NBU as part of the government's plan to reform the national banking sector. The sale will create greater transparency; encourage the use of modern technologies and management techniques, and help to tap international capital markets, improve the quality of services, achieve greater independence for the bank and make the bank more responsible to shareholders for its final results.

Ownership Structure

In March 1993, the bank was registered as a banking institution wholly owned by the government of the Republic of Uzbekistan.

Funding Sources

The bank's funding sources largely include authorized capital, resource funds and other funds; accounts of clients; credits from other banks; capital from companies, banks and corporations in other counties; profits from bonds and securities; and the savings of residents. The government also lends money to the bank and provides guarantees for loans. However, the government is not required by law to pay the bank's debt, except for those debts for which the government takes responsibility.

Operational Data

As of December 31, 2013, the bank's assets consisted of UZS 11,227,362 million (USD 5,098 million), of which the share of earning assets reached 83%. Significant weight in the asset structure falls on credit operations, which constitute 59.5% of the bank's total net assets. At the end of 2014, the bank's assets totaled UZS 12,831,110 million (USD 5,132 million), its liabilities equaled UZS 11,726,389 million (USD 4,690 million) and its equity was UZS 1,104,721 million (USD 442 million). As of December 31, 2013, the bank's assets consisted of UZS 11,286,234 million (USD 5,643 million). Its total equity at the end of 2013 was UZS 1,012,614 million (USD 506 million). In 2013, the bank's net profit of 2013 was UZS 102,181 million (USD 51 million). At the end of 2013, the bank's ROA was 0.9%, and its ROE was 10.1%. Its total equity at the end of 2013 was UZS 1,012,614 million (USD 502 million). The bank's total gross loan portfolio at the end of 2013 was UZS 6,822,294 million (USD 3,650 million), which represented an increase of 30% compared with the prior year. The longest loan maturity is 15 years.

On May 3, 2013, the bank was rated by Moody's Investors Service as B1/B2/E +/ NP and on November 26, 2013, the bank was rated by Standard & Poor's as B +/B. All rating organizations rated the bank as stable. By April 2015, no new rating had been published for Uzbekistan's sovereign credit by Moody's, S&P or Fitch.

Business Models and Products

The NBU engages in both wholesale and retail lending. The bank serves more than 70% of Uzbekistan's foreign trade turnover, offering guarantees, forfeiting, factoring and direct lending to domestic exporters. Using credit lines offered by the EBRD, AsDB and IFC, the bank finances investment projects involving the construction, modernization and technical re-equipment of industries as well as the purchase of raw materials. The NBU is the largest investment bank in Uzbekistan, and its portfolio includes equity stakes in aircraft manufacturers and companies in the textile and food industries, agribusiness, transport and tourism, as well as the financial sector. In particular, the bank makes a special effort to support SMEs. Moreover, the NBU provides traditional retail services and is the established leader in terms of private deposits; to continually increase that amount, the bank relies on both innovative products and a high level of public trust in the national banking system.

The bank's products can be divided into 3 categories: products for individuals, projects for small and private businesses, and projects for corporate clients, including money transfers, microcredit, project financing and other products.

Supervision

The bank is directly supervised by the government. Its council members include the finance minister of Uzbekistan, the minister of foreign economic relations, and other individuals. The leaders of the bank are the chairman and the deputy chairman of the board.

Box 4 – 2　The NBU Received an International Award for "Sustainable Project Financing"

In 2014, the NBU won an international award for "Sustainable Project Financing". More than 200 banks and financial institutions from dozens of countries participated in the contest. The certificate was awarded to the bank based on a construction project for the electrified railway "Angren-Pap".

To engage in sustainable development, the NBU has focused on several infrastructure projects. The bank took a landmark step in financing the construction of electrified railway line "Angren-Pap", which is 124 kilometers in length.

The project ensured that no irreparable harm was done to the environment during construction and that there were no settlements for rare species of indigenous plants or animals in the area. Because the location was carefully selected, the land used is not suitable for agriculture. Several other measures were also taken to ensure that the surrounding areas were not affected.

One of the major environmental benefits of the "Angren-Pap" project is that it reduces CO_2 emissions by more than half as a result of the redistribution of freight traffic.

The project contributes to the livelihood of more than 900 families and creates further income-generating opportunities for the population in the Fergana Valley. It also connects local residents with other communities and provides them with easier access to facilities outside of their region. The project reduces the travelling time of the local population and contributes to social cohesion.

The "Angren-Pap" project provides numerous economic benefits to Uzbekistan.

> In addition to creating employment, the project reduces the transportation cost for cargo, which in turn reduces the cost of goods and contributes to enhancing the competitiveness of Uzbekistan's economy.

Development Bank of Mongolia (DBM)

General Information

The Development Bank of Mongolia (DBM) was established on May 12, 2011, as a development policy bank. The bank is located in Ulaanbaatar, the capital of Mongolia. Its establishment was based on Resolution No. 195, which was issued by the government on July 20, 2010, and the Law of the Development Bank of Mongolia, which was passed on February 10, 2011, with the aim of formalizing, manipulating and observing the DBM. As a 100% government-owned financial institution, the DBM serves as a key instrument for the implementation of state policy on industrial and infrastructure development projects. The bank aims to promote regional development, assist in the reduction of urban-rural disparities and facilitate strategic projects co-financed with foreign and domestic investors.

The DBM has an average of 79 staff members and a board that consists of nine members appointed by the government for a maximum fixed term of three years. The DBM conducts business under the direct supervision of the Cabinet, which is the highest institution of government administration in Mongolia; it is also under observation by the Ministry of Economic Development and the Ministry of Finance.

Mission and Strategy

The mission of the DBM is "to foster the economic and infrastructure development of Mongolia by providing long-term financing for policy-oriented projects consistent with the government's macroeconomic development strategy as well as to encourage sustainable economic development, support the value-added products industry and propagate modern financial solutions and ideas".

According to DBM law, the bank has the responsibility to finance large projects and programs. The Mongolian parliament approves a list of projects and programs every year, and the DBM Law stipulates that the bank is to provide loans for these project, whereas projects without a government guarantee must be examined by the DBM board.

The DBM follows several different strategies: (i) financing the most important sectors (energy, transmission lines, the processing industry and infrastructure) by providing medium-or long-term loans and other financial solutions; (ii) introducing internal and external investment and promoting foreign investment; (iii) encouraging investment in areas that can optimize the structure of the economy, for instance, supporting export industries and new export enterprises by increasing their competitiveness; (iv) supporting the sustainable development of society by bridging the urban/rural divide, increasing jobs and introducing good governance principles; and (v) cooperating with both renowned institutions in the financial sector and other organizations.

Ownership

As a 100% state-owned bank, the DBM is supported by the government in three major ways. First, the bank was incorporated under Mongolian law. The government of Mongolia and parliament use the law to support, lead and supervise the bank in the financing of programs and projects approved by parliament. Second, the bank obtains financing directly from the government at an interest rate (4.79%) that is lower than the market rate. Therefore, the bank is able to provide loans at lower interest rates and for longer maturities. Moreover, the government of Mongolia uses its sovereign status to guarantee loans. "All loans to be repaid from the state budget are guaranteed by the government and have the same credit rating as the government of Mongolia"; thus, each individual loan has no risk of loss.

Funding Sources

The DBM's funding sources include medium-term notes issued by the DBM and financing borrowed from the government of Mongolia. The bank completed documentation for the EMTN (Euro Medium-Term Note program) and successfully sold USD 580 million of five-year notes with a coupon of 5.75%, guaranteed by the sovereign, in March 2012.

Later in 2012, the government of Mongolia issued the "Chinggis Bond", which was worth USD 1.5 billion and had a relatively low coupon of 5.25% over 10 years (4.25% for the 5-year bond). The bond is aimed at financing major projects and programs and boosting industry and infrastructure in Mongolia (see Box 4 – 3 for more information).

In addition, in late 2013, a 10-year Samurai bond denominated in yen was issued by the DBM to gain access to Japanese capital market. It was the first issue of a Samurai bond by a Mongolian institution, and the DBM is the first institution with a B rating to be guaranteed for Samurai bond. Moreover, the bank has signed numerous memorandums of understanding with foreign financial institutions such as the China Development Bank (CDB) and the Kuwait Fund for Arab Economic Development.

The key financing sectors are mining, auto roads, construction materials, energy, railways, air transportation and engineering utilities. Most of the proceeds from the Chinggis Bond are used for road construction, while the largest DBM funding investment supports Erdenes Tavan Tolgoi (ETT), which is a subsidiary of Erdenes MGL, a government-owned company specializing in mining.

At the end of 2014, the DBM had total equity of MNT 246,536 million (USD 1,306 million). On July 17, 2014, Moody's Investors Service downgraded Mongolia's foreign currency government bond rating from B1 to B2, and the outlook has since remained negative. In a related rating action, Moody's downgraded the senior unsecured rating of the DBM from B1 to B2; again, the outlook remains negative. Because the DBM's payment obligations carry a credit guarantee from the government of Mongolia, its debt obligations justify a rating at the same level.

Box 4-3 Chinggis Bond: Transformative Investments vs. Debt Sustainability

Similar to China and many other developing economies, Mongolia experienced continuous and rapid GDP growth that peaked at 17.3% in 2011. However, the situation changed significantly in 2012. Parliament passed into law a limit on the amount of foreign investment in major economic areas, insisting that Mongolian ownership should be at least 50% in all corporations. The law significantly dampened the enthusiasm of foreign investors. Meanwhile, China, which is Mongolia's largest target market, gradually reduced its imports of carbon and coal, which contributed to a deceleration of Mongolia's economic growth. In addition, the country's inferior internal infrastructure further hampered economic development. A poor infrastructure encourages little investment, and a lack of money leads to a poor investment environment. This vicious circle must be addressed by Mongolia's government.

To manage the situation, Mongolia's government found it necessary to attract and mobilize a large amount of money from the capital market. At the end of 2012, the government issued a bond, known as the "Chinggis Bond", in the international market via the DBM.

The "Chinggis Bond" is the first national bond issued by the government of Mongolia in the international market, and it raised USD 1.5 billion for the government. The bond is aimed at financing major projects and programs as well as boosting industry and infrastructure in Mongolia.

What was the development impact of the "Chinggis Bond"?

On the one hand, the "Chinggis Bond" has been celebrated as a success for the following reasons:

First, the bond has supported several large infrastructure construction programs. "The New Railroad" program, which aimed to increase the exportation of mining products by building 1,800 km of railroad, received a total loan of USD 400 million.

Second, the bond has increased Mongolia's foreign exchange reserves and boosted investor confidence in the country's economic performance. The bond not only has reached its targeted revenue amount but is also "ten times oversubscribed", indicating that the demand for bonds was 10 times greater than the supply.

Finally, the bond has improved living standards in the country. For example, the "Buyant Ukhaan-1" District was financed to provide 1,764 apartments to young families, elders and civil workers at a relatively low price ($1,280,000 ₮ / m^2$).

However, some concerns have arisen. Both the World Bank and the IMF have recently cautioned the government that its expansionary fiscal and monetary policies could threaten the stability of the economy. In December 2013, the ratings agencies revised the country's outlook from stable to negative.

Operational Data

At the end of 2014, the DBM had total equity of MNT 246,536 million (USD 1,306 million), which indicates 20% growth from 2013's figure of MNT 143,879 million

(USD 88 million). The total assets of the DBM at the end of 2013 were MNT 3,230,870 million (USD 1,968 million) compared with MNT 5,506,034 million (USD 2,917 million) in 2014. Total liabilities were MNT 5,259,497 million (USD 2,786 million) at the end of 2014 and MNT 3,086,990 million (USD 1,880 million) in 2013.

The total comprehensive income for 2014 was MNT 102,657 million (USD 54 million). This is a remarkable progress, since the total comprehensive income for 2013 was MNT 26,888 million (USD 16 million).

The DBM's ROA was -0.60% at the end of 2012, 0.80% at the end of 2013 and 0.50% in the first quarter of 2014. The bank's ROE was -8.50% at the end of 2012, 18.70% at the end of 2013. The capital adequacy ratio (CAR) was 12.80% at the end of 2013.

Business Models and Products

The DBM participates in development projects primarily in three ways. The first is through debt financing. Direct loans are available for small and medium-sized projects when such financing is legal. For larger projects, the bank is capable of providing or arranging co-financing with multilateral agencies, such as the World Bank, and it can also arrange international syndicated loans. Second, the bank can provide equity financing if a project requires strategic investment. Third, the bank can provide consulting services to structure a financing scheme, find relevant sources of funding, structure a project and negotiate with international financing sources for Mongolian companies.

Corporate Governance and Regulation

The DBM has a board that consists of nine members; the current chairperson is B. Shinebaatar /Б. Шинэбаатар/, who is the secretary general of the Department of Economic Development. All nine board members are appointed by the government of

Mongolia; six of them are governors from different ministries, and the other three are selected from the Bank of Mongolia, the Department of Local Business and Industries and the Committee of Mongolian Banks. The chief executive officer (CEO) is nominated by the board and approved by the General Meeting of Shareholders, which represents the government. The current CEO is N. Munhbat /Н. Мөнхбат/, who leads five departments: Credit, Investment, Assets & Liabilities, Risk management and supervision Monitoring. The Risk Management Department is required to identify, measure and manage both financial and non-financial risks while regularly reporting to the board and CEO. The board is responsible for monitoring risks and ensuring proper bank operations.

Bank Pembangunan Malaysia Berhad (BPMB)

General Information

Incorporated in 1973, the Bank Pembangunan Malaysia Berhad (BPMB) commenced operations on June 8, 1974. BPMB was incorporated under the Companies Act of 1965. Its registered office is in Kuala Lumpur.

Mission and Strategy

BPMB's original objective was to assist entrepreneurs involved in small and medium-sized industries through the provision of various financing facilities, entrepreneur training and advisory services.

"Today, BPMB is mandated to provide medium-to-long-term financing for Islamic and conventional facilities in capital-intensive industries, which include infrastructure projects and the maritime, science and technology, and oil and gas sectors."

Ownership

BPMB is wholly owned by the Malaysian government through the Ministry of Finance

(MOF) and the Federal Lands Commissioner.

Funding Sources

Historically, BPMB has primarily relied on the government to support its financing activities. However, the bank has gradually diversified its financing through (i) deposits from the general public, (ii) loans from other institutions and debt issuance in local markets, and (iii) government support from direct budget transfers with various types of funds and compensations as well as guarantees of notes and loans. For instance, in 2013, BPMB received MYR 120 million (USD 36.60 million) in compensation from the government. The government guarantees BPMB's debt, including infrastructure notes and all loans from the Employees Provident Fund (EPF). The proportions of funding sources are: deposits from customers: paid-in capital: government transfers: borrowed from other FIs: redeemable notes = 7,430: 3,039: 120: 311: 3,025.

Operational Data

BPMB lends directly only to final customers. The BPMB Group's total assets increased to MYR 29.25 billion (USD 8.92 billion) at the end of 2013. Total equity showed a considerable increase to MYR 7.59 billion (USD 2.31 billion) in 2013, largely because of the net profit recorded during the financial year. The group's total net loans, advances and financing amounted to MYR 24.21 billion (USD 7.38 billion). BPMB also has strategic investments through its two subsidiaries. For the financial year ending in 2013, BPMB's ROA was 1.74% and its ROE was 6.65%. The gross impaired loan ratio at the end of 2013 was 10.17% and the net impaired loan ratio was 4.19%. The Bank Negara Malaysia (the Malaysian central bank, BNM) has imposed several regulatory capital requirements whereby the bank must have an absolute minimum capital of MYR 300 million (USD 83.58 million) and a minimum risk-weighted capital ratio (RWCR) of 8% at all times. To further strengthen the capital position of the bank through a progressive and systematic accumulation of the reserve fund, the minimum RWCR under both normal and stress scenarios shall not be less than 20% and 12% respectively. The interest rate on loans ranges from 6.8% to 10%. The maximum loan term maturity is 20 years.

Business Models and Products

BPMB lends to organizations in several subsectors, including agribusiness, construction, industry/manufacturing, services, infrastructure, energy, education, health and maritime. The industries receiving the most investments are (i) construction; (ii) electricity, gas and water supply; and (iii) transport, storage and communication. In addition, BPMB has the Tourism Infrastructure Fund (TIF) and the Tourism Infrastructure Development Fund (TIDF) that support the government's mission of developing and boosting the tourism industry. The Maritime Fund and the Maritime Development Fund (MDF) provide financial assistance to new and existing companies involved in shipping, ship-building, marine, oil- and gas-related activities and services. The target markets include the government, SMEs' and all corporations. The bank offers loans for working capital, bridge or short-term loans, long-term loans and syndicated loans through conventional and Islamic securities (Susuk issuance and Islamic CP&MTN programs).

Governance and Supervision

The government, particularly the Ministry of Finance, continuously supports and assists BPMB. The bank also receives guidance and advice from BNM. BPMB's corporate governance is subject to BNM's guidelines on corporate governance for DFIs and other primary legislative and regulatory provisions. The Islamic banking activity of BPMB operates on a window basis and is governed by the Shari'ah Governance Framework (SGF) for Islamic Institutions issued by BNM in 2011. The prudential limits are the same as in the prudential rules. BPMB is legally required to be audited by Ernst & Young.

Development Bank of the Philippines (DBP)

General Information

The Development Bank of the Philippines (DBP), headquartered in Makati, is a state-owned development financing institution that is tasked with a pivotal role in the quest for sustainable growth and development. The bank originally served only development programs until 1995, when it was granted an expanded banking license and attained universal banking status.

The DBP's board of directors comprises nine members, including two independent directors. All members are appointed by the Philippine president. Jose A. Nuñez, Jr. is the current chairman. Buenaventura is the vice chairman as well the president and CEO.

Mission and Strategy

The mission of the DBP is policy oriented: "to raise the level of competitiveness of the economy for sustainable growth; support infrastructure development, responsible entrepreneurship, efficient social services and protection of the environment; and promote and maintain the highest standards of service and corporate governance among its customer constituencies". Its primary objective is to provide banking services, principally to cater to the medium-and-long-term needs of agricultural and industrial enterprises, with an emphasis on small and medium-scale industries.

Corporate Governance

The DBP is entirely funded and controlled by the government of the Philippines. The bank can be considered as a state-owned institution with strong viability and even sustainability.

The fact that the DBP receives the same rating as government debt subtly implies that since the DBP plays a crucial public role in supporting the country's development, it is expected to be provided with sufficient and timely support if it encounters significant financial distress.

Funding Source

The major source of the DBP's funding is deposits, which account for 61.75% of its total assets. The primitive capital accounts for only approximately 2.82% of its funding.

Operational Data

Several figures from 2014 are disclosed as follows: The DBP's total assets were PHP 475.36 billion (USD 10,616 million), and its net income was PHP 5.18 billion (USD 115.67 million). The ROA/ROE in 2013 was 1.33%/12.73%, which was significantly lower than the average ratio in the banking industry in the Philippines, which was 2.0%/15.4%. Finally, the NPL ratio was 3.34%, which was close to the average.

Business Models and Products

The bank offers various products, including banking investment, deposits, trade products, treasury products, remittance products, trust services and electronic banking. Moreover, the DBP also offers financing services. Its loan portfolio in 2013 was largely divided into two sectors: first priority areas (45.37%) and other priority areas (54.63%). First priority areas consist of four sub-sectors: infrastructure and logistics (63.36%), environment (17.77%), micro, small and medium enterprises (MSMEs, 14.31%), and social services (4.57%). The other priority areas include manufacturing (39.44%), wholesale and retail trade (28.44%), and public administration and defense (18.91%).

Corporate Governance and Regulation

The DBP's board consists of independent directors, an executive committee and various functional committees, including audit and compliance, risk oversight, trust, IT management, governance, human resources and development advocacy. Moreover, the management committee, the credit committee and the asset and liability management committee are responsible for management affairs.

The DBP is regulated by Republic Act No. 7353, which is also known and cited as the "Rural Act of 1992". According to section 3 of the Act, "the Monetary Board of the Central Bank of Philippines shall formulate the necessary rules and regulations… and supervise the operation of such banks." However, as the DBP has been licensed as a common bank since 1995, it should be regulated the same as other private commercial banks.

In conclusion, the DBP successfully engages in market competition without protection from the government, which enables it to provide loans for SMEs and for enterprises in other development-related sectors. In addition, the benefits of cooperation with MFIs experienced by the DBP may imply that the government, compared to the private sector, is ineffective in collecting credit information about SMEs. The DBP is considered as a success because of the bilateral exploitation of its comparative advantages: goverment versus market and public versus private.

Industrial Development Bank of India (IDBI)

General Information

The Industrial Development Bank of India, or IDBI Bank Ltd., whose headquarters is located in Mumbai, was created as a DFI in 1964 under the Industrial Development Bank of India Act. It thereafter became a commercial bank in 2004, and it is currently a universal bank offering personalized banking and financial solutions in the retail and corporate banking areas throughout India as well as from a branch in Dubai. The board of directors consists of nine people, including five independent directors. Shri M. S. Raghavan, who was appointed by the government of India, is the current chairman as well the managing director. The board focuses on the important functional areas of the bank. As a board-managed organization, responsibility for the day-to-day management of bank operations is vested with the chairman and managing director as well as the deputy managing directors.

Mission and strategy

The mission of the IDBI is multi-dimensional. It includes "delighting customers with our excellent service and comprehensive suite of best-in-class financial solutions; touching more people's lives with our expanding retail footprint while maintaining our excellence on corporate and infrastructure financing; continuing to act in an ethical, transparent and responsible manner, becoming the role model for corporate governance; deploying world class technology, systems and processes to improve business efficiency and exceed customers' expectations; encouraging a positive, dynamic and performance-driven work culture to nurture employees, grow them and build a passionate and committed work force; expanding our global presence; and relentlessly striving to become a greener bank."

Ownership

The major shareholder of the IDBI is the government of India, which holds 76.5% of the total shares. Other shares are owned by insurance companies (9.65%), individual shareholders (6.47%) and foreign institutional investors (2.9%). In general, no evidence indicates that there is a specific government budget for the IDBI. However, during the last five years, the bank was infused with capital from the government of India three times and the government's shareholding increased from 52.67% to 76.5%. The government does not guarantee the bank's debt payments or infuse money for bad debt.

Funding Source

The major source of funding for the IDBI is deposits, which account for 71.7% of its total assets. Most of the deposits are term deposits (77.4%) to ensure that it has sufficient rigidity of assets. The IDBI's rating by S&P is BB + , whereas the rating for India's sovereign debt is BBB-, which likely implies that IDBI's debt is believed to be supported by the government.

Operational Data

Several figures from financial year 2014 are disclosed below. The IDBI's total assets were approximately INR 3.29 trillion (USD 54,779 million) and its net income was INR 1,112.14 billion (USD 1,867.15 million). The IDBI's return on assets/equity ratio in 2014 was 0.41%/5.57%, which is significantly lower than the average ratio, which was 0.80%/11.70% in the banking industry in India. Finally, the net interest margin was 2.17% and the non-performing assets ratio was 4.9%, which is slightly higher than the average ratio of 4.0% in India.

Business Models and Products

The bank operates through two distinct business groups: corporate and retail, with separate departments for retail banking, priority sector groups (MSE and agri-business), infrastructure and corporate banking. The amount of the bank's gross advance portfolio is 2.03 trillion rupees (USD 33,845 million), which comprises the Corporate Banking Group (47.81%), Infrastructure Lending (24.73%), the Retail Banking Group (18.68%) and the Priority Sector (8.48%).

Several recent key business decisions have been made by the IDBI; one such decision was to expand the bank's branch network. In 2014, the bank added 309 new branches, with the total number of branches increasing to 1,388. Meanwhile, the bank has deepened and widened its corporate banking and investment banking relationships. In addition, it has focused aggressively on priority sector lending (PSL), which includes loans to weaker sectors such as agriculture, MSMEs, housing and education.

Corporate Governance and Regulation

The IDBI's principle of corporate governance is to serve in the best interests of its stakeholders. Responsibility for maintaining a high governance standard lies on the board of directors and various board committees. In addition, the bank has 13 functional committees: audit, business review, executive, shareholder, fraud monitoring, risk management, CSR, customer service, information technology, remuneration, HR steering, nomination and recovery review.

The bank is primarily regulated by two acts: the Companies Act of 1956 and the Banking Regulation Act of 1949. The IDBI is regulated as normal commercial banks and follows the regulations that requests by the authority. The bank discloses its regulatory reports every season under Basel III.

In general, IDBI aims to diversify its business and optimize its asset portfolio rather than being solely dedicated to economic development. The bank's cooperation with the government reduces its information costs and in turn increases the effective disbursement of its funding. This cooperation ameliorates and eases the problems induced by a lack of accessibility in unbanked and rural areas and in turn offers assistance for economic development.

Industrial Development Bank of Turkey (TSKB)

General Information

Türkiye Sınai Kalkınma Bankası A. Ş (TSKB, Industrial Development Bank of Turkey, hereinafter referred to as "the bank") is Turkey's first privately owned development and investment bank and was established in 1950 by the Council of Ministers Resolution Number 3/11203 with the support of the World Bank, the Turkey Republic (T. R.) government, the T. R. Central Bank and commercial banks. The headquarters of the TSKB started its journey in 1950 by financing private sector investments in Turkey and, today, the TSBK provides loans and project financing to corporations in different fields with the goal of promoting sustainable development.

The board of directors of the bank is chaired by Adnan Bali. The bank's senior management consists of the following divisions: Project Appraisal, Evaluation and Financial Institutions Coordination, Corporate Banking and Project Finance, Financial Control, Budget Planning and Investor Relations, Treasury and Human Resources, Loans, Information Technology and Operations, Enterprise Architecture, Corporate Finance and Economic Research, General Secretariat and Internal Systems.

The bank's headquarters is located in Istanbul; it has four subsidiaries and six affiliates in Izmir and Ankara. According to the classification included in Banking Law No. 5411, the bank was established as a development and investment bank. The bank is not licensed to accept deposits.

Mission and Strategy

The TSKB's mission is to promote Turkey's sustainable development and to "supply entrepreneurs with medium-and-long-term financing, brokerage and advisory support; play a continuous role in the development of the capital markets in Turkey; and create increasingly more added value for its shareholders, customers, employees, and all other stakeholders."

The bank's strategy is to (i) support the sustainable development (sustainability financing) of corporations in different fields, (ii) provide entrepreneurs with money and capital market brokerage and advisory support, (iii) ensure sustainable profitability and growth, (iv) strengthen the corporate structure, and (v) communicate effectively with stakeholders.

Ownership

The bank does not use government subsidies. In addition, it has no intangible assets acquired through government grants. The T. İş Bankası A.Ş. (İş Bank) Group owns 50% of the shares and controls the bank's capital directly or indirectly. T. Vakıflar Bankası T. A. O. owns 8.38% of the shares, and other institutions and individuals own the remaining 41.62%.

Funding Sources

As a development and investment bank, the bank obtains most of its funding from abroad. The bank obtains loans from domestic and foreign financial institutions and borrows from the money market or the issuance of securities in domestic and foreign markets.

In the past five years, the government has transferred no grants to repay the bank for NPLs. However, the Turkish Treasury provides guarantees for some of the bank's multilateral funds. The bank obtains financing from the capital market. Its ratings are Baa3 (Moody's) and BBB (Fitch).

Operational Data

In 2014, the TSKB increased its total assets to TRY 15,700 million (USD 6,732 million) and its total loans to TRY 10,980 million (USD 4,708 million), with annual growth of 21.6% and 19.7%, respectively. The bank's equity capital reached TRY 2,287.89 million (USD 981 million), which was a 21.4% increase in 2014 compared with the previous year, and its average annual ROE was 17.7%. The bank's ROA was 2.6%. Its average annual interest rate on loans was 4.33% and its NPL ratio was 0.15%.

The TSKB's net profit reached TRY 369.19 million (USD 158.3 million) in 2014, representing yearly growth of 13.3%. In addition, the total resources obtained by the TSKB from the international markets exceeded USD 1,400 million in 2014. In addition, the headquarters signed an agreement with the International Finance Corporation for a subordinated loan of TRY 116.61 (USD 50 million).

As of the end of 2014, a total of TRY 5,014 million (USD 2,150 million) was provided for financing sustainable investments, which play an important role in the TSKB's total loan portfolio, with a share of 52%. In this regard, TRY 3,032 million (USD 1,300 million) was disbursed for renewable energy, TRY 977.2 million (USD 419 million) for energy and resource efficiency and environmental investments, and TRY 536.4 million (USD 230 million) for sustainable tourism.

Business Models and Products

The TSKB's business can be separated into three main parts: corporate banking, investment banking, and consultancy.

Corporate banking includes: (i) corporate lending (industrial investments, energy and resource efficiency, environmental protection investments, renewable energy, sustainable tourism, education and health investments, and multilateral funds); and (ii) other credit products (wholesale banking and SME financing, foreign trade financing, country-ECA credits, working capital finance and leasing).

Investment banking includes: (i) corporate finance (IPO preparation and execution, bond issue underwriting, mergers and acquisitions, asset purchases and sales, and privatization consultancy); (ii) money and capital markets (equity brokerage services, fixed income securities brokerage services, FX transactions, repo transactions, warrant and certificate trading, derivative market trading, forex leveraged trading, loans against securities, asset management, and investment advisory); (iii) derivative and structured products (forwards, options, caps and floors, swaps, and swaptions); and (iv) economic research (daily bulletins and sectorial research).

Consultancy includes: (i) strategic financial consultancy; (ii) real estate appraisal; and (iii) sustainability and environmental consulting.

Corporate Governance

The TSKB's Audit Committee is composed of two non-executive board members. The duties and responsibilities of the Audit Committee are to establish internal audit and risk management systems in compliance with legal and internal regulations. Risk management at the TSKB aims to provide an uninterrupted and systematic flow of information for bank management's decision-making processes by using state-of-the-art analytical methods to scientifically guide TSKB's operations. The TSKB is committed to full compliance with current laws and regulations in Turkey pertaining to money laundering and terrorism financing. The bank has completely incorporated all essential controls, early warnings, and other mechanisms into its business processes.

The Corporate Governance Committee is also composed of two non-executive board members. Corporate governance and full compliance with the requirements of the law provide TSKB with the strength to power sustainable economic performance, a framework for ethical and fair competition, and an essential tool to consider and balance stakeholders' interests.

Having increased its corporate governance rating score to 9.44 as a result of its performance in fully complying with the Chase Manhattan Bank's Corporate Governance Principles amended in 2014, the TSKB has once again been awarded "The Company with the Highest Corporate Governance Rating Score in the Build-in Self-test Corporate Governance Index."

Box 4 – 4 The TSKB as a Sustainable Bank

The TSKB thinks globally and always strives to devise and conform to best practices when addressing environmental and sustainability-related issues. For this reason, climate change, the environment, and sustainability are all strongly integrated into the TSKB's corporate strategy and business principles. The bank's sustainability journey began in 1980 and was not only integrated into its strategy but also internalized by its employees.

The TSKB has structured its sustainability approach in the following four dimensions:

1. Minimizing the environmental risks arising from its lending activities: the external environmental impacts of TSKB;

2. Defining, controlling and reducing the TSKB's internal environmental impacts arising from its operational services: the systematic management of electricity, water, natural gas usage, paper consumption and CO_2 emissions;

3. Emphasizing the TSKB's products and services for sustainable banking: financing renewable energy, energy efficiency and environment investments; and

4. Continuously informing all TSKB employees and stakeholders and encouraging them to actively participate in processes and increase their awareness of the environment, to participate in combatting climate change and to promote a low-carbon economy.

The TSKB provides financial support and consultancy for the transition of the Turkish private sector to lower-carbon and more efficient production levels. The TSKB has played a pioneering role in Turkey's banking sector and continues to work toward sustainable development in Turkey.

Agricultural Bank of Turkey (TCZB)

General Information

TÜRKİYE CUMHURİYETİ ZİRAAT BANKASI (ZİRAAT BANK, hereinafter referred to as "the bank") is a commercial bank in Turkey that is fully owned by the Turkish Undersecretariat of Treasury. Having started its banking operations as a national bank in 1863 funded by the government, Ziraat Bank is Turkey's strongest and most deeply rooted bank. According to Budget Law No. 444 enacted by Parliament, the bank was converted from a state institution into a welfare funds joint-stock company in 1888. The sole shareholder of the bank is the Prime Ministry Undersecretariat of Treasury ("Treasury") of the Republic of Turkey. The board of directors is chaired by Muharrem KARSLI. The bank's head office is located in Ankara and it conducts activities in a total of 1,708 branches (both domestic and abroad), representing the largest branch network in and around Turkey. By the end of 2014, the bank had a 12.4% market share—the largest in the banking sector—and was ranked first among Turkish banks.

Mission and Strategy

Ziraat Bank's mission is "to be a bank that understands customer needs and expectations, thereby offering them the best solutions and value proposition from the most appropriate channel; a bank that brings to every segment of society a wide range of products and services in the fastest, most effective way through its extensive network of branches and alternative distribution channels; a bank that operates with profitability and productivity at global standards by recognizing its ethical values and social responsibility; a bank that holds customer satisfaction to be more important than anything else."

The bank's strategies are (i) banking for everyone (including being a "Morale Bank" that derives satisfaction and happiness from working with its customers, providing universal service at the same high level of quality throughout the world, managing its agricultural—particularly industrial agricultural—financing more effectively, and ensuring organic growth in the local and global distribution network), (ii) effective banking (including ensuring the optimization of sectorial distribution in corporate customer portfolios, proactively managing credit quality through more effective credit processes, and ensuring effective business and expenditure management), and (iii) being a global player (including securing a rapid increase in the share of the foreign trade transaction sector; providing global-level value to customers; more effectively integrating with the international financial structure; and being present in the markets of North Africa, the Middle East, the Gulf Region and the Far East).

Governmental Support

The TCZB is a bank owned by the government. However, no government incentives were utilized by the bank as of the balance sheet date.

Funding Sources

The bank's main funding sources are Turkish lira deposits, repurchase agreements, issued securities, shareholders' equity and government funds transferred from the budget. The bank also receives funds from ministerial offices and other public resources to the Bank by means of legislative and administrative decisions. Deposit, non-deposit sources and equity account for 62%, 23%, and 12% of the TCZB's liabilities, respectively.

Operation Data

By the end of 2014, the TCZB had expanded its total assets to USD 106.17 billion and its total loans to USD 60.85 billion. The bank's equity capital had reached USD

12. 24 billion, and the average annual ROE was 19.0%. The bank's ROA was recorded as 1.8%. Its average annual interest rate of loans was 5.17% and the NPL ratio was 1.9%.

The percentages of top 100 and top 200 cash loans in the total cash loan portfolio are 22% and 27%, respectively. The percentages of top 100 and top 200 non-cash loans in the total non-cash loan portfolio are 61% and 73%, respectively. The percentages of top 100 and top 200 cash and non-cash loans in the total cash and non-cash loan portfolio are 27% and 33%, respectively. The bank posted a net profit of USD 1.41 billion for recent period and became the most profitable bank in the sector.

Business Models and Products

Because the bank is the primary financial institution meeting the financing needs of the agricultural sector in Turkey, it subsidizes individuals and institutions operating in the agricultural sector by mediating the usage of fund-originated loans in addition to agricultural operations and investment loans from its own sources for vegetable and animal production, fishery products and agricultural mechanization directly to producers and to the Union of Agricultural Credit Corporations.

The bank's business is separated into three main parts: retail, SME and commercial. The retail part includes deposit products, investment products, loans, cards, payment, services, insurance, pensions and direct banking. The SME part includes deposit products, investment products, loans, foreign trade, cards, cash management and POS services. The commercial part includes deposit products, investment products, cash loans, non-cash loans, foreign sourced loans, foreign trade, cards, and cash management.

Corporate Governance

Senior management consists of Internal Systems, the Chief Executive Officer, Information Technologies (IT) Management, Retail Banking, Financial Coordination, International Banking, Human Resources, Loan Allocation and Management, Loan Policies, Operational Transactions and Marketing.

The bank's board of directors is responsible for establishing and maintaining effective internal control over financial reporting to prevent misstatements resulting from error or fraud and for selecting and applying appropriate accounting policies in compliance with the "Regulation on Accounting Applications for Banks and Safeguarding of Documents" published on the Official Gazette No. 26333 dated November 1, 2006, Turkish accounting standards, Turkish financial reporting standards and other regulations, interpretations and circulars published by the Banking Regulation and Supervision Agency (BRSA) on accounting and financial reporting principles.

Box 4–5 Exclusive Expertise and Know-How in Primary Industry

One major challenge faced by the Turkish economy is a proportional imbalance within its primary industry—crop production takes too much resource, whereas forestry, fishery and animal husbandry develop slowly, which indicates the unreasonable industrial structure of the primary industry, poor management, and the need for improvement.

As a bank owned by the Treasury and originally founded to support the development of the Turkish primary industry, the TCZB has made agricultural funding a high priority. The bank initiated a new strategy to "address upper segments of the value chain by focusing on agro-industrial loans." In 2014, the TCZB allocated 27% of its non-retail loans to agriculture, which includes not only farming but also forestry, fishery and animal husbandry (see Figure 4.1).

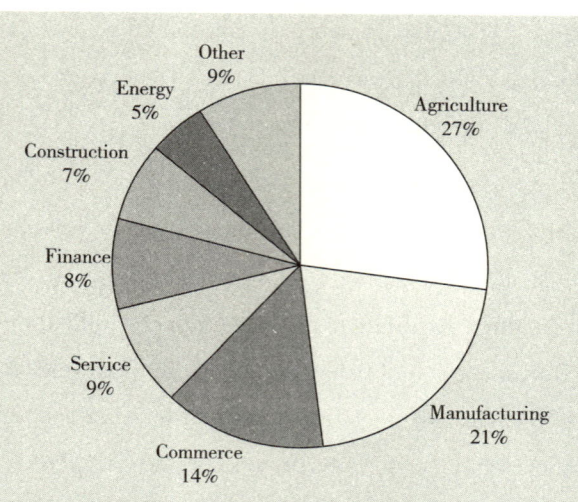

Figure 4.1 Breakdown of Non-Retail Loan Book by Sector, 2014

Source: These charts are extracted from "Investor Presentation Q4 2014 – TCZB," p. 11

- Agriculture 27%
- Manufacturing 21%
- Commerce 14%
- Service 9%
- Finance 8%
- Construction 7%
- Energy 5%
- Other 9%

Among its various efforts to support agriculture, the TCZB also provides agricultural insurance supported by the state. Within the scope of State-Supported Agricultural Insurance, the key features are as follows:

- For Crop Produce Insurance, 25% of the premium payable by the holder is paid in advance, with remainder rest collected at harvest end (at the latest). (Advance payments are not payable for policies taken out with the bank.)

- For Greenhouse Insurance, 10% of the premium payable by the holder is paid in advance, with the remainder collected at the end of a specified term.

- For Animal Life, Poultry and Aquaculture Products Insurance, 25% of the premium payable by the holder is paid in advance, with the remainder collected in a maximum of five installments.

This case illustrates the role of DFIs in upgrading the industry in accordance with the development strategy of those countries based on their expertise.

Part one Overview of Development Financing

Brazilian Development Bank (BNDES)

General Information

The Brazilian Economic Development Bank (BNDES) was established as a government agency on June 20, 1952, under Law 1628, to develop and implement national economic development policies. The agency was converted into a state-owned company under private law, according to Law 5662, on June 21, 1971. Situated in Rio de Janeiro, Brazil, the BNDES has three integral subsidiaries: FINAME (for financing purchases, sales operations, exports of Brazilian machinery and equipment, and imports of goods of the same nature produced overseas), BNDESPAR (for conducting capitalization operations of undertakings controlled by private groups consistent with the BNDES' plans and policies) in Brazil, and BNDES PLC (for increasing the bank's visibility in the international financial community and effectively supporting Brazilian companies undergoing the internationalization process or those searching for opportunities in the international market) in London. The board of directors comprises nine members: the president, the vice president and seven directors, all appointed by the president of the Republic and subject to dismissal at his sole discretion. Figure 4.2 is the BNDES's organizational chart. Because of its vast international operations in countries in Africa, Latin America and the Caribbean, economists around the world recognize that the BNDES is a key financial organization in Brazil.

Mission and Strategy

The bank's mission is "to foster sustainable and competitive development in the Brazilian economy, generating employment while reducing social and regional inequalities". The BNDES offers several financial support mechanisms to Brazilian companies of all sizes as well as to public administration entities, enabling investments in

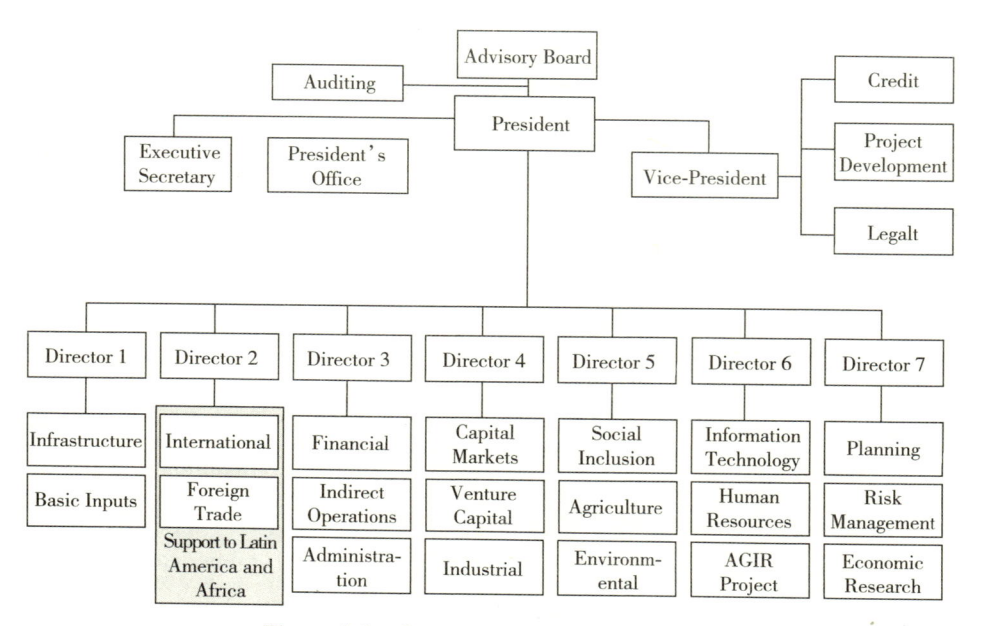

Figure 4.2 Organizational Chart, BNDES

all economic sectors, and the bank emphasizes three factors that it considers strategic: innovation, local development and socio-environmental development.

Governmental Support

The bank is a state-owned company—a federal public company associated with the Ministry of Development, Industry and Trade. The government supports the BNDES's low-cost financing through the Brazilian National Treasury.

Funding Sources

Local credit in Brazil is concentrated in the short term; therefore, the BNDES must seek alternative fundraising solutions to support long-term investment projects. The return on financing operations is its primary funding source. Since 2009, the Brazilian National Treasury has been the most significant source of funding. In 2014, within the boundaries of Law No. 13,000/14, the National Treasury transferred BRL 60.0 billion (USD 22.6 billion) to the BNDES. In order to support the BNDES' increasing disbursements, the Brazilian National Treasury granted a BRL 105 billion (USD 60.3 million) loan in 2009, a BRL 107 billion (USD 63.7 million) loan in 2010, a BRL 50 billion (USD 26.6 million) loan in 2011 and a BRL 55 billion (USD 26.8 billion) loan in 2012. In addition, the BNDES also has the following sources of funding: the Workers' Assistance Fund (FAT); corporate shareholding; foreign fundraising on the international capitals market, as well as multilateral entities such as the Inter-American Development Bank (IDB) and the World Bank; besides fundraising on the domestic market through its integral subsidiary, BNDESPar. Figure 4.3 shows the proportions of funding sources at the end of 2012.

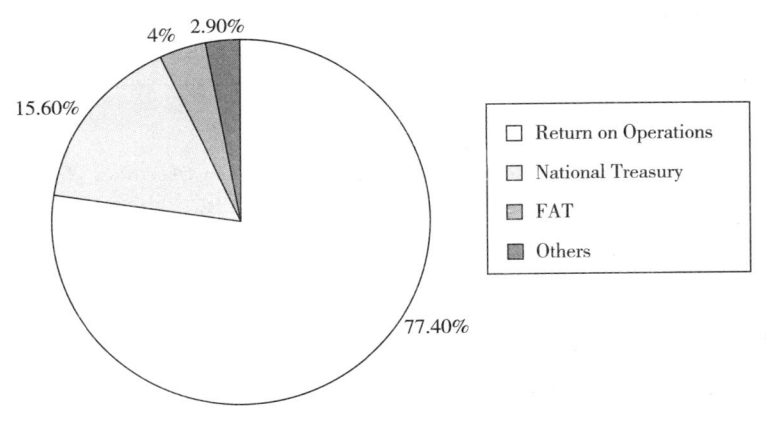

Figure 4.3 The Proportion of Funding Sources at the End of 2012

Operational Data

In December 2014, the shareholders' equity was BRL 66.3 billion (USD 24,916 million). The net profit was BRL 8,594 million (USD 3,231 million) in 2014, representing an increase from BRL 8,150 million (USD 3,453 million) in 2013. The ROA was 1.03%, and the ROE was 13.05%. The NPL/total loans ratio was

0.01%, the same as in December 2013. Table 4.1 and Table 4.2 show some selected financed ratios in December 2014.

Table 4.1 Selected Financed Ratios from balance sheet in December of 2013 and 2014

BRL million, except percentage

Balance Sheet Ratios	Dec/14	Dec/13
Total Assets	877,219	782,043
Shareholders' Equity	66,276	60,626
Shareholders' Equity/Total Assets	7.56%	7.75%
Loans, net of allowance/Total Assets	74.24%	72.28%
Nonperforming loans/Total Loans[1]	0.01%	0.01%
Allowance for losses/Total Loans[1]	0.49%	0.56%
Renegotiated credits/Total Loans[1]	0.66%	1.17%
Allowance for losses/Nonperforming Loans[1]	45.76	46.42

Note: 1 includes loans and interbank onlendings.

Table 4.2 Selected Financed Ratios from income statement in December of 2013 and 2014

BRL million, except percentages

Income Ratios	2014	2013
Net Income	8,594	8,150
ROA (Net Income/Total Assets$_{average}$)	1.03%	1.10%
ROE (Net Income/Shareholders' Equity$_{average}$)	13.05%	16.51%
Return on Equity Investments	3.53%	2.96%

Business Models, Products and Supervision

The BNDES finances projects based on criteria that prioritize development with social harmony, job creation and income. The bank's operations cover most economic activity sectors. Below are the types of projects supported by the BNDES:

(ⅰ) The BNDES provides long-term finance to fund industrial investments and infrastructure. "Investment projects aiming at expanding the Brazilian industrial sector (including the cattle-raising and agriculture sector) are heavily promoted. The objective of the BNDES's efforts is to meet three significant challenges: expanding industry's production capacity; increasing exports; and advancing innovation capacity, which is an essential growth factor in a globalized world. The BNDES's policy is driven by the Production Development Policy Guidelines established by the federal government."

(ii) The BNDES provides financial service to segments such as cattle-raising and agriculture, trade, services and tourism, culture, social and urban development, innovation, the preservation of the environment and the protection of special communities, including Brazil's indigenous communities.

(iii) The BNDES's will invest in large companies according to the government's policies.

(iv) The BNDES operates as an underwriter of bonds and securities—such as shares and debentures of publicly listed companies or those of companies that may enter the capitals market in the medium term—including internationalization and the restructuring of operations in competitive companies, mergers and incorporations. Within this context, the priority is given to small and medium-sized innovative companies that may receive direct participation or participation through closed-end investment funds and that, as a result of their operation in each region or sector, offer a broader reach for operations, thereby enabling the leverage of private resources for capital in such companies.

(v) As the main financing agent of the largest South American country, the BNDES pays special attention to international trade through financing mechanisms for exports of Brazilian products and services. Increasing the international presence of Brazilian companies abroad is also considered. The BNDES offers support for foreign trade and for the internationalization of Brazilian companies.

The BNDES's support aims to implement, modernize or expand the undertakings of companies from nearly all economic sectors, including innovation, the environment, culture, infrastructure, industry, exports of Brazilian machinery, equipment and services, in addition to banking/financial activities, weapon trade, motels, saunas and establishments for adult entertainment and gambling, among others. The bank offers financial support to companies of any size in the country. "The partnership with financial institutions and agencies established around the country facilitates the dissemination of credit, enabling greater access to BNDES's resources". Figure 4.4 shows the disbursement by main sectors.

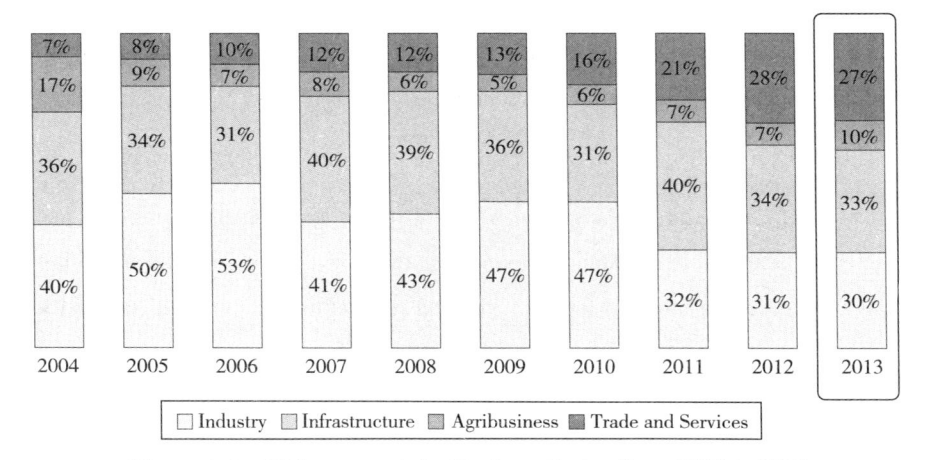

Figure 4.4 Disbursements by Business Sector from 2004 to 2013

The BNDES's disbursement is spread throughout large areas in Brazil. Figure 4.5 shows the disbursement by region.

The requests for financing that the bank receives undergo a series of procedures to conduct project analysis and selection, which involves preliminary consultation, classification, project presentation, project analysis and disbursements. Preliminary consultation is a entrepreneur's first step; subsequently, a pre-assessment of the company's capacity is conducted to execute the project. In the event that the financing is approved, a classification letter indicates which department of the BNDES's operational divisions will be responsible for analyzing and structuring the operation,

Figure 4. 5   Disbursements by Region in 2013

which will guide the company in sending information and additional necessary documentation. The project presented is analyzed by the competent operational division, which creates and sends the project analysis report for appraisal to the managing director of the Operational Division, who in turn submits it to the BNDES's board of directors for assessment, which is conducted in weekly meetings. Once all conditions are met, the first disbursement of resources is conducted as stated in the contract. During the entire term of the financing contract, follow-up on the economic-financial status of the company is performed.

The BNDES has several tools to finance the investment needs of its clients on a long-term basis, such as financing, allocation of non-reimbursable resources and the subscription of securities. The BNDES project financing is earmarked for the financial structuring of investment projects and contractually supported by the cash flow of this project. Assets and receivables may serve as guarantees of this same undertaking. "And in some specific cases, financial support may be provided in a mixed manner by means of financing to a part of a project and through the subscription of securities to another part of it". Requests for loans can be made directly, indirectly or in a mixed manner depending on the type of support used: the direct operation is conducted directly with BNDES or through an agent, the indirect operation is performed by accredited financial institutions or through the use of a BNDES card and the mixed operations combine both the direct and the indirect manners.

"The BNDES's Internal Auditing division, which is linked directly to the Advisory Board, coordinates all of the BNDES System's communication with external control and supervisory organizations, such as the Office of the Comptroller General and Brazilian Central Bank."

Corporate Governance

The senior body of the BNDES is the Advisory Board, which comprises ten members appointed by the president of the Republic of Brazil. A member is nominated by each of the following: the Minister of Planning, Budgeting and Management; the Minister of Labor and Employment; the Minister of Finance; and the Minister of Foreign Affairs. The Minister of Development, Industry and Foreign Trade nominates the remaining members. Their term of office lasts for three years and the board president is elected among these members. The Advisory Board also includes a representative of the BNDES's staff, along with a deputy, who is a substitute in the absence of the representative, and the president of the BNDES, who performs the duties of vice president of the Advisory Board.

The Auditing Committee is responsible for auditing activities, and the Fiscal Council is responsible for examining and issuing opinions on balance sheets and other financial statements, for rendering the annual accounts of the BNDES's board of directors and for performing other duties not stipulated in the Corporations Act.

Venezuelan Economic and Social Development Bank (BANDES)

General Information

The Venezuelan Economic and Social Development Bank (BANDES; in Spanish,

Banco de Desarrollo Económico y Social de Venezuela) is a state-owned and state-controlled economic development bank in Venezuela. The original Venezuelan Investment Fund (FIV in Spanish) was transformed into the BANDES in 2001. The bank's headquarters is located in Caracas, the capital of Venezuela. BANDES was incorporated under several laws, including the Decree on the Rank, Value and Force of Law of Venezuela Economic and Social Development Bank (BANDES).

The Minister of Finance of Venezuela is responsible for the stewardship of BANDES. The bank's board is composed of seven members: one president, who is also the president of the BANDES, and six directors and their alternates. The Minister of Finance is free to appoint and to remove all of them. The executive board meets at least twice each month and meets when convened by the president or requested by at least two members. The president is responsible for the administration of BANDES and is the legal representative of the bank. On February 5, 2014, Simon Zerpa was appointed president of BANDES.

Since 2006, BANDES has been establishing representative offices in the Republics of Ecuador and Nicaragua. On March 24, 2007, the Chinese Venezuelan Joint Fund (FCCV) was created under BANDES's administration. BANDES also has a subsidiary in Uruguay.

Mission and Strategy

According to the law, BANDES "promotes economic and social development by technical and financial support to national and international socio-productive investments in accordance with the Outline Plan for Economic and Social Development of the Nation." The bank also values the principles of justice, equity and solidarity.

Ownership

The bank is 100% owned by the state.

Funding Sources

The bank depends primarily on borrowing from other financial institutions. In 2013, its debts to domestic financial institutions were VEF 2.51 billion (USD 0.4 billion), and those to foreign institutions were VEF 140.93 billion (USD 22.43 billion), accounting for 1.61% and 90.4% of total liabilities, respectively. The paid-in capital experienced growth in 2009 and 2010, reaching nearly VEF 8.87 billion (USD 1.41 billion) in 2013.

No explicit rule states that the government assists in reducing the NPL ratio or offers a debt grantee for the bank.

Operational Data

The bank lends both wholesale and retail. In 2013, the bank's interest rate was nearly 15%. The longest domestic loan maturity was 10 years, whereas for international funds, the amortization term was up to 20 years. Total assets were VEF 182.79 billion (USD 29.09 billion), and total equity was VEF 26.94 billion (USD 4.29 billion) in June 2013. The ROA and ROE were 2.61% and 17.82%, respectively, in the same month. The NPL ratio was 10.88% in June 2013.

Business Models and Products

According to the law, BANDES can perform several general operations and concessional operations. According to Article 6 – 9, BANDES is authorized to perform the following tasks:

- Establish funds for specific goals with its own equity. The money used for the creation of these funds cannot exceed 25% of the budget of BANDES. The bank also directly or indirectly finances short-, medium-and-long-term projects. The amount used for the financing operation will be fixed by the executive board.

- Sign consulting contracts, correspondent contracts and trusts with public or private institutions.

- Perform concessional operations: the bank can engage in concessional operations with its own money, which cannot exceed 5% of the pre-tax net profit.

- Constitute or participate in companies or funds of venture capital with an amount no higher than 20% of the anterior net profit. The board will fix the exact percentage.

- Conduct programs and perform operations in international cooperation and financing.

- Lend specialized funds to regional key programs and projects.

- Offer direct or indirect technical and financial assistance to help improve channels of access to credit for the development of micro, small, or medium-sized enterprises and any other form of association; aid can also be given to agencies and entities of the public sector and private sector.

- Solicit and contract national and international financing.

- Release securities in domestic or foreign currency in the internal or external market, which should be maintained within the limits of permitted indebtedness established by the Law.

- Grant sureties, securities and other guarantees in cases and in the manner determined by the board, with a cumulative amount that cannot exceed 10% of the bank's liquid assets.

- Perform custody of materialized and dematerialized securities.

The BANDES has also announced that it prioritizes the manufacturing and tourism industries. In terms of international operation, the bank focuses primarily on Latin America, particularly South America. The credits offered by the BANDES are associated with the characteristics of the activities themselves. Interest rates are, according to ownership of the means of production, 6% to 10% in manufacturing and 5% to 9% in tourism. The maximum period is ten years for fixed assets (excluding transport). The bank posts collateral that backs these loans. All credits must be at least half of the loan amount prior to the first disbursement.

Governance and Supervision

The BANDES is not subject to the restrictions of the General Law on Banks and Other Financial Institutions in terms of the placement of liquidities and resources that are not invested. Its credit operations should be subject only to the requirements established by the Decree on the rank, value and force of law and the financing policy. The bank is subject to the supervision of the Superintendent of Banks and Other Financial institutions, as other commercial banks are.

Box 4 – 6   Financing the Manufacturing Sector in the Context of an Economic Shock

Venezuela's economy suffered a setback since June 2014 as a result of the dramatic fall in oil prices in the international market. The country used all means to ensure its economic stability and to promote social development. To that end, the BANDES awarded credits to companies in the manufacturing sector to increase productive capacities and promote economic growth.

On October 9, 2014, the BANDES awarded VEF 50 million (USD 8 million) in funding to companies in the manufacturing sector, with the expectation that the profit-earning capacities would be enhanced primarily through the acquisition of machinery and equipment, raw materials, supplies and working capital.

The beneficiary companies were Tableros y Transformadores C.A. in Sucre state, with funding of approximately VEF 17 million (USD 2.71 million); Tasty Pack Corporation C.A. in Carabobo, with more than VEF 21 million (USD 3.34 million); and Procesadora Los Pirineos in Falcon state, with more than VEF 14 million (USD 2.23 million).

Part one   Overview of Development Financing

Tableros y Transformadores C.A.

According to Mark Millan, the president of the company, resources would be allocated to the acquisition of a new building and raw material. He stated that 50% of production would be delivered to Corpoelec as part of an agreement to improve the national electricity system. Because of this new funding, production capacity would increase from 2,000 transformers per year to 6,000 in the near future. The company also expects to increase its working force from 14 to 22 employees.

Tasty Pack Corporation C.A.

According to Juan Carlos Martinez, director of Tasty Pack Corporation C.A., this funding allowed the company to increase its number of product lines and productive capabilities (from 65% to 95%) through the acquisition of machinery that will automate work. "We are eager to begin a new stage. We want to produce bread, tortillas, pita bread, puff pastry and puff pastry discs, products that will be distributed to people at a low cost," he stated.

Tasty Pack C.A. recently increased its human capital, creating more than 40 direct jobs and 130 indirect jobs, which had a positive effect in the community. Alongside its major trading partners, such as Industrias Diana, Tasty Pack C.A. has been contributing to improving the nation's food security.

This case shows that DFIs can serve as a cushion in mitigating economic shocks by stimulating growth and creating jobs.

Industrial Development and Workers Bank of Egypt (IDWBE)

General Information

The Industrial Developmentand Workers Bank of Egypt was initially established in

1947 to provide specialized financing for the private industrial sector. In 1971, it merged with Bank of Alexandria and became a specialized department for micro-lending. In 1976, the bank was re-established as the Industrial Development Bank of Egypt as an autonomous specialized financial institution focusing on providing structured finance to the newly emerging private sector industrial projects. In November 2008, the Egyptian Workers Bank was merged into the IDBE under the name of "Industrial Development & Workers Bank of Egypt" (IDWBE) to create a stronger financial institution capable of providing distinctive banking services to Egyptian industry. The shareholder structure changed to become 84.4% for the Ministry of Finance, 3.3% for the public sector and 12.3% for the private sector. The head office of IDWBE is in Cairo, with 19 branches throughout the country. The chairman of the bank is El-Sayed Mohamed El-Kosayer, with another eight members on the board.

Mission and Strategy

The bank's mission is "to promote, enhance and service the Egyptian private industrial sector, with special emphasis being placed on small and medium-sized industrial enterprises (SMIEs)." Realizing the importance of the industrial sector, particularly small and medium-sized industrial enterprises (SMIEs), as a catalyst for invigorating the national economy, the bank has always been a forerunner in financing SMIEs. This activity was complemented by its efforts to expand a variety of technical, marketing and financial services. The strategy of the bank is to promote, enhance and service the Egyptian private industrial sector, with an emphasis on SMIEs. Supported by a stable medium-and-long-term funding base and a business and product development team, IDWBE is uniquely poised to extend a multitude of diversified tailored products and services designed to meet the requirements and needs of depositors, entrepreneurs and businesses. The bank's vision is to become a leader in its field of specialty and to be operationally dynamic and proactive in economic and industrial reforms, customer oriented, technologically advanced, financially strong and profitable. In addition, the bank aims to provide continuous financial, technical and marketing support to new and existing small and medium-sized industrial projects, thus ensuring their sustained growth and competitiveness in a highly dynamic market.

Government Support

The bank is 84.4% owned by the Ministry of Finance. With this ownership structure, the bank has enjoyed a considerable level of support from the government, which is a main rating driver for the bank. The bank was promised a cash injection from its sole shareholder in 2006 to help the bank clean up its balance sheet and make necessary provisions. The bank also has ready access to three credit lines from the Central Bank of Egypt (CBE), with EGP 500 million (USD 87.67 million), and it has priority (empowered by CBE) over all other banks operating in Egypt, including other public sector banks, with regard to redeeming assets or exercising mortgages.

Funding Sources

The bank's funding is primarily obtained from deposits and interbank funding.

Size, Profitability, and Asset Quality

Total bank assets have been increasing, reaching EGP 3,524,736,000 (USD 642.6 million) by the end of 2009. The largest portion of assets in 2009 was in loans and advances, which accounted for 76.48% of the total. By the end of 2009, the total shareholders' equity of the bank amounted to EGP 858 million (USD 156.23 million). The ROA and ROE were −2.25% and −7.44%, respectively, in 2008, which were not satisfactory. However, the ROA and ROE improved, reaching 0.01% and 0.02%, respectively, in 2009. The gross NPL ratio was high, and the bank exerted efforts to decrease this ratio. As a result, the gross NPL ratio declined from 74% in 2008 to 63% in 2009. The bank did not make great profits because of the high ratio of gross NPLs, and the net profit for 2009 was EGP 181,000 (USD 87.67 million). The bank's capital adequacy ratio (CAR) was 44.86% for the same period.

Business Models and Products

The bank has three main product lines: saving instruments, credit lines and retailing bank programs. With saving instruments, the bank offers interest rates of 5.875% to 7.25% for time deposits from 1 to 12 months, and for saving accounts, it offers interest rates of 7.5% for 12 months and 7% for 6 months. The bank's credit lines involve a variety of programs, such as assisting industrial projects in complying with environment laws at an interest rate of 2.5%. Through retail banking programs, the bank provides many products to support individuals. For example, the bank offers an education loan to employees in the government, the public business sector and the professionals at an interest rate of 9%; the minimum loan amount is EGP 2,000, and the maximum amount is EGP 30,000.

The bank's target markets include construction, manufacturing, energy, and health. In addition to its core specialized banking business, the IDWBE extends the following services to its clients: project evaluation, financial engineering, feasibility studies and the disposal of assets on behalf of its clients.

Corporate Governance

The bank does not specify its corporate governance structure on its official websites or in its annual reports. However, in 2009, the bank continued to upgrade its Information Technology System and enhance its Management Information System (MIS) to closely monitor and measure its business performance and efficiency over all the bank and other lines. In addition, the bank focused on improving, relocating and expanding its branches network to reach and better serve its clients' needs by covering most of Egypt's industrial cities. New branches were to be opened in Helwan, El-Obour, El-Mahala El-Koubra and Quesna.

Development Bank of Southern Africa (DBSA)

General Information

The Development Bank of Southern Africa (DBSA) is a wholly state-owned financial institution that was established in 1983. DBSA is incorporated under The Development Bank of Southern Africa Act, 1997 (Act No. 13 of 1997). Other relevant mandates include The Public Finance Management Act, 1999 (Act No. 1 of 1999), and the Companies Act of South Africa, 2008 (Act No. 71 of 2008). The DBSA headquarters is located in Johannesburg, South Africa. Consisting of 425 employees, the bank is operated under the system of the board and the executive management committee. The board chairman is Jabu Moleketi and the CEO is Patrick Dlamini.

Mission and Strategy

The bank aims to accelerate sustainable socio-economic development and to improve the quality of life of the people of the Southern African Development Community (SADC) by providing financial and non-financial investments in the infrastructure sectors.

The bank's general agenda is premised by its vision, mission and values. Vision: a prosperous and integrated region, progressively free of poverty and dependence. Mission: to advance the development impact in the region by expanding access to development finance and effectively integrating and implementing sustainable development solutions. Values: high performance, shared vision, integrity, innovation, and service orientation.

The bank's mission, defined by its mandate, the DBSA Act (No. 13 of 1997), is as follows: "promote economic development and growth, human resources development and institutional capacity in the region; support sustainable development projects and programs in the region; focus on infrastructure and leverage the private sector."

Ownership

The government of the Republic of South Africa—in particular, the Ministry of Finance—is the sole shareholder of DBSA.

Funding Sources

The years 2013/2014 witnessed a new round of government recapitalization of ZAR 2,400 million (USD 228 million). However, no direct evidence can prove that this recapitalization aimed to solve the NPL problems, although the bank indeed had a difficult time in 2012/2013.

The bank's credit ratings remained in line with the sovereign rating. At the end of 2014, Standard & Poor's downgraded South Africa's sovereign credit rating by a notch to BBB-, and Fitch ratings lowered the country's credit rating outlook from stable to negative. Being linked to the sovereign rating, the DBSA was affected by these moves.

Operational Data

In the context of the rapid development and emerging challenges of sub-Saharan Africa, DBSA achieved remarkable results across most of its business sectors in the year 2014. Total disbursements multiplied by 39 percent, from ZAR 9.2 billion (USD 1 billion) to ZAR 12.7 billion (USD 1.2 billion), which contributed to the growth in total assets from ZAR 54.0 billion (USD 5.85 billion) in the previous year to ZAR 63.8 billion (USD 6.06 billion). Total liabilities and total equity also increased from ZAR 37.3 billion (USD 4.04 billion) and ZAR 16.8 billion (USD 1.81 billion) in the previous year to ZAR 42.9 billion (USD 4.07 billion) and ZAR 19.9 million (USD 1.89 billion), respectively.

Meanwhile, the DBSA returned to be profitable with a net income of ZAR 787 million (USD 75 million) compared with a loss of ZAR 826 million (USD 89 million) in 2012/2013. Its ROA increased to 1.6% in 2014 from the 2013 level of 1.3%, and its ROE increased to 4.3% in 2014 from its 2013 level of −4.8%. Moreover, the asset quality of the bank improved; the gross NPL ratio was reduced to 5.8% in 2014 from 7.3% in 2013.

The average annual interest on loans in 2014 was approximately 7.69%. The maturity of development loans ranged from within 1 year to more than 14 years. Loans with durations longer than 14 years constituted 8.35% of the total development loans ZAR 4,379.69 million (USD 415.90 million) out of ZAR 52,449.85 million (USD 4,980.72 million). Table 4.3 shows the amount of loans with different durations.

Table 4.3 Maturity Analysis of Development Loans, DBSA, USD millions

	2014	2013
<1 yr	651.87	664.49
1 – 2 yrs	420.62	425.78
2 – 3 yrs	433.90	420.30
3 – 4 yrs	360.90	434.09
4 – 9 yrs	1,601.49	1,599.09
9 – 14 yrs	1,087.94	647.21
>14 yrs	415.90	676.37

Business Models and Products

The business of the DBSA served both the wholesale and retail tracks with a pool of target customers involving DFIs, governments and private entities. The DBSA operates its business in a loop under the concept of financial sustainability. It begins with a secure funding source and continues with the implementation of developmental investment projects. For revaluation, the bank receives key financial indicators, such as interest income and non-interest income. Finally, it ploughs back profits for a new round of business.

In total, the DBSA provided ZAR 12.7 billion (USD 1.21 billion) in loans in 2013/14, a new record from a previous high of ZAR 9.3 billion (USD 977 million) in 2008/09, which included 116 projects and covered 13 nations. The bank concentrated its efforts on four key sectors: energy (ZAR 6.7 billion/USD 636 million, 53%), transportation (ZAR 2.3 billion/USD 218 million, 18%), water (ZAR 989 million/USD 94 million, 8%) and communications (ZAR 652 million/USD 62 million, 5%) (see Figure 4.6). Specifically, ZAR 9.2 billion/USD 874 million of total disbursements was spent on domestic financing, and the remainder was spent on international projects (ZAR 3.6 million/USD 342 million). Regarding its international financing business, its geographical scope is expected to move northward from the Sub-Saharan area to other parts of Africa in the next three years. Previously, its international investment primarily flowed to SADC members, including Angola, Botswana, the Democratic Republic of Congo, Lesotho, Malawi, Mauritius, Mozambique, Namibia, Swaziland, Tanzania, Zambia and Zimbabwe. Disbursement in Angola constituted 16.4% percent of the total disbursement this year, followed by Zimbabwe.

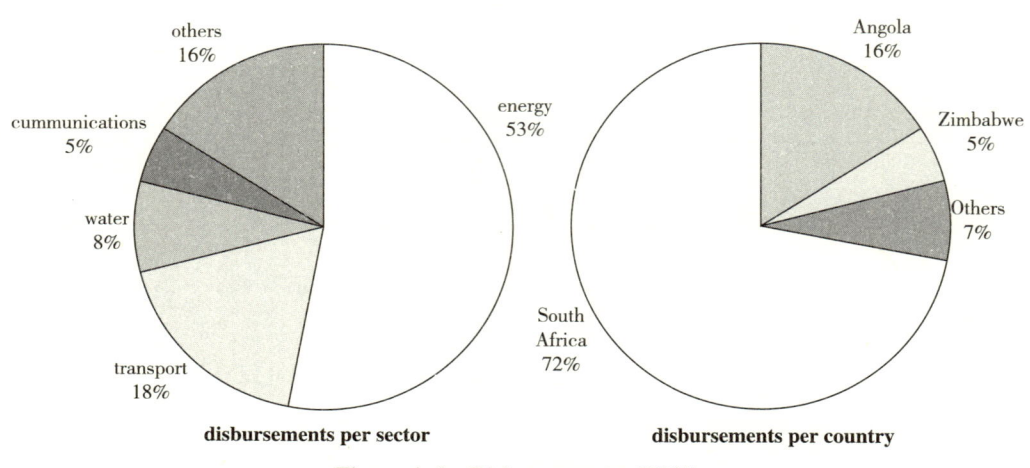

Figure 4.6   Disbursements, DBSA

Governance and Regulation

The DBSA is supervised by the Ministry of Finance of South Africa's government, whereas commercial banks in South Africa are governed by the South African Reserve bank. Furthermore, as a public financial entity, the DBSA follows the Public Finance Management Act and Sections 27 to 31 of the Companies Act, in addition to other acts and mandates that govern the DBSA and commercial banks.

Box 4 – 7 The Green Fund

In the 21st century, dominated by environmental problems and climate change, the transformation to a green economy, defined as "improving humans' well-being and social equity while significantly reducing environmental risks and ecological scarcities", is a compelling challenge for all countries worldwide.

The Green Fund is a unique, newly established national fund that seeks to support green initiatives to assist South Africa's transition to a low-carbon, resource-efficient and climate-resilient development path delivering high-impact economic, environmental and social benefits. The DBSA manages the Green Fund on behalf of the Department of Environmental Affairs (DEA) of the South African government.

Established in April 2012, the Fund aims to promote three main areas—green cities and towns, low-carbon economy and natural resource management—by providing various financial and non-financial services. The financial support provided by the Green Fund primarily takes the form of recoverable and non-recoverable grants, loans with concessional rates and terms, and equity.

During 2013/2014, the Fund approved 27 projects at a value of ZAR 339.8 million (USD 32 million), bringing the amount of total approvals to date to ZAR 671.1 million (USD 64 million). Commitments for the year amounted to ZAR 232.6 million (USD 22 million), and disbursements increased significantly to ZAR 189.3 million (USD 18 million), a relative increase of 539.3%.

Of the 49 projects approved by the Green Fund since its establishment, 26 belong to investment projects, 16 belong to research projects, and 7 belong to capacity development projects (see Figure 4.7).

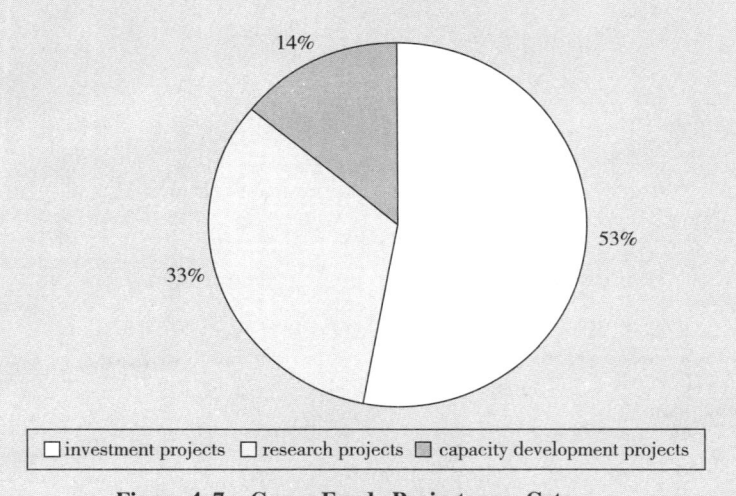

Figure 4.7 Green Funds Projects per Category

Recently, the DBSA Green Fund sponsored a program co-developed by the Uitenhage-Despatch Development Initiative (UDDI) and the Climate Innovation Centre of South Africa (CIC). The project aimed to provide financial, incubation and other business support services to entrepreneurs or small business experimenting with the development of low-carbon technologies in the Eastern Cape and the Nelson Mandela Bay area. Qualified small businesses and entrepreneurs should benefit from the company recruitment, technical and business support, the provision of office space for SMMEs, training, finance, commercialization, and legal and intellectual property services offered by UDDI and CIC. To this end, the program is also working to promote the green economy through SMME development in Uitenhage and in the greater Eastern Cape region.

The review report of the Green Fund projects based on the site visits of 14 approved projects shows that the projects have contributed economic, social and environmental benefits. For instance, more than ZAR 35 million (USD 3.3 million) of economical profits is expected, approximately 14,957 jobs will be created, and carbon emissions will be reduced by 100,693 tons.

This case illustrates the power of national funds, based on the collaboration between the government and DBSA, to leverage environmental projects in developing countries.

Chapter 5　China-Related DFIs

Acknowledging the important role of development financing in serving national strategies and supporting socioeconomic development, the Communist Party of China (CPC) and the Chinese government has proposed a series of crucial initiatives and established the necessary institutional arrangements to promote development financing since 2013. This indicates that development financing in China has entered a new phase.

Below are key milestones in the development of China-led DFIs.

On November 11, 2013, the Third Plenary Session of the CPC's 18th Central Committee noted, "we will set up development-oriented financial institutions, accelerate the construction of infrastructure connecting China with neighboring countries and regions, and work hard to build a Silk Road Economic Belt and a Maritime Silk Road, so as to form a new pattern of all-round opening".

On April 2, 2014, the State Council executive meeting decided to boost shantytown (dilapidated houses) renovation projects by bringing into full play the financing role of state credit-based, breakeven development-oriented financial institutions that are committed to national strategies.

In a meeting on April 25, 2014, the Political Bureau of the CPC Central Committee proposed the use of development financing in supporting shantytown renovation projects.

In its eighth meeting, which convened on November 4, 2014, the Central Finance

Leading Group studied the Silk Road Economic Belt and Maritime Silk Road and stated that the unique advantages and role of development financing and policy-based finance must be fully used.

In the Report on the Work of the Government that was delivered on March 5, 2015, Premier Li Keqiang emphasized the role of development financing and policy-based finance in increasing the provision of public goods.

In March 2015, the State Council approved the reform plans for the China Development Bank (CDB), emphasizing that the development-oriented CDB should enhance its operation in line with increasing market dynamics and globalization, play a more positive role in stabilizing economic growth and adjusting economic structure, and further scale up support for priority sectors and underprivileged regions.

This chapter focuses on China-related DFIs, including CDB, and recent initiatives—the Asian Infrastructure Investment Bank (AIIB), the BRICS New Development Bank, and the Silk Road Fund.

China Development Bank (CDB)

General Information

Established in 1994 and headquartered in Beijing, CDB was incorporated as China Development Bank Corporation on December 11, 2008. On April 12, 2015, the State Council officially ratified the reform plan of CDB. According to this reform plan, CDB will develop into a development-oriented financial institution with adequate capital, strict internal control, secure operation and strong competitiveness in the near future.

CDB's shareholders are the Ministry of Finance (MoF), Central Huijin Investment Ltd. (Huijin) and the National Council for Social Security Fund (NCSSF). The shareholders' details as of the end of 2014 are as follows: MoF (50.18%), Central Huijin (47.63%), and NCSSF (2.19%).

Currently, there are 11 members on the Board of Directors of CDB. Mr. Hu Huaibang is Chairman, and Mr. Zheng Zhijie is President. There are 10 members in the executive management. The Chairman and other major board members are approved by the Board of Directors and the China Banking Regulatory Commission (CBRC). CDB is also subject to the supervision of the People's Bank of China and the CBRC. CDB must comply with the same prudential rules as other domestic commercial banks and is legally required to be audited by a professional external auditor (Deloitte).

As of 2014, the organizational structure of CDB consists of 31 divisions and departments, including the Executive Office, Center for Financial Research & Development, Treasury & Financial Market Department, Risk Management Department, Business Development Department, Global Cooperation Department, Loan Management Department and some other major departments.

CDB currently has 37 domestic branches and five overseas entities, including, e.g., the Beijing branch, the Tianjin branch, the Shanghai branch, the Shenzhen branch, the Hong Kong branch, the Cairo representative office, the Moscow representative office and the Rio de Janeiro representative office.

Besides, CDB has two wholly owned subsidiaries, CDB Capital Co., Ltd. and CDB Securities Co., Ltd. Established in August 2009, CDB Capital Co., Ltd. is primarily engaged in direct investment, private equity funds, investment consultancy and accounting services. Established in August 2010, CDB Securities Co., Ltd. is mainly engaged in the business of brokering, underwriting or dealing in securities and investment consultancy. CDB also has two holding subsidiaries, CDB Leasing Co., Ltd. (established in May 2008 and engaged in financial leasing) and China-Africa Development Fund (launched in June 2007 as an investment fund focusing on Afri-

Part one　Overview of Development Financing

can investments). Furthermore, in an effort to expand inclusive finance, accelerate the development of rural economy and promote SMEs, CDB has acquired predominant holdings in thirteen village banks and bought two others. Collectively, these village banks have an asset of CNY15. 31 billion and an outstanding loan of CNY7. 25 billion.

CDB has employed 8,723 people worldwide by the end of 2014.

Mission and Strategy

As a development financing institution created by the government, CDB provides medium-to-long-term financing facilities that assist in the development of a robust economy and a healthy, prosperous community. It aligns its business focus with national economic development strategy and allocates resources to break through bottlenecks in China's economic and social development by leveraging development financing tools.

CDB carries out its mission through the following actions:

- Supporting the development of national infrastructure, basic industries, key emerging sectors, and national priority projects;

- Promoting coordinated regional development and upgrading industrial transformation while bolstering the new urbanization program;

- Developing inclusive finance by financing low-income housing and other initiatives that are focused on livelihood improvement; and

- Facilitating China's cross-border investment and global business cooperation.

CDB is committed to market-based practices that stimulate solid performance, financial robustness, sustainable growth and a healthy risk appetite; it strives to achieve eminence in development finance to help sustain the sound development of economy and society.

Strategy for 2014

In the beginning of 2014, the Chairman of CDB, Hu Huaibang, noted that in 2014, CDB would strive to make progress on a stable basis and follow the direction of advancing development financing, deepening the reform of CDB and contributing to national reforms. On the one hand, CDB should support the government's efforts to promote the development of urban infrastructure, affordable housing projects, industrial restructuring and global cooperation. On the other hand, CDB should strengthen its capability to serve national strategies by improving management mechanisms, bolstering risk management and laying the groundwork for quality development. The President of CDB, Zheng Zhijie, mapped out the work for 2014, stating that CDB should take full advantage of financial leverage to shore up support for the new type of urbanization; lend strong support to the development of agriculture, forestry and water conservancy; advance developments in education, healthcare and provisions for the elderly; and assist in the construction of the Silk Road Economic Belt and Maritime Silk Road.

Business Performance

At the end of 2014, the total assets of CDB exceeded CNY 10 trillion (USD 1.61 trillion), registering an increase of 26%; its total outstanding loans amounted to CNY 7.94 trillion (USD 1.28 trillion); and its net profits rose steadily to CNY 97.7 billion (USD 15.74 billion). Its risk management was further reinforced. At the end of 2014, the gross non-performing loan ratio (NPL) was 0.65%, a level that was well within 1% for 39 consecutive seasons, testifying to CDB's leading position in asset quality. Moreover, CDB's ROA was 1.06%, its ROE was 15.63%, and its capital adequacy ratio (CAR) was 11.88%. CDB's total equity capital was CNY 680,164 million (USD 109,585.94 million), and its average annual interest rate on loans was 5.84%.

In line with the development goals set forth in early 2014, CDB largely supported socioeconomic development:

In supporting the new type of urbanization, CDB extended an aggregate loan of CNY 1.11 trillion (USD 178.84 billion), or 60% of the total CNY-denominated loans, to the urbanization effort.

In supporting regional coordinated development, CDB's new loans to the central and western regions in 2014 totaled CNY 462.9 billion (USD 74.58 billion), accounting for 66%, whereas new loans to the Northeast Industrial Base were CNY 79.6 billion (USD 12.82billion), accounting for 11%. New outstanding loans made to Tibet and Tibetan-inhabited areas in four provinces during the year totaled CNY 14.7 billion (USD 2.37 billion), whereas new outstanding loans to Xinjiang amounted to CNY 21.8 billion (USD 3.51billion).

In supporting the construction of major infrastructure projects, CDB made loans of CNY 119.5 billion (USD 19.25 billion) and CNY 81.4 billion (USD 13.11 billion) for railway and water conservancy projects, respectively. CDB also offered financing assistance for a number of national priority projects, including the highway network, passenger-dedicated railway lines, oil and gas infrastructure, coal processing, new-energy-based power generation and water resources projects.

In an effort to promote economic restructuring, CDB partook in the establishment of the China Integrated Circuit Industry Investment Fund (CICIIF) and, notably, granted loans of CNY 218.2 billion (USD 35.16 billion) and CNY 42.5 billion (USD 6.85 billion) to the strategic burgeoning sectors and cultural sectors. The outstanding loans to environmental protection and energy conservation projects stood at CNY 958.5 billion (USD 154.43 billion), up by 7.2% year-on-year.

To explore new models in financial services supporting shantytown renovation project, CDB established a housing finance division. CDB offered CNY 408.6 billion (USD 65.83 billion) in loans for urban renewal projects this year, up by nearly

300% year-on-year, accounting for a market share of over 80%. Overall, CDB has provided financial assistance for the rehabilitation and renovation of more than 900 million square meters of shantytown areas, benefiting 9.16 million families, or more than 28.57 million persons. In 2014, CDB was awarded the annual "Best Bank for Excellence in Supporting Shantytown Renovation" by the newspaper *Financial News* and the Institute of Finance and Banking with the Chinese Academy of Social Sciences (CASS).

At the end of 2014, CDB had provided student loans amounting to CNY 69.2 billion (USD 11.15 billion) (representing more than 80% share of the total national student loan market), covering 2,732 colleges and universities throughout 26 provinces (or autonomous regions and municipalities directly under the central government).

By the end of 2014, CDB's outstanding loan portfolios dedicated to SMEs had reached CNY 2.47 trillion (USD 397.96 billion), CNY 1.03 trillion (USD 165.95 billion) of which was accounted for by small and micro businesses. These loan portfolios have helped SMEs, micro and individual businesses, farmers and various social groups, including start-up youth and raid off workers, and covered roughly twenty industries, including the manufacturing industry, agribusiness, forestry, husbandry and fisheries.

By the close of 2014, CDB had outstanding foreign currency loans of USD 267 billion and an offshore yuan-denominated loan balance of CNY 56.4 billion (USD 9.09 billion), which further cemented its status as a pillar of cross-border financing in China. In lending all possible support and backing to the "One Belt, One Road" initiative and promoting interconnection with neighboring countries, CDB has delivered loans of more than USD 120 billion to relevant countries. CDB has also devoted considerable efforts to facilitate the export of energy exploitation, telecommunications, nuclear power and high-speed rail products.

Part one Overview of Development Financing

Funding Sources

CDB raises funding primarily by issuing bonds based on national credit. The conversion of nation credit into bonds is a means of funneling scattered capital into one reservoir from which national priority sectors and underprivileged regions draw to achieve faster development. CDB offered its first bonds in the interbank bond market in 1998 and is now the second largest bond issuer (next only to the MoF) in the bond market of China.

In 2014, CDB issued CNY 1.175 trillion (USD 189.31 billion) in yuan-denominated bonds through diversified channels and in different markets in 2014, with more than CNY 10 trillion (USD 1.61 trillion) accumulative renminbi debts issued.

In 2014, CDB achieved two important breakthroughs in bond trading. The first was CDB's issuance of CNY 2 billion (USD 322.23 million) offshore yuan bonds in London (see details below). It represented the first time such quasi-sovereign / CNY bonds issued on the London market. The second was the offering of financial bonds to individuals. From May 6 to 8, 2014, CDB put its first tranche of over-the-counter financial bonds of CNY 2 billion (USD 322.23 million) for sale through ICBC. These bonds had a one-year maturity, and the nominal value of each bond was CNY 100, with its interest rate at 4.5%. It was estimated that individual investors and non-financial institutions subscribed to CNY 1.545 billion (USD 248.93 million) and CNY 455 million (USD 73.31 million), respectively. The single largest individual subscription amounted to CNY 25 million (USD 4.03 million). As the first over-the-counter financial bonds ever issued in China, these bonds offered by CDB add another choice for public investment in financial bonds.

China Association for the Promotion of Development Financing (CAPDF)

As China's first and single nationwide association in the field of development financing, the China Association for the Promotion of Development Financing (CAPDF) was established in April 2013 initiated by CDB. CAPDF's mission is to sum up the pros and cons of China's development financing, promote theoretical research and institutional innovation in the field of development financing. CAPDF also aims to apply principles and approaches of development financing to promoting market liberalization, market incubation and institutional reform. CAPDF aims to foster exchanges and cooperation among DFIs worldwide. Mr. Chen Yuan, vice chairman of Chinese People's Political Consultative Conference (CPPCC) and CDB's former chairman, was elected as the president of CAPDF by member delegates. The principal leaders of CDB, such as Mr. Hu Huaibang and Mr. Zheng Zhijie, were elected as vice presidents.

By the end of 2014, CAPDF has inducted 8,000 members, which are mostly large enterprises and research institutes involved in the field of development financing. Mobilizing and integrating member resources, CAPDF has organized eighteen consecutive lectures and launched two clubs (the Cultural Finance Club and the Energy Finance Club). Moreover, CAPDF has also undertaken massive efforts in ramping up the cooperation between state-owned enterprises and private firms along the industrial chain, attracting diverse and modern companies to support infrastructure construction, industrial development and employment generation in poverty-stricken regions and to build up collaboration between CAPDF and international development financing institutions.

The highlights of CDB operations in 2014 are as follows: the establishment of the housing finance division (see Box 5 – 1), the issuance of CNY 2 billion (USD 322.23 million) offshore bonds in London (see Box 5 – 2), the participation in the establishment of the integrated circuit industry investment fund (see Box 5 – 3), the program of poverty alleviation in the Wuling region (see Box 5 – 4) and the promotion of the securitization of credit assets (see Box 5 – 5).

Box 5 – 1   Establishing Housing Finance Division

In late July 2014, CDB established the Housing Finance Division in compliance with the requirements of the State Council. The Housing Finance Division was intended to manage the housing finance business in an intensive, professional manner for a long-term sustainable development by capitalizing on the role development financing played in market construction, institutional improvement, financing and brainstorming (i. e., provision of planning and financing support). This division's line of business focuses on extending loans to shantytown renovation and urban infrastructure projects and on fulfilling soft loan collection and re-loaning services (within approved quotas) for financing shantytown renovation and urban infrastructure projects.

CDB's support for shantytown renovation dates from 2004, when shantytown areas were addressed in the Liaoning Province. The chief measures started with driving the government's role in resource allocation and introducing market-oriented borrowers. Then, CDB made loans to the borrowers, who then put the renovation projects into motion. In this way, a major source of social capital was mobilized. The result was impressive. It took only 21 months for fourteen cities of the Liaoning Province to accomplish the goal of relocating 1.2 million families from low-lying and dilapidated shanties to modern facilities. In 2013, the Chinese government put forward a plan to renovate 10 million shanties within five years. In light of these plans, the establishment of the Housing Finance Division is all the more significant, because it will guarantee a steady supply of capital for affordable housing projects, alleviate monetary bottlenecks to shantytown renovation projects and, thus, help improve housing security and affordability. On an incidental note, as a momentous reform in Chinese housing finance, the establishment of CDB's Housing Finance Division was one of the top ten Chinese banking news stories of 2014.

Box 5-2 Issuance of CNY 2 Billion Offshore Bonds in London

On September 12, 2014, the Sixth China-UK Economic and Financial Dialogue (EFD) took place in London. China and the UK agreed that the issuance of CNY-denominated government and quasigovernment bonds in the UK would support the development of the CNY offshore markets and agreed to explore ways to support liquidity and efficiency in offshore CNY bond markets. As a first step, CDB has successfully issued CNY 2 billion (USD 322.23 million) bonds in London, and the UK announced its intention to issue an CNY bond and to use the proceeds to finance the UK government reserves of foreign currency. The UK will become the first Western country to issue an overseas CNY bond.

On the same day, CDB made its first offering of CNY 2 billion (USD 322.23 million) overseas bonds in London, consisting of three kinds of off shore bonds: CNY 600 million (USD 96.67 million) with 3-year maturity at 3.35%, CNY 500 million (USD 80.56 million) with 5-year maturity at 3.6%, and CNY 900 million (USD 145.01 million) with 10-year maturity at 4.35%. At a subscription ratio of 2:1, this bond offering was met with robust demand from global investors, while European investors claiming nearly 30% of the issue. The initial offering of the Chinese quasi-sovereign CNY bonds in London marked another landmark development for the offshore CNY markets and demonstrated the positive results of the deepening Sino-British financial cooperation.

As a bond bank, CDB raises the bulk of its funds through the issuance of bonds. CDB has heretofore offered a bond issue totaling more than CNY 10 trillion (USD 1.61 trillion), accounting for roughly one-fifth of the domestic bond market. From 2007 (when CDB offered the first dim sum bonds in Hong Kong) to 2014 (when CDB placed CNY bonds for sale in London), CDB issued overseas bonds totaling CNY 20. 8 billion (USD 3. 35 million), imparting tremendous momentum to the development of offshore CNY markets.

Box 5 – 3 Participation in the Establishment of Integrated Circuit Industry Investment Fund (CICIIF)

In 2014, the Chinese government promulgated "Guidelines to Promote National Integrated Circuit Industry Development", defining the IC industry as the core of the information technology industry and the strategic, fundamental and pioneering industry underpinning socioeconomic development. As specified in the guidelines, it is necessary to establish a national industrial development fund that aims to attract large enterprises, financial institutions and social capital. The IC industry takes center stage in the guidelines with respect to accelerating the industrial transformation and upgrading. On September 24, the Integrated Circuit Industry Investment Fund (CICIIF) was formally inaugurated as part of the agreement signed by China Development Bank Capital Corporation Ltd. (CDBC, a wholly-owned subsidiary of CDB), China National Tobacco Corporation (CNTC), Beijing E-Town International Investment & Development Co., Ltd (BEIID) and China Mobile Communications Corporation. According to media sources, during Phase I, CICIIF is worth CNY 120 billion (USD 19. 33 billion), of which CNY 36 billion (USD 5. 80 billion) will be provided by state finance, CNY 32 billion (USD 5. 16 million) by CDBC, CNY 10 billion (USD 1. 61 million) by BEIID and the remaining CNY 42 billion (USD 6. 77 million) by public funding. CDB's participation in the establishment of CICIIF highlights the important role that the development financing could play in pushing forward renewed industrialization and informatization in China.

Box 5 – 4   Poverty Alleviation in the Wuling Region

Straddling the borders of Hubei, Hunan, Chongqing and Guizhou Province, the Wuling region is home to many minorities and connects immense swaths of poverty. CDB is committed to injecting vitality and vigor into this region by assisting in industry-, infrastructure- and education-based poverty eradication efforts.

In Yinjiang County, Guizhou, for example, CDB assisted in the anti-poverty effort in the form of "four platforms plus one union". The "four platforms" are the financing platform, which handles CDB's credit funds and financially supports qualified SMEs; the loan guarantee platform, which is responsible for examining loan application materials and performing pre-/post-guarantee checks; the management platform, which assists eligible loanees in applying for loans and accessing credit; and the publication platform, which publicizes loanees' names, credit lines and other information. The "one union" is the credit union that is part and parcel of creating a sound credit system. By the end of 2014, CDB had provided agricultural loans of CNY 131.4 million (USD 21.17million) in support of Yinjiang's rural tourism and associated industries of special foods (edible fungi, tea and chickens laying green-shell eggs). For instance, in 2011, in partnership with the Poverty Alleviation and Development Office of the Guizhou Province, CDB offered a local edible fungi cooperative (based in Banxi Town, Yinjiang) a loan of CNY 1 million (USD 0.16 million) bearing interest rate at merely 1 percent per annum. At present, the fungi farmers' per capita income has increased by CNY 25,000 (USD 4,027.92). In supporting the development of the tourist infrastructure of the Huayuan County, Hunan Province, CDB partnered with the local government under Public Private Partnership (PPP) mode, forming a special purpose vehicle (SPV) to provide a CNY 260 million (USD 41.89 million) loan to finance infrastructure projects, with proceeds of ticket sales and service and real estate transactions as reimbursements for the loan. By the end of 2014, the CDB Hunan branch had extended loans of CNY 84.57 billion (USD 13.63 billion) to the Wuling region, of which CNY 1.95 billion (USD 314.18 million) went to leading corporations as well as medium, small and micro enterprises (MSMEs), while CNY 19.27 billion (USD 3.10 million) was directed to finance projects for highways, rural trunk roads, water conservancy, power grids, urban road networks, indemnificatory housing and comprehensive land utilization. In addition, the CDB Hunan branch had granted CNY 1.53 billion (USD 246.51 million) student loans to financially deserving students.

The pro-poverty-relief efforts in the Wuling region are simply a brief epitome of CDB's commitment in a wide variety of provinces. In May 2014, CDB signed an agreement called the Collaborative Agreement on Poverty Alleviation through Development-oriented Finance with the State Council Leading Group on Poverty Alleviation and Development (LGOPA). In this agreement, CDB agreed to ratchet up funding for specialty industries, infrastructure construction, education and other critical areas. By late 2014, CDB had extended infrastructure loans of more than CNY 1.3 trillion (USD 209.45 million) to poverty-stricken areas and CNY 14.98 billion (USD 2.41 billion) to students in 405 state-level impoverished counties. Simply stated, CDB has spared no efforts and resources in poverty alleviation, a global policy task for and challenge to countries worldwide.

> **Box 5-5   CDB's Promotion for Securitization of Credit Assets**
>
> The securitization of credit assets is a process in which credit assets with poor liquidity but potential growth prospects are pooled together and repackaged to be sold in the form of securities. Importantly, in the process, the existing surplus liquidity is unleashed to push forward the development of the real economy.
>
> In August 2013, the Chinese government expanded a pilot program for securitizing credit assets, with the objective of channeling the surplus capital funds into the underprivileged economic sectors and priority industries. As a forerunner and one of the foremost participants in China's securitization of credit assets, CDB is ranked first in domestic banking markets in terms of bond issuance frequency, size and format. During this pilot phase, CDB has floated securities of CNY 101.3 billion (USD 16.73 billion) in ten series, accounting for 34.2% of the total market share. For good measure, all redeemed securities are free from defaults and management errors. Most of the unleashed surplus liquidity has been shifted into priority and underprivileged sectors. Particularly, a surplus capital of CNY 51 billion (USD 8.42 billion) was diverted into railway projects, providing fertile ground for institutional reform in financing railway construction.

The Asian Infrastructure Investment Bank (AIIB)

General Information

The Asian Infrastructure Investment Bank (AIIB) is a strategic conception that was first put forward by the Chinese President Xi Jinping and Premier Li Keqiang during their respective visits to Southeast Asian countries in October 2013.

On October 21, 2014, 21 Asian countries (including, e. g., Bangladesh, Brunei, India, and Pakistan) signed a Memorandum of Understanding (MOU) to establish the AIIB. According to this MOU, the authorized capital of AIIB will be USD 100 billion, and Beijing was elected as the future headquarters. Soon thereafter, Indonesia also signed this MOU and became the 22nd Prospective Founding Members (PFMs).

On March 12, 2015, the United Kingdom officially proclaimed that it would join the AIIB. After the UK, France, Italy and Germany all successively joined the AIIB. As of April 15, 2015, there are 57 PFMs: Australia, Austria, Azerbaijan, Bangladesh, Brazil, Brunei, Cambodia, China, Denmark, Egypt, Finland, France, Georgia, Germany, Iceland, India, Indonesia, Iran, Israel, Italy, Jordan, Kazakhstan, Kuwait, Kyrgyzstan, Laos, Luxembourg, Malaysia, Maldives, Malta, Mongolia, Myanmar, Nepal, the Netherlands, New Zealand, Norway, Oman, Pakistan, the Philippines, Poland, Portugal, Qatar, the Republic of Korea, Russia, Saudi Arabia, Singapore, South Africa, Spain, Sri Lanka, Sweden, Switzerland, Tajikistan, Thailand, Turkey, UAE, the UK, Uzbekistan, and Vietnam.

As of now, Japan's government stated that Japan has no intention to join the AIIB. The US proclaimed that it would welcome the China-led AIIB "as long as it complements existing institutions and adopts high governance standards". However, the US has not officially stated whether it has intentions to join the AIIB now or in the future.

Five discussions among PFMs on the establishment of the AIIB have taken place in Kunming, Mumbai, Almaty, Beijing and Singapore. It is anticipated that the Articles of Agreement (AOA) will be finalized and open for PFMs this June. The AOA is expected to be in force and the AIIB is expected to be fully established by the end of 2015.

Mission and Strategy

According to the "MOU on The Establishment of AIIB" and AIIB's official website, the AIIB will "be a new multilateral development bank (MDB) designed to provide financial support for infrastructure development and regional connectivity in Asia".

To achieve this mission, the AIIB will "focus on the development of infrastructure and other productive sectors in Asia, which may include energy and power, transportation and telecommunication, rural infrastructure, agriculture development, urban development and logistics. All AIIB investments will be in line with the Bank's business strategy and policies which would be approved by the Board." Moreover, the AIIB claimed that it will collaborate closely with multilateral and bilateral development partners, including the World Bank Group and the Asian Development Bank (AsDB).

Before the official establishment of the AIIB, the operational strategy and priority areas of engagement can be revised or further refined by its governing boards in the future as circumstances may warrant.

The Timeline of the AIIB

- The AIIB firstly put forward by the Chinese President Xi Jinping and Premier Li Keqiang during their respective visits to Southeast Asian countries in October 2013.

- On October 21, 2014, 21 Asian countries (including Bangladesh, Brunei, India, Paristan and etc.) Signed a Memorandum of Understanding (MOU) to establish the AIIB.

- On March 12, 2015, the UK officially proclaimed that it will join in the AIIB. After the UK, France, Italy and Gemany all successively joined the AIIB.

- As of April 15, 2015, there are 57 PFMs.

- As of May 2015, five discussions among PFMs on the establishment of the AIIB have taken place in Kunming, Mumbai, Almaty, Beijing and Singapore.

- It is anticipated that the AOA will be finalized and signed by PFMs in June 2015.

- The AOA is expected to be in force and the AIIB to be fully established by the end of 2015.

Ownership and Funding Sources

According to the MOU, the authorized capital of the AIIB will be USD 100 billion. As a regional development financing, the AIIB's regional members will be the majority shareholders and the non-regional members will hold smaller equity shares. The AIIB's official website claims that "this shareholding arrangement reflects the commitment and ownership of regional members while providing non-regional members the opportunity to participate actively".

In addition to the capital subscribed by members, the AIIB will "raise funds primarily through the issuance of bonds in financial markets as well as through the interbank market transactions and other financial instruments. It can also establish and administer trust funds and special funds".

Business Models and Products

According to the AIIB's official website, the main financial products of the AIIB will include loans, equity investments and guarantees. It is also anticipated that the AIIB may have the capacity to offer technical assistance.

The AIIB is expected to build on the "lessons" and experiences of the existing multilateral development banks and the private sector. Therefore, its corporate governance will be lean, clean and green. "Lean" means that the AIIB will attempt to maintain a small and efficient management team and highly skilled staff. "Clean" means that the AIIB will be transparent and never tolerate corruption. Finally, "green" means that the AIIB will respect the environment.

The New Development Bank of BRICS

General Information

The New Development Bankof BRICS (NDB BRICS), formerly referred to as the

BRICS Development Bank, is a multilateral development financing institution operated by BRICS states (Brazil, Russia, India, China and South Africa).

The NDB was initiated at the fourth BRICS Summit in New Delhi in 2012 and subsequently announced in the fifth BRICS Summit in Durban in 2013. During the sixth Summit of Heads of State and of Government of BRICS, held in Brazil's Fortaleza and Brasília, the BRICS countries declared that BRICS and other emerging market economies and developing countries (EMDCs) continue to face significant financing constraints to address infrastructure gaps and sustainable development needs. For this reason, the BRICS signed the agreement to establish the NDB.

According to the Fortaleza Declaration, the NDB will be headquartered in Shanghai, China. As the AOA stated, there will be a regional office in Johannesburg (South Africa).

The Timeline of New Development Bank BRICS (NDB BRICS)

- The NDB was initiated at the fourth BRICS Summit in New Delhi in March 2012.
- The NDB was announced at the fifth BRICS Summit in Durban in March 2013.
- During the sixth Summit of BRICS, held in Fortaleza and Brasília in July 2014, the BRICS countries signed an agreement to establish the NDB.
- The NDB will be fully operational in 2016.

Mission and Strategy

Regarding the mission, the AOA of the NDB claimed that "the Bank shall mobilize resources for infrastructure and sustainable development projects in BRICS and other emerging economies and developing countries, complementing the existing efforts of multilateral and regional financial institutions for global growth and development."

Directed by this mission, the NDB will put stress on the following issues:

- Support public and private projects through loans, guarantees, equity participation and other financial instruments;

- Provide technical assistance for the preparation and implementation of infrastructure and sustainable development projects to be supported by the Bank;

- Support infrastructure and sustainable development projects involving more than one country;

- Establish, or be entrusted with the administration of, Special Funds designed to serve its purpose;

- Cooperate with other existing international organizations and financial entities.

Ownership and Corporate Governance

According to the Agreement, the NDB will have an initial subscribed capital of USD 50 billion and an initial authorized capital of USD 100 billion. The initial subscribed capital will be equally contributed by the five founding members.

Articlesix of the AOA states that the voting power of each member will be equivalent to its subscribed shares in the capital stock of this bank. The initial authorized capital is equally distributed among the five founding members; thus, all members will have equal voting power. Unlike the World Bank, which assigns votes based on capital share, none of the members in the NDB, will have veto power. The AOA also claims that the NDB will publish an annual report that contains audited statements of the accounts.

The bank will have a board of governors, a board of directors, a president and vice presidents. The board of governors will elect a president from one of the founding members on a rational basis. In addition to the president, there will be at least one vice president from each founding member except the country represented by the president. The vice presidents should be appointed by the board of governors on the recommendation of the president. The president and vice presidents will serve a five-year term.

The Silk Road Fund

General Information

On November 4, 2014, Chinese President Xi Jinping first put forward the Silk Road Fund concept during the eighth Meeting of the Central Finance Leading Group. On November 8, 2014, President Xi officially proclaimed that China would offer USD 40 billion to establish the Silk Road Fund to be headquartered in Beijing.

In accordance with the Company Law of the PRC, the Silk Road Fund Limited Liability Company (LLC) completed its business registration on December 29, 2014. According to the information published by the State Administration of Industry and Commerce (SAIC), the initial capital of the Silk Road Fund is contributed by the direct foreign exchange reserve investment, the China Investment Corporation, the Export-Import Bank of China and CDB.

Because the Silk Road Fund LLC is not an international organization, there are no member states. However, as a company, the Silk Road Fund LLC will be open to both domestic and international investors.

The Timeline of the Silk Road Fund

- Chinese President Xi Jinping first put forward the Silk Road Fund during the eighth Meeting of Central Finance Leading Group in November 4, 2014.

- President Xi offcially proclaimed that China would offer USD 40 billion to establish the Silk Road Fund.

- In accordance with the Company Law of the PRC, the Silk Road Fund Limited Liability Company (LLC) completed its business registration on December 29, 2014.

- During President Xi Jinping's state visit to Pakistan, the Silk Road Fund LLC, China Three Gorges Group and the Pakistan signed the Karot Hydropower Project.

Mission and Strategy

President Xi Jinping claimed that the Silk Road Fund, along with the AIIB, will support the "One Belt, One Road" strategic conception. Specifically, President Xi elaborated that the Silk Road Fund would support "One Belt, One Road" directly based on Chinese financial strength.

Ownership and Funding Sources

The initial capital of the Silk Road Fund is contributed by the chinese foreign exchange reserve investment (USD 6.5 billion), the China Investment Corporation (USD 1.5 billion), the Export-Import Bank of China (USD 1.5 billion) and CDB (USD 0.5 billion) (see Figure 5.1).

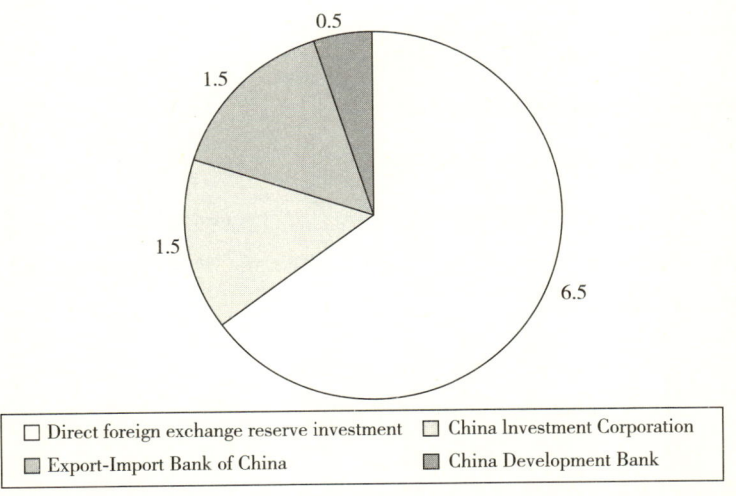

Figure 5.1 Funding Sources of the Initial Capital of the Silk Road Fund LLC (USD billion)

The Silk Road Fund will invest in stocks, debt, funding loans etc. and will establish joint investment funds with international developmental institutions and financial institutions. The Fund will also have asset entrusted management, entrusted overseas investment and other business ratified by the State Council.

Business Models and Products

For reasonable returns and medium-/long-term sustainable development, the Silk Road Fund will invest in infrastructure, resource exploitation, industry cooperation, financial cooperation and other fields through marketing operations.

The business scope of the Silk Road Fund will focus primarily on:

- Investments in stocks, debt, funding loans etc. ;
- The establishment of joint investment funds with international developmental institutions and financial institutions;
- Asset entrusted management and entrusted overseas investment, etc. ;
- Other business ratified by the State Council.

Corporate Governance

The Silk Road Fund Limited Liability Company (LLC) completed its business registration (Registration No. 100000000045300) at the end of 2014. Jin Qi, who was the Assistant President of the People's Bank of China, was appointed the first president of the Silk Road Fund.

There are four shareholders: Export-Import Bank of China, Buttonwood Investment Platform Co., LTD, Seres Investment Co., LTD, and CDB Capital Co., LTD. There are 10 members on the Board of Directors.

There are 10 members on the Board of Directors: Jin Qi (Chairman), Wang Yanzhi (CEO), Liu Jinsong, Fan Haibin, Liu Wei, Guo Tingting, Zhang Qing, Tian Jinchen, Yuan Xingyong, and Hu Xuehao.

Box 5-6 Karot Hydropower Project in Pakistan

Pakistan is facing severe power shortages—largely because few individuals or government departments, including the military, pay for electricity. In 2013, the country's National Planning Commission estimated that the lack of energy possibly reduced annual economic growth by at least two percent. However, Pakistan does not have sufficient financial power to support the development of energy generation infrastructure.

The Ministry of Planning, Development & Reform (Pakistan) claimed that improving energy supply conditions and further supporting economic growth are priorities of the Pakistani government. Developing hydropower for economic growth is also one part of the Guiding Principles of the Water Resources Development Annual Plan.

The site at Karot has been identified as a potential power site by the Water and Power Development Authority (WAPDA) since November 1984. However, since the identification of this site, no further substantial development took place until 2014, when a group of Pakistani and Chinese investors was finally willing to finance this hydropower project.

The feasibility report was completed in March 2014. Because "the project is likely to improve agriculture in this arid area, rather than having a negative impact," the Karot Project was immediately approved by the Environmental Protection Agency-Punjab in March 2015.

On April 21, 2015, during President Xi Jinping's state visit to Pakistan, the Silk Road Fund LLC, China Three Gorges and Pakistan formally signed the Karot Hydropower Project.

As a USD 1.65 billion project, the Silk Road Fund will help the South Asian country upgrade its power supply and improve its economic performance. Along with the Export-Import Bank of China, another major lender of this project, the Silk Road Fund will provide capital for this project by investing in a subsidiary of the China Three Gorges Cooperation (China Three Gorges South Asia Investment Limited).

With the development of this project, on April 22, 2015, the International Finance Corporation (IFC), one member of the World Bank Group, the China Three Gorges Cooperation, and the China Three Gorges South Asia Investment Limited signed the Shareholder Agreement. Thus, the IFC and the Silk Road Fund both became shareholders of the China Three Gorges South Asia Investment Limited simultaneously. The Xinhua Net noted that the ICF can enhance the partners' confidence and attract more investments forcefully. Thus, the joining of IFC will also prompt further investments in the Silk Road Fund.

The expected outcome of the project is as follows.

First, according to the report of Xinhua Net, the Karot Hydropower Project has a designed installed capacity of 720,000 kw and generates 3.213 billion kw-hours of power per year. This project will begin at the end of this year and is expected to be completed in 2020. According to the Wall Street Journal, the Karot Project will be run by the Chinese side for 30 years before being handed over to the Pakistani side.

Furthermore, the Silk Road Fund will invest in hydropower projects in the region with a combined power-generating capacity up to 3,350 megawatts to improve the power supply condition as well as to prompt economic growth, people's living standard and social stability in Pakistan.

Third, Jin Qi, Chairman of the Fund, stated that this project and further projects will support the development of Chinese high-tech and equipment manufacturing industries by helping enterprises move overseas.

Fourth, this project is also the priority of the development of the broader "China-Pakistan Economic Corridor", which starts from Kashgar in China's northwestern territory of Xinjiang and ends at the Pakistani port of Gwadar. As outlined in the joint statement issued by the governments of China and Pakistan, the Silk Road Fund will actively expand financing opportunities for other projects under the framework of the China-Pakistan Economic Corridor. This project and further investments will boost Pakistan's economic growth and may provide an additional route for China to import oil from the Middle East.

Finally, the Silk Road Fund is one part of the nation's commitments to the "One Belt, One Road" initiative. As the first overseas investment since its establishment last December, the Karot Project will also prompt the whole initiative in the long term.

The cooperation between the IFC and the Silk Road Fund in Pakistan signals the beginning of the cooperation between China's "One Belt, One Road" strategic initiative and the World Bank Group. The tight and successful cooperation between the IFC and the Silk Road Fund may attract increasingly more international developmental financial institutions to cooperate with the Fund and to attract increasingly more capital to the Asian infrastructure field.

Chapter 6 Associations of DFIs

In this chapter, we introduce three associations of DFIs. These associations are not development banks, but they are organized by development banks. They build networks for development banks; share practices among development banks; identify and develop joint business opportunities; share know-how and best practice experiences for mutual learning; promote research on development banks; and help development banks communicate with government, with industry and with one another. The associations organize conferences and publish data and research reports; they are a part of the international development bank community.

Long-Term Investors Club (LTIC)

Members of LTIC

The LTIC currently consists of 18 members: the Bank GospodarstwaKrajowego (BGK), China Development Bank (CDB), La Caixa Bank, Caisse des Dépôts et Consignations (CDC), Caisse de dépôt et placement du Québec, Cassa Depositi e Prestiti (CDP), Caisse de Dépôt et de Gestion (CDG), Caixa Econômica Federal (CEF), Development bank of Japan Inc. (DBJ), European Investment Bank (EIB), Instituto de Crédito Oficial (ICO), Infrastructure Development Finance Company Ltd (IDFC), Japan Bank for International Cooperation (JBIC), Kreditanstalt für Wiederaufbau (KfW), Mubadala Development Company, Ontario Municipal

Employees Retirement System (OMERS), Teachers Insurance and Annuity Association-College Retirement Equities Fund (TIAA CREF), Industrial Development Bank of Turkey (TSKB), and Bank for Development and Foreign Economic Affairs (Vnesheconombank).

The Club has two categories of members: the *founding members* are CDC, CDP, KfW, and EIB; the *members* are any long-term financial institution admitted to the Club in accordance with the charter provisions.

The LTIC also enjoys partnerships with several other organizations: the OECD, the World Economic Forum, Eurofi, the Long-Term Infrastructure Investors Association (LTIIA), and European Long-Term Investors (ELTI).

Mission and Strategy

The club's objectives are the following:

- To share best practices among long-term investors, to strengthen their network and to increase long-term investors' non-financial value through their membership;

- To promote academic research on long-term investments and to contribute to public and professional debates;

- To assist in communications with political stakeholders of long-term investors and to assist each member in pursuing its investment policies;

- To facilitate joint initiatives in connection with projects and investments.

Activities of Information Exchange

Conference on: "Investing in Long-Term Europe: Relaunching Fixed, Network and Social Infrastructure" (Rome, December 12 – 13, 2014)

This conference was jointly organized by the Italian Banking Insurance and Finance Federation, the OECD, the LTIC and the CDP. The conference was organized in association with the Italian EU presidency, the European Long-Term Investors Association, the Official Monetary and Financial Institutions Forum, Integrate, and the Italian Council of the European Movement.

The conference lasted for two days on four topics in three rounds of debating:

Topic 1: Investing in long-term Europe. Where do we stand? Progress made and next steps. Speakers discussed topics such as *"investing in long-term Europe"* and *"how to create a more favorable financial and non-financial regulatory framework for long-term investment in the EU."*

Topic 2: The response of institutions, industry and civil society. Speakers discussed topics such as *"the role of institutional investors in financing long-term investment"* and *"infrastructure investment at a global asset level."*

Topic 3: Retuning the European public-private partnership agenda. Speakers discussed topics such as *"financing transport infrastructure in Europe"* and *"financing energy infrastructure in Europe."*

Topic 4: The unexplored business of social infrastructure.

Three rounds of debates included debating the demand side, debating the supply side and debating the role of the institutional side.

Fourth LTIC International Conference an "Growth and Employment: The role of long-term investors" (Luxembourg, October 8, 2012)

The Luxembourg Conference was held at the European Investment Bank under the aegis of the EU Presidency and on the margins of the Eurogroup and Ecofin meetings. The main themes of the conference were dedicated to growth and employment, addressing public policy-related issues and focusing on what actions should be taken to improve the provision of long-term finance in specific sectors that are crucial for growth and employment.

During the course of the conference, two main topics were discussed: *"growth and long-term financing"* and *"energy, climate change and long-term investment."*

International Development Finance Club (IDFC)

IDFC Members

According to its official website, the IDFC has 23 members. Its members are geographically widespread:

(i) In Europe: Black Sea Trade and Development Bank (BSTDB), Agence Française de Développement (AFD), the Croatian Bank for Reconstruction and Development (HBOR), KfW Bankengruppe, the Industrial Development Bank of Turkey (TSKB) and Vnesheconombank (VEB);

(ii) In Central and South America: Nacional Financiera (NAFIN), Development Bank of Latin America (CAF), Central American Bank for Economic Integration (BCIE/CABEI), Bancoldex S. A., Corporación Financiera de Desarrollo S. A. (COFIDE), Banco Nacional de Desenvolvimento Econômico e Social (BNDES) and Banco Estado (BE);

(iii) In Africa: Caisse de Dépôt et de Gestion (CDG), Development Bank of Southern Africa (DBSA), Banque Ouest Africaine de Développement (BOAD), the Eastern and Southern Africa Trade and Development Bank (PTA);

(iv) In Asia and MENA: Small Industries Development Bank of India (SIDBI), Indonesia Exim Bank, China Development Bank (CDB), Islamic Corporation for the Development of the Private Sector (ICD), Korea Finance Corporation (KoFC) and Japan International Cooperation Agency (JICA).

In 2010 when the IDFC was founded, the total commitments of the 19 founding members of the IDFC amounted to approximately USD 390 billion. Within the IDFC, the highest commitments in 2010 came from KfW (Germany; USD 108 billion) and BNDES (Brazil; USD 105 billion).

Mission and Strategy

The IDFC's objectives are as follows:

- Setting the agenda by joining forces and networking on issues of common interest;
- Identifying and developing joint business opportunities;
- Sharing know-how and best practice experiences for mutual learning.

History and Governance

Founded in 2010, the IDFC is a young organization. Following the first meeting of the development bank CEOs in 2010, several participating institutions suggested formalizing their cooperation. They confirmed the need for a regular exchange and decision forum on a CEO level that could help national and sub-regional development banks strengthen their voice in an environment dominated by multilateral financing institutions. Thus, the IDFC was established as an association of like-minded development banks. The club has a distinct legal personality, but membership carries no legally binding obligations other than those expressly mentioned in the IDFC charter. Members operate within the framework of the development policies in their respective countries and assist their respective governments in fulfilling their national and international commitments within the framework established by their constitutional documents.

The organizational structure of the IDFC has intentionally remained simple and lean:

(i) The annual meeting is a meeting of all club members, each represented by its CEO or designated representative.

(ii) A steering group is composed of chairperson and vice chairpersons. It is elected by all the members for a two-year term and is responsible for the preparation and follow-up of the annual meeting and any other business. The group convenes at least twice annually.

(iii) A secretariat is appointed by the chairperson and is hosted and funded by the members whose CEO is the chairperson. The secretariat is responsible for communicating on behalf of the club upon request from the steering group. The secretariat organizes and administers the work of the club and coordinates the implementation of decisions made at the annual meeting.

(iv) Delegates are appointed by each member to serve as transmitter contacts between the secretariat and member institutions. They are responsible for all communication and exchanges with the secretariat.

(v) A working group is appointed at the annual meeting on an ad hoc basis to research and prepare specific topics in which the club is currently engaged and to develop relevant information and documentation.

Activities of Information Exchange

Climate Finance Forum (Paris, March 31, 2015)

The members of the IDFC participated in this forum, which has resulted in major advances in ensuring IDFC in practical fight against the climate change.

First IDFC Annual Meeting (Tokyo, October 14, 2012)

The IDFC members participated in the annual meeting where they reached a consensus on the members, mission and workings of the IDFC. The 2012 work program of the IDFC was successful, resulting in the "IDFC Green Finance Mapping Report" and the "Position Paper on Leverage Private and Public Funds". The IDFC members agreed on a new work program for 2013. The IDFC will highlight its activities on the overarching theme of sustainable development with a special focus on green development and social development. Green development includes but is not limited to the sectors of (green) infrastructure, renewable energy and energy efficiency. SME development and social inclusion through poverty reduction are principal channels of the club's activities in the field of social development.

World Federation of Development Financing Institutions (WFDFI)

Members of WFDFI

The World Federation of Development Financing Institutions (WFDFI) is a global organization of development banks. The WFDFI has the following categories of members:

Regional members include ordinary regional members. Regional associations of DFIs are endowed with a legal personality. In total, the Federation contains four ordinary regional members: the African Association of Development Finance Institutions (AADFI), the Association of Development Financing Institutions in Asia and the Pacific (ADFIAP), the Association of National Development Finance Institutions in Member Countries of the Islamic Development Bank (ADFIMI) and the Latin American Association of Development Financing Institutions (ALIDE). Temporary regional members are DFIs of countries where there is as yet no regional associations.

Special members are international institutions or organizations (of the world, regional or sub-regional status) interested in development financing, national associations of DFIs where such associations exist, and non-DFIs wishing to assist the Federation in achieving its goal by supporting its programs.

Individual members: Distinguished persons who, through their interest or participation, support the Federation in the accomplishment of its aims and activities.

Honorary members: Persons, who have performed outstanding services in the field of development banking or in related fields of economic development, may be elected honorary members of the Federation with the approval of the Council of Governors.

AADFI: In March 1975, at a meeting in Abidjan, a decision was made by the African Development Bank (AfDB) to create AADFI, the African Association of Development Finance Institutions, by designating George Aithnard of Togo, one of the AfDB's senior officials, as secretary general of AADFI and providing him with office space and a small staff in the building of the AfDB. In May 1975, in Dakar, its first General Assembly was held. The first president was August Daubrey of the Ivory Coast. Since then, AADFI has had seven secretary generals, with Magatte Wade from Senegal currently holding this position since 2000.

ADFIAP: The Association of Development Financing Institutions in Asia and the Pacific (ADFIAP) is the focal point of all development banks and other financial institutions engaged in the financing of sustainable development in the Asia-Pacific region. Founded in 1976, the ADFIAP presently has 117 member institutions in 42 countries and territories. The Asian Development Bank (AsDB) is a special member of the Association. The ADFIAP is also a founding member of the 328-member, 154-country World Federation of Development Financing Institutions (WFDFI) composed of similar regional associations in Africa, Latin America, and the Middle East. The ADFIAP is a non-governmental organization with a consultative status with the United Nation's Economic and Social Council. The ADFIAP is the 2008 Overall Winner (developing country category) of the "Associations Making a Better World Award" of the American Society of Association Executives and the Center for Association Leadership. The ADFIAP is a non-stock and non-profit international organization with headquarters in Manila in the Philippines.

ADFIMI: The Association of National Development Finance Institutions in member countries of the Islamic Development Bank (IsDB) is a regional association of DFIs established as an autonomous and independent international organization. At the 11th IsDB Board of Governors Meeting (Amman, March 1986), a provisional constituent assembly of DFI representatives was elected to establish the ADFIMI. The association commenced the operations in September 1987 at its headquarters in Istanbul, Turkey, upon being given the status of an international organization by the Turkish government.

ALIDE: ALIDE is the international organization that represents the development banking system of Latin America and the Caribbean. Established in 1968, the organization has its permanent headquarters in Lima, Peru. Its aim is to promote the cohesion, communication and participation of development banks and DFIs in economic, financial and social fields in the region. The organization has a varied membership comprising institutions that operate on the financing-for-development arena, including active, associate and collaborating members. ALIDE has 80 members from 31 countries (regional and non-regional) and international financial organizations as well as multilateral development banks. ALIDE is also a founding member of the World Federation of Development Financing Institutions. ALIDE is now ISO 9001: 2008 certified.

History and Governance

In June 1979, at a UNIDO development bank conference in Zurich, AADFI, ADFI-AP and ALIDE, jointly with KfW of Germany, signed an agreement to establish the World Federation of Development Financing Institutions (WFDFI). Its first governors were Willi F. L. Engel of KfW, Frankfurt; René Amichia of AADFI, Ivory Coast; Tomás Pastoriza of ALIDE, Dominican Republic; and Vicente R. Jayme of ADFIAP, the Philippines. At the end of 1979, the WFDFI opened its secretariat at the Instituto de Crédito Oficial (ICO) in Madrid, which was then headed by Rafael Bermejo Blanco.

José Elías Gallegos became its first secretary general. Since then, the Federation has had eleven secretary generals. The WFDFI's headquarters was in Madrid from 1979 until 1994, when a decision was made to give WFDFI a rotating secretariat in which the secretariat role was served by each regional association for a three-year period. The secretariat was with ADFIAP in Manila from 1995 to 1998 for three years, and it then moved to ADFIMI in Istanbul from 1999 to 2002, with Orhan Sagci from Turkey serving as secretary general. In May 2002, Rommel Acevedo, secretary general of

ALIDE, became secretary general of WFDFI until 2009. Octavio B. Peralta of ADFIAP was elected secretary general of WDDFI in Istanbul in 2009 for a period of three years commencing January 1, 2010.

Nuri Birtek, secretary general of ADFIMI, is the present WFDFI secretary general after being elected at the BOG meeting in Tokyo, Japan, on October 11, 2012. He is serving as secretary general for three years beginning on January 1, 2013.

General Assembly

The supreme body is composed of the chairmen/CEOs of the ordinary regional members, who hold all the authority necessary to accomplish the aims of the Federation. The assembly has the following specific powers:

- To examine and approve the annual report of the board of governors.
- To confirm the admission of members and decide on their suspension or expulsion.
- To allocate the assets of the Federation in the event of dissolution.
- To examine any other matters submitted for consideration by the board of governors.

Board of Governors

The governing body is composed of the secretaries general of each of the ordinary regional members, holding the following specific duties and powers:

- To convene the Ordinary General Assembly.
- To elect and appoint the secretary general.
- To review and approve plans, programs and budgets of the Federation, as proposed by the secretary general.
- To determine powers and authority of the officers of the board of governors and of the secretary general.

- In general, to be responsible for overall supervision of the general secretariat and the secretary general.
- To appoint committees or individuals to perform specific tasks for the purpose of advancing the work of the Federation.
- To implement or establish the implementation of the instructions transmitted by the General Assembly.

Management

The management of the Federation is conducted by the general secretariat under the direction of the secretary general, who is the CEO of the WFDFI. The general secretariat performs its duties in accordance with the policies, procedures and budgets approved by the board of governors.

Activities of Information Exchange

Joint International Development Forum: "Collaborative Entrepreneur Development, A Determinant in a Challenging Business Ecosystem" (Royale Chulan Hotel, KL, Malaysia, October 20 -21, 2014)

In this one-and-a-half day event, ADFIMI-SME Bank Joint International Development Forum 2014, addressed the following four topics:

- Topic 1: Beyond financing—A Game Rule Changer in Shaping and Sustaining High-Growth Entrepreneurs. This Forum discussed some of the key strategic issues and proposals and their limitations as experienced by both the financing institutions and by entrepreneurs at large.
- Topic 2: Innovation—The Value Creation Tool in a Changing Business Ecosystem. This Forum discussed new innovative approaches in value-added process. Such approaches could not only ensure that the financial institutions stay relevant in the marketplace but also encourage entrepreneurs to continue creating value by means of blended investment packaging through such structural levels of collaboration.

- Topic 3: Managing Risks—Alternative Models in a Collaborative Entrepreneurial Environment. The Forum discussed experiences and offered alternative models related to the prerequisites for actions and their implications, as experienced by some leading financiers and entrepreneurs in managing inherent investment business risks.

- Topic 4: Cross-Border Engagement—The Challenges to the DFIs' and SMEs' Collaboration in Sustaining Growth. The Forum discussed related challenges and explored the means of addressing these issues in the context of initiating structured networks of a collaborative DFI-SME environment.

Joint AfDB/AADFI General Assembly Workshop: "Strengthening the Effectiveness of National Development Finance Institutions" (May 28, 2013, Marrakech, Morocco)

The AfDB/AADFI Annual Joint Workshop attempted to answer the fundamental question of how to enhance the role of African DFIs in promoting economic and social development. In this regard, the workshop focused on the rationale and missions of African DFIs and discussed international best practices in prudential regulation and supervision; the corporate management of risks, including environmental and social risks; and the measurement and monitoring of results.

Part Two   Analysis and Outlook of Development Financing Institutions

Part Two will build on the overview of DFIs to focus on the analysis and outlook of DFIs. Chapter 7 will provide the readers with an overall picture of the structure and trends of the entire group of the sample institutions. Chapter 8 will use case studies to elaborate three strategic roles that DFIs can play in realizing a transformative development agenda, namely, long-term planning, market incubation and convening power in creating public-private synergies.

Part Two Analysis and Outlook of Development Financing Institutions

Chapter 7 Structure and Trends of Global Development Financial Institutions

Chapter 2 – 6 presents detailed descriptions of each development financial institution (DFI) in our sample. Chapter 7 will provide the readers with an overall picture of the structure and trends of the entire group of the sample institutions.

As shown in Part One, our sample is composed of 30 DFIs, including eight multilateral development banks, 18 national development banks and four China-related DFIs. This sample represents the most important development finance institutions in the world, especially in Asia as a geographic region of greatest interest in the present report. However, because these institutions are not randomly selected and the sample size is not sufficient for more detailed analyses, the results of the following statistical analysis only represent the general features of the sample institutions.

Structure

This section describes the structure of the DFIs in our sample, using a horizontal comparison. Most of the statistics that are presented in this section utilize data from 2014.

Establishment

The DFIs in our sample cover various geographic areas across the globe. Of the eight multinational DFIs, one providesservice worldwide, whereas the seven other institutions provide service at the regional level, e. g., Africa, Asia, North and Latin America, Europe, Europe/Asia, the Caribbean region and Islamic countries. Of the 18 national development banks, three are in Europe, three in Russia and Former Soviet republics, eight in Asia, two in Latin America and two in Africa. The four China-related DFIs are located in China.

An interesting finding of this research is the age distribution of the DFIs. A large number of DFIs were established in the periods 1945 – 1985 and 2000 – 2014. This indicates that the world experienced two major waves of DFI establishment. The first wave came after World War II, while the second wave arrived after the beginning of the 21st century.

The age distributions reveals that, first, a large number of DFIs were established more than 30 years ago and have been operating since then; and second, another large number of new DFIs were established at the beginning of the 21st century, despite the wave of privatization of state-owned financial institutes in some countries (see Figure 7.1).

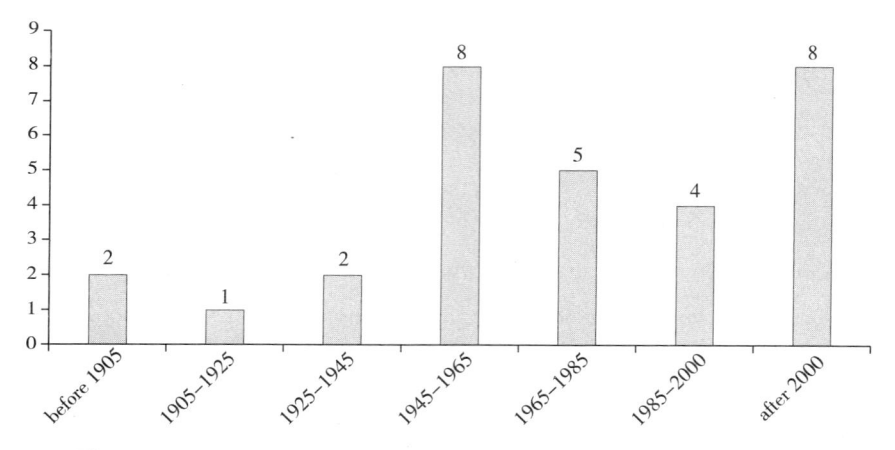

Figure 7.1 Age Distribution of DFIs, Number of Bank Establishments

Note: Data include 30 development banks.

Size of the DFIs

The size of DFIs can be measured by the scale of their asset, equity and loan portfolios, which reflect the scale and the global importance of the development financing industry.

Data on individual DFIs show that the assets of most DFIs grew in the period between 2006 and 2013. Among the DFIs in the sample, CDB had the largest increase in total assets, as measured in terms of both level and growth, followed by KfW. Currently, CDB is the largest and KfW is the second largest DFI in the world in terms of total assets.

Figure 7.2 shows the assets of individual DFIs. The small box in Figure 7.2 magnifies the data for the group of DFIs with smaller assets.

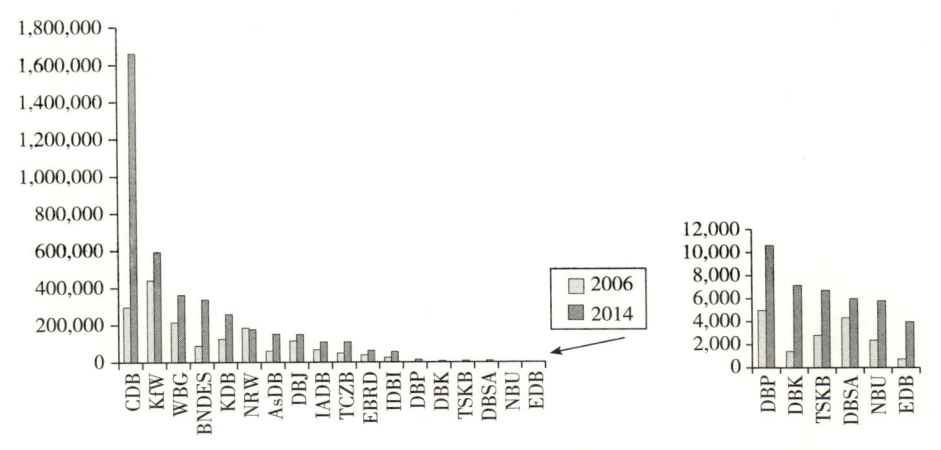

Figure 7.2 Assets of Individual DFIs, 2006 and 2014, USD million

At the end of 2014, the DFIs in our sample reported total assets of USD 4.25 trillion. Of the DFIs, CDB reached USD 1.66 trillion in total assets in 2014. We group DFIs into small (less than USD 1 billion), medium (USD 1 – 9.9 billion), large (USD 10 – 99.9 billion) and super large (more than USD 100 billion) groups. The share of the super large group rose to 38% at the end of 2013, from 27% at the end of 2006 (see Figure 7.3).

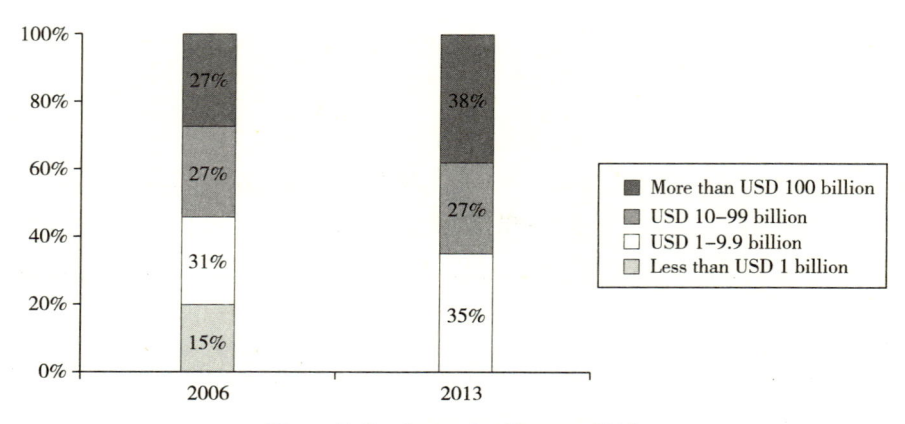

Figure 7.3 Assets by Group, 2013

Note: 26 FIs' data available.

The equity of the DFIs in our sample also experienced a strong increase from 2006 to 2014. CDB showed the greatest increase in equity compared with the other DFIs in the group (see Figure 7.4).

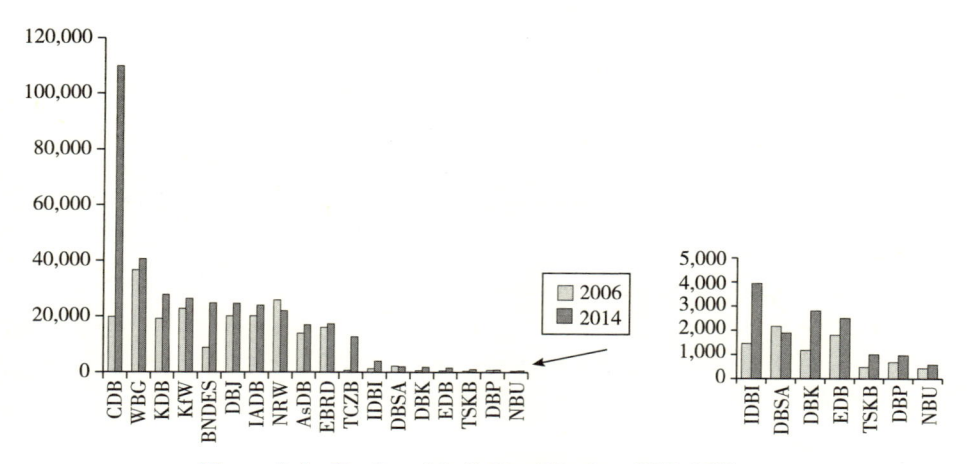

Figure 7.4 Equity of Individual Banks, USD Million

The total gross loan portfolio of the DFIs, for which data are available (which includes most of the DFIs), increased greatly from 2006 to in 2014. In terms of individual banks in the sample, again, CDB had the largest loan portfolio and the highest growth between 2006 and 2014 (see Figure 7.5).

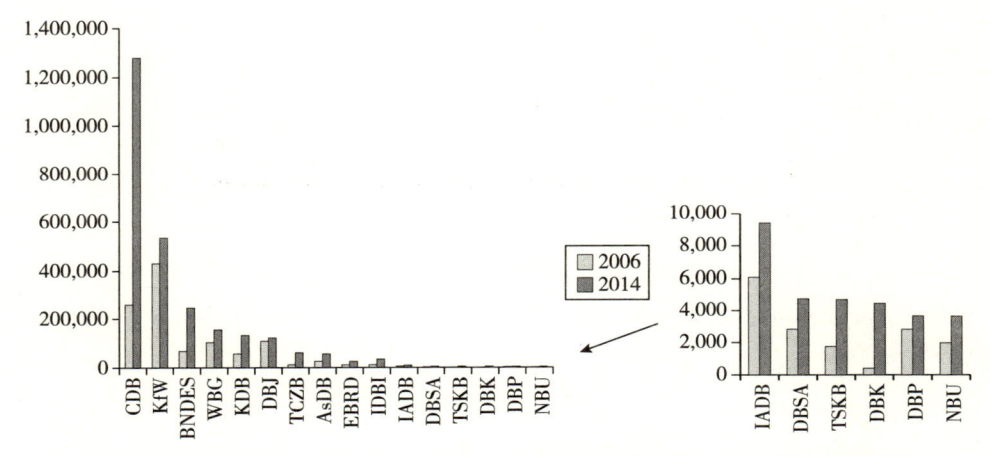

Figure 7.5 Total Gross Loan Portfolio, Individual DFIs, 2014, USD Million

Overall, the DFIs experienced dramatic growth over the past several years, as measured by their total assets, total equity and loan portfolio. Some of the DFIs became super large financial institutions and major players in the world financial market.

Ownership and Government Support

Most of the national DFIs in the sample are owned or supported by the government. In most of the cases, the government provides the strategic directions and appoints DFI's senior management. However, government ownership takes diversified forms, and not all of the DFIs in the sample are entirely owned by the government.

The government provides strong support to DFIs. Of the institutions in our sample, 82% of the DFIs receive direct budget transfers from the government (see Figure 7.6).

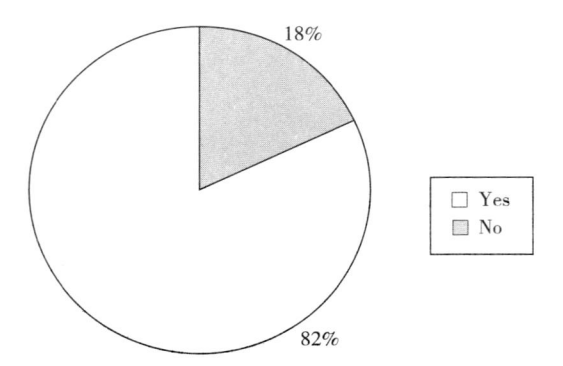

Figure 7.6 Direct Budget Transfers from Government
Note: 17 national DFIs' data available.

However, if governmental transfers were eliminated, most of the DFIs would still be able to operate on a sustainable basis with their own generated income (see Figure 7.7).

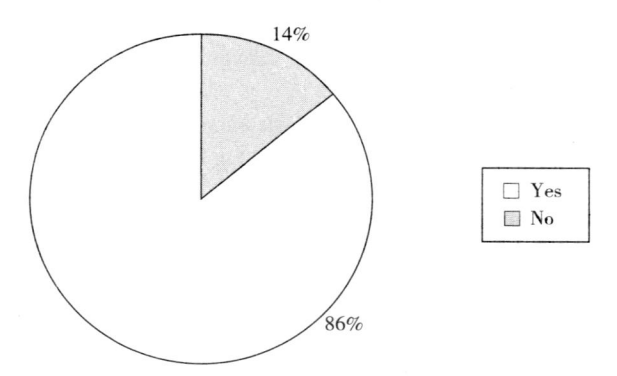

Figure 7.7 Operate with Own Income
Note: 14 national DFIs' data available.

Our data show that the governments guarantee the debts of 16 among the 19 national DFIs. Our data also show that 85% of the DFIs in the sample received governmental funds, subsidies or transfers to cover losses or strengthen their financial situation in the past five years.

Funding

DFIs have diversified sources of funding, including taking deposits from the public, borrowing from other financial institutions, issuing debt in the domestic and international markets, receiving budget transfers from the government and using their own equity.

Most of the DFIs in the sample can borrow from other financial institutions or issue debt in local markets. Most of the DFIs receive direct budget transfers from the government (see the previous section). Some of the DFIs receive governmental funds, subsidies or transfers to cover losses or strengthen their financial situation.

Unlike regular commercial financial institutions, more than half of the DFIs do not take public deposits as a source of funding. By not taking deposits from the public, DFIs can focus on the lending operations and avoid competition with regular commercial banks (see Figure 7.8).

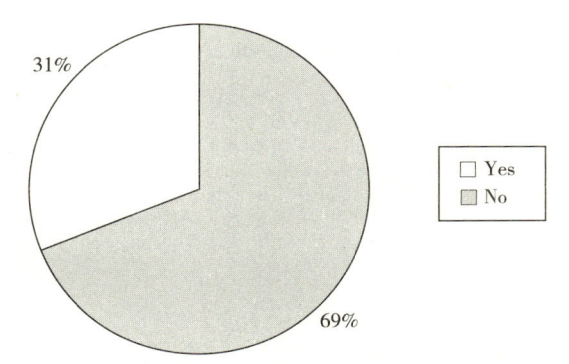

Figure 7.8 Percentage of the Institutes Taking Deposits from the Public
Note: 26 DFIs included.

Business Models

The DFIs have created and adopted a wide range of business models and serve different types of clients. Through these business models, the DFIs realize their development mandates.

DFIs perform their lending operations through retail (lending directly to end customers) wholesale (lending to other financial institutions which subsequently lend to end customers) or both. In our sample, 8% of the DFIs solely engage in wholesale lending, 23% of them solely engage in retail lending and 69% of them engage in both wholesale and retail lending (see Figure 7.9).

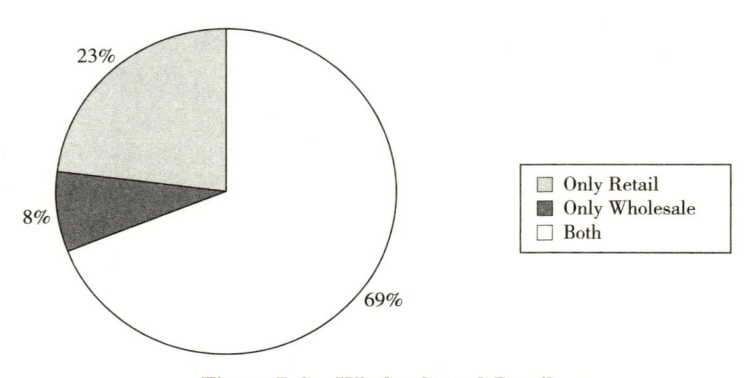

Figure 7.9 Wholesale and Retail

Note: 26 DFIs' data available.

The DFIs in our sample lend in multiple subsectors. Most of the DFIs lend in construction (100%), energy (96%) and infrastructure (96%). Other sub-sectors that the DFIs often lend in are industry/manufacturing, services, agribusiness and health (see Figure 7.10).

Most of the DFIs choose micro, small and medium enterprises, countries and large private corporations as their target markets, followed by other financial institutions, other state owned enterprises, individuals and households as well as start-ups (see Figure 7.11).

The DFIs offer their customers various types of lending products. The most common types of loans that DFIs offer are long-term loans bridge or short-term loans, and syn-

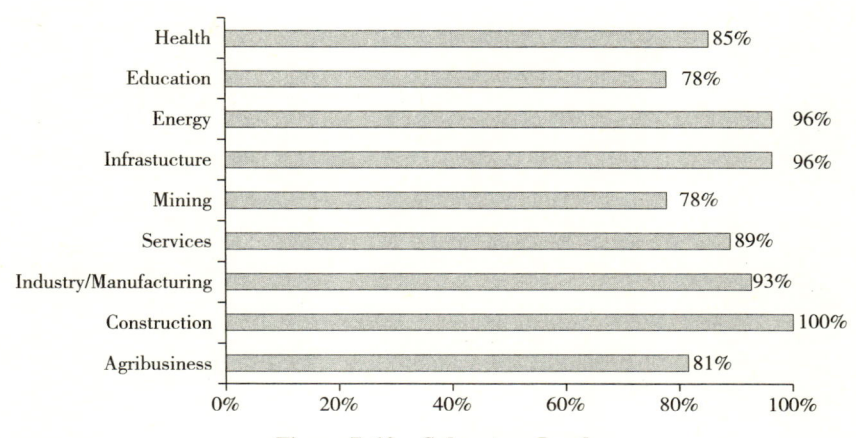

Figure 7.10   Subsectors Lend

- Health 85%
- Education 78%
- Energy 96%
- Infrastucture 96%
- Mining 78%
- Services 89%
- Industry/Manufacturing 93%
- Construction 100%
- Agribusiness 81%

Note: 27 DFIs' data included.

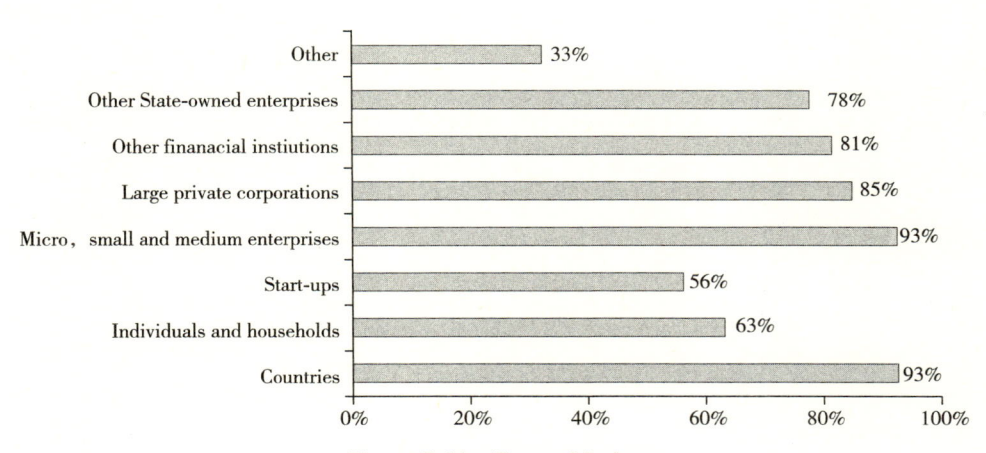

Figure 7.11   Target Market

- Other 33%
- Other State-owned enterprises 78%
- Other finanacial instiutions 81%
- Large private corporations 85%
- Micro, small and medium enterprises 93%
- Start-ups 56%
- Individuals and households 63%
- Countries 93%

Note: 27 DFIs' data included.

dicated loans, which are offered by 89%, 81% and 81% of the DFIs in the sample, respectively. Other commonly offered loans are loans for working capital and loans for start-up activities (see Figure 7.12).

The average annual interest rates that the DFIs offer to their customers are typically lower than the interest rate that is offered by regular commercial banks. The average

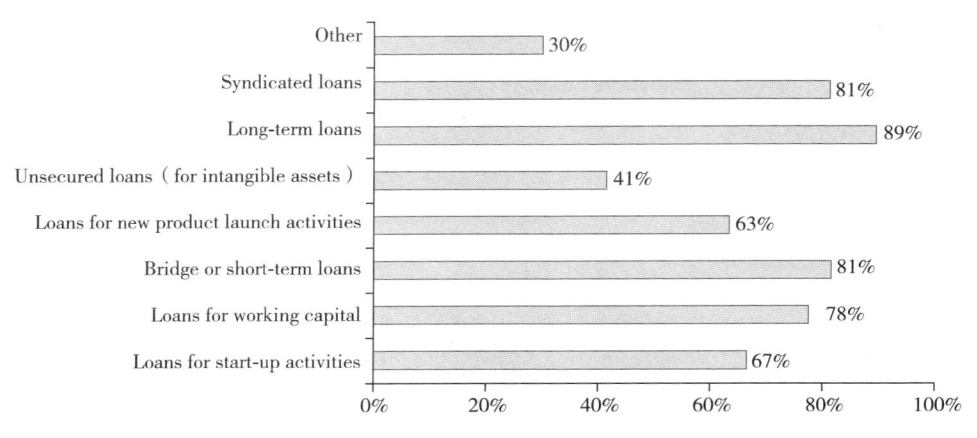

Figure 7.12 Lending Products

- Other: 30%
- Syndicated loans: 81%
- Long-term loans: 89%
- Unsecured loans (for intangible assets): 41%
- Loans for new product launch activities: 63%
- Bridge or short-term loans: 81%
- Loans for working capital: 78%
- Loans for start-up activities: 67%

Note: 27 DFIs' data included.

of the interest rates in our sample is 5.1%. According to our data, 15 of the DFIs provide loans at subsidized interest rates (below market interest rates).

The DFIs in our sample also offers other financial products, including loan guarantees, trust services, money transfers, microinsurance, savings accounts and deposit accounts (see Figure 7.13).

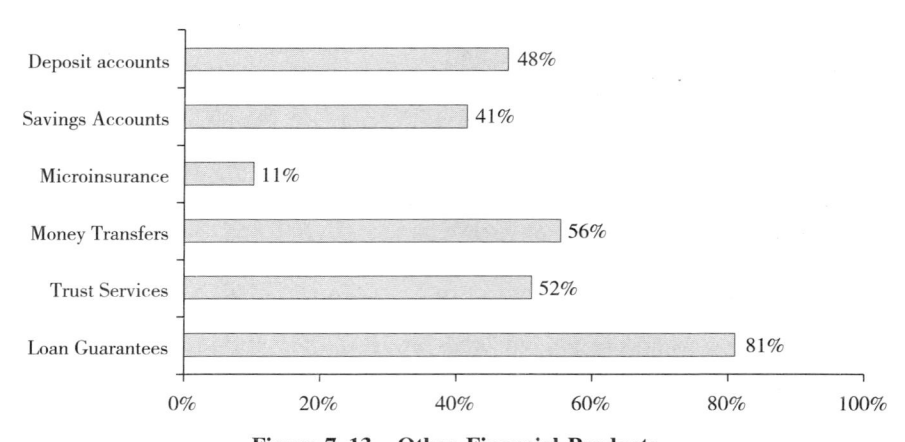

Figure 7.13 Other Financial Products

- Deposit accounts: 48%
- Savings Accounts: 41%
- Microinsurance: 11%
- Money Transfers: 56%
- Trust Services: 52%
- Loan Guarantees: 81%

Note: 27 DFIs' data included.

DFIs offer long-term loans to their customers. Our data reveal the maximum maturity of the loans that the DFIs in the sample offer to their customers. Approximately 42% of the 19 DFIs that provides information on the maximum maturity of their loans, offer loans with a maturity of more than 21 years, and 42% of them provide loans with a maximum maturity of 11 – 20 years (see Figure 7.14).

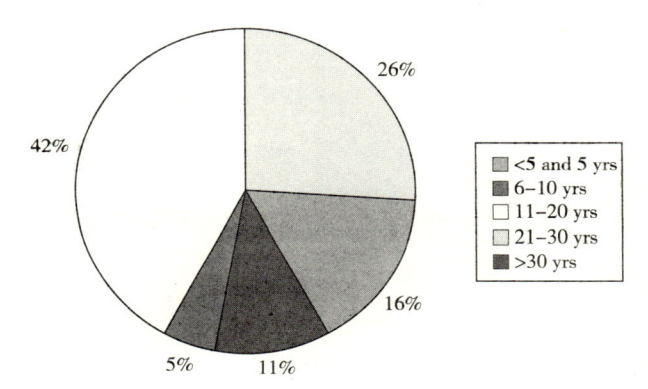

Figure 7.14 Maximum Loan Term, in Years, % of DFIs

Note: 19 DFIs' data available.

Profitability and Asset Quality

Although profit maximization is not the objective of the DFIs, many DFIs attempt to improve their profitability and asset quality.

Indicating the amount of earnings that were generated from invested capital (assets), the return on assets (ROA) is an indicator of how profitable a company is relative to its total assets. ROA gives an idea on how efficiently the management uses its assets to generate earnings. Calculated by dividing a company's annual earnings by its total assets, ROA is displayed as a percentage. ROA values for public companies can vary substantially and are highly dependent on the industry and the country in question. To avoid mistakes in measurement, we compare a national DFI's ROA against the average ROA in its home country. Figure 7.15 depicts these differences. Although some of the DFIs present value below the average ROA of their home country, most of the DFIs in the sample have ROA values above that of their home country (i. e., most DFIs in our sample perform better than other banks on average in terms of ROA). The data show that over half of the national DFIs outperformed the average ROA values of their home countries, which indicates that these DFIs had good earnings performance in 2014.

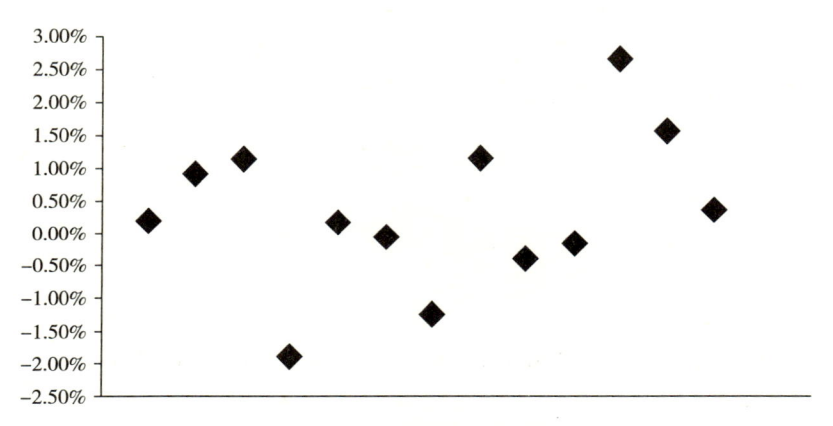

Figure 7.15 ROA, 2016, Compared with All Banks in the Same Country

Source: ROA of banks in a specific country in this table and ROE, NPL in Figure 7.16 and Figure 7.17 is from http: //www. helgilibrary. com/sectors/index/banking, and Bankscope Country Reports, "The Economist Intelligence Unit," May 9, 2015, retrieved at https: //bankscope. bvdinfo. com/version – 201556/ Search. EIUCountryReports. serv? _ CID = 4&context = 2X88BC5YQBB3M2Q.

Return on equity (ROE) measures the rate of return on the ownership interest (shareholders' equity) of common stock owners and, thus, measures a firm's efficiency at generating profits from each unit of shareholder equity. ROE shows how well a company uses investments to generate earnings growth. An analysis of ROE for the sample DFIs reveals that more DFIs' ROE were lower than the average for all banks in home country (see Figure 7.16).

We collected the non-performing loans (NPL) ratios for the DFIs. NPL is an indicator of the asset quality. We calculated the difference between a DFI's NPL ratio and

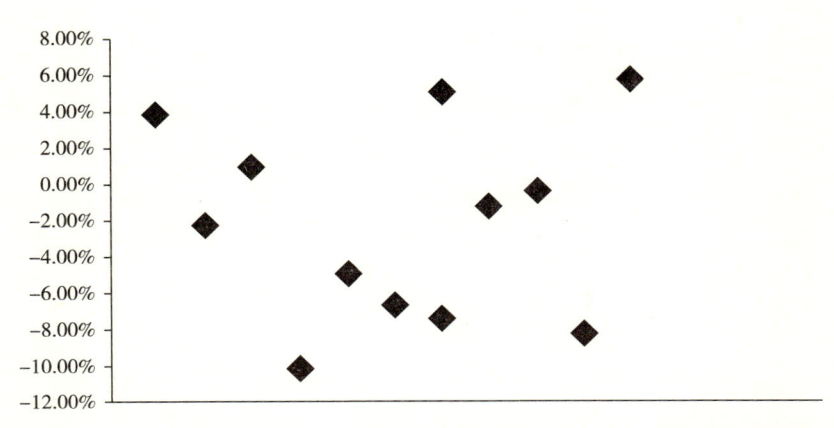

Figure 7.16 Average ROE, Compared with the Average of All Banks in Home

that of its home country's average in banking industry. The results show that 7 of the 11 DFIs had a lower NPL than their home country average, which is consistent with the World Bank's findings in 2012 (see Figure 7.17).

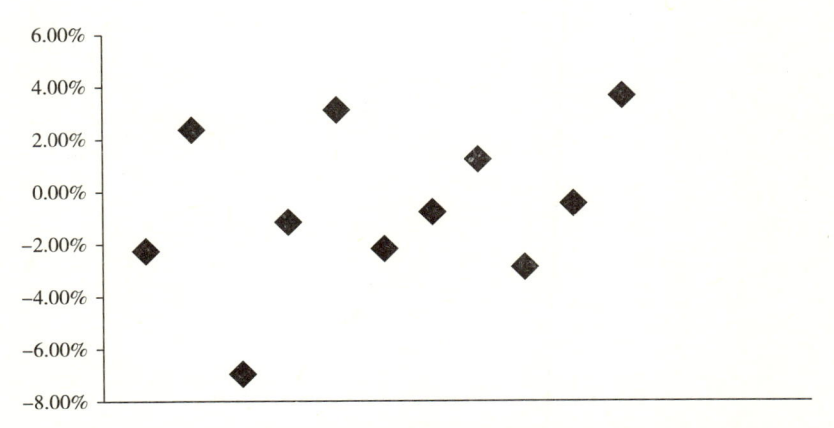

Figure 7.17 Non-Performing Loans, Compared with the Average of Home Country Banking Industry

Although the DFIs do not pursue profit maximization, most of them make profits and some of them perform better than the average performance in their home country.

Corporate Governance and Regulation

It is extremely important for DFIs to improve their corporate governance. The challenge that DFIs face in corporate governance is rooted in the DFI's characteristics. Because most of the DFIs are owned and controlled by the government, their corporate governance could be more complex than that of regular commercial banks. The nature of non-profit maximum and good economic performance may also conflict with each other. Our data show that many DFIs are attempting to improve their corporate governance, by being more transparent regarding information disclosure and by creating an efficient supervision-management structure.

All established DFIs in our sample have a risk management (or equivalent) unit that is responsible for identifying, monitoring and managing the risks in the institution's operations.

Most of the DFIs in our sample disclose information on the corporate governance and regulation to the public at least once per year. All of them disclose audited financial statements to the public. However, not all of them disclose information concerning their governance, risk management framework, off-balance-sheet items and capital adequacy (see Figure 7.18).

Category	Percentage
Regulatory capital and capital adequacy ratio	54%
Governance and risk management framework	93%
Off-balance sheet items	89%
Audited financial statements	100%

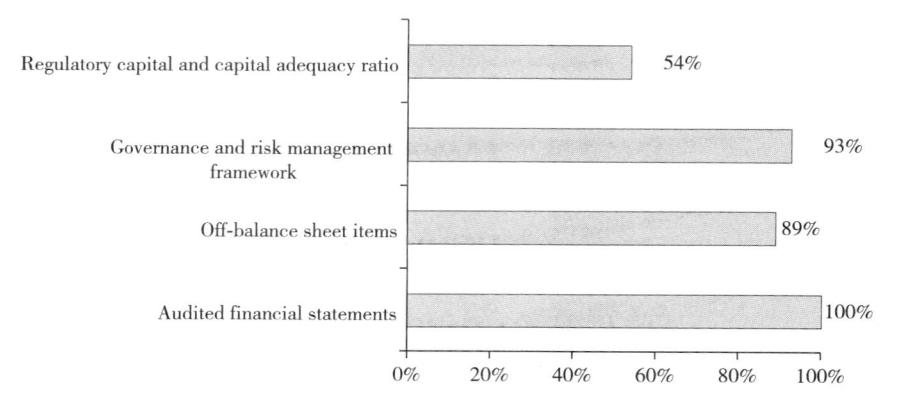

Figure 7.18 Disclosure to the Public

Note: 27 DFIs included.

Of the national DFIs in our sample, 58.3% are required to comply with the same standards of prudential supervision that private commercial financial institutions must comply with, whereas the remaining 41.7% of DFIs are subject to other standards (see Figure 7.19).

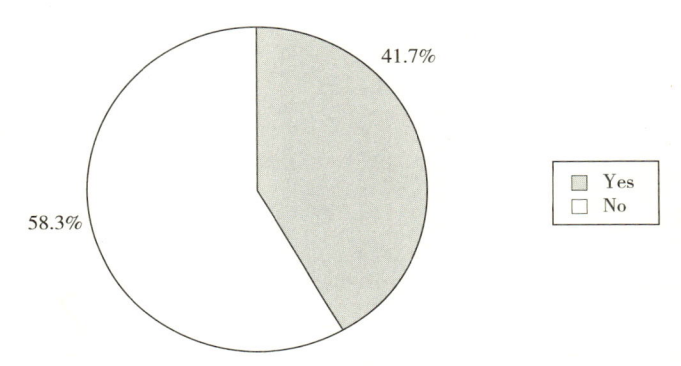

Figure 7.19 Same Prudential Rules

Note: 24 DFIs data available.

Our sample also shows that 77% of the DFIs are legally required to be audited by a professional external auditor.

Trends

In the first 15 years of the 21st century, the world economy experienced both boom and recession, especially the financial crisis from 2007 to 2009. During this period, the DFIs achieved dramatic growth. The DFIs also improved their performance in many fields during this period of fast growth. This section uses our available data to indicate some global trends in the development finance industry.

Tremendous Increase in the Size of DFIs

The combined total assets of the sample DFIs increased significantly to USD 4.27 trillion in 2014, from USD 2.03 trillion in 2006. The growth in total assets increased continuously, with the exception of a slight slowdown during the financial crisis in 2009 (see Figure 7.20).

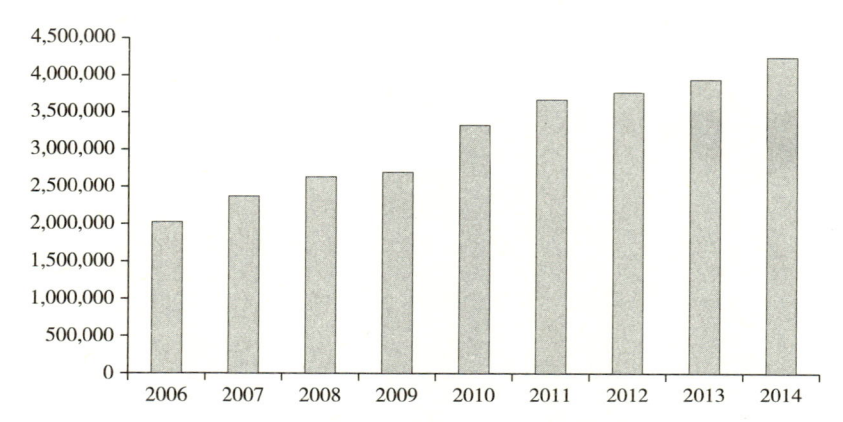

Figure 7.20　Combined Total Assets, 2006 – 2014, UDS Million

On average, DFIs now represent for a large portion of the entire financial system. Analysis shows that the DFIs in our sample accounted approximately 6.27% of the assets of all banking institutions in the world in 2012 (see Figure 7.21).

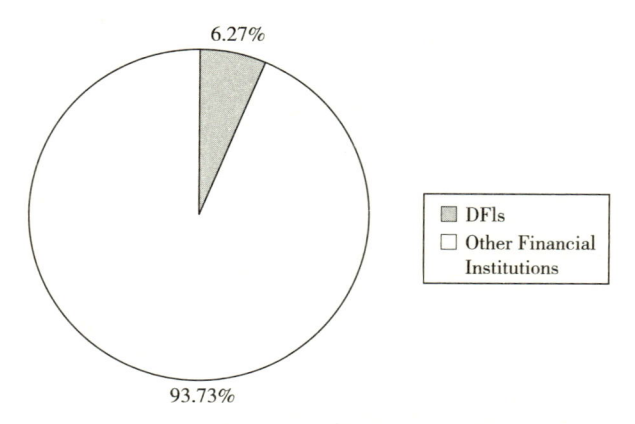

Figure 7.21　Share of Asset, DFIs vs. All Banking Institutes

Source: Helgilibrary, "Banking Asset", retrieved May 12, 2015, http://www.helgilibrary.com/indicators/index/bank-assets-usd

The total equity and gross loan portfolio of the sample DFIs follow the same pattern as that of total assets during the period 2006 – 2014 (see Figure 7.22).

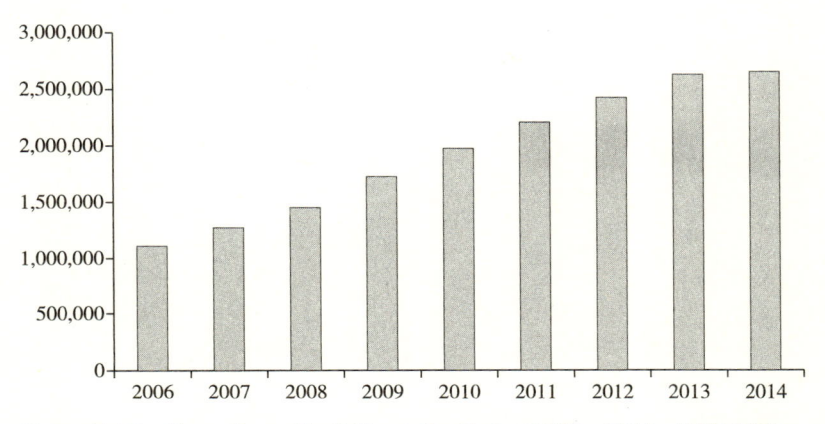

Figure 7.22 Gross Loan Portfolio at the End of 2006 – 2014, USD Million

Overall, the DFIs in our sample enjoyed continuous growth in their total assets, total equity and gross loan portfolios from 2006 to 2014. The global financial crisis from 2007 to 2009 did not halt the strong growth of the world's major DFIs. On the contrary, the DFIs' activities have a pronounced countercyclical effect.

Improved Operations

While experiencing rapid growth, the performance of the DFIs improved during the period from 2006 to 2014, with some fluctuations (see Figure 7.23). The mathematical average ROE of sample DFIs returned to a high level after the slowdown in 2008 and 2011 – 2012. The average ROA increased in 2014 but remained lower than the peak before the financial crisis.

Follow the peak before and during the financial crisis, the average NPL ratio decreased. When the financial crisis ended, the NPL ratio of most of the DFIs declined to a normal level (see Figure 7.24).

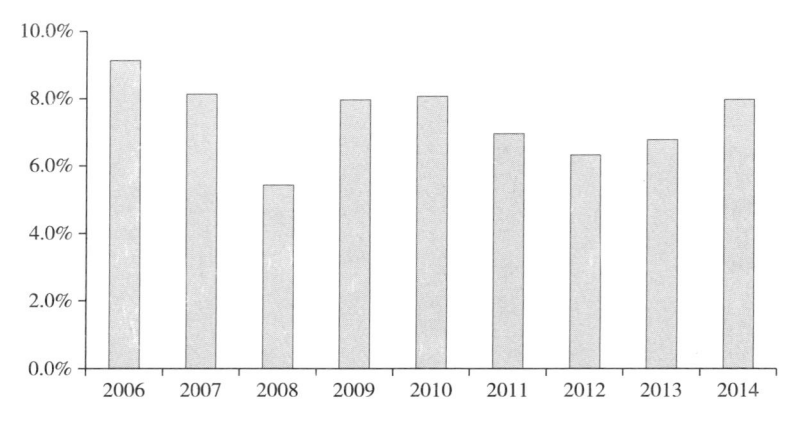

Figure 7. 23   Average ROE, 2006 – 2014

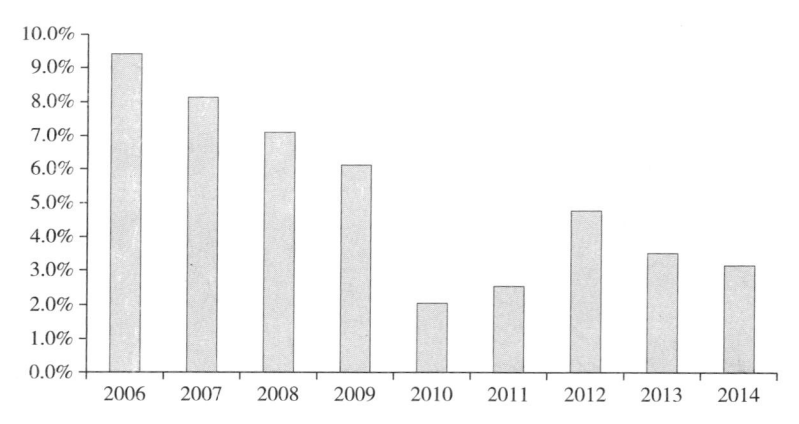

Figure 7. 24   Average Non-Performing Loans Ratio, 2006 – 2014

Conclusions

Although the DFIs in our sample have wide diversified characteristics, they exhibit certain common patterns.

- The DFIs experienced dramatic growth in the past several years, as measured by their total assets, total equity and loan portfolio. The asset, equity and portfolios of most individual DFIs grew in this period of rapid growth. Of the DFIs in the sample, CDB had the largest increase in total assets and total equity, as measured in terms of both level and growth.

- Most of the national DFIs in our sample are wholly owned by the state. The governments provide strong support to DFIs. However, the governmental support also adopted different forms.

- DFIs have diversified sources of funding, including taking deposits from the public, borrowing from other financial institutions, issuing debt in the domestic and international markets, receiving budget transfers from the government and using own equity.

- The DFIs have created and adopted a wide range of business models and serve different types of clients. DFIs perform their lending operations through retail, wholesale or both. Currently, DFIs are focusing on a number of strategic investment areas, for which commercial banks cannot provide long-term financing. Using these business models, DFIs help governments to reallocate resources and eliminate bottlenecks obstructing economic development.

- It is extremely important for DFIs to improve their corporate governance. In the past several years, the DFIs have improved their operations in dynamic global economic environment and redesigned their interior management and supervision structures.

- During the global financial crisis, the DFIs played an important role in stabilizing the financial market and the entire economy. After the financial crisis, the DFIs' performance improved, although some of the indicators have not returned to their pre-crisis peaks.

Chapter 8　The Role of DFIs in a Transformation Agenda

This chapter uses case studies to elaborate the three strategic roles that DFIs can play in realizing a transformative development agenda, namely, long-term planning, market incubation and convening power in creating public-private synergies. The purpose here is not to define the "best" practice; rather, the purpose is to foster mutual learning among DFIs to better cope with development challenges in an innovative way.

Long-Term Planning

A comprehensive long-term plan is pivotal to achieving economic transformation. In contrast to the traditional state planning in a command economy, the starting point of long-term planning by DFIs is an economy's factor endowments—which is "given at any specific time and changeable over time". The aim is to identify the economy's comparative advantages and crucial bottlenecks to promote a dynamic process of industrial upgrading and economic diversification. Driven by a grand vision, long-term planning can help in the design of medium-term strategies and short-term work plans to create "hard" and "soft" infrastructure to enable transforming economies to move up on the economic ladder.

This part will first examine how the China Development Bank prioritizes planning to facilitate economic transformation in China and abroad. Then, it will explore how the

African Development Bank deploys planning to help African economies to realize the African Union Transformation Plan's long-term vision of the entire continent achieving middle-income status by the year 2063.

The Case of China Development Bank (CDB)

As early as 2003, China Development Bank (CDB) determined that "planning must take precedence". Since 2006, when the nation's Eleventh Five-Year Plan began, CDB has been working constructively in close cooperation with relevant authorities and agencies to promote planning. In 2009, CDB created a planning division, and all of its branches established a planning department. The Planning Research Institute and the Planning Commission for Scientific Development that were established in later years were also part of CDB's consistent endeavors in this regard. In an effort to develop a preliminary framework for business planning and implementation, CDB focuses on the systematic facilitation of domestic planning, targeted at various regional sectors and strategic clienteles, and seeks to develop diverse international planning regimes, such as transnational consultative cooperation on drafting national plans and bilateral collaboration in planning practices. Accordingly, CDB is moving toward working though a system that encompasses national and transnational as well as intra- and inter-industry dimensions.

As an important feature of development financing, the notion of planning taking precedence represents an important means of developing foresight and proactiveness in promoting middle-and-long-term investment and financing. In practice, by prioritizing the needs of governments at all levels and key clientele groups, CDB is fully committed to national economic and diplomatic strategies, coordinated regional development, industrial restructuring and constructions in the priority sectors. CDB also strives to provide top-notch brainstorming services, to advance bank-government and bank-corporate cooperation through collaboration in planning and to diversify its approaches to translating national strategies into action. Moreover, by capitalizing on its financing advantage and utilizing development financing theories, CDB accentuates the importance of ameliorating credit and market conditions, streamlines its financing patterns and programs, and embarks on a series of major projects. In this way, a planned development will dovetail effectively with downstream business activities. Furthermore, by succeeding in forging a distinct brand of systematic planned financing, CDB has substantially contributed to the enrichment of national planning. CDB holds that planning must take precedence, an important feature that distinguishes development financing from commercial finance, and considers this a core competitive strength in both expanding its cooperation with outside partners and guarding against risks. Thus, the notion that planning takes precedence is assuming increasing importance in the boost that development financing provides for national strategies.

In concrete terms, CDB regards planning as a systematic project that straddles a variety of areas and disciplines. Regarding regional and urban planning, it is important to consider issues (such as urban size, functional partitioning, industrial composition and infrastructure distribution) on the basis of determining the extent to which natural resources and the environment can be sustained. With respect to industrial planning, it is essential to restructure industrial planning in consonance with local natural resource endowments, to place technological research and development at the forefront and to place ample emphasis on the financing and credit systems that underlie industrial activities. Concerning social planning, it is vital to focus on population and human development while regulating the allocation of infrastructure such as education, medical care and culture. With respect to market planning, it is imperative for developing countries to make strenuous efforts to establish and enforce highly efficient market mechanisms. Apropos of planning in financing, it is necessary to mobilize social capital to deliver the financing required for economic development. In terms of planning for wealth creation, it is of foremost importance to design schemes that will benefit the majority of the people. Given all of these factors, the regional planning takes center stage because of its instrumental role in industrial and social development, whereas the market planning serves a fundamental and pervasive role.

Two examples of how the CDB conducts development planning in China (see Box 8 – 1) and abroad (see Box 8 – 2 and Box 8 – 3) are presented below.

Box 8 – 1 Planning for the Coastal Economic Belt in Liaoning

Nicknamed the "Oriental Ruhr", Liaoning Province is northeastern China's only coastal border province and has long been an important industrial base in China. In 2005, the Liaoning provincial government initiated as development policy entitled "Three Points, One Line" that targets Changxing Island, Yingkou City and Jinzhou Gulf (all within the Bohai Economic Rim) and sought to enlist CDB's support. After completing its investigation, CDB considered that, considering the natural and geographical advantages of Liaoning Province, a fully developed coastal Liaoning would have a positive effect on the economic restructuring of Liaoning's old industrial base and the economic revitalization of northeastern China. The policy of "Three Points, One Line" should be developed into a more holistic strategy of "Five Points, One Line", with Dandong Industrial Park, Dalian Huayuankou Industrial Park and two other cities (Huludao and Panjin) being incorporated into the overall plan for the Liaoning Coastal Economic Belt. The Liaoning provincial government and CDB reached a consensus and jointly created a steering team to oversee the planning and formulation of the "Five Points, One Line" strategy (see Figure 8.1).

Figure 8.1 Planning for Liaoning Coastal Economic Belt, the "Five Points and One Line" Strategy

In endorsing the planning process, CDB extended an assistance loan of CNY 600,000 to the Liaoning provincial government. In March 2007, the Liaoning Coastal Economic Belt Development Plan (the Plan) was concluded and, following the approval of the State Council in 2009, was elevated to a national strategy. In an effort to support the implementation of the Plan, CDB conducted a systematic financing analysis and estimated that it would spend three to five years raising CNY 30 billion to support the infrastructure projects and establish investment and financing platforms to attract businesses. By late 2012, the entire CNY 30 billion credit line was already extended and all of the planned key projects were already in the pipeline.

From the initial suggestion that planning must take precedence to the close of the

Twelfth Five-Year Plan, CDB helped elevate a total of 53 regional planning and development initiatives to national strategies. These initiatives involved a wide range of regions and sectors, such as the Pearl Delta Region, the Yangtze Delta Region, Guanzhong-Tianshui Economic Zone, the Wuhan Metropolitan Area, Greater Changsha Metropolitan Region, the Tumen River Economic Development Area, coastal Jiangsu, Guangxi Beibu Gulf and Zhejiang Marine Economy Development Demonstration Zone. CDB also participated in the formulation and execution of national strategies and agendas, such as the "One Belt and One Road" initiative, the Beijing-Tianjin-Hebei Coordinated Development Program and the National New-Type Urbanization Plan.

Box 8 – 2 CDB's International Outreach: The Case of Venezuela

CDB believes that planning can spearhead economic reform and development in other countries and cooperation in policy planning will assist in ascertaining development strategies, implementing major projects, avoiding blind investment and redundant construction, promoting sustainable and general economic growth, and reinforcing the endogenous dynamics of socioeconomic development.

In 2010, as requested by the Venezuelan Government, CDB began to provide planning and consultancy services to Venezuela. In keeping with its working procedure, CDB dispatched a team of experts to Venezuela to conduct intensive surveys and research. As a result, in accordance with the Venezuelan Government's requirement that the overall planning coincides with the six-year tenure for each administration, CDB mapped out a set of plans to be executed in three successive stages (2010 – 2012, 2013 – 2018, and 2019 – 2030). This planning package consists of an overall master plan for socioeconomic development and detailed consultative programs covering eight sectors (i. e., agriculture, housing and urban development, industrial development, public transportation, electric power and hydrocarbon fuels, mining, fiscal finance). The planning package, which was subjected to multiple amendments under the advise of the Venezuelan Government, was eventually submitted to the Venezuelan Government and received considerable acclaim. Later, during an investigative visit to China by a high-level Venezuelan delegation comprising cabinet ministers and experts, CDB invited officials from several Chinese ministries to present the planning information on China's Twelfth Five-Year Plan. Furthermore, the delegation was taken to more than ten Chinese conglomerates for field investigations to enrich the content and forms of bilateral planning and financing cooperation.

Box 8 – 3   CDB's International Outreach: The Case of Sweden

In addition to cooperation with developing countries, CDB is committed to cooperate on policy planning with countries with developed market economies.

During a visit to Sweden in March 2010, as part of then Vice President Xi Jinping's retinue, Mr. Chen Yuan, then the Chairman of CDB, signed the "Cooperative Memorandum on Development Financing" with the Swedish Trade & Invest Council (STIC). This memorandum signified the beginning of cooperation between a Chinese financial institution and the Swedish Government in development financing. In an effort to implement the requirements stipulated in the memorandum, CDB and STIC signed a cooperation agreement on policy planning in Beijing in March 2011, making Sweden the first nation to sign such an agreement with CDB. The bilateral agreement is intended to galvanize economic cooperation between China and Sweden through a platform emphasizing policy planning, and to eliminate bottlenecks that hamper the linkage of enterprises with potential projects, and prioritize the first set of items, such as wind power and clean energy, mineral resources and hi-tech SMEs. As per the signed agreement, CDB and STIC co-hosted a symposium on Sweden's internal development. CDB also assigned a team of top Chinese planners to conduct field surveys in Sweden. CDB also interacted extensively with several Swedish government agencies (Swedish Transport Administration, Swedish Energy Agency, Swedish Governmental Agency for Innovation Systems and Geological Survey of Sweden) and a large number of key enterprises before suggesting a cooperation proposal that outlined projects. Initial estimates of the total investment for all the projects are upwards of USD 40 billion. As an added effort, Sino-Swedish investment forums on cooperation in policy planning were convoked both in China and Sweden in a further effort to increase the number of cooperative initiatives in investment and financing. In these forums, enterprises from China and Sweden exchanged information on projects that require funding signed cooperation agreements between many leading Chinese enterprises and their counterparts in Sweden. Both the Chinese Ambassador and the Commercial Counselor to Sweden expressed great appreciation for CDB's positive attitude and initiative in promoting Sino-Swedish economic relations through cooperation in policy planning, commenting that such cooperation represented an important financial innovation and would serve as a lodestar and exemplar for enterprises to strengthen cooperation in the context of economic globalization.

The Case of the African Development Bank (AfDB)

Similar to China, African economies aspire to take off and fly higher. Africa is now the world's second fastest-growing continent. Amidst seismic shifts in the global economy, Africa has defied the pessimists by accelerating its economic development. However, these advances have been tempered by infrastructure deficits, old and new conflicts, youth unemployment and growing inequality. In the face of these compelling challenges, long-term planning is critical to sustaining growth and fostering the structural change and economic transformation that will enable the continent to join global value chains.

The AfDB places itself at the center of Africa's transformation. In this context, "transformation means diversifying the sources of economic growth and opportunity in a way that promotes higher productivity, resulting in sustained and inclusive economic growth. It also means supporting the development of industries that increase the impact of the existing sources of comparative advantage and enhance Africa's global competitive position."

Vision setting is the first step. In 2006, a Panel of Eminent Persons helped the AfDB chart a vision for the African continent and a path for the organization. *Investing in Africa's Future—The African Development Bank in the 21st Century*, in turn, inspired the strategic choices that guided the Bank's work from 2008 to 2012. In this vision, Africa sees itself becoming a prosperous continent with high-quality growth that creates more employment opportunities for all, especially women and youth. Hence, sound policies and better infrastructure will drive Africa's transformation by improving the conditions for private sector development and boosting investment, entrepreneurship and micro, small and medium enterprises.

Formulating medium-term strategies is a critical step. In 2013, the AfDB established a new decade-long strategy—*At the Center of Africa's Transformation: Strategy for 2013 – 2022* (in short, the Strategy). The aim of this strategy is to ensure that the growth is inclusive and "green" to broaden and deepen the process of transformation. To realize these two objectives, the Strategy outlines five operational priorities for the AfDB to guide its work and improve the quality of growth in Africa: (i) infrastructure development, (ii) regional economic integration, (iii) private sector development, (iv) governance and accountability, (v) skills and technology. In implementing its ten-year Strategy, the AfDB will pay particular attention to three areas of special emphasis: fragile states, agriculture and food security, and gender.

Country-led national strategies are indispensable to effective interventions by the AfDB. The AfDB formulated a five-year Country Strategy Paper for its borrowing countries.

Box 8-4 Ethiopia: Country Strategy Paper 2011-2015

Ethiopia, officially known as the Federa.

Democratic Republic of Ethiopia is located in the Horn of Africa. Ethiopia is the most populous landlocked country in the world and the second-most populous nation on the African continent. Its capital and largest city is Addis Ababa. The Government of Ethiopia launched a Growth and Transformation Plan (GTP) in 2010 in response to the challenges of poverty reduction and economic transformation. This plan was borne out of the Government's vision to propel Ethiopia into middle income country status by 2025.

To realize the above vision, the AfDB worked with the Government to formulate a new Country Strategy Paper (CSP) covering a period of 2011-2015. This paper is aligned with the GTP and articulates how the AfDB plans to support its implementation.

The CSP first analyzed challenges and opportunites under Ethiopia's context and prospects and then tailored its support to the country-specific circumstances with a special focus on two key pillars: (i) support for improved access to infrastructure, and (ii) support for enhanced access and accountability in basic services and improving the business climate.

After setting the priorities, the AfDB specified its deliverables and targets: "the Bank proposes to use a combination of project and programmatic instruments, including budget support for Protection of Basic Services. The African Development Fund Partial Risk Guarantee could also be deployed, where feasible, to support Private Sector Participation in infrastructure development. Consistent with Bank Group policy, cross-cutting issues—gender, HIV/AIDS and environment (including climate change) will be given attention in the design of all operations."

The AfDB then further identified five major risks that may affect the CSP's implementation and the achievement of the GTP objectives. These risks included: (i) high vulnerability to exogenous shocks, (ii) weak institutional capacity, (iii) financing and macro-economic risks, (iv) governance, and (v) regional insecurity.

The AfDB was confident that "The new CSP for Ethiopia is timely and aligned to the GTP, which seeks to achieve further reduction in poverty and lay the foundation for Ethiopia to reach middle income status."

Aligned with the country-driven GTP, the CSP helped Ethiopia's economy to grow by 9.7% in 2012/13, which made Ethiopia one of Africa's top-performing economies.

Market Incubation

DFIs are strategically positioned to develop investor confidence to incubate the market for large-scale transformative investments to achieve sustainable development with three key pillars of economic, social and environmental developments. DFIs can act as first-movers in assuming risks, overcoming misperceptions or even disillusionment, and developing investor confidence to leverage private financing.

This section will explore three examples of DFIs that rely on sovereign creditworthiness to nurture conquered risks in underdeveloped markets, advanced frontier markets and green bond markets.

Conquering Risks in Underdeveloped Markets

In the 1990s, at the height of privatization, free-market believers predicted the death of multilateral development banks' (MDBs') involvement in private infrastructure financing, because they believed that the private markets could fully address the challenge. This prediction was not fulfilled, because the needs are too great, the challenges are too numerous and the gaps remain too plentiful. Rather than dying out or outright exiting from infrastructure financing, the MDBs have played a pivotal role in providing long-term finance deals, especially in vital but structurally and contractually complex, that could not attract commercial bank debt.

Below, we use the example of the Asian Development Bank (AsDB) to illustrate how the MDBs conquer risks in less developed markets to leverage private capital in infrastructure financing.

Box 8-5 How AsDB Conquers Risks in Underdeveloped Project Finance Markets in Asia

One of the AsDB's priorities is the neglected project finance markets of Asia. According to an AsDB study, Asia's infrastructure needs amount to approximately

USD 800 billion per year. "There are, of course, overwhelming needs across Asia, but they are perhaps most acutely felt in the less developed markets, where local banks are least able to respond and international banks are hesitant."

AsDB's very different perception and management of political risk has allowed it to finance a telecom licensee in Afghanistan, a transmission line in Cambodia and a multi-billion dollar petrochemical plant in Uzbekistan, amongst many other projects. Furthermore, when possible, it has used its products and its presence to entice otherwise-hesitant commercial banks, as it did with its B loan and political risk guarantees for the cell phone company in Afghanistan.

"Taking the early challenge"

Going where commercial banks may fear to tread does not only apply to adventurous geographies. The AsDB also seeks to lead the market in areas that "may initially be perceived as technically or structurally risky." Here are some recent examples:

- In India and in Thailand, the AsDB has helped lead the solar project financing markets by lending to the first large photovoltaic solar farms and, very recently in India, the world's largest linear Fresnel concentrated solar power project.

- In Indonesia, the AsDB helped lead the financing of the first private geothermal project in that country for well over a decade. With that financing test case proven, several more geothermal projects are in the works.

"Pushing the market"

Financing projects are a key focus of the AsDB. However, even as the AsDB expands its private infrastructure financing, its direct funding, while filling gaps and realizing projects, remains "a drop in the bucket of overall Asian project financing needs." The AsDB increasingly measures itself according to how many dollars of private money it mobilizes rather than its own dollars. This means mobilizing money through the AsDB's presence (that is, the "halo effect" of perceived risk mitigation from its presence in the deal), through its products (the AsDB targets much wider deployment of B loans, political and partial risk guarantees, and risk participations) and through selectively adopting a different risk profile than commercial banks (longer tenures, different slices of debt, early and wider use of equity and so forth when a project is in need and banking constraints justify the risk). Furthermore, it includes "pushing beyond the commercial bank markets to stimulate the still-largely-dormant project bond markets."

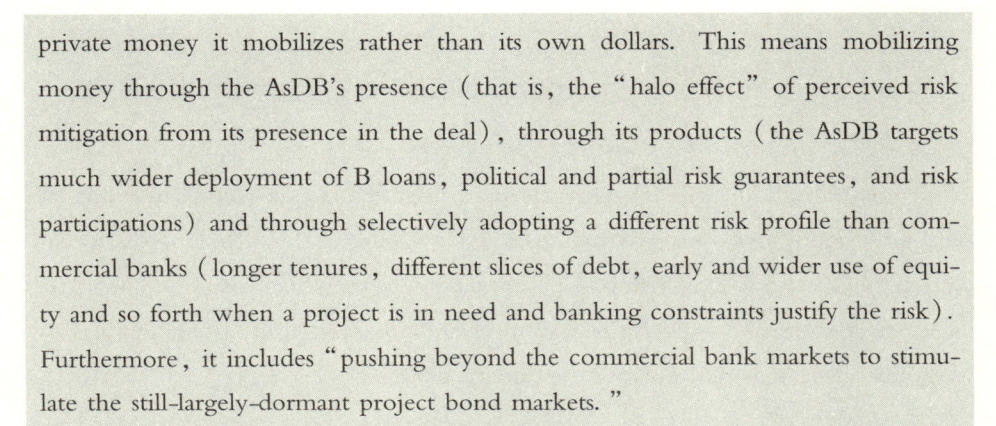

"Creating more and better projects"

A much-debated topic is whether there is a dearth of financing for private infrastructure projects in Asia or whether there is a dearth of good projects to be financed. The discussants often decide that the latter is the case. "From making the political case for public private partnerships (PPPs), to helping set up PPP centers and enabling laws and regulations, to helping governments pick, structure, tender, and award private infrastructure concessions, the AsDB is substantially stepping up its work and focusing on the heavy lifting of stimulating quality project finance supply. And the AsDB will then continue to work with the market to finance many of those projects."

Advancing Frontier Markets

Innovations in frontier markets often entail high risk, which deters the flow of funds to develop novel products. A delay in innovations further exacerbates the gloomy outlook, thereby suppressing innovations. To break this vicious circle, the risk-taking development financing is crucial to push the frontier of burgeoning markets.

Below, we provide an example of how the EBRD helps to foster the innovation and production capacities of the pharmaceutical industry.

Box 8-6 Financing Pharmaceutical Production by the EBRD

As a flourishing industry, the pharmaceutical industry has developed into one of the most innovation-intensive industries (see Figure 8.2). R&D activities in health and medicine have reduced the mortality rate (see Figure 8.3). The pharmaceutical industry is expected to lead to not only higher quality of life but also economic growth, innovation and production capacities.

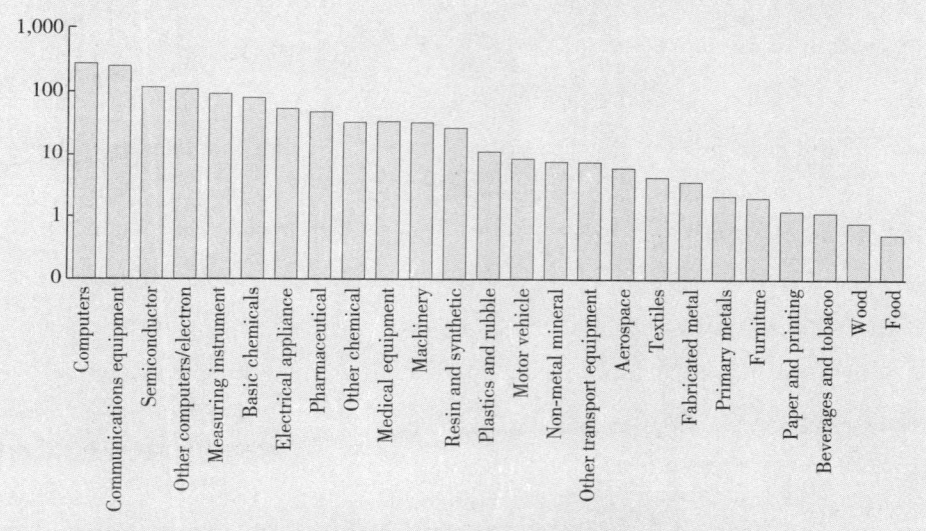

Figure 8.2 Innovation Intensity of Various Industries

However, for most medicine producers, funding is a major problem that limits the release of new products. For example, it was reported that only 8% of Jordan medical firms could adequately receive funds for the development of products.

To solve this problem and promote the healthy development of the pharmaceutical industry in member countries, the EBRD has funded medical companies. In

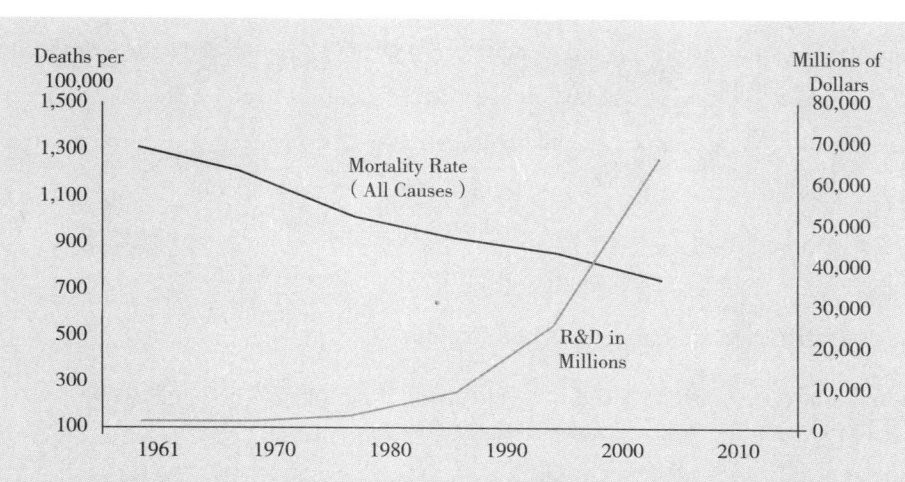

Figure 8.3 Correlation between R&D in medicine and mortality rate

2014, 9% of new investments were in the pharmaceutical field. For the first time, the Jordanian Government and the EBRD cooperated to invest in medical companies to expand production capability and conduct research on a range of novel products. Croatia has also participated in cooperation with the EBRD, including its leading pharmaceutical company, Jadran Galenski Laboratorij. The EBRD has also invested in Ukraine.

Below, we provide specific examples of how the EBRD helps to advance the frontier in the pharmaceutical industry.

1. Pharmaceutical Group Hikma in Jordan

In April 2014, Hikma, a pharmaceutical company in Jordan, was provided with a loan of USD 50 million by the EBRD. The EBRD's financing would enable Hikma "to continue its Jordanian operations efficiently and to upgrade the manufacturing standards of its operating subsidiaries in the SEMED region."

It was expected that not only would more novel medicine be developed but also that intellectual property would be protected in a more integral legal framework.

According to the statement and design of the EBRD, this loan would contribute to the future growth of Hikma through "the acquisition of intellectual property rights (IPRs)", which is generally considered to be a major incentive for pharmaceutical companies to continue researching and developing innovative products. The future plan of this project included offering highly effective medicine at affordable cost across the Southern and Eastern Mediterranean (SEMED) region.

2. Jadran Galenski Laboratorij in Croatia

Jadran Galenski Laboratorij (JGL) is a Croatian company that aims to become a world leader in the sterile solutions segment. In November 2014, the EBRD provided a long-term working capital multi-currency loan of up to EUR 20 million (USD 24.90 million) to JGL.

This investment was expected to double the company's production capacity. To achieve this goal, JGL expected to expand its facilities with the construction of a new "Pharma Valley", which would "double its output in sterile solutions and create 100 new jobs." In addition, the loan would be complemented by a EUR 32.7 million (USD 40.71 million) loan offered by the Croatian Development Bank, HBOR.

3. Farmak in Ukraine

The EBRD realized the great potential of the Ukrainian medical market and that the existing problem was that the industry needed better access to financing. To deepen the collaboration with Ukraine in this field, in December 2014, Farmak, a Ukrainian pharmaceutical company received its third loan from EBRD with a maximum facility of EUR 8.5 million (USD 10.29 million). The EBRD promised to provide working capital and access to hard currency.

Thus far, more than EUR 95 million (USD 115.05 million) in funding for pharmaceuticals has been spent in Ukraine, compared with a total of over EUR 500 million (USD 605. 52 million) in the region of operations. The aim of this financing project was to advance medical technologies and make every effort to decrease the cost of pharmaceutical products, making them affordable to more people in need.

In summary, the EBRD is investing to advance the frontier market of the pharmaceutical industry. Because locally manufactured medicines are scarce in the Middle East and North Africa (MENA), the pharmaceutical manufacturing industry is in great demand and the potential of the commercial market in this field is considerable.

Nurturing Green Bond Markets

The dire consequences of climate change defy national boundaries and demand drastic action to reduce greenhouse gas emissions to achieve a smooth transition to a low-carbon and resilient economy. The world is barreling down a path toward a 4-degree temperature increase at the end of the century, if the global community fails to act on climate change. This would trigger a cascade of cataclysmic changes that include extreme heat waves, declining global food stocks and a sea-level rise that will affect hundreds of millions of people. The consequences threaten the existence of the human species. Therefore, it is no overstatement that the transition to a low-carbon economy is one of the most significant challenges that humanity has ever had to face.

Yet, the supply of climate finance falls well short of the vast demand. According to the Climate Policy Initiative, annual global climate finance flows totaled approximately USD 331 billion in 2013, falling USD 28 billion below 2012 levels. The cumulative gap between available and required financing is growing, placing globally agreed temperature goals at risk and increasing the likelihood of costly climate impacts.

To fill the financing gap, public sectors must play a proactive role in leveraging private investments. While many investors are concerned with the effects of climate change and specifically seek to make a difference by supporting climate change-related projects, private investors often shy away from unknown risks in uncharted areas, resulting in inaction.

To overcome this bottleneck, DFIs have two comparative advantages in incubating "green bond" markets. First, DFIs typically enjoy sovereign crediworthiness that can help to mitigate risks that deter the entry of private sector actors. Second, DFIs possess expertise to better manage projects to develop a proven track record of successes.

Below, we provide two examples of how DFIs develop green bond markets. One is a multilateral development bank—the World Bank—which initiated the green bond market that is now soaring, and the other is a national development bank—the NRW.

Box 8-7 The World Bank Initiated and Incubated Green Bond Markets

Addressing climate change requires unprecedented global cooperation across borders. The World Bank Group is helping to support developing countries and contributing to a global solution.

In 2008, the World Bank launched its "Strategic Framework for Development and Climate Change" to help stimulate and coordinate public and private sector activities in this area. The World Bank Green Bond is an example of the type of innovation that the World Bank is attempting to encourage within this framework.

The World Bank Green Bond raises funds from fixed-income investors to support World Bank lending for eligible projects that seek to mitigate climate change or help affected people adapt to it. Eligible projects are selected by World Bank environment specialists and meet specific criteria for low-carbon development.

These criteria underwent an independent review by the Center for International Climate and Environmental Research at the University of Oslo (CICERO). CICERO concurred that, combined with the governance structure of the World Bank and safeguards for its projects, these activities provided a sound basis for selecting climate-friendly projects.

"For investors, World Bank Green Bonds are an opportunity to invest in climate solutions through a triple-A rated fixed income product. The credit quality of the Green Bonds is the same as for any other World Bank bonds. Repayment of the bond is not linked to the credit or performance of the projects, and investors do not assume the specific project risk. Investors benefit from the Triple-A credit of the World Bank, as well as from the due diligence process of the World Bank for its activities."

In 2014, the World Bank had a record year for green bond issuances, raising a total of nearly USD 3 billion in fiscal year 2014 (July 2013 to June 2014). With its first green bond issued for fiscal year 2015—a green bond linked to a sustainable equity index—the World Bank's total issuance reached USD 6.4 billion through 68 bonds in 17 currencies, supporting 62 projects in 20 countries (see Figure 8.4).

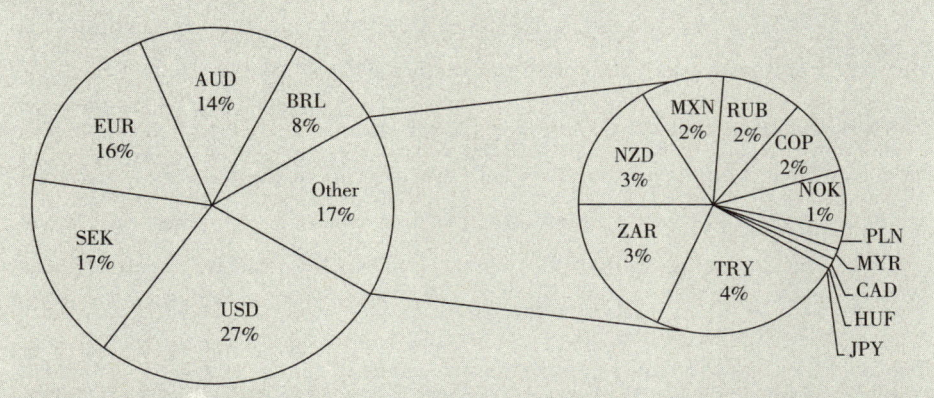

Figure 8.7 Outstanding World Bank Green Bonds by Currency (As of July 31, 2014)

Note: Of the US $ eq. 6.4 billion issued, US $ eq. 5.3 billion is outstanding in 17 currencies.

The strong demand for World Bank green bonds is accompanied by a significant increase in the overall green bond market. By July 2014, green bond issuance well exceeded USD 20 billion—twice the amount of the green bonds issued in 2013.

Box 8-8 NRWB Green Bond

To deploy innovative methods to raise more green investments, North Rhine-Westphalia Bank (NRWB) aims to raise funds under the Green Bond program exclusively to refinance previously defined environmental promotion projects.

Following its debut in 2013, NRWB successfully issued its second Green Bond, a EUR 500 million (USD 605.52 million) four-year transaction in October 2014. While "Water" and "Energy" were again chosen as the focal fields, the focus in 2014 was placed on "Energy", with approximately EUR 370 million (USD 448.08 million) being earmarked for investments in this area.

To be selected and designated for funding from the Green Bond 2014, projects needed to fulfill a specific profile, including a commitment date in the current calendar year and relevance in terms of the themes defined for the Green Bond.

NRWB assured investors that the proceeds from the Green Bond would be used to fund loans that would be granted in 2014 for projects in the fields of water management, energy efficiency, renewable energy and electric transportation. Development projects totaling EUR 500 million (USD 605.52 million) were financed with the help of NRWB's Green Bond:

The objective was to make a contribution to reducing carbon emissions and improving water quality. The Bank used the proceeds from the Green Bond to facilitate the construction of more than 20 wind turbine generators, replace local transport vehicles with more environmentally friendly models and invest in more energy-efficient and resource-efficient production plants, to list a few projects. Proceeds of EUR 130 million (USD 157.43 million) from the 2014 Green Bond were used to help to create a modern and effective sewage system and to considerably improve water quality and biodiversity and, hence, environmental quality in general.

For the first time, the Bank had the environmental benefit and the quality of the projects chosen for the 2014 Green Bond analyzed and assessed by an external rating agency.

Looking ahead, developing more rigorous standards for green bonds is crucial to scaling up this innovative financial instrument to channel more private capital toward green growth.

Convening Power in Creating Public-Private Synergies

DFIs are ideal candidates for forging synergies between the public and private sectors. Addressing complex development challenges is often beyond the capacity of a single finance provider. DFIs can provide a platform that provides governments, multilateral development banks, private sector investors and financiers with opportunities to collaborate.

Below, we provide four examples of how DFIs, multilateral and national, help to utilize a wide range of financial instruments and contribute to a knowledge-sharing platform to bring together diverse expertise. A brief introduction of the four cases is as follows:

- the World Bank created the Global Infrastructure Facility to offer governments, multilateral development banks, private sector investors and financiers a new way to collaborate on complex projects that no single institution could pursue alone (see Box 8-9);

- the Islamic Development Bank designed a "Triple-Win" mechanism to work with philanthropies to address a pressing development challenge (see Box 8 – 10); and
- the Industrial Development Bank of India (IDBI) works with credit rating agencies and microfinance institutions to offer finance to small-/medium-sized enterprises (SMEs) (see Box 8 – 11).

Box 8 – 9　The World Bank's Global Infrastructure Facility

The World Bank Group created the Global Infrastructure Facility (GIF)—a global open platform—that will facilitate the preparation and structuring of complex infrastructure PPPs to mobilize private sector and institutional investor capitals. From the beginning to the end of a project, the GIF platform will provide support by drawing on its array of technical and advisory partners, which will include private investors, to ensure that well-structured and bankable infrastructure projects are brought to market. Its unique collaborative approach has already won strong support from institutional investors. Its aim is to provide integrated support—using the wide range of skills and resources available within the World Bank Group and in the public and private sectors—to unlock a credible pipeline of viable and bankable public private partnership projects in emerging markets and developing economies to help meet the infrastructure challenge.

In the inaugural event for the GIF in October 2014, the World Bank President, Jim Yong Kim, stated, "The GIF was being designed to tap into expertise from within and outside of the Bank Group to deliver complex public-private infrastructure projects that no single institution could address on its own."

The GIF paves the way for a wide range of finance providers to help fill infrastructure gaps in the developing world: USD 1 trillion per year in additional investment needed through 2020. One of the most recent examples is taking place in Quito, Ecuador, where a construction began during fiscal year 2014 on an underground metro line that is expected to ease congestion and reduce pollution in a city that has a population of 1.6 million people and is surrounded by volcanoes. When completed in late 2018, the 23-kilometer metro will have the capacity to transport 360,000 passengers per day.

The financing of the project came from a unique collaboration between IBRD, the Andean Development Corporation (CAF), the European Investment Bank (EIB) and the Inter-American Development Bank (IDB), along with Ecuador's municipal and national governments. For the first time, the four multilateral agencies, together with the national and municipal governments, joined forces to finance the construction of the first line of the Quito Metro, which will require an investment of USD 1.5 billion.

"For the first time in the history of the World Bank, it is working with the EIB, IDB and CAF under the leadership of the Municipal team that is implementing the project. This will be an example for other cities and countries that could benefit from this experience," said Hasan Tuluy, World Bank Vice President for Latin America and the Caribbean.

Spanning 23 kilometers and 15 stations—six of which will be integrated with the Metrobus-Q network—the first metro line will have the capacity to transport 360,000 passengers daily. Thus, Quito will have the best metro system in the Americas. The metro will save USD 14 million in fuel annually, directly generate 1,800 jobs, link the north and south of the city and invigorate the economy. The Quito metro will enable inhabitants to travel between the north and south of the city in approximately half an hour. It will set new standards for transport in the Ecuadorean capital, which currently has a high and growing demand for efficient public transport.

Box 8 – 10 The Islamic Development Bank's Triple-Win Mechanism

In the wake of the recent global financial crisis, especially because it resulted in tighter aid budgets and a greater urgency for financing global public goods, it is important to promote many innovative modes to leverage financial resources in the market to finance developing countries' agriculture, nutrition, education, energy, infrastructure and climate projects.

To achieve this objective, the Vice President of Operations led a Bank-wide team to engineer an innovative "Triple-Win" Financing Mechanism after months of negotiations and interactions with the Bill and Melinda Gates Foundation (Gates Foundation) in 2012.

This mechanism is exemplified in a pilot project in which the Islamic Development Bank (IsDB) offered all the resources needed to close the financing gap to support national responses to polio eradication in Pakistan as part of the Global Polio Eradication Initiative (GPEI). Additionally, the Gates Foundation and the IsDB have declared their support for the eradication of polio in Nigeria and Afghanistan and they will then extend the use of the financing mechanism to pursue the eradication of malaria and overcome food insecurity. This enables the Bank to tap into its ordinary resources to augment its concessional pool and thereby extend a large amount of financing to a member country to address a pressing development challenge, while the member country pays only the principal and the Gates Foundation pays the mark-up and/or the service fee.

This may appear to be similar to the "buy down" mechanism and the "loan conversion" model that the Gates Foundation had with the World Bank Group and the Japan International Cooperation Agency (JICA), respectively. However, this newly engineered innovative financing mechanism is different, because "its use in the Pakistan Polio Program is the first time that such a mechanism is being utilized by an International Financing Institution (IFI) to avail considerable amount of ordinary resources, softened through philanthropic contributions, to social sector programs/projects in a developing country."

A prominent benefit of the "Triple-Win" innovative financing mechanism is its contribution to the ongoing reflections on the future of concessional financing, as global circumstances change, aid budgets tighten and the urgency of financing global public goods increases. Through the new financing mechanism, concessional funding could be increased if the grant allocation of the World Bank's International Development Association (IDA) African Development Fund could be used as mark-up subsidy funds to leverage the large amount of financial resources in the market, which could become considerably greater than the initial grant amount.

In summary, this new and innovative financing mechanism, which complies with the Islamic modes of financing, holds promise for millions of people as more concessionary financing is made available to developing countries in Africa and Asia.

Box 8–11　The Industrial Development Bank of India's SME Financing

For SMEs, the most challenging issue is to address the problems that arise from information asymmetry. On the lending side, the banks would be unlikely to offer financing to SMEs because the business scales of SMEs are too small to be normalized, exacerbating the banks' difficulty in inspecting the business. In addition, the lack of economic scale and management ability may lead the SMEs to have lower profitability. On the borrowing side, the difficulty of inspection increases the likelihood that SMEs with lower profitability will default, which runs the risk of their free riding on other better-performing SMEs given a common interest rate. In short, the problem of information asymmetry increases the risk that banks face when engaging in SME business. With these factors as common knowledge for both sides, the final result would be a contract that consists of exorbitantly high interest rates and a few borrowers with terrible credit quality.

The challenge of financing SMEs lies in determining how to reduce the magnitude of information asymmetry to enhance the creditworthiness of SMEs to gain better access to finance. Below, we provide two examples of how the IDBI collaborates with credit rating agencies and microfinance institutions to enable SMEs to obtain financing on a sustained basis.

To obtain a better understanding and thereby differentiate the credit risk in the pool of SMEs, the IDBI corporates with rating agencies in India. For instance, IDBI, which was the largest shareholder until March 2015, corporates with CARE (Credit Analysis & Research), which is the second largest rating agency in India.

CARE tailors its rating methods to the special characteristics of SMEs. It essentially considers parameters that are crucial for solvency and profitability. In addition to these parameters, CARE examines the form of capital and unsecured loans from promoters' own sources to support their operations. According to those variables, the SMEs are classified into several credit levels and, in turn, the bank determines its loan scheme based on the rating. CARE suggests that banks that are interested in SMEs' business can establish a separate framework with relatively lower interest rates.

In addition to cooperating with rating agencies, the IDBI collaborates with the

MFIs (Microfinance Institutions). Through collaboration, each institution can take advantage of the strength of the other to achieve its own goals. MFIs have intimate knowledge of MSEs but lack adequate funds for releasing loans to these MSEs that are in need of such loans. The IDBI has adequate funds but is unable to address the information asymmetry. Hence, there is ample room for mutual support.

For instance, IDBI has partnered with Bandhan—the largest MFI in India—to expand its business to unbanked areas. As microfinance is an important source of financial services for small entrepreneurs that lack access to finance, the bank has extended credit to nearly all the major MFIs that have a presence in major parts of the country. In particular, IDBI bought farm loans that amounted to INR 50 million (USD 0.98 million) from Bandhan in 2012, which is the largest securitization to date. For IDBI, loans are then pooled and securitized and then sold to investors. For Bandhan, this deal helped it to deploy cash flows to the poor without borrowing from banks, which improves SMEs' access to financing (see Figure 8.5).

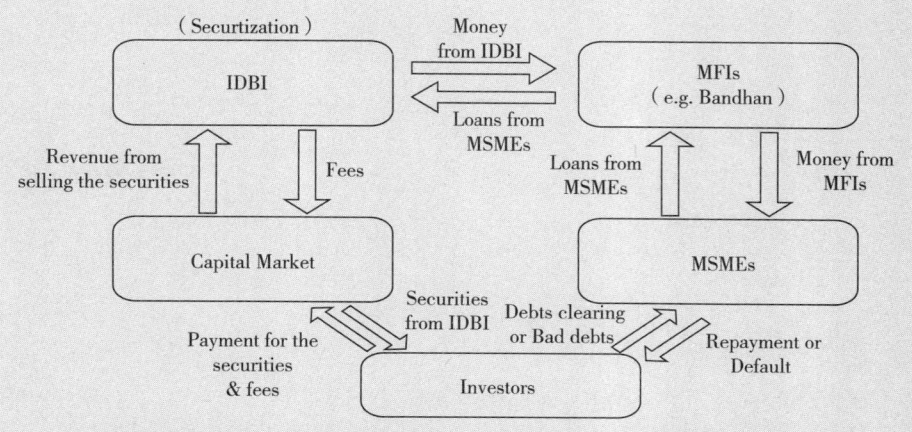

Figure 8.5 The Market Operation Diagram of the IDBI-MFI Cooperation

Yet, the path to innovation is not always smooth. According to a report prepared by Nirmal Bang for IDBI, both the declines in net interest rate by 15% (year-on-year percentage, YoY) and in margin by 0.42% YoY are due to the deliberate attempt to increase SME loan portfolios in the first quarter of 2015.

In essence, DFIs are well positioned to play the three strategic roles necessary to address development financing challenges. These strategic roles include long-term planning, market incubation and convening power to facilitate public-private co-operation. The above case studies show that, while the path to innovation is bumpy, it holds great potential for realizing a transformation agenda.

Part Two Analysis and Outlook of Development Financing Institutions

Chapter 9 Conclusion

We live in an era of transformation. A forward-looking analysis of development financing needs highlights the three major trends heralding new opportunities and challenges:

- deepening regional integration demands catalytic and demonstrative financing to initiate transformative projects;
- accelerating industrialization and urbanization calls for long-term finance;
- scalable sustainable development financing entails market incubation.

To turn the above challenges into opportunity, DFIs are uniquely positioned to play three key strategic roles in realizing a transforming agenda:

- long-term planning guided by a grand vision;
- relying on sovereign creditworthiness to incubate market creditworthiness;
- convening power in creating public-private synergies.

Looking across the selected DFIs worldwide, a promising trend is taking hold. Specifically, in the wake of the recent financial crisis, governments are strengthening DFIs' role in fulfilling pivotal strategic development goals such as stabilizing financial systems, upgrading industrial structures, innovating technologies, promoting long-term finance and incubating frontier markets in the transition to green economy. This upbeat prospect defies a gloomy prediction that DFIs would die out in the wave of privatization.

To harness the growing financial power of DFIs as a positive force, mutual trust and reciprocal cooperation are the keys to foster win-win partnerships and innovations at the national, regional and global levels. History shows that promoting trust and cooperation is necessary. In the 1970s, when countries increased their support for national DFIs, fierce competition, if not well managed, had led to financial arms races. These occur when DFIs compete to match the financial terms of their foreign rivals, drawing on official credit support to win sales without regard to the financial means or political risks of the debtors/buyers. This can easily result in a race-to-the-bottom in the absence of coordination and discipline. To avoid repeating historical mistakes, mutual trust and cooperation among DFIs are pivotal to healthy competition and win-win partnerships to unleash the great potential of DFIs for achieving a transformation agenda.

Looking ahead, cooperation among DFIs can take place in the following key areas:

First, to foster mutual learning on innovations of development ideas and practices. The shared goal of DFIs is to promote sustainable development and inclusive growth on the national, regional and global levels. Policy forums and collaborative research can be held regularly to promote mutual learning on how to innovate development ideas and practices of DFIs to better cope with significant challenges.

Second, to strengthen cooperation in promoting long-term finance. Long-term finance is a critical financial instrument for stabilizing financial markets, mitigating cyclical economic shocks and building public infrastructure. Transformative projects are often complex and large-scale, demanding to create synergies among diverse finance providers.

Third, to promote cooperation in the field of development planning. Formulating development planning is indispensable for identifying factor endowments and comparative advantages, tailoring development strategies to accommodate specific circumstances and reducing blind investments and repetitive construction. Fostering cooperation in the area of development planning can help to strengthen the rigor and feasibility of development planning, improve interconnectivity among different countries and regions as well as lay the foundation for other forms of cooperation within and across different regions.

Fourth, to mobilize development financing to build industrial parks and cross-border economic cooperation zones in order to pioneer in technological innovations and industrial upgrading. Aligned with development planning, DFIs can provide enterprises with stable and low-cost financing to facilitate innovations in a wide range of fields including agriculture, manufacturing, energies, green investments and technological development.

Last but not least, to strengthen cooperation in building international creditworthiness systems. DFIs can foster peer learning on how to use sovereign creditworthiness to cultivate market and social creditworthiness systems. DFIs can also work together to improve the system of risk identification, early warning, prevention and crisis management, to create an exchange and cooperation mechanism of addressing cross-border risks and crisis and to strengthen the capacity of international financial system in mitigating risks.

In conclusion, this inaugural report opens a new era of mutual learning and cooperation among DFIs in an effort to promote their win-win partnerships to achieve a transformative development agenda.

Acronyms and Abbreviations

Abbreviation	Full Name
AADFI	African Association of Development Finance Institutions
ACF	EURASEC Anti-crisis Fund
ADF	African Development Fund
ADFIAP	Association of Development Financing Institutions in Asia and the Pacific
ADFIMI	Association of National Development Finance Institutions in Member Countries of the Islamic Development Bank
AFD	Agence Française de Développement
AfDB	The African Development Bank
AIIB	Asian Infrastructure Investment Bank
ALIDE	La Asociación Latinoamericana de Instituciones Financieras para el Desarrollo/ Latin American Association of Development Financing Institutions
AOA	Articles of Agreement
AsDB	The Asian Development Bank
AUM	Assets under Management
BANDES	Banco de Desarrollo Económico y Social de Venezuela /Venezuelan Economic and Social Development Bank
BCIE/CABEI	Banco Centroamericano de Integración Económica/Central American Bank for Economic Integration
BE	Banco Estado

(continued)

Abbreviation	Full Name
BEIID	Beijing E-Town International Investment & Development Co., Ltd
BGK	Bank GospodarstwaKrajowego
BiH	Biomass boiler plant in Bosnia and Herzegovina
BIST	Build-in Self-test
BMCs	Borrowing Member Countries
BMUB	Bundesministerium für Umwelt, Naturschutz, Bau und Reaktorsicherheit/Federal Ministry for the Environment, Nature Conservation, Building and Nuclear Safety
BMZ	Bundesministerium für wirtschaftliche Zusammenarbeit und Entwicklung/Federal Ministry for Economic Cooperation and Development
BNDES	Banco Nacional de Desenvolvimento Econômico e Social/Brazilian Development Bank
BNM	Bank Negara Malaysia/The Malaysian Central Bank
BOAD	Banque Ouest Africaine de Développement
BOG	Board of Governors
BPMB	Bank Pembangunan Malaysia Berhad
BRD	Bundesrepublik Deutschland/Federal Republic of Germany
BRICS	Brazil, Russia, India, China and South Africa
BRSA	Banking Regulation and Supervision Agency
BSTDB	Black Sea Trade and Development Bank
CAF	Corporación Andina de Fomento/Development Bank of Latin America
CAR	Capital Adequacy Ratio
CARE	Credit Analysis & Research
Caribbean DB	Caribbean Development Bank
CASS	Chinese Academy of Social Sciences
CBE	Central Bank of Egypt

(continued)

Abbreviation	Full Name
CBRC	China Banking Regulatory Commission
CDB	China Development Bank
CDC	Caisse des Dépôts et Consignations
CDG	Caisse de Dépôt et de Gestion
CDP	Cassa Depositi e Prestiti
CEO	Chief Executive Officer
CIC	Climate Innovation Centre of South Africa
CICA	Confidence Building Measures in Asia
CICERO	Center for International Climate and Environmental Research at the University of Oslo
CICIIF	China Integrated Circuit Industry Investment Fund
CNP	Caisse Nationale de' Prévoyance
CNTC	China National Tobacco Corporation
COFIDE	Corporación Financiera de Desarrollo S. A.
CP	Commercial Paper
CPC	Communist Party of China
CSP	Country Strategy Paper
CTF	Clean Technology Fund
DBJ	Development Bank of Japan
DBK	Development Bank of Kazakhstan
DBM	Development Bank of Mongolia
DBP	Development Bank of the Philippines
DBSA	Development Bank of Southern Africa
DEA	Department of Environmental Affairs
DEG	Deutsche Investitions-und Entwicklungsgesellschaft/German Investment and Development Company

(continued)

Abbreviation	Full Name
Dena	Deutsche Energie-Agentur GmbH/Germany Energy Agency GmbH
DF	Development Financing
DFIs	Development Financial Institutions
EBRD	European Bank for Reconstruction and Development
ECP	Euro Commercial Paper
EDB	Eurasian Development Bank
EFD	Economic and Financial Dialogue
EIB	European Investment Bank
ELTI	European Long-Term Investors
EMDCs	Emerging Markets Economies and Developing Countries
EMTN	Euro Medium Term Note program
EPF	Employees Provident Fund
ERP	Enterprise Resource Planning
ETCs	Early Transition Countries
ETT	Erdenes Tavan Tolgoi
EU	Europe Union
EVSL	Enhanced Variable Spread Loan
FCCV	Fondo Conjunto Chino Venezolano/Chinese Venezuelan Joint Fund
FIID	Forced Industrial-Innovative Development
FIV	Fondo de Inversiones de Venezuela/Venezuelan Investment Fund
FuB	Finanzierungs-und Beratungsgesellschaft mbH/Financing and Consulting mbH
FX	Foreign Exchange
GBA(W)	Global Banking Alliance for Women
GIF	Global Infrastructure Facility
GmbH	Gesellschaft mit beschränkter Haftung/Company with limited liability

(continued)

Abbreviation	Full Name
GPEI	Global Polio Eradication Initiative
GTP	Growth and Transformation Plan
GVCs	Global Value Chains
HBOR	Hrvatska banka za obnovu i razvitak/Croatian Bank for Reconstruction and Development
HPP	Hydroelectric Power Plant
Huijin	Central Huijin Investment Ltd.
IADB	Inter-American Development Bank
IBRD	International Bank for Reconstruction and Development
ICBC	Industrial and Commercial Bank of China
ICD	Islamic Corporation for the Development of the Private Sector
ICO	Instituto de Crédito Oficial
NGOs	Non-Government Organizations
ICSID	International Centre for Settlement of Investment Disputes
ICT	Information and Communications Technology
IDA	International Development Association
IADB	Inter-American Development Bank
IDFC	International Development Finance Club
IDWBE	Industrial Development & Workers Bank of Egypt
IFC	International Finance Corporation
IFI	International Financing Institution
IFRs	International Financial Reports Standards
IIC/IAIC	Inter-American Investment Corporation
IMF	International Monetary Fund
IPEX	International Project and Export Finance

(continued)

Abbreviation	Full Name
IPO	Initial Public Offering
IPRs	Intellectual Property Rights
IsDB	The Islamic Development Bank
IT	Information Technology
JDB	Japan Development Bank
JGL	Jadran Galenski Laboratorij
JICA	Japan International Cooperation Agency
JSC	Joint Stock Company
KDB	Korea Development Bank
KDBFG	Korea Development Bank Financial Group
KfW	Kreditanstalt für Wiederaufbau/Reconstruction Credit Institute
KIAMCO	Korea Infrastructure Investments Asset Management
KICB	Kyrgyz Investment and Credit Bank
KMT	Kuo Min Tang
KoFC	Korea Finance Corporation
KTZ	Kazakhstan Temir Zholy/Kazakhstan National Railway Company
LICs	Low Income Countries
LLC	Limited Liability Company
LTIC	Long-Term Investors Club
LTIIA	Long-Term Infrastructure Investors Association
M&A	Merges and Acquisitions
mbH	mit beschränkter Haftung/limited liability
MDBs	Multilateral Development Banks
MDF	Maritime Development Fund
MENA	Middle East and North Africa

(continued)

Abbreviation	Full Name
MF	Maritime Fund
MFIs	Microfinance Institutions
MIF	Multilateral Investment Fund of the IDB Group
MIGA	Multilateral Investment Guarantee Agency
MIS	Management Information System
MOF	Ministry of Finance
MOU	Memorandum of Understanding
MSMEs	Micro Small and Medium Enterprises
MTBS	Medium Term Business Strategy
MTN	Medium Term Note
MW	Million Watt
NAFIN	Nacional Financiera
NBK	National Bank of Kazakhstan
NBU	National Bank for Foreign Economic Activity of the Republic of Uzbekistan/National Bank of Uzbekistan
NCSSF	National Council for Social Security Fund
NDB BRICS	New Development Bank of BRICS
NDFIs	National Development Finance Institutions
NPA	Non-performing advance
NPL	Non-performing loan
NRWB	North Rhine-Westphalia Bank
NTF	Nigeria Trust Fund
OCR	Ordinary capital resources
OMERS	Ontario Municipal Employees Retirement System
PFM	Prospective Founding Members
POS	Point of Sales

(continued)

Abbreviation	Full Name
PPP	Public Private Partnership
PSL	Priority Sector Lending
ROA	Return on Assets
ROE	Return on Equity
ROK	Republic of Korea
RWCR	Risk-Weighted Credit Ratio
S&P	Standard and Poor
SADC	Southern African Development Community
SAIC	State Administration of Industry and Commerce
SEI	Sustainable Energy Initiative
SEMED	Southern and Eastern Mediterranean
SEMED	The Southern and Eastern Mediterranean
SGF	Shariah Governance Framework
Sida	Swedish International Development Cooperation Agency
SIDBI	Small Industries Development Bank of India
SMEs	Small and Medium-sized Enterprises
SMIEs	Small and Medium Industrial Enterprises
SPV	Special Purpose Vehicle
SSF	Shareholder Special Fund
STIC	Swedish Trade & Invest Council
Tbg	Technologie-Beteiligungs-Gesellschaft mbH/Technology and Equity Investment Company mbH
TCZB	Türkiye Cumhuriyeti Ziraat Bankası/ Agricultural Bank of Turkey
TIAA CREF	Teachers Insurance and Annuity Association-College Retirement Equities Fund
TIDF	Tourism Infrastructure Development Fund

(continued)

Abbreviation	Full Name
TIF	Tourism Infrastructure Fund
TR	Turkey Republic
TSKB	Turkiye Sinai Kalkinma Bankasi/Industrial Development Bank of Turkey
UDDI	Uitenhage-Despatch Development Initiative
UNIDO	United Nations Industrial Development Organization
VEB	Vnesheconombank/Bank for Development and Foreign Economic Affairs
WAPDA	Water and Power Development Authority
WB	World Bank
WBG	The World Bank Group
WFDFI	World Federation of Development Financing Institutions
YoY	Year over year

Acronyms and Abbreviations

Europe
- **CDC** — Caisse des Dépôts et Consignations, Paris, France
- **EBRD** — European Bank for Reconstruction and Development, London, United Kingdom

Europe
- **KfW** — Kreditanstalt für Wiederaufbau/Reconstruction Credit Institute, Frankfurt, Germany
- **NRW.BANK** — NRW.BANK, Dusseldorf and Münster, Germany
- **VEB** — Bank for Development and Foreign Economic Affairs, Moscow, Russian Federation

Central Asia
- **NBU** — National Bank for Foreign Economic Activity of the Republic of Uzbekistan, Tashkent, Republic of Uzbekistan
- **EDB** — Eurasian Development Bank, Almaty, Kazakhstan
- **DBK** — Development Bank of Kazakhstan, Astana, Kazakhstan
- **DBM** — Development Bank of Mongolia, Ulaanbaatar, Mongolia

China
- **CDB** — China Development Bank, Beijing, China
- **AIIB** — The Asian Infrastructure Investment Bank, Beijing, China
- **Silkroad Fund** — The Silkroad Fund, Beijing, China
- **NDB BRICS** — The New Development Bank of BRICS, Shanghai, China

America
- **BNDES** — The Brazilian Development Bank, Rio de Janeiro, Brazil
- **BANDES** — The Venezuelan Economic and Social Development Bank, Caracas, DC., Venezuela
- **Caribbean DB** — Caribbean Development Bank, St. Michael, Barbados
- **WBG** — World Bank Group, Washington DC, United States
- **IADB** — Inter-American Development Bank, Washington DC, United States

Africa
- **DBSA** — Development Bank of Southern Africa, Johannesburg, South Africa
- **IDWBE** — Industrial Development & Workers Bank of Egypt, Cairo, Egypt
- **AfDB** — The African Development Bank, Abidjan, Côte d'Ivoire

West Asia and South Asia
- **IDBI** — Industrial Development Bank of India, Mumbai, India
- **IsDB** — Islamic Development Bank, Jeddah, Kingdom of Saudi Arabia
- **TCZB** — Agricultural Bank of Turkey, Ankara, Turkey
- **TSKB** — Industrial Development Bank of Turkey, Istanbul, Turkey

East Asia and Southeast Asia
- **DBJ** — Development Bank of Japan, Tokyo, Japan
- **KDB** — Korea Development Bank, Seoul, Republic of Korea
- **DBP** — Development Bank of the Philippines, Makati City, Philippines
- **AsDB** — The Asian Development Bank, Manila, Philippines
- **BPMB** — Bank Pembangunan Malaysia Berhad, Kuala Lumpur, Malaysia

Acknowledgements

This report was co-written by China Association for the Promotion of Development Financing (CADF), who initiated the project, and the National School of Development (NSD) at Peking University. The authors gratefully acknowledge the unstinting support from China Development Bank (CDB), the Multilateral Interim Secretariat of Asian Infrastructure Investment Bank (AIIB), and Silk Road Fund, etc.

For data collection we thank NSD students—Cheng Yuanjia, Chu Bo, Li Zhe, Liu Chang, Jiang Zhuo, Jin Dehong, Liu Mengjing, Liu Shuangcheng, Lv Xiaoxuan, Ma Shiqi, Qu Boya, Sha Fan, Song Meijing, Wang Longlin, Wang Xiaowen, Wei Liping, Wu Keqian, Wu Shilei, Yu Jie, Zhong Yang, Zhou Yusi, Zhou Yue, etc.—for their contributions to gathering basic information about each development financing institution. Special thanks go to Ms. Zhao Pusheng, whose organizing work was most helpful. The report also benefited from the direct assistance by CDB colleagues including Pan Chenglong, Yang Limei, Zuo Wei, Gu Yang, You Wei, Chen Fei, Wu Liangyun, Chen Xiaopeng, Yang Lihua, and Li Baishan, as well as Sun Xue from the Multilateral Interim Secretariat of AIIB and Xie Jing, Feng Yanqiu, Zhou Ying from Silk Road Fund, in compiling information. In addition, we appreciate the hard work of all the translators and proofreaders who rendered the original English report into Chinese: PKU students Gong Ning, Han Xuan, Hou Guodong, Li Hongda, Lu Junyan, Ren Yicheng, Wang Panpan, Tang Shichen, Zheng Jie, Zou Jingxian, and CADF colleagues Li Jiefeng, Ren Jining, Shen Wei, Yan Jie, Tang Fen, Qi Shuang, Chen Yinghui and Zhang Jucheng. We would also like to acknowledge the valuable contributions of CDB management —deputy director of Policy Research Department, Liu Jin, and deputy director of Center for Financial Research & Development, Zou Lixing— to the perfection of the report by offering crucial suggestions.

As a result of collective efforts, the report incorporated the originality and commitments of all people mentioned above. It was their professionalism and team work, their courage when faced with challenges in pioneering tasks, their faith in and contributions to the international cooperation of development financing that made the report possible.

Any comment or advice on the report will be highly appreciated.

For further information, please contact the authors:

Zhang Fan (zhangfan@nsd.pku.edu.cn)

Xu Jiajun (jiajunxu@nsd.pku.edu.cn)

Wang Chunlai (hrb_wangchunlai@cdb.cn)

References

Annual Report

AfDB, *AfDB Annual Report 2013*, 2013.

AsDB, *ADB Annual Report 2014*, 2014.

BANDES, *Published Balance Sheet at the Semi-annual Close on June 30, 2013 and December 31, 2012*, 2013.

BNDES, *Annual Report of 2013*.

BNDES, *Management Report of 2014*.

Caribbean DB, *Caribbean DB Annual Report 2012*, 2012.

Caribbean DB, *Caribbean DB Annual Report 2013 Vol 1*, 2013.

Caribbean DB, *Caribbean DB Annual Report 2013 Vol 2*, 2013.

CDB, *Annual Report 2013*, 2014.

CDB, *Annual Report 2014*, 2015.

CDC, *CDC investor presentation*, 2015.

CDC, *Corporate Social Responsibility Report 2013*, 2014.

CDC, *Financial report 2012*, 2013.

CDC, *Financial report 2013*, 2014.

CDC, *Fitch CDC Full rating report*, 2015.

DBK, *2013 Annual Report of Development Bank of Kazakhstan*, 2014.

DBK, *2014 Financial Report of Development Bank of Kazakhstan*, 2015.

DBK, *Reference Book of Development Bank of Kazakhstan* (Справочник _ английский), 2015.

DBP, *Annual Report 2013*, pp. 4.

Development Bank of Mongolia, *Financial Statements and Independent Auditor's Report*, 2014.

Development Bank of Mongolia, *Interim Report 2014*, 2014.

Development Bank of Southern Africa, *DBSA Integrated Annual Report 05/06*, 2006.

Development Bank of Southern Africa, *DBSA Integrated Annual Report 06/07*, 2007.

Development Bank of Southern Africa, *DBSA Integrated Annual Report 13/14*, 2014.

EBRD, *EBRD Annual Report 2013*, 2013.

EBRD, *EBRD Donor Report 2013*, 2013.

EBRD, *EBRD Financial Report 2011*, 2011.

EBRD, *EBRD Financial Report 2012*, 2012.

EBRD, *EBRD Financial Report 2013*, 2013.

EBRD, *EBRD Financial Report 2014*, 2014.

EDB, *EDB 2013 Annual Report*, 2013.

EDB, *EDB Financial Statements 2014*, 2014.

IADB, *IDB 2014 Annual Report The Year in Review*, 2014.

IDBI, *Annual Report 2013 – 2014*.

Industrial Development & Workers Bank of Egypt, *Balance Sheet 2009*, 2010.

IsDB, *IsDB Annual Report 2013*, 2013.

KDB Financial Group, "Affiliates Overview," from KDB Financial Group Annual Report 2010.

KDB, "KDB at a Glance," from KDB Annual Report 2014.

KDB, "Trans-Mission of New KDB," from KDB Annual Report 2014.

KfW, *Annual Report 2013*, 2014.

KfW, *Financial Report 2013*, 2014.

KfW, *Financial Report 2014*, 2015.

KfW, *Laws concerning KfW, Article 11 Legal status*, 2006.

KfW, *Laws concerning KfW, Article 1a Guarantee of the Federal Republic*, 2006.

KfW, *Present Itself*, 2015.

Ministry of Planning, Development & Reform, Pakistan, "Annual Plan 2014 – 15", Ministry of Planning, Development & Reform, 2014.

NBU, *Annual report of 2013*, 2014.

NBU, *Financial report of 2014*, 2015.

NBU, *Rules of the bank*, 2015.

NRW. BANK, *Financial Report 2011*, 2012.

NRW. BANK, *Financial Report 2013*, 2014.

NRW. BANK, *Financial Report 2014*, 2015.

NRW. BANK, *Fitch Full Rating Report NRW. BANK*, 2014.

NRW. BANK, *Statutes of NRW. BANK*, 2014.

TSKB, "2014: Communication on Progress," *from TSKB Annual Report 2014.*

TSKB, "*Programme Response Investor CDP-2014,*" *from TSKB Annual Report 2014.*

TSKB, "Unconsolidated financial statements As of and For the Year Ended 31 December 2014," *from TSKB Annual Report 2014.*

VEB, *Annual report 2013*, 2014.

VEB, *Development banking in Russia*, 2014.

VEB, *Federal Law "Bank for Development and Foreign Economic Affairs. (Vnesheconombank)"*, 2007.

World Bank, *Annual Report 2014.*

World Bank, *Enterprise Survey 2010*, 2010.

World Bank, *World Bank Annual Report 2014*, 2014.

Ziraat Bank, *Agricultural Bank of Turkey Publicity Announced Unconsolidated Financial Statement Together with Independent Auditor's Report*, December 31, 2014.

Books and Articles

ACET, *Growth with Depth. 2014 African Transformation Report.* Ghana: The African Center for Economic Transformation, 2014.

ADB/ADBI, *Infrastructure for a Seamless Asia*, Tokyo: Asian Development Bank Institute, 2009.

AfDB, *At the Center of Africa's Transformation: Strategy for 2013-2022.* The African Development Bank, 2013.

Boyce, James K., and Léonce Ndikumana, *Africa's Odious Debts: How Foreign Loans and Capital Flight Bled a Continent*, Zed Books, 2011.

Chandy, Laurence, Akio Hosono, Homi J. Kharas, and Johannes F. Linn, eds.,

Getting to Scale: How to Bring Development Solutions to Millions of Poor People. Brookings Institution Press, 2012.

CDB, *The History of China Development Bank*, Beijing: China Financial Publishing House 2013.

CDB, *Theories and Practices on Planning for Scientific Development*, Beijing: China Financial & Economic Publishing House, 2013.

Chen, Yuan, *Aligning State and Market*, Beijing: CITIC Publishing House, 2012.

G20/OECD High-Level Principles of Long-Term Investment Financing by Institutional Investors, September 2013.

G20/OECD Report on Effective Approaches to Support Implementation of the G20/OECD High-Level Principles on Long-Term Investment Financing by Institutional Investors, November 2014.

G-30, *Long-term Finance and Economic Growth*, Washington, D. C. : Group of 30, 2013.

Gutierrez, Eva, Heinz P. Rudolph, Theodore Homa, and Enrique Blanco Beneit, Development Banks: Role and Mechanisms to Increase their Efficiency. Washington, DC, World Bank Policy Research Series, 2011.

International Islamic Financial Market, "Sukuk Report: A Comprehensive Study of the Global Sukuk Market," November, 2014.

Islamic Development Bank Group, "39 Years in the Service of Development," May, 2013.

Kay, John, *The Kay Review of UK Equity Markets and Long-Term Decision Making*, 2012.

Kharas, Homi, Annalisa Prizzon, and Andrew Rogerson, *Financing the Post*-2015 *Sustainable Development Goals: A Rough Roadmap*. ODI Working Paper, 2014.

Lin, Justin Yifu, *New Structural Economics: A Framework for Rethinking Development and Policy.* Washington DC: World Bank, 2012.

Lin, Justin Yifu, *The Quest for Prosperity: How Developing Countries can Take off,* Princeton and Oxford: Princeton University Press, 2012.

Luna-Martinez, José de, and Carlos Leonardo Vicente, "Global Survey of Development Banks," *World Bank Policy Research Working Paper,* 2012.

Mazzucato, Mariana, *The Entrepreneurial State: Debunking Public vs. Private Sector Myths.* New York: Anthem Press, 2013.

Middle East Rating & Investors Service, *Banking Analysis for Industrial Development Bank of Egypt (IDBE),* May 2006.

Moss, Todd, and Benjamin Leo, *IDA at 65: Heading Toward Retirement or a Fragile Lease on Life?* . Center for Global Development Working Paper 246, 2011.

OECD, *Fragile States 2014: Domestic Revenue Mobilization in Fragile States,* 2014, p. 16.

OECD, Institutional investors and long-term investment, accessed 30 April 2015, http://www.oecd.org/pensions/private-pensions/institutionalinvestorsandlong-terminvestment.htm.

OECD, *Mapping Channels to Mobilize Institutional Investment in Sustainable Energy,* 2015.

Official Gazette, "Decree with Rank, Value and Force of Law of Venezuela Economic and Social Development Bank (Bandes)," *Official Gazette of the Bolivarian Republic of Venezuela,* No. 5,890 Special, July 31, 2008.

Overseas Development Institute, "The European Bank for Reconstruction and Development," Overseas Development Institute briefing paper, September, 1990.

Rudolph, Heinz, *State Financial Institutions: Mandates, Governance, and Beyond,*

Washington, DC, World Bank Policy Research Series 5141, 2007.

The United Nations' High Level Panel on the Post-2015 Development Agenda, "A New Global Partnership: Eradicate Poverty and Transform Economies through Sustainable Development," 2013.

United Nations, *Report of the Intergovernmental Committee of Experts on Sustainable Development Financing*, 2014.

Wade, Robert, *Governing the Market: Economic Theory and the Role of Government in East Asian Industrialization*, Princeton, NJ; Oxford: Princeton University Press, 2004.

World Bank, *Long-Term Investment Financing for Growth and Development: Umbrella Paper*, Presented to the Meeting of the G20 Ministers of Finance and Central Bank Governors, February 2013, Moscow, Russia, February 2013.

World Bank, *Transformation through Infrastructure*, World Bank Group Infrastructure Strategy Update fiscal year 2012-15.

World Bank, World Development Indicators, 2014.

Xu, Jiajun and Richard Carey, *The Renaissance of Public Entrepreneurship: Governing Development Finance in a Transforming World*, Background Research Paper for the High Level Panel on the Post-2015 Development Agenda, 2013.

Xu, Jiajun and Richard Carey, "Modernising Global Reporting Systems: How to Enhance Sustainable Development Financing for Low-Income Countries?," *Institute of Development Studies Evidence Paper*, 2015, forthcoming.

Xu, Jiajun and Richard Carey, "Post-2015 Global Governance of Official Development Finance: Harnessing The Renaissance Of Public Entrepreneurship," Special Issue on "The Post-2015 Moment: Towards Sustainable Development Goals and a New Global Development Paradigm" in *Journal of International Development*, August 2015, forthcoming.

Xu, Jiajun and Richard Carey, "The Renaissance of Public Entrepreneurship: a fresh look at China's official finance in Africa," working paper, 2015.

Xu, Jiajun, *Beyond Business as Usual: Turning Challenges into Opportunities in Post-2015 Development Financing Strategies.* Global Policy Journal (op-ed), 2013.

Ziraat Bank, "Investor Presentation December 2014," 2014.

신용평가서<한국 산업 은행 AAA 재무 제표 기준일:2013 년 12 월 31 일 평가일: 2014 년 10 월 22 일> 한국 신용 평가 주식 회사 (Korean Rating Agency Rating report "Korea Development Bank: AAA; Financial statements as of Dec 31, 2013; Assessment as of Oct 31, 2014")

熊长水:《韩国产业银行资金筹措的分析与借鉴》[J] 广东金融, 1996 年, pp. 34-35. Xiong Changshui, "Analysis and Lesson of the fund raising of KDB"; Guangdong Finance, 1996, pp. 34 – 35.

Global Development Financing Report 2015

All requests, questions, and comments should be directed to:

WANGChunlai: hrb_ wangchunlai@cdb.cn

ZHANGFan: zhangfan@nsd.pku.edu.cn

XUJiajun: jiajunxu@nsd.pku.edu.cn